YANKEE CITY SERIES VOLUME 5

PUBLISHED ON THE RICHARD TELLER CRANE, JR.,
MEMORIAL FUND

THE YANKEE CITY SERIES IS DEDICATED TO

CORNELIUS CRANE

EACH VOLUME IN THE YANKEE CITY SERIES IS
COMPLETE IN ITSELF

YANKEE CITY SERIES

1. W. Lloyd Warner and Paul S. Lunt

   The Social Life of a Modern Community

2. W. Lloyd Warner and Paul S. Lunt

   The Status System of a Modern Community

3. W. Lloyd Warner and Leo Srole

   The Social Systems of American Ethnic Groups

4. W. Lloyd Warner and J. O. Low

   The Social System of the Modern Factory. The Strike: a Social Analysis

5. W. Lloyd Warner

   The Living and the Dead. A Study of the Symbolic Life of Americans

THE LIVING

AND THE DEAD

A Study of the Symbolic Life of Americans

W. Lloyd Warner

GREENWOOD PRESS, PUBLISHERS
WESTPORT, CONNECTICUT

Library of Congress Cataloging in Publication Data

Warner, William Lloyd, 1898-1970.
   The living and the dead.

    Reprint of the ed. published by Yale University Press,
New Haven, which was issued as v. 5 of Yankee City
series.
    Bibliography: p.
    Includes index.
    1. United States--Civilization--1945-
2. United States--Social life and customs--1945-
3. Symbolism. I. Title. II. Series: Yankee City
series ; v. 5.
[E169.02.W34 1975]   973.92   75-11495
ISBN 0-8371-8194-1

Originally published in 1959 by Yale University Press,
New Haven

Reprinted with the permission of Yale University Press

Reprinted in 1975 by Greenwood Press, Inc.,
51 Riverside Avenue, Westport, CT 06880

Library of Congress catalog card number 75-11495
ISBN 0-8371-8194-1

Printed in the United States of America

10 9 8 7 6 5 4 3 2

TO MILDRED HALL WARNER

CONTENTS

TABLES

CHARTS

PART I

POLITICS AND SYMBOLIC USAGE

INTRODUCTION

From the earliest beginnings of their inquiries into the nature of primitive and civilized collectivities social anthropologists and sociologists have studied the meanings and functions of man's symbolic life. Émile Durkheim's interpretation of the collective representations of Australian totemism, Sir James Frazer's treatment in *The Golden Bough* of the symbolic significance of the pagan religions that preceded Christianity, Malinowski's research on the meanings and functions of the Trobriand Islanders' economic rituals, and Sapir's work on the languages of the world are a few noteworthy examples.

Broadly speaking and for the present, symbols may be defined as "things which stand for or express something else." They are signs of meaning and include much of our cultural equipment, including the words and meanings of language; the pictures, sounds, and gestures of the arts; the creeds, beliefs, and rituals of religion; and most of what is communicated by word and act in our everyday existence. All signs and their meanings (words, for example) which conceptually or expressively refer to something beyond the sign itself are symbols. Symbols are substitutes for all *known* real and imaginary actions, things, and the relations among them. They stand for and express feelings and beliefs about men and what they do, about the world and what happens in it. What they stand for may or may not exist. What they stand for may or may not be true, for what they express may be no more than a feeling, an illusion, a myth, or a vague sensation falsely interpreted. On the other hand, that for which they stand may be as real and objectively verifiable as the Rock of Gibraltar. (In large part this and the following paragraph are repeated and developed in Chapter 15.)

3

The essential components of a symbol are the sign and its meaning, the former usually being the outward perceptible form which is culturally identifiable and recognizable, the latter being the interpretation of the sign, usually composed of concepts of what is being interpreted and the positive and negative values and feelings which "cluster about" the sign. The sign's meaning may refer to other objects or express and evoke feelings. The values and feelings may relate to the inner world of the person or be projected outward on the social and natural worlds beyond.

The present volume investigates the meanings and functions of some of the symbols of contemporary America. It is the result of field research on our political and historical symbols, on those of the elite and the commoner, on those of the living and the dead, holy days and holidays, and the "myths" and rituals of Christianity. Throughout the book our concern will be to interpret the meanings and social functions of these and other American symbol systems.

Although the research was done on one community and consequently, in a limited sense, the results hold only for it, the nature of symbolic life in this country is such that, despite important variations, the basic meanings of our secular and religious symbols are much the same in all regions. When one studies political campaigns, Memorial Day rites, or the significance of the Mass in New England or the Far West, much of what is learned holds for the rest of the nation. The methods used in this and the previous volumes follow those used in *Black Civilization.* [139a]

From one point of view, human culture is a symbolic organization of the remembered experiences of the dead past as newly felt and understood by the living members of the collectivity. The human condition of individual mortality and the comparative immortality of our species make most of our communication and collective activities in the larger sense a vast exchange of understanding between the living and the dead. Language, religion, art, science, morality, and our knowledge of ourselves and the world around us, being parts of our culture, are meaningful symbol systems which the living generations have inherited from those now gone. We use these symbols briefly, modify them or not, and then pass them on to those who succeed us. Thus, in fact, communication between living and dead individuals maintains continuity of culture for the species. Secular symbols probably more often emphasize the living present; sacred symbols appear to be more concerned with death, with the past of the species and the future of the individual.

The first four volumes of this series presented more data than this one; emphasis here is on theory and interpretation. We shall start our inquiry with the more secular symbols and move to the most sacred, ending with an examination of symbols generally and their significance in the mental life of man. As the book proceeds it moves from chapters which are more factual to those which are more abstract, theoretical, and general in their significance, the last three being entirely concerned with symbolic theory and methods for its study.

The use of the term *sacred* in this connection brings up a point about which the general reader may find explanation helpful. Certain terms are used throughout the text in a somewhat specialized sense which may depart from the reader's connotations or experience of common parlance. Thus *sacred* is applied not only to Divine Being and the central experience and sacraments of Christian faith, but to objects and phases of life to which the special reverence arising from religions in general has been extended. This intends no discourtesy or profanation but is simply the sociologist's way of finding a term of contrast to objects and experience of purely secular origin.

Other terms also used in a somewhat special sense, beginning in this section, are *ethnic, non-rational,* or *non-logical,* and the use of *masculine* and *feminine* to denote the quality of symbols. *Ethnic,* whose usage according to Webster denotes racial differences as opposed to national or cultural ones, is employed simply for people of foreign background recent enough to cohere as a group or consciously retain some of that character —there being no convenient noun or adjective in the language for this purpose. *Non-rational* or *non-logical* symbols are those which arise out of the basic individual and cultural assumptions, more often unconscious than not, from which most social action springs. They supply the solid core of mental and emotional life of each individual and group. This does not mean they are irrational or maladaptive, or that man cannot often think in a reasonable way about them, but rather that they do not have their source in his rational processes. When they come into play, such factors as data, evidence, proof, and the facts and procedures of rational thought in action are apt to be secondary or unimportant. *Masculine* and *feminine* symbols are words, gestures, pictures, and the like whose meanings may denote bodily differences or the actions of the two sexes, or they may be culturally defined meanings which connote one sex or the other—for example, those that evoke notions of virility are likely to be considered masculine, while those expressive of the abundance of nature, vegetation, and nurture are more likely to be feminine.

In the Introductions to later sections of the book a few other terms will be noted. Readers interested in the research basis of the class divisions of Yankee City (three main classes, each having an upper and lower phase) are referred to Volume 1 of the "Yankee City Series." For those interested in what the people were like in each class the "profiles" should be read (*ibid.*, pp. 128–201). For the statistical characteristics, pages 422–50 of the same volume should be consulted.

The evidence on which the political chapters about Mr. Muldoon in Part I are based is varied and extensive. It includes many interviews with him, his friends, and his enemies throughout the several years of our field work in Yankee City. One research document on Mr. Muldoon assembled by Mr. Paul Lunt consisted of over a thousand typewritten pages. It covered his political career from 1927, when he ran successfully for mayor, to 1935, when the field research was concluded. In this document were full transcripts from the local and Boston papers, his autobiography, as well as many other materials generously supplied by Mr. Muldoon. Altogether we kept in touch with his activities through some thirty years and fifteen mayoralty campaigns in their entirety.

Since the publication of *The Last Hurrah*, some people believe they see a close parallel between Muldoon and the hero of O'Connor's novel. The resemblance is at best superficial—they are both Catholic Irish, both mayors (Yankee City and Boston), and both in politics. But whereas the hero of *The Last Hurrah* was believed to be dishonest and a cunning politician, Biggy Muldoon is puritanically honest and, in the popular and invidious sense of the word, not a "politician." For the record, the chapters on Muldoon in this book were written and used in mimeographed form for seminars well before the novel was published.

For the convenience of the reader and in order to avoid a multitude of footnotes, references to source material are by bracketed numbers indicating items in the Bibliography, where the customary publishing data will be found. Where more than one reference to a single work is involved, the page numbers are given in brief footnotes to the text.

CHAPTER 1

BIGGY MULDOON, A POLITICAL HERO

The Symbolic Role of the Hero

Our present story is concerned with the good and evil fortunes of Biggy Muldoon. It tells why all of Yankee City, where he was elected mayor, and millions of people throughout the United States became emotionally involved in his political and private life. It attempts to explain how the joy, anger, and sorrow they experienced in his spectacular triumphs and bitter defeats helped to develop and expand, yet control and limit, his career. Many of the crucial factors operating in his political life have always been powerful in the political and social life of America. If we can learn the meaning of his career we may gain deeper insight into some of the more important aspects of American politics.

Biggy Muldoon, the "Yankee City Bad Boy," is a big-shouldered, two-fisted, red-haired Irishman. He was born down by the river on the wrong side of the tracks, the only child of Irish-Catholic immigrant parents. Once a street-fighter, a brawler, and an all-round tough guy, he was arrested by the police for shooting dice, profane and abusive language, fighting, and other rough behavior distasteful to the pious and respectable.

Yankee City, where Biggy was born and grew up, is a New England community of some 17,000 people which spreads in a thin line along the banks and mouth of a large river. Its history goes back to the beginnings of English occupation of this continent. Although originally a sea culture, early in the last century it turned its energies and skills into the manufacture of textiles, shoes, and silverware. It is now a modern New England manufacturing community.[1] For many generations the "Old Families" on Hill Street, founded on the economic power inherited from the wealth of their seagoing ancestors, have been the upper class, where they are now joined—in lesser status—

1. See "Yankee City Series," Vols. 1 and 4.

by the "New Families" whose money is more recently acquired from manufacturing. Beneath them the solid middle and large lower classes, each divided into two levels for our purpose, complete the total of six social classes in the town.

It is a dignified, quiet New England city. Some say it is more conservative than sedate Philadelphia, more historically minded and conscious of its glorious past than Brahmin Boston. It regards any break in decorum or deviation from good form with extreme disapproval. Since the town first grew into a city its mayors have personified the virtues admired by its better citizens. Successful candidates for the office have been men socially situated well above the common level; some have come to the position from careers that earned them national recognition. Although sometimes subject to criticism, all have enjoyed solid reputations in the community. For the honor of being mayor of his home city each of these prominent and successful men—one a former Attorney General of the United States—was willing to risk possible defeat by the local voters.

Despite Biggy's background and the traditions of the office and city, he was nominated and elected by the voters of Yankee City to be mayor. They gave him a very substantial majority, until then the largest ever received by any candidate. He was voted into office in preference to a respectable, conservative incumbent whose life conformed to all the better usages of Yankee City, a man who lived on the social heights of Hill Street and belonged to "the better class" of the town.

Moreover, from shortly before his first election and for several years after, his political fortunes received intense and continued treatment in the great metropolitan newspapers, national magazines, and radio systems. Clearly such an extraordinary reversal of the political traditions of the town and the strong feelings Biggy aroused among millions of Americans throughout the country indicate that some of the vital forces in American life were at work. As research men studying the community where this political drama was played, we asked ourselves what its significance might be to us as scientists and to Americans generally. We believed that if we were fortunate enough to learn some of the answers we would acquire a better understanding of how and why Americans think, talk, and act the way they do. This analysis of Biggy's career tells what we

learned. Although economic factors, among others, were involved, economic discontent and distress do not explain his defeat of the other candidate, for the city at the time was
prosperous. There had been no change in local politics to account for his unpredicted victory. The political principles for
which he stood—lower taxes, efficient and honest government,
and a square deal for everyone—while commendable, are not
of the stuff that arouses the electorate of a conservative city to
political revolt or brings representatives of the great mass
media of the nation hurrying to a small community to report to
their millions of readers what a Biggy Muldoon is doing to his
home town. He did not have a formal political organization to
help him; the other candidate did. His opponent, while mayor,
had not alienated any large block of voters who could become Biggy's natural followers. He had voted against prohibition—but Biggy was an ardent pro-liquor man. His opponent was for Sunday motion pictures—but so was Biggy.
Moreover, he stood for other, similar activities which were not
to the liking of many respectable people of Yankee City. Yet
they elected him mayor.

It might appear that this was the kind of man who could
have been elected earlier had he but tried; that, if given the
opportunity, Yankee City would have favored him as a pleasant
escape from the restraints of its middle-class propriety and
aristocratic conservatism. But this explanation, too, is wrong,
since he had been an unsuccessful candidate in previous elections for minor office. At the time of his first victory in a
mayoralty contest he was thirty-one years old. Ten years
earlier, at twenty-one, he had run for councilman in a field of
six and came in sixth. He then ran for similar positions several
times and was badly defeated, once coming in twelfth in a field
of fourteen. A year before his triumph as mayor he had again
stood for election as councilman of his ward, receiving an em-
barrassingly small number of votes, 47 in all. Yet twelve months
later, when he was elected mayor with a grand total of 2,852 to
his opponent's 2,357, the people of his ward contributed 355
votes to his victory. Something had happened to bring about
this change. But what?

The explanation of the triumph of Biggy Muldoon is not to
be found among the ordinary reasons given for political vic-

tories. The succeeding events of his career, briefly sketched, will help to bring the problem into rounded view. At the end of his first two-year term he ran again. This time a number of prominent men had been informally selected to run against him and thereby divide his vote. One was a powerful and highly respected member of a very old family in Yankee City. Once again Biggy won, but this time by a reduced majority, defeating his nearest opponent by the narrow margin of 40 votes. He next ran for the state senate in the hope of gaining more recognition among the state's electorate, and lost this election. Thereafter he ran again for mayor and was badly defeated, losing by over a thousand votes to one of the Hill Streeters, a man in the "right" tradition who enjoyed a high position in the community.

When he was first elected mayor Biggy's percentage of the vote was so unprecedentedly large, his backing so strong, and the interest in him as a public man so great among the people of Yankee City, the state, and for that matter the nation, that he publicly announced his intention to run for governor or for the United States Senate and voiced his ultimate ambition to be President. Given the evidence and the time when we examined it, his hopes and expectations were well within the bounds of any strong man's dreams. But the dreams were not realized.

Biggy is still a major factor in Yankee City politics. He has run in every election for mayor since his first, sixteen in all. Of these contests he has won six and lost ten. By custom in Yankee City, a field of several men try out in the primary to determine which two will be candidates in the final election, which is non-partisan. In every election save one Biggy has been one of the two finalists. Yet with the exception of 1935 he was not elected mayor again after his first two victories until 1949; at present he is again mayor of the city.

From this brief and limited review of his affairs several obvious but fundamental questions emerge about the rise of Biggy Muldoon. The social behavior resulting in his elections and defeats and the kind of role he has played are not wholly unknown in the local, state, or national elections of the United States. The political careers of such men as Al Smith, Huey Long, Fiorello La Guardia, and—for certain purposes—such names as William Jennings Bryan, Andrew Jackson, and even Abraham Lincoln must be considered.

The crucial questions to be answered are:

Why did Biggy Muldoon rise to local and national fame?

Why did he gain political power?

What prevented Biggy from going beyond the political apex he quickly achieved as mayor to the higher positions in state and nation to which he aspired? Men far less talented and much less able than Biggy occupy places in the halls of Congress and our national life. Why did he lose the power and position he had achieved?

Despite his defeats, why, since the first great days of his political career, has he retained the affection and respect of a solid core of voters and the dislike and even hatred of a powerful group in his community? Why do many of the city's voters continue to love a hated Biggy Muldoon? And why have his enemies failed to achieve his ultimate and decisive defeat— failed to destroy him as a political force in Yankee City?

Several kinds of evidence are needed to answer these questions.

The social and psychological evidence required is diverse and complex. We must know the essential and immediate facts of his career and the campaigns by which he was first elected and then defeated. Knowledge of the structure and condition of the society at the time is of great importance. The way he conceived of himself in the social world in which he lived—the personality of Biggy Muldoon, who played the principal role in the drama of the bitter elections for mayor—and the continuing development of his personality as well as the social circumstances largely responsible for what he became, are all relevant.[2]

2. Mr. Muldoon generously collaborated with the research. For the many interviews we had with him, for his permission to use some of his correspondence and his autobiography to help us understand the significance of his political activities, we are deeply indebted. Paul Lunt was principally responsible for the excellent relations we had with Mr. Muldoon. The field work of Mr. Robert Snider, now of the Conservation Foundation in New York; Dr. Burleigh Gardner, President of Social Research, Inc., Chicago; Professor Solon Kimball, now at Teachers College, Columbia University; and Professor Conrad Arensberg of Barnard College, Columbia University—all student field workers at the time— added further evidence that contributed to our understanding of politics in Yankee City.

Above all, the meaning of the symbols of political attack and defense wielded by Biggy and his opponents in their struggle for power, and their effect upon Biggy himself, his political foes, and the people of Yankee City and the country at large, are crucial and of the highest significance.

Before examining at close range the evidence in these divers categories, a general hypothesis consisting of several propositions may be offered to keep our attention focused on relevant factors and to guide our investigation.

It goes without saying that a hero always expresses fundamental and important themes of the culture in which he is found; this is no less true in historical or contemporary America than elsewhere. Each theme is a symbolic statement which relates and organizes some of the beliefs and values of a community or a nation to each other and to the group. Rational thought is not the real source of evocative symbols or the themes, values, and beliefs expressed by them. The creation of heroic forms, their crystallization around actual persons, makes these themes and the beliefs and values they represent manifest in a human being. [71a] In this way they easily become emotionally and convincingly understandable to everyone, with personal meaning to the child as well as to the mature, to the unlettered and the lowly as well as to the educated few. These social beliefs and values have a universal significance to the members of a culture because the basic emotional structure of each person is largely acquired and formed in childhood from his earliest intimate experiences as a new member of a society. Each growing individual sees, feels, and hears beliefs and values not as abstract concepts and principles but as integral, personal parts of loved or disliked persons whom he experiences through social and personal interaction. The child's strongest feelings are very often directed to other individuals who are part of his immediate environment, and to his own self as an integral part of this intimate personal environment. Abstract principles, precepts, and moral judgments are consequently more easily felt and understood, and more highly valued, when met in a human being endowed with a symbolic form that expresses them. Obviously the "hero" is ideally suited to this role.

The functions of a hero for the individuals who believe in

him are related to, but different from, his functions for the society. He functions in at least three significant ways for members of the group. His actual presence stimulates those who believe in him to project their own private feelings and beliefs directly on him. His presence also serves as a model for their imitation and learning and for the measurement of their own moral inadequacies. Further, the hero arouses the hopes and fears of those who believe in him, and he energizes and gives social direction to some of their anxieties.

The hero clearly has internal as well as external significance for individual members of a group. The inner world of each is forever in danger of sinking into the malaise and disquiet of personal chaos. It is in constant need of the moral strength, intellectual stability, and hard realities of the social order which lie both within and beyond each of us. The belief in a hero helps single members of a group to relate themselves more effectively to each other and to the general and more universal beliefs and values of the whole society. Privately, the presence of a hero organizes the individual's hopes and fears and expresses them in a meaningful way, both for him and for the society. The belief in a hero can release the individual from anxiety and reward him with a faith that his hopes are, or are about to be, realized. Such belief is always exciting and reassuring to the individual in his private world, but the excitement is greatly increased when, from the evidence of his senses and the physical presence of his hero, he can publicly validate his faith. Heroes and hero-worship are integral parts of any complex, changing society; which is to say that heroes must always be present in the cultures of nations and civilizations, whether ancient or contemporary.

Let us now return to Biggy Muldoon, the man who became a hero.

The writer believes that Biggy, through a set of circumstances and a sequence of events presently to be related, was transformed in the minds of many in Yankee City from the mundane referential image they had of him as another tough kid from the wrong side of the tracks into a type of symbolic hero much beloved by Americans. For them he became the champion of the people, the strong man who attacks the proud and powerful and protects the poor and lowly. In their minds he conformed for a while to all the necessary criteria for this heroic role. Then, through other events, for some who had faith in him he lost his hero's stature; they joined those who thought of him as contemptible and a fool or a villain, and came to hate him in large enough numbers to bring about his defeat.

I believe that through it all Biggy, the person, changed very little. Though later facets of his behavior may have gone beyond people's first reckoning, ironically he stayed very much the same live, vibrant man, Biggy Muldoon. What did change were the symbols, and their component beliefs and values, that were attached to him in a political drama in which he played the leading role, symbols that first made him a hero—perhaps even something of a martyr—and then for many, for a time, turned him into a "fool" and even a "traitor" to his town. The distribution of these negative and positive symbols in the electorate and in the national mass media changed as time went by and as the sequence of incidents in his dramatic career had their effect.

The life and times of Biggy Muldoon easily divide into three major parts: the early formative one of preparation and training for the central role he later played; that role itself, in the highly dramatic second period which began with the Hill Street episode and ended after he served two terms as the town's chief executive; and the last period, beginning with his defeat for a third term and continuing until the present time. It will be one of our principal problems to learn why Biggy has continued to hold such a strong appeal for a substantial portion of the electorate and why a large percentage have opposed him. But our primary concern will be with his first two victories and subsequent defeat.

The Rise of a Hero

Mary Muldoon, Biggy's mother, arrived in Yankee City from Ireland as a seventeen-year-old country girl with ten dollars in her pocket. She was an ambitious and very determined young woman. She worked for a time as a domestic in the Judge Sampson house, a "beautiful mansion" in the aristocratic Hill Street section of town. Judge Sampson, a former mayor, was a member of the so-called superior class of the city.

Mary Muldoon married and, shortly before her husband went back to his native land, gave birth to her only child, Thomas Ignatius Muldoon, who subsequently became known to all as Biggy. During her early career Mrs. Muldoon worked as a cook and as an employee of a shoe factory. She saved her money and in time opened a little store in the front of her small house. During World War I a tip from a well-placed friend showed her how she could borrow money and, with the help of her savings, buy sugar and flour in carload quantities. With these profits and others arising from war inflation she accumulated considerable capital. She invested in real estate. Among other buildings, she acquired a jail abandoned by the city—the jail where she had once served time for refusing to pay for a license for Biggy's stray dog (a few years after that episode Biggy had also been incarcerated in the same jail). Somewhat later, when the Sampson house came on the market, she borrowed money and, with Biggy, purchased it. They made a home of the sheriff's quarters and lived there together—it gratified their strong sense of humor and irony. But Mrs. Muldoon's far from easy life ended in a heart attack not long after.

Biggy, meanwhile, had grown into a hard-muscled, tough-fibered boy. Although he "ran wild," his mother's moral influence was so strong on his life that he never drank or smoked. She also taught him to attack his enemies and, being of humble Irish origin, to define them as those who occupy the seats of the mighty. Perhaps he would have learned most of this anyway, for the district in which he grew up teaches its children to be aggressive and prizes physical violence as the means of solving problems.

Biggy took charge of the family property shortly before his mother's death and attempted on several occasions to get a permit from the mayor and the city council to move the Sampson house, destroy its garden and terrace, as well as the wall about it, and put up a filling station. Viewed purely from the commercial angle it was perhaps a reasonable venture. But each time the authorities refused. He then tried other tactics.

One morning the gentle people of Hill Street awakened to find large, highly colored circus posters, advertising a Wild West show, covering the chaste walls of the Sampson mansion. A few days later Biggy tore down the walls of the terraced garden. Of its stone slabs he fashioned gravestones, placing them at the heads of suitably shaped mounds of earth. The names of the members of the council and of the mayor, many of them Hill Streeters, were written on the headstones. The garden, in the most prominent place in Yankee City, had been turned into a graveyard to mock the enemies where the rude and the vulgar could laugh at them. The trucks and vehicles that removed the wall and earth from the garden had signs which announced their ownership as "The Biggy Muldoon Destruction Company." While the soil was being removed one of the veterans' organizations, having no members above the lower-middle class, paraded in the town. Biggy gave them permission to place their chapter's American flag over the house, and there it waved.

Obviously indignation was very intense on Hill Street. The circus was persuaded by state officials through indirect channels to take down the posters, but a few days later the indignation of Hill Street swelled to outrage, for hanging from the windows and high gables of the proud old house were several rows of bedroom crockery and, beneath them, a large sign which read: THE SPIRIT OF YANKEE CITY. Lindbergh had recently flown the Atlantic, thrilling all Americans with pride in their scientific progress and in American ability to triumph over the limitations of time and space. It will be recalled that the *Spirit of St. Louis* was the plane that made the historic flight. Everyone in Yankee City knew that certain great families on Hill Street clung so tenaciously to the ways of their forefathers that they had refused to install the amenities of modern plumbing. A few still used outside privies, gas lighting, and tin bathtubs because they disapproved of "all this modern nonsense." Biggy's allusion was clear.

He tried again to get a permit for his filling station, but when he went to the mayor's office he became so angry from the tongue-lashing given him by this official that he struck him, or, as he said, "socked the so-and-so on the jaw." He was arrested, sentenced on several charges, and served two months in jail—the county jail this time.

Previous to this on several occasions, as we have noted, Biggy had run for city councilman and had been defeated. Less than a year from the time of the jail sentence, after some hesitation, he ran for mayor. The announcement of his candidacy drew the attention of a metropolitan paper in Boston. A long front-page story was printed when he became one of the two candidates chosen in the primary for the "run-off" in the final election. The article immediately attracted great interest. It told of Biggy's struggle with Hill Street and referred to him as Yankee City's Bad Boy. The story in general had a favorable and positive, although gently humorous, turn. Immediately other papers in Boston, New York, and other large cities sent their reporters to Yankee City; their shrewd editors knew a good story when they saw it. The dramatic tale of the rebel, the man from the wrong side of the tracks who hated cops, socked mayors, challenged the high and mighty, and thumbed his nose at the rich and powerful, was told repeatedly in news columns throughout the United States and Canada. The stories described how he was running for mayor of Yankee City, then controlled by the Hill Streeters, by telling his highly placed foes he'd throw them out and run the town in his own fashion. With the realization that here was a dream hero come to life, functionaries of radio, motion pictures, and stage were rushed to Yankee City and Biggy's name was soon known from coast to coast. He was a welcome relief from the usual bad news found on the front pages or in the newsreels. People far and wide who had never heard of his home town loved Biggy and laughed at the discomfort of his high-born enemies, or reacted with indignation and contempt and predicted that he would "get what he deserved."

Soon after his first election Biggy again applied to the city council for a permit to sell gasoline and permission to cut down the ancient elms which blocked the entrance to his proposed filling station. Both requests were immediately refused. The next day Biggy cut down the trees, started the installation of the storage tank, and soon was selling gas to thousands of people who came from everywhere to see and shake hands with the celebrated Biggy Muldoon, then hurried home to tell their friends what the Yankee City Bad Boy had said to them as he filled their gas tanks.

Hill Street quickly retaliated. Biggy was arrested, tried, and convicted. He was sentenced to two months at hard labor and fined over four hundred dollars. He conducted the affairs of the mayor's office from a cell in the county jail. Newsreel cameras took pictures of him there, while the papers carried his jail story to millions of people across the continent.

When he was released—two days before the local election—over forty thousand people gathered around and about the jail to welcome him and a great parade was spontaneously formed to carry him in triumph back to his home. When they arrived in Yankee City Biggy delivered a speech which blasted his enemies, told of his martyrdom, and urged the election of his friends to the city council. The citizens of Yankee City responded: every one of Biggy's candidates was elected and all his opponents defeated. The council soon changed the zoning law. Biggy triumphantly—yet anticlimactically for those emotionally involved in the struggle—sold his gas station for $41,000 to one of the great oil companies. The battle of Hill Street was over.

Biggy Muldoon Tells Who He Is

Before exploring the important influence of the town itself on the drama of Biggy Muldoon we must let Biggy tell his own story. His autobiography, composed with editorial assistance just after his first election, was run as a serial in several issues of a Boston paper. It aroused such interest that privilege to publish was requested by several papers in the South, the Middle West, and Canada as well as New England. The following excerpts represent only a fraction of the original, but they give in synoptic form some of the most significant parts. Judging from Muldoon's later writings and our interviews with him, the story told is very much his own. His vivid prose gives a clear view of his conception of himself and the world around him. Though some of what he says must have been difficult to tell, unlike most people in self-revelations he writes and speaks, with little or no effort to suppress evidence, a straightforward, candid account of his life.

They call me "Biggy" Muldoon, the roughneck mayor.

They say I hate cops, favor my friends, and am down on bankers.

It's all true, and there's plenty worse to tell of me. I've been in jail. I've been a street corner loafer, a hobo, a dishwasher, a gob, and a fighter. I cuss and I hold grudges. I don't change my shirt every day.

The cops have arrested me for almost everything a two-fisted, red-headed kid could do except get drunk or something crooked. I've never bothered with rum, and even the lads that hate my shadow wouldn't say I wasn't honest. I got lonesome sometimes when I was a kid. My mother worked, and she worked hard. Part of the time she was in the shoeshop. Part of the time she hired out as cook. For all she could do, I ran kind of wild, but I had my blue spells. That's how it came I picked up a tramp puppy. He was a mess. I called him "Bo"—short for "Hobo." I was sort of sorry for him. I didn't know then I'd be a hobo myself later.

The cops got wise that "Bo" hadn't a license. Ma and Bo got pinched. Of course, I was too young to be responsible, so my mother got the summons. She had to go to court and they fined her $5. Ma was Irish, too. She gave them a piece of her mind and told them they'd die of old age before they got a nickel.

"Pay up or go to jail," they warned her.

She went to jail—with more than $100 in cash in her pocket. They kept her locked up for eight days!

To me it was a hell of a thing. I was all broke up. I got rid of the dog. I'll never live another eight days as tough as those . . . And I won't forget that the cops were the cause of it all.

That's enough about the cops. . . . Anyhow, they'll pick on no kids and mutts while I'm mayor. And I'm not kissing any of them.

I'm accused of having it in for bankers. I think that most of them get away with murder. They're dead but they won't lie down. What they've got they figure to keep and they don't give the young fellows a look-in.

That other fellow from Yankee City, Mr. W. L. Garrison, was quite a fellow. As a kid, I thought he was the greatest man in history, next to Julius Caesar. He thought he had done something worth telling about and telling about right—so Caesar wrote the piece himself. It was at high school that I got acquainted with Julius Caesar. I thought he was the works. He wasn't afraid to admit it himself.

I'm also supposed to be a woman-hater. That's the bunk. I like 'em—in their place. We guys at school thought girls were something like puppy dogs. We looked down on them. But when I got in the Navy I looked the senoritas over in Cuba and Puerto Rico. The spiggoti girls weren't half bad-looking. The only trouble with them was they thought every year was leap year. The first party I ever went on ashore at Santa Cruz del Sur, wherever the hell that was, I had to jump out of a second-story window to keep my independence.

After high school I went to an academy for part of a year. Then the war started. I tried to enlist in the Navy. They wouldn't let me—couldn't pass the physical exams—and me a husky guy. I went on the bus to the West Coast to try to get in out there. I was a hell of a high-class hobo. I was what the jungle gangs know as a "time-table bum," a "fast bo," and on the best trains. I crossed the continent three times while I was bumming. I'm not ashamed of it—bumming. There isn't a soul to tell you what you ought to do and what you ought not. There isn't any bull-throwing. You've got your two fists and your nerve and that's all you need. When you feel like going you go. When you feel like stopping you stop.

Nobody yet ever called me a "mamma's boy." Some of those, though, who picked on my mother, and some of those who talk now about my mother will have cause to remember that I'm Mary Muldoon's boy.

After Ma was dead I remembered her advice. She'd told me over and over that I oughtn't to go off half-cocked. She'd begged me to get my feet solid before I swung on anybody.

It was worry and grief that murdered my mother. I was partly to blame. I'd tried to do something—be somebody. The folks that ran things were bound that they'd bust me. They didn't mind if they busted my mother at the same time. The term I served in Salem jail for whacking the mayor was hell for my mother.

I'm still sore about the deal they handed me that time in the court. I understand the judge was told confidentially that Yankee City felt I ought to have a chance to "rest my head." I got a sixty-day jail sentence. That was a rough sixty days. If I had been a gunman or a burglar or a thief, I'd have had a chance to get favors . . . Not Biggy. I was chambermaid to horses, and I was a permanent member of the fertilizer shovelling squad.

They razz me for living in the old jail property. I'm kind of thin-skinned about that. I like the place. I own it. It's my home. It was my mother's home. I've never been a roomer in somebody else's shack. I'm not beginning now.

There's something more to be said about the jail building. The part I use is the residence that was built for the sheriff. Talk about your historic mansions. Mine was moss green when the "antique" Sampson place I'm supposed to have ruined was still woods. One of these days I'm going to renovate it, fix up the grounds, and have a house that nobody in Yankee City can turn his nose up at. Such as it is, the jail building is my castle. I'll stay in it.

The Muldoons, my mother and me, were always the sort of people the real old-time moth-eaten Yankees figured they could get along easy without. We were always struggling along with the funny notion that, this being a free country, a family that tended to its business, worked like hell, and banked its jack ought to get a fair break with the community.

But the codfish aristocrats, the nice ladies and gentlemen whose granddads made their piles in decent trades like importing niggers or transporting rum, wanted Yankee City to stay quaint and little, and dead. Commerce was all right in Yankee City so long as it knew its place. There wasn't any real objection to there being a population of enough working folks to make the place livable. But when an old Irish woman and a redheaded Irish kid that didn't know enough to tip his hat to white people invested real dough in new industries—wow, what a howl went up!

When I make my pile—and I will—I want to leave Yankee City a memorial of Biggy Muldoon. It won't be a monument in a cemetery. It will be a first-rate, up-to-the-minute indoor swimming pool, built somewhere along the bank of the river. It will be open and free all the year around with an instructor there to teach swimming and rescue work. I want Yankee City to be a place where any red-headed, two-fisted kid will be given a fair break to be somebody. No matter who their mothers and fathers are, I want kids to grow up without the tossing around that made me the roughneck I am supposed to be. I want them to grow up proud of their home town, proud of its history, and proud of their chance to look out for its future.

The Political and Social Worlds of Biggy Muldoon

Much of what Biggy was as a man, and what made him significant to his friends and foes in Yankee City, can be better understood by a brief examination of certain selected parts of the social world in which he rose to fame, particularly the political and status conditions in which he operated during his political career.

The community in which his rise and fall took place was more than a setting for the drama. The forces acting within it helped to create his personality; they were the all-powerful feelings and beliefs that functioned in his career like Fate in the lives of Greek tragic heroes. Indeed, a good case could be made demonstrating that the flaws in the characters of Greek tragedy and the fates they suffered were no more than the basic precepts and principles of their society, its social logics, operating in the dramas and in the beliefs and values of the audience who watched them. Since Greek dramas are still powerful— for Oedipus Rex can bring tears to the eyes of modern audiences—it seems probable that these same fates and flaws operate in the lives of contemporary men.

Biggy's able and ambitious mother, like most new arrivals from the old country, started at the bottom of the social heap. Biggy's early formative experiences and training took place there. The community of Yankee City, with its American way of life, has several social classes (see pp. 6 and 9), forming subcultures which have powerful effects on the attitudes of all members of the community. We have noted the modest size and general historical background of the city. Most of the upper class live in the Hill Street area or extensions of it in the new and Old Town districts. The two upper classes, the birth aristocracy and the new elite, together were only 3 per cent of the population at the time of our research. Ten per cent were upper-middle, 28 per cent lower-middle, 33 per cent were upper-lower, and 25 per cent at the lowest level.[3] The region from which Biggy emerged has a statistically significant high concentration of lower-class people and an equally significant small number from the upper and middle classes. Approximately half of the 400 houses designated as mansions are concentrated in the Hill Street area and its extensions. Biggy came up from a region of little streets and little houses, both ordinarily in poor condition. The mansions are owned in significantly high numbers by families from the Levels Above the Common Man; the little people from the wrong side of the tracks live in houses classed as being, more often than not, in bad condition. The mansions on the heights of Hill Street, as well as the name of the region itself, consequently often in fact as well as symbolically denote families that enjoy superior social status.

At the top of the Yankee City governmental organization— a hierarchy of elected and appointed officials—are the mayor and council, elected every two years. Each of the six wards of the city elects one member to the council, while the city at large elects the other five. The candidates for mayor and council run on non-partisan tickets. These two *sets* of candidates are similar in quality and background.

The voters are unequally distributed among the six social classes, the lowest varying greatly in population and in the way they think and act in the politics of the town. The two upper classes, with 3 per cent of the total population, had 2.9 per cent of the total number of registered voters. The two middle classes registered and voted in larger proportions than their percentage of the population: with 38.3 per cent of the total population they represented 48.4 per cent of the registered voters. In the lower classes, the upper-lower person revealed himself as up-and-coming politically compared to the class beneath him: the upper-lower class had about the same percentage of voters as representation in the total population, whereas the lower-lower class, with slightly over 25 per cent

3. See Warner [139c], 203.

of the population, had less than 15 per cent of the voters.[4] Of the latter class the clammers are a picturesque group, living down on the clam flats or across the river in a community largely their own. Their shanties are often banked by seaweed and sea grasses to keep out the cold of winter. They are the remnants of the old sea culture of the town when it was a shipping and fishing center, and until Biggy's advent were for the most part inarticulate politically.

The normal political behavior of the lower-lower group before Biggy arrived on the scene fitted into the general way they participated in all the life of the community. They were decidedly apathetic to political appeals. The great majority rarely took the trouble to vote. Interviews demonstrated that they were often indifferent to the point of not knowing an election was pending or caring little about the candidate, the issues, or the outcome. Of the few who voted, most felt that it would have little or no consequence to their own existence because the candidates ordinarily did not represent their interests. It may be observed in general that the organizations which stir others into action in voting rarely reach these people. The symbols that will appeal to and energize all other levels, including the hard-working members of the upper-lower class, have only a minimal appeal to the private and public worlds of those who live at the Level Below the Common Man. Something more is needed to get to them. Different kinds of organizations and associations must be used, with different symbols and appeals, to pull these people out of their apathy and indifference and bring them to the voting booth.

As regards Biggy's personal life, perhaps the most significant events in his career as boy and man in Yankee City were his several arrests by the police and his conviction by the courts for crimes of physical violence and other infractions not explicitly violent but still expressive of aggression against the respectability and superiority of the higher social levels of Yankee City. An inspection of the proportion of arrests of members of the six classes, when related to Biggy's own troubles with the police, tells a significant story. Sixty-five per cent of all the arrests appearing on the police records of Yankee City were from the lowest social level of the community,

4. See Vol. *1* of this series.

a class with 25 per cent of the population. Ninety per cent of those arrested were from the two lowest classes, 58 per cent of the population. Less than 3 per cent were in the three upper classes with 13 per cent of the inhabitants. Biggy's arrests and convictions were not those of an aberrant individual. They fit neatly and tightly into the conventional pattern established by the relations of the police and the higher political authority to the lower levels of the ethnic groups at the bottom of the heap in Yankee City.

These percentages obviously sharpen the social drama and status significance of Biggy's arrests. When in his informal speeches to the people of his district he told them he was "going to tell the cops where the hell to get off," he spoke words whose meaning and values they could enjoy with an intensity experienced perhaps by no other level of American. Traditionally and informally most Americans are believed not to like "cops" and are reputed to take satisfaction in seeing these symbols of authority brought low; but no level has as much provocation to take pleasure in seeing "cops shoved around" as those at the bottom who are most vulnerable to them. The long-suffering Biggy, who had a history of arrests himself and whose mother had gone to prison rather than give the cops and the courts five dollars for a dog tag, was a man who "everyone said" would know how to act when he "got to be the man who was boss over the cops." The people at the lower levels of the society, the clammers—particularly those who had registered for the first time and were about to vote in large numbers—were delighted to read in one of the great Boston papers that Biggy had said, "A cop who made a lot of talk about voters who went to register and called them wharf rats, drunkards, and bums, is going to be publicly reprimanded," and "a couple of cops who thought they were pretty smart are going to get the cemetery beat where they will have a lot of other dead ones for company." When Biggy was elected mayor and "walked down to the cop station to tell a few flatfeet something for their own good," a multitude of followers in fact, and more in their fantasies, walked beside him and enjoyed the tongue-lashing given the cops as Biggy "put them in their places" and told them "where the hell to get off." The great crowd of his followers who carried the traditional red fire that night, and cheered at his inauguration while Biggy told Yankee City and the world what he was going to do now that he and his kind were "top dogs," took in very clearly the significance of at least one man's behavior: the policeman who had once arrested Biggy now stood obediently holding his hat, ready to provide more service for the "boss man."

Many other social conditions were among the forces that operated in the structure of the community and in Biggy's personality and influenced what happened. But those reviewed provide us with most of the necessary background for understanding what occurred during the conflict on Hill Street and his later political career.

CHAPTER 2

THE SYMBOLS AND FACTS

OF POLITICAL CONFLICT

The Symbols of Attack

The great leaders of the multitude have often used the evocative and dramatic power of the simple parable to arouse the masses; its traditional symbols are deeply rooted in the common core of experience, in precept and example felt by all men. Biggy, in the Hill Street episode and those following it, manipulated far more dramatic and compelling symbols to center favorable attention on himself and his aspirations. This social drama made the difficult abstractions and conflicting values underlying his argument significant to the great body of the people. It is doubtful whether the figurative words of a parable could have equaled its effectiveness.

·If we think of the whole series of incidents as centering around the backdrop of the mansion, Biggy can be easily seen as an impresario producing and directing a public spectacle, in which he is also the principal actor, for the entertainment and edification of the masses. He had a story to tell, an argument to win, and a goal to achieve. With masterful instinctive artistry, his choice of symbols and mounting episodes, each topping the other, accomplished his ends, defeated his enemies, and gained the recognition and the economic and political goals at which he aimed.

To what extent Biggy *explicitly* understood the significance of the symbols and anticipated the kind of impact they might have on Yankee City and the United States cannot be established. But it can be said that he felt their significance and, with the skill and insight of the artist, fashioned his burlesque in such a way as to outrage only the superior few and a minority (although a substantial one) of the common people. His pageant delighted a large proportion of ordinary persons. His great skill appears even more remarkable when it is recalled that at this time he made such remarks as "They're dead but they won't lie down," about respected men, some of whose names had also been written on the Hill Street gravestones. Clearly, although humorously put, his hostility carried an unconscious death threat; but most of what he did and said was so well disguised, both to himself and to others, and seemingly "unreal," that it aroused no strong fears or anxiety but, instead, the appropriate laughter. Just as the slang stereotype "drop dead" is often used for amusement, so Biggy's symbolic idioms aroused pleasurable feelings and meanings rather than fear in those who viewed his spectacle. But still the use of these symbols out of their context stretched the bounds of propriety almost beyond the limits of easy permissiveness into areas where anger and disgust dominate the response of the people.

The flamboyant circus posters with which Biggy covered the walls of the Hill Street mansion advertised a well-known Wild West Show. Their gaudy colors, rampant lions and tigers, rodeos with cowboys and bucking broncos, trapezes alive with the buxom forms of lady acrobats, all conveyed the young explosive vigor of untamed frontier country. They aroused the youthful free fantasies of all ages. But such posters ordinarily tell their gay and devil-may-care stories on the sides of old barns, abandoned dwellings, outhouses, or billboards and other objects of low status. Their excitement, while suggesting festival, and their gaiety, while appealing to almost everyone, are secular, profane, and beyond the realm of private life. They are for the public; they advertise spectacles not for the exclusive few but for the masses, where payment makes anyone as good as anybody else.

Although appealing to everyone, these shows and posters largely depend on exciting the imagination of the crowd, the hoi polloi, the common man. They tell of fun and reckless excitement, of "death-defying acts" where actors take a chance; they are not concerned with the safety and quiet where people live a life of order, respectability, and tranquil uneventfulness. Risk-taking is something more than an investment which results in a coupon clipped from a bond.

Such posters now were plastered over an elegant structure in an area of the highest status significance. Symbols common, secular, and profane were attached to—and covered—those which were private, superior, and "sacred." Thus a superior, private, in some sense sacred world was symbolically transfigured into a common, public, and inferior secular one.

Moreover the untamed, raucous symbols of the "Wild West" were in stark opposition to the quiet walls of the mansion of conservative old-family class and historically well-disciplined Hill Street. Thus symbols of the vigor of youth, of newness and the future, were dramatically placed in dominating opposition to those of the old, the familiar, and the past—the untamed and the unregulated against tamed domesticity. To state fully what Biggy accomplished by his action would require a very long essay. Yet what he meant was established for the common people in one dramatic moment. The posters disrespectfully said, in the most forceful circumstances, that the past was interfering with the progress of the new technology—of filling stations, of the automobile age, and the pressing demands of the future. Nor was response wanting. The circus advertising man who wrote Biggy to thank him for the use of this point of vantage said, "The cloth banners on your residence caused our show to get a world of publicity." One of the kids who went to the circus did even better: "Those old kill-joys up there always try to stop things. They don't want any of us to have any fun." Biggy's plea for what he claimed as the demands of an advancing technology against the dead hand of proper usage had been positively interrelated in people's feeling with fun, impulse excitement, and desire of almost everyone to have a good time.

The gravestones made from the stone slabs of the terrace wall, the grave mounds fashioned from the lawn, and the likeness of an ancient cemetery formed in the garden, transformed sacred symbols into profane and comic objects. The whole history of Western ceremonial tells of days of festival when sacred symbols are used profanely for the laughter and entertainment of the masses; but it also often speaks of the pain and effort of constituted authorities to reduce or eliminate such outbursts. Attempts to confine such revelry to the narrow, respectable limits of appointed times and places are never completely successful.

The grave and its stone headpiece, marking the end of a life and the dead remains of a once live body, are the visible and permanent signs of a sacred ceremony, the funeral or *rite de*

passage which symbolically translates the body from the world
of the living to that of the dead and helps to re-establish the
relations of living members of the group to each other and to
the memory of the dead. The name on the gravestone is more
than a mark of respect for a dead person. Seen in the context
of the sacred ceremonial, the funeral, and the consecrated
ground of the cemetery, the name of the departed becomes the
'ultimate symbol which helps to relate the secular living to the
sacred dead. It is a sign that the dead are eternally related to
deity and to the sacred world. Accordingly, gravestones and
the cemetery are two of the very few most dramatic and powerful symbols referring to the ideal parts of our past and reaffirming our respect for our traditions.

The grave and the gravestone are of particular significance
in a status society. Since the upper-upper-class position is
greatly dependent on lineage to validate its claims to superiority and its position at the apex of the class system, the graveyard is often the ultimate demonstration and source of social
power. The names of a long line of ancestors composing a
superior lineage are "eternally" located on the gravestones
within the protection of the cemetery—visible and confirmatory
proof to its still living members of old family, birth aristocracy,
and their high position in the community. As the Yankee City
Herald said, Biggy's cemetery bore "a remarkable resemblance
to an ancient graveyard." The emphasis upon the very old
cemetery related the spectacle he had contrived immediately
and directly to the old families and reduced its connection with
modern and contemporary graveyards. Thus the mansion with
its garden, the cemetery with its graves—two great symbols
of membership in the upper class—were combined in a single
composition for the vulgar laughter of the crowd. They became
a kind of symbolic pantomime or charade. This episode, it will
be remembered, immediately followed upon that of the circus
posters. It was a fitting and satisfactory answer to the question
in the minds of most people in Yankee City: What would Biggy
do next to torment his Hill Street enemies?

Moreover—and on the other hand—the grave is an unan-
swerable symbol of the equality of men. As a repository of the
remains of those who have lived, it is a reminder that all men
must die and give up their earthly claims to prestige and

power. Funeral sermons and Memorial Day orations are eloquent with allusion to the fact that "six feet of earth make all men equal." Christian doctrine declares that all souls are equal in the sight of God; in the absolute reckoning of supernatural values and beliefs the cemetery and its graves are equalitarian and democratic, while in the secular reckoning of the living they help to establish claims of rank and status. In Biggy's graveyard the headstones, instead of validating high status, were signs that reduced such claims to a joke for the amusement of the common crowd.

The next sets of symbols displayed, with the emotionally charged building as a backdrop and timed to the expectations aroused by the previous scenes, demonstrated that, like any gifted writer and producer of comic drama, Biggy could make each act cap the last.

The display of the old-fashioned chamber pots from the ridgepole and windows of the mansion and the sign referring to them as the "Spirit of Yankee City" achieved a new peak in the growing excitement he aroused, and a new extreme in the use of emotionally powerful symbols whose appeal reached into the deeper psychological levels, often beyond the limits of social acceptance. Whereas the impact of the gravestone episode came largely from his attack on the upper class by the transferral of revered objects from a respected to a comic context, the next incident's great impact came from the degradation of an upper-class house, symbolic of superiority, to inferior and unclean levels. The chamber pots obviously referred to excretory behavior and aroused anal feelings. They mocked the house and the upper-class world for which it stood with the whole array of dirty excretory jokes in which men and their claims to moral and social respectability are made to appear ridiculous and absurd. The force of tens of thousands of humorous anal stories, told and retold for many millennia in human culture, was here released by Biggy and directed against his enemies. The human feelings of animal inferiority and the contempt and distaste everyone learns very early as part of his cleanliness training now became part of his attack.

No doubt there are symbols other than the chamber pots that might have derogated the traditional values of the upper class, but none could so easily and effectively have aroused ribald laughter. The excretory and anal aspects of the crockery theme reintroduced another motif into Biggy's struggle with the superior people of Hill Street. Just as all men are equal "in six feet of earth," so are they equal and reduced to the same unclean and very human level in their need to defecate. That the feces of each man, whether high or low, are equally repulsive and unclean and smell equally unpleasant is the point of many well-known and much appreciated American jokes. The scatological symbols employed are not for the drawing rooms of the superior or the gathering places of the respectable, but the underlying moral statements of the values of democracy and equality are to be found in some of the more profound declarations of the founding fathers.

Scatological humor plainly styled and openly stated, although accepted and sometimes appreciated by the higher levels, is most enjoyed by the levels at the lower extreme of American life. The superior classes are most likely to respond to subtle sexual jokes, less to bluntly told sexual ones, and least to anal ones where the humor largely depends on explicit and conscious use of fecal symbols.

Death and the corruption of the grave have always been objects of terror and awe as well as laughter and ridicule in American, English, and general European tradition. By his elaborate charade Biggy mobilized the enormous power of graveyard and barnyard humor against the upper-class symbol of the mansion. Looked at from a distance, such humor may be funny to all levels, but *felt* within the context of Yankee City it was modified by the assertion of class values operating in the community. Most people of the middle classes may have laughed momentarily, but they could not officially approve of his humor or go so far as to vote for him.

But here we must modify our previous remarks, for perhaps the most significant characteristic of Biggy's scatological humor and the art he used generally in his spectacle of the mansion on Hill Street was the style he used to express them. Given his exuberance, the strength of his hostility, and the openness of his aggression (it must be remembered that he "socked the mayor in the jaw" and struck other public officials), it might be assumed that he would overstep the acceptable limits and repel almost everyone. Let us suppose he had forgotten all physical restraint, as with the mayor, and had smeared the walls of the house with feces to express his contempt and hostility. Humor would have been lost and mere disgust resulted. Chamber pots as originally used in the society were not only objects of necessity and utility but also forms of self-respect which surrounded the physical act with propriety and reduced its offensiveness to a minimum. While reducing shame and embarrassment they helped increase the satisfaction and pleasure usually experienced but seldom admitted. The chamber pot increased man's sense of being a person and helped to disguise his animal nature. Although Biggy's joke was excretory and animal, it was, in fact, told with more decorum than is at first realized.

Biggy's style of attack, his symbolic rhetoric, despite its explosive and violent qualities, although offensive to many, was always confined within certain limits of tradition—limits outrageously stretched beyond the boundaries of staid propriety. His chamber pots were old-fashioned, directly comparable to Chick Sales' outhouse humor: household artifacts that could be used as excretory symbols, but still symbols rather than facts. Biggy used them like a great actor, thereby escaping the condemnation of many for telling dirty and offensive jokes. For large numbers of people he kept the theme and its point within the realm of what is considered funny rather than embarrassing and disgusting.

But the degrading excretory theme, although important and reaching depths greater than the others, was not in fact the most powerful and immediately potent one aroused by the episode. The chamber pots were anachronistic relics of a former period. They were "artistic" reminders of a past that technological invention had made obsolete for most people in the town. By the legend under his exhibit Biggy told his more elegant fellow townsfolk, "Some of you people don't want electric lights, gas, airplanes, or any of the twentieth century improvements and inventions. Just the same way some of you don't want me . . ." The resistance to the inventions of a new technology could not have been better illustrated than by this allusion to the known backwardness of certain members of the ruling group in the matter of household plumbing.

The picture of Lindbergh as the "Lone Eagle" with the

athletic Rupert Brooke face hung in the homes and offices of thousands of Americans, and all over the country rhapsodic poetry and editorial prose had poured out in tribute to the "unconquerable youth" whose adventure and daring symbolized man's progress. The flight over the forbidding Atlantic represented man's need for triumph over great obstacles; it also symbolized his freedom from old frustrations and release from past confinements. Thousands of editorials spoke of its promise for the future and evoked feelings of human progress and ability. The plane itself—the *Spirit of St. Louis*—embodied achievement and American technological advance; it became the symbol of the promise of a better world, identified in the optimistic twenties as the "Spirit of America." Lindbergh and his plane were powerful symbols to every citizen of what an American should strive to be. The ancient chamber pots and the traditions of the old families to which they referred in Biggy's derogatory lampoon did not conform to this ideal that surged in the emotions of the people.

Another important American theme emerges from the incident. Lindbergh, the Lone Eagle, who flew high and far, was universally thought of as a once unknown mechanic and small-town aviator who, struggling against great odds, had acquired the skill to fly and finally accumulated enough money to finance his flight to Paris. The American theme of a country where everybody has his chance was embodied in this unknown boy who had succeeded in his inalienable American right to make good, who had landed at the top and received the acclaim of presidents and kings.

Lindbergh had been given his chance. Biggy had been thwarted by the anachronistic spirit of Hill Street. It cannot be proved that Biggy fancied himself another Lindbergh. Yet the pantomime he fashioned symbolically identified him with America's greatest contemporary hero. As he said just before his first election, "I only want my chance to show what I can do." The "dead ones" symbolically portrayed in their graves, who stopped progress and prevented him from having his filling station, personified the values represented by the ancient bedroom crockery. Perhaps it is not too much to say that the contents of these two kinds of symbolic repository were identified as one in the non-logical world of the unconscious.

In addition, the "Biggy Muldoon Destruction Company" speaks for itself. The American flag flying over the mansion, aside from its shock value, reminded the people that this symbol was superior to all other American symbols; it told its own story of the power and triumph of ordinary folk over the strength and prestige of the wealthy and superior. The fundamental themes of hostility to superior levels and the basic precept that all men are created equal were stressed and reiterated in every incident of the Hill Street spectacle.

It is small wonder that to many people in Yankee City Biggy himself soon embodied the values and beliefs which were intrinsic parts of the several incidents: Riverbrook against Hill Street, the rights of the common man against the privileges of the superior, the equality of opportunity and birth against the inequality of inherited wealth and aristocracy. None of these social themes could be felt or mentioned in Yankee City without the figure of Biggy Muldoon entering and increasing the emotional heat of all present. Biggy was no longer just another man from the river flats but "a man of the people," a hero or villain according to the role assigned to him by each member of his audience as part of his new symbolic significance.

If the message of a marching song is a more telling argument than the reasoning of a proposition, then the triumphant acts of a flesh-and-blood champion of the people in a drama of real life carry the final, validating force of a knockout blow. Through Biggy and the drama he created, the common people and lower class of Yankee City told the high and mighty ones living on Hill Street to go to hell and made them like it. Later some of them did this in the comparative safety of voting for Biggy and thus approving his smashing attacks on the political power of the higher classes and the symbols of their great prestige. What he did openly as a hero, common men could do vicariously; when he "socked" authority and respectability on the jaw and knocked the mayor to the floor, or when he tore an ugly wound in the mellow beauty of Hill Street and pulled down an old mansion from its lofty status, they, by identifying with him, could feel a deep satisfaction, a rare one for those who seem helpless and are frustrated because of humble position. They could laugh when Biggy assaulted the dignity of sedate Hill Street. Later, voting for him and his men, they were able to seize the instrument of political power. Biggy's show was something more than buffoonery to entertain the masses.

The Several Clusters of Symbols and Their Themes

It does not take a psychological expert to understand something of what motivated Biggy Muldoon and to know why he refused, or failed, to respond to some of the conflicting influences that were exerted on him. A deep love of an only son for his mother is apparent. Her love and restraining hand, inwardly realized, became permanent parts of Biggy's self. The character of the mother, hard-working, aggressive, hostile to authority and to the superior, is easily seen in the son. His mother's experiences at the hands of the powerful people of Yankee City were felt painfully by him as if they were his own.

The fighting and open violence and his attacks on the police he boasts about are not only psychological manifestations but expressions of what the social traditions of his ethnic and class cultures had taught him. The restless energy which drove his mother as a seventeen-year-old girl to leave her family and home in Ireland and migrate to America was continued to the son. The desire not to be subordinated but to dominate, and his considerable preoccupation with himself, are everywhere apparent in what he says and does. His heroes—Julius Caesar, the conqueror and dictator who wrote "a piece about himself," and William Lloyd Garrison, who attacked the powerful slave-owners and championed the ideals of human freedom and equality—represent logically contradictory concepts but emotionally compatible virtues. Despite the rational opposition of these two sets of values, Biggy greatly admired, and was attracted by, each of them. It may be observed that both have some of the characteristics of martyrs.

When the long list of persons and things he attacked during his first two campaigns and terms in office is placed beside the much shorter one of those he approved and loved, the larger role Biggy played in the symbolic and social life of the town soon becomes apparent. The values and beliefs of the status groups which were for and against him are expressed in the symbols used. Their several meanings fit into larger clusters of significance and have a place in the meaning of the social world of Yankee City and America.

The first and most obvious targets of his attack were the persons and symbols of political authority, among them the police, the fire chief, the mayor, the city council, the superintendent of schools, and jails and jailers. Lawyers, judges, and prosecuting and state's attorneys were part of this list. Almost any role or status of authority and some of the apparatus of local government and law enforcement are involved. The ordinary conventional resistance of Americans to authority was carried to an extreme; yet Biggy placed this dangerous attack within the same framework of comic-strip humor. The laughter of children and grown-ups at the comic mass symbols of an earlier period—the Captain and the Katzenjammer Kids, Buster Brown, Happy Hooligan, the Keystone Cops—and many contemporary ones such as Mickey Mouse and Donald Duck, was turned on the people who occupied authoritative positions in real life. Many of the traditional fantasies and the private and unconscious feelings of joy in being able to attack authority were released in some people, while in others the fears of what may happen when authority is attacked aroused them to fight Biggy.

He also attacked the bankers, the trust and loan companies, the Chamber of Commerce and the manufacturers' association, as well as the bosses he had personally worked for. They occupied a position similar to that of the political group, for they wielded powerful authority in the economic world. The attack on these figures was verbal, not physical or visual as in the symbols used on Hill Street. Just as the police and the political authorities, in Biggy's mind, had made him and his mother suffer when he was young, so had the bankers and the economically strong. Yet Biggy and his mother, despite opposition, had done well financially. They owned several important pieces of income property. Biggy's announcement that he was "damn well off" clearly said he was not among the "wage slaves" or economically frustrated. He wanted more money, and as a competent enterpriser he knew how to get it. He was not bucking private enterprise so much as the system and power inherited by the old families.

Other objects he attacked were "foreigners," "hypocrites,"

"immoral people," and young men who were not drafted and did not enlist. The symbolic pattern is not so clear in this list as in the others, but the theme of not being a good member of the group runs throughout. The "foreigners" he felt ambivalent about; he wanted them to be good Americans and then they were "just as good as anybody else." The others, including the hypocrites, immoral people, and the young men "whose fathers kept them out of uniform," were largely people from the higher levels of Yankee City society. They were attacked for their moral delinquencies, but were particularly reprehensible because most of them belonged to the symbolic cluster he called the "codfish aristocracy." The intense feeling aroused by such attacks, although enhanced by the belief that they were unethical or immoral, sprang more from a sense of inequality and injustice and status frustration among his followers than from moral disapproval.

The elms, old gardens, the Sampson mansion, lace-curtain Irish, Hill Street and the codfish aristocrats, all from the upper levels of the social-class system of Yankee City, form a logically heterogeneous but non-logically homogeneous group. Since they are at the focal center of his attack we have examined them in the context of the conflict. The significance of trees and mansion as a ramified symbol we will explore separately.

The list of loved objects is important and revealing. Biggy's mother stands in a class by herself. She was loved, admired, and respected by her son in a way perhaps that only the widowed mother of an only child can be. She was feared and at times defied, but was deeply loved and served as a model for much of what he did. In another category were his boyhood friends, hobo comrades, and his Navy pals. All were former members of intimate face-to-face clique groups. All were particularly loved in an atmosphere of youthful defiance of authority and symbolized some of the feelings he had about being young, free, and autonomous.

Another cluster includes the clammers, his cur dog "Bo," workers on strike, a prisoner up on charges of murder, prisoners generally, and Al Smith, William Lloyd Garrison, and Andrew Jackson. Biggy identified with all of them either as an underdog himself or as a champion of the underdog. The significance of the list, of course, parallels the previous one.

Still another group would include fighters, Julius Caesar, football, the Navy, those who enlisted and fought in World War I, and technological progress generally. Among other common values here expressed are competition, aggression, dominance, and success.

Biggy also had a deep love for Yankee City, particularly for the streets along the river. Perhaps most interesting of all was his identification with the taxpayers and his liking for schoolteachers. Since he was a large taxpayer himself and a man of property, the former feeling is easily understood. It might be supposed that, because of their authoritative role, he would have disliked teachers, but his liking for them seems to be connected with their understanding of his boyhood deviltry. Few of the people, statuses, or symbols he liked belong to the experiences of adult life. Even the taxpayers may reflect his memory of his mother's often reiterated claims of being a large taxpayer in Yankee City. His mother, his native city, his childhood neighborhood, and his friends are at the core of his positive feelings.

To the list of positive objects must be added the jail, once a prison to his mother and himself, now his much beloved and admired home. Since he now owned it, this former symbol of authority was his to do with as he willed.

Biggy Muldoon spent three periods in jail. These experiences embittered him and increased his hostility toward authority, but the several days his mother spent in jail for refusing to pay for a license for his stray dog grieved and angered him far more than his own incarcerations. When the judge sentenced him for cutting down the elm trees he said he'd "run for governor and fire the judge," and when he did time for hitting the mayor, he said that when he got to be mayor he would fire the superintendent of the jail. When he did indeed become mayor he did not forget the time he and his mother spent in the local jail and retaliated by firing certain officials and giving some of the "cops" menial and distasteful tasks.

The purchase of the jail was an economic action, no doubt judged by the criteria of economic risk-taking; yet it was a source of great satisfaction to Biggy and Mrs. Muldoon to control the symbol of their humiliation. The symbolic significance of the act becomes even more apparent when it is remembered that they lived in the sheriff's quarters, where they now had liberty to come and go as they pleased. The people of Yankee City at the time did not miss the point; they were excited by it, many being pleased with the idea of former prisoners owning and controlling the jail that had held them captive. The purchase of the Sampson house where Mrs. Muldoon had once worked as a domestic easily fits into this same symbolic category. Economically it was a good buy, but the social significance of ownership by one who had once served there was not overlooked by the citizens of the town.

Biggy dramatized some of the basic conflicts of our society, perhaps most specifically those around technological change. Symbolically he supported the values of progress and change against those of conservatism, which supports the moral, aesthetic, and intellectual worth of the past. The conflict between the technology and the conservative mores of the past in a democratic society makes the manners and morals of the old-family status vulnerable to attack, particularly by the distortions of satire and burlesque. When matched against the symbols of old family and the past, the symbols of youth and new technology with its discoveries and inventions, intertwined as one in a changing world where "progress" is a highly valued process, are very formidable.

This force is felt particularly by common men who have ambition for higher status. Once the economic barriers have been conquered by mobile men, only acceptance by the aristocracy—that always necessary legitimizing of the personal success of the mobile man and his family—keeps them from being triumphant. Here lies the possibility of conflict. Those who have been at the top for only one or two generations are likely to be the very people who in fact and symbol oppose the social and economic advance of men beneath them. There is a desperate need for such a class to control the processes by which people enter, and become part of, their group. It is also necessary for their security and stability that they exercise a considerable control over the forces (or channels) which produce successfully mobile people. The low birth rate at the top requires continual recruitment to fill their superior ranks. As long as they dominate the tacit agreements which constitute the rules for social and economic success at their own level, they and their forms of behavior are secure. When the principles by which they establish control are threatened, they and their whole way of life face destruction. The basic power of the old-family class is their right to accept a few sheep of peculiar whiteness and reject all others who try for admission. Because of this power, in effect, they control how an ambitious family will spend its money, the social rituals its members will adopt, the charities and philanthropies, arts, and other similar highly regarded behavior they will support; the associations and churches they will join and maintain, and, for many mobile families, the beliefs about the world and themselves that they will accept and make their own.

Biggy Muldoon had challenged all this and invited the little people of Yankee City and the world to join him. The elegant and forbidding presence of the mansion and its walled gardens and the great moral and economic power and prestige of embattled Hill Street had not intimidated him. He behaved socially in character as a man from the wrong side of the tracks: he used a violent style of attack to settle arguments. The metropolitan papers which frequently reprinted (to the delight of their mass audiences) the story he told a reporter, that he did not go in for boxing but only bare-knuckled street fighting, caught one important aspect of Biggy which, among many, identified him with this class. But his faith in money, hard work, saving and investing capital, and taking a risk was something else again. Benjamin Franklin, a charter member of the middle class and phrase-maker for it, would have admired and sponsored the Biggy who believed in enterprise and making money and wanted no "socialist" nonsense about "dividing my money in half." Economically Biggy was a middle-class man and conformed to the central precepts of that part of the success story.

But he did not want, as a reward for such splendid successful enterprise, to marry the boss's daughter—that symbol of acceptance by, and submission to, the social authority of the upper class. Nor did he make any other moves for social acceptance; rather, he regarded all advances he made as attacks on the upper class and everything they and those who emulated them stood for. Biggy was not an economic but a social rebel,

who vigorously assaulted the social, not the economic, foundations of superiority. The contradictions between his economic
and social ideologies created a seeming paradox which confused
both his foes and many of his followers. On the other hand, it
protected him from serious charges of being a "goddamned
bolshevik" who wanted to overthrow the American way of life.
The fact that he was willing to pay the price demanded for
economic success, but not for social acceptance, was of fundamental importance in determining his successes and failures.

We have examined some of the meanings of Biggy's treatment of the Hill Street mansion. We must now return to the
significance of the house itself.

The Hill Street Mansion and Garden: Objects of Biggy's Violence

At the time Biggy and his mother purchased it, the Sampson mansion rested securely within its pleasant and spacious
garden, which spread across the highlands marking the summit of Hill Street. Surrounded by a terraced wall of heavy
granite slabs, the estate was effectively separated from the
public highway below. The wall shut out the world of common
people from the superior and well-bred life of the few. The
ancient elms growing along the street at the side of the house
made a part of the long rows of elms bordering Hill Street to
form a great canopy stretching for miles along that broad
avenue.

The beauty of the tree-lined street and the common sentiment of its residents for the venerable elms unify the homes of
Hill Street in the minds of its people, the fine old trees providing an outward symbol of that superior region's self-regard.
The trees themselves are part of a planting that physically and
symbolically interrelates the contemporary families and their
homes with the larger cultured world of their dwelling area, and
this whole world with the values and beliefs of an upper-class
style of life through past generations. In the living presence
of the elms, the past lives too. Hill Street is the most important
public symbol of the upper classes of Yankee City.

Although rows of fine trees are the hallmark of old New
England towns and villages, it cannot be denied that in a fair-

sized city, in the residential section, they constitute a public expression of the presence of upper-class manners and gentle refinement. Here on Hill Street, their age and the agreeable and historic style of most of the houses give eloquent testimony that good form, good breeding, and a proper ritualistic consumption of wealth have been and are being maintained by the families who have lived there for generations. The historical markers on many of the houses, placed there at the time of the three-hundredth anniversary of the state, tell of their continued claims to superiority, the ultimate mark of old family. An authoritative book written by one of the owners, consisting of pictures and histories of the great houses of the city, most of them on Hill Street, provides final and clinching evidence. It shows the houses and their gardens and displays the art of doorways, fireplaces, stairways. Beyond the selection of the oldest houses connected with great days of the past, as well as elegant and architecturally significant mansions built by the wealth of the early Yankee City merchants when the town was a great seaport, the most significant characteristic of the book is the genealogy of owners proudly claimed by each house. Beside the picture of each is a list of owners and their period of ownership, validating and legitimizing its claim to superiority by the same social form as the lineage of old families.

A house with its landscaping and architecture is usually the very heart of the technical and symbolic apparatus necessary for the maintenance of self-regard in upper-class personality, and for the persistence of the culture of the group which occupies this social level. The decor, furnishings, paintings, and their arrangements in the various rooms where the family life is differentiated and defined are all symbolic objects belonging to a subculture which expresses to those who occupy the house, and those who frequent or know about it, the nature of the inner world of each person living there. The symbols not only refer to the manners and morals of the subculture and express the significance of the people and their way of life, but also evoke and maintain in people sentiments about who they are and what they must do to retain their superior images of themselves and keep before them an interesting and gratifying vision of the superiority of their world. The subjects of the paintings on the wall of a living room often directly refer to an ancestor, and to his and their superior position. They may evoke sentiments and express values which reinforce the learning of childhood within the private worlds of the family members, or strengthen the present solidarity of the family by indirectly relating its members more closely to each other and tying each more closely to a shared ancestor.

The upper classes in our culture have characteristically taken unto themselves, and have had yielded to them by most of the society, the principal role of fostering the arts and cultivating the taste necessary for their existence. Since these classes are rarely sufficiently creative to supply the artists necessary for the survival of the great arts, they patronize artists and often by social recognition or marriage recruit many of them to be members of their own level. The presence and control of objects of art provide a permanent mirror of superiority into which the upper classes can look and always see what they believe to be their own excellence, thus reinforcing one of their principal claims to superiority, their belief in their own good taste.

Landscaping transforms the surroundings of the house into a superior aesthetic form, functioning for the exterior setting much as the beauty of furnishings and decor for the interior. To have significance for status purposes, a garden must reflect taste and an understanding of beauty; the owner must have suitable knowledge of shrubs and plants—better still, the garden, its trees and flowers, should have their own superior history.

The old-family tradition demands understatement about outward forms, particularly personal possessions. The perfect expression of the "ideal" should be avoided for it is often the mark of the parvenu, driven by his feelings of anxiety that "he won't do it right" while running from his inner sense of inferiority, to have everything perfect about the house and "all the parts fitting in perfect harmony." The presence of such values and fears is also the reason interior decorators are numerous and well-paid in this society. The often expressed hostility and contempt for them is symbolically similar to that generally felt for undertakers—each is felt to be necessary to cover human pain and inadequacy.

Many of the better houses are occupied by lower-upper or

new-family people without family lineage. Since they have been able to become the proud owners of houses whose lineage strengthens unspoken claims for recognition the owners feel they themselves deserve, they too belong to a culture founded on inherited achievements.

The purchase of such a house is not only a display of wealth and a public statement of a family's economic position but a demonstration that the family knows how to live according to a code of manners and can conform to the stylized pattern that makes up their way of life. A good house is one of the most important symbols upward-mobile people can use to transform money into claims of superior behavior which may be acceptable to the top levels of the society. Such a house and garden can be a staging area from which a family may increase its participation with, and ultimately be included in, the upper class.

Despite what the theorists say, conspicuous expenditure *per se* is insufficient to achieve this end. The form and manner in which conspicuous expenditure is made determine its efficacy for advancement in status. It can end all hopes for those who are upward-mobile, simply by the manner in which it is carried out. Only when a house encloses a style of existence that conforms to its outward form, and when its inner way of life has been recognized and accepted through the intimate participation of its owners with the top group, does it cease to be no more than a claim to upper-class status and become a symbol of the actually achieved status of the family.

The social position of the children of upper-class families, as in other classes, is entirely dependent on that of the parents. The economic position of the family is ordinarily, though not always, dependent on the husband and father; but the maintenance of the private life of the family and its status are usually centered in the wife and mother. Family life is planned and organized around her, and as the lady of the house she often becomes the gracious symbol of the family's way of life.

Given its physical form, it is easy to understand why the house has come to be regarded in the study of symbolism as feminine rather than masculine. For other non-logical reasons, it is also no cause for wonder that a garden is considered a feminine rather than a masculine symbol. The most private and protected part of social life that is shared by two or more

people is the family; the most intimate relation, highly protected by secrecy, is the sexual one between husband and wife.
The sexuality of the woman is guarded by many restrictions
and taboos. They help to make her the most significant person
in the continuing life of our culture and the subcultures of the
social classes. The enclosed and concealed physical character
of her sexual being is further enclosed by convention and, for
some Christians, transformed into a sacred mystery. The core
of all family life in America, particularly that of the upper-
upper class, is the person of the wife and mother. She is usually
the most important factor in the formation of the growing
child's personality and the transmitter of some of the basic
values and attitudes which are the foundations of the learning
determining the class to which her children belong. The persistence of the culture of a social class as a way of life is partly
founded on her strength as wife and mother within the protec-
tive spiritual walls of family and the material ones of the
house.

If the enclosed, inner world of a house and garden is feminine
and a symbol of aloof superiority, the outer world of a Hill
Street is a mixed symbol at once of feminine grace and privacy
and of masculine dominance and superiority. This avenue is the
present symbolic expression of the past glory of Yankee City
when it was one of the great aggressive trading cities of New
England, a port which built and sent its sailing ships to fight
and trade all over the world. When the ships returned, Hill
Street received a major share of their wealth, for the ship-
owners and wealthy merchants lived in many of its houses.

The separation of the inner and outer worlds of particular
homes and the general dwelling area into feminine and masculine symbols is worth exploring. The early period of Hill Street
and Yankee City's glory was more masculine and aggressive,
the whole order dominated by the values and virtues our culture
commonly ascribes to males. The sailing ships, classed symbolically as female, were part of a larger world dominated and
run by men. In the economic life of the time they occupied a
symbolic position similar to that held by the houses, then and
now, in the life of the town. They were owned by men and, as
economic objects, were under their control and protection. Essentially, this parallels the position of most upper-class women

in our society; during most of their lives they are economically dependent upon and socially protected by men.

It should be mentioned that the book on the houses of Yankee City and their lineage has a few appended pictures of the great ships built and sailed from the city in the time of her maritime greatness—the ideal and sometimes actual source of the inherited wealth of some of her old families. Their inclusion with the houses built by the same wealth and by the skills of the same carpenters and craftsmen appears not to be a coincidence. Each is a perfect symbol of inherited upper-class status and refers to basic facts of the social and economic life of the town's past. Each evokes sentiments proper and necessary for the continuance of the culture of this upper-class group. The mansions of Hill Street are the most important symbols of a cherished and highly prized way of life. The deepest sentiments about what a man is and what he is to others are rooted within their walls.

When Biggy attacked the mansion he attacked the most potent symbol of the superior classes of Yankee City; he struck at their very foundations. Not only did he violate the house and threaten the values attached to Hill Street as well as old-family sentiment, but he injured and threatened the deeper unconscious emotions felt for that protected place where wives and mothers live, whose persons are the emotional center of the group and the channel through which social forms and symbols persist, for they train the young in their particular usages.

Biggy's removal of the great house and substitution of a commercial filling station were simple utilitarian acts. The increased use of cars on Constitution Avenue, part of an interstate highway, made the gas station a good business risk. The traditional values protecting Hill Street were breached as part of the social changes resulting from the progress of the automobile and other technological improvement. The mansion on Hill Street served the few and excluded the many; payment could not buy entrance into it. The filling station, a commercial and technological machine, served and included everyone. It was not endowed with "social" prestige. It was frankly for profit rather than for the spending and display of wealth to establish a family's claims to superior status.

Of all these acts which were transposed into the realm of

evocative symbols, the cutting of the great trunks of the ancient elms went deepest and pervaded most fully the conscious and unconscious life of the members of Yankee City society. Trees have long been symbols of man's vitality and of his hopes for eternal life. The tree is an evocative symbol, important in legend and religion and in poetry and the art of the theatre; it is an essential part of our cultural context as people. Its significance for all life and its symbolic interdependence with man's existence, enhanced by sentiments of the agricultural societies which were our cultural forebears, are deeply rooted in the very beginnings of man's social existence. Frazer's *Golden Bough* is a literary and scientific monument marking the significance of the tree in man's feelings and beliefs about himself and what he is.

To the author of the *Cherry Orchard* what happened at Hill Street and Constitution Avenue would have been easy to understand. In the Chekhov drama, it will be recalled, the merchant who had risen from serfdom to affluence purchased the orchard from a decaying aristocratic family. A new railway had given the land a new kind of social value. The self-made man who bought the cherry orchard declares that it can be "cut up . . . into building lots" and great profits made. He reminds all who will listen that "my father was your father's serf." For the aristocrats, the orchard is the past living in the present and in each of them. "When I walk through . . . in the evening or at night," one of them says, "the rugged bark on the trees glows with a dim light and the cherry trees seem to see all that happened a hundred and two hundred years ago." Just before the sound of the axe announces the climax and end of the play, the merchant Lopokhin cries, "I have bought the property where my father and my grandfather were slaves."

On the morning Biggy cut down the elms an old man who lived on Hill Street passed by. It was said he cried openly and wiped the tears from his eyes as he continued down the street. One of his friends told us, "For a person like me, born and brought up in Yankee City, walking under the elms on Hill Street is always an experience. Sometimes I'm in another world; I'm back talking to my grandfather and listening to all the fine things he used to say. Those trees are like people, the people I used to know, the kind of people my parents were."

CHAPTER 3

MASS MEDIA: THE TRANSFORMATION

OF A POLITICAL HERO

Mask for a Hero

Biggy Muldoon's fight with Hill Street was played before two highly interested audiences. The local ones, the citizens of Yankee City, consisted of those who participated as actors in the drama and those who, acting as a kind of chorus, watched and commented as the plot unfolded. Among them were the Hill Street crowd, the lace-curtain Irish, and the ordinary little people, Yankee and ethnic, who lived down by the river. For the national audience Yankee City itself, through the symbols of the mass media, became a stage where a human drama of intense interest was being played, yet no one of the audience was directly involved. Each vicariously experienced what happened by reading about it in the great metropolitan papers and magazines, seeing it in a newsreel, or hearing it over the radio. Biggy became a topic of dinner-table conversation, barbershop gossip, a part of gay and ribald talk in the speakeasies throughout the nation.

The Yankee City audience at first viewed him as one kind of character in the plot: a public personality fashioned by events and through experiences with members of the town. Later they saw him and the other members of his drama in a different light, characters whose lines had been rewritten by the national media of communication. Here he became something more than he had been and was applauded accordingly. The local effect of this outside influence was considerable. It was felt directly, for about half the newspapers sold in Yankee City came from metropolitan sources.[1]

To the local audience, despite its laughter, this was a serious play, a tragedy or a drama of triumph according to the time and necessities of those who watched. If so minded,

1. See "Yankee City Series," Vol. 1.

they could laugh, and laugh hard, when Biggy made his opponents ridiculous; but beneath the laughter, and often beside it, were anxious feelings that what was happening demanded sober consideration. The responsibilities of the citizen were involved in what should be felt about each event.

For the audience in the world beyond Yankee City, Biggy's drama was either light comedy or slapstick. The hero could be liked and enjoyed by everyone because he laid his paddle across the fat posteriors of the rich, upset the self-respect of the respectable, and dumped their power and authority on the floor. Yet no one needed to feel responsible for what happened; everyone could have fun. Childhood fantasies of kicking adult authority in the pants, of breaking loose from subordination and the restraint of respectability, were vicariously felt. For the general audience Biggy was the little guy, the "small fry" in them, still rebelling against the jail-like constraints of adult responsibility. He was also the embodiment of their distrust and concern about the rigid moral attitudes of the middle class. But above all he was a symbol of revolt against the imposition of these moral restraints by the powerful middle class; through him, without fear of punishment, they had a good time raising hell before the pained gaze of the respectable.

In Yankee City a part of the figure of Biggy Muldoon was inescapably true, real, an actual person—but in Memphis or Peoria or Pittsburgh he was a glorious clown or a figure of light comedy, though still the hero of the show and a man his audience could respect. They liked and trusted him as "an honest man doing his damnedest." Second thoughts that might arise in the minds of the serious about not wanting "that kind of thing to happen in my town" could be easily dropped because Biggy was not there. For many, perhaps most, it was easy to say, "what this town of ours needs is a Biggy Muldoon, maybe he'd stir things up and get rid of the damned stuffed shirts and crooked politicians who are running things." For such people in Yankee City the trouble with Biggy was that he was in Yankee City.

For many in both audiences Biggy's actions, his friends, and his enemies had been transformed into something more than a drama by the metropolitan papers and national mass media. Perhaps the whole might be called a contemporary collective ritual, its participants characters in a collective rite in which everyone symbolically participated. The characters under different names have appeared in thousands of plays and legends and stories, told straight or with humor, that everyone has heard and seen. The hero, dominant and positive symbol of countless folktales—lodged securely in everyone's pleasant private fantasies and the mythical embodiment of a people's hopes —as champion of the oppressed goes forth to battle. He attacks the position of the powerful few and of those who arouse the fears and anxiety of the many. Those in power fight back, and with their superior weapons capture the hero, incarcerate him, and for a time defeat and disgrace him. But one knows that by his indomitable courage and herculean determination, and with the help of the little people, he will once again attack the fortresses of the mighty, in the end defeating his enemies and winning a great victory for the common people. This drama, continuously modified to meet the needs of the time, older than the records of history, is a public myth often capable of empirical validation, and· a private fantasy deeply embedded in the conscious imagery of all Americans.

For a brief time, in the heyday of Biggy's fame, Yankee City became one of the many small stages where America watches the current but passing heroes of the national scene act out a drama whose cast and plot express the varying sentiments, values, and symbolic themes of our people and the system of social relations which organizes and controls us. Through newspapers, magazines, radio, and motion picture, events in that city were conveyed to the world in the form of a drama which did not necessarily correspond in cold fact to what those events and persons really were; nor did its representations present an exact image of the social world of Yankee City. [79]

The contemporary storytellers whose mass art maintains the living continuity of myth and legend in our society and contributes to the integration and persistence of the culture work under far more difficult circumstances than the storytellers of bygone days. Formerly, fables, legends, and myths could be told as if they were true—because they *should* be true, and the imaginations and fantasies of their audiences unquestioningly accepted them. Heroes and villains and their plots and solutions conformed to traditional convention, and for the audience as well as the storyteller who entertained them, defined the proper role of each character and determined how these symbolic beings should be related to each other. The artist and the members of his audience, although different persons, were products of the same social matrix, with closely corresponding beliefs, values, and expectancies about each other and the world in which they lived. The symbols and themes used to arouse anxiety or assuage fear, and the masks and ritualistic plots of the drama which evoked the hopes and fears of their audiences, needed only the artistry of the entertainers and the sanction of conformity to the conventions of the culture to be assured eager acceptance.

The audience believed a tale or a drama was true and conformed to *their* reality if it fell within the confines of sanctioned collective representations. The close fit of the private image and the public symbol provided the conviction of reality while arousing the private emotions of the individual and at the same time controlling them. The collective representations were evaluated beliefs sanctioned by the whole moral and social order. Their private fantasies being controlled more fully by the collective representations of their society, early storytellers easily projected their private imagery on the tales they told and into the folk dramas they presented. Their own private images often were no more than minute individual variations of those in the public domain. Consequently the need of evidence, of induction and rational empirical testing, was greatly reduced.

Today the reporter is trained to be objective, accurate, and to get the facts about the people and events that make a news story. The more recently developed mass media use these same criteria and insist on rules of evidence as guides for their field men who report on current events. The instant repercussions of a modern libel law, as well as the potential embarrassments inherent in a modern system of communications only too ready to point out and publish any discrepancies of fact, sharpen this rule.

Despite the intrusion of modern canons of accuracy and the infusion of the spirit of rationality into newspapers and other mass media, a casual listing of the prevailing selection of stories and the simplest analysis of the criteria of a "good story" that will hold readers and perhaps build circulation demonstrate that the "objective" coverage of what happens every day to the people of the world is dominated by the basic wishes, the hopes and fears, the non-logical symbolic themes and folk beliefs of the people who buy and read the papers. The degree of rationality and accuracy exhibited in the news stories of a paper or magazine is in direct relation to the degree of rational values of its audience. The audiences of mass media vary by age, sex, education, social class, urbanity, and many other social characteristics. Those who have been trained to respect rationality and objective reporting and to expect accurate coverage of events usually read papers and magazines which carry more stories of this character and have corresponding policies. [76b] Even these papers print news accounts often filled with evocative, non-logical symbols rather than logical and empirical ones—symbols arousing the feelings and cultural beliefs of the reader rather than pointing out the factual flow of human actions in the event reported.

The fact is, the contemporary newsman must tell his story much as did his progenitors. His tale must arouse and hold the interest of his readers; he must hold out the same kind of symbols to their fears and hopes as did his predecessors. There must be villains and heroes in every paper, and the story lines must conform to the usage of suspense, conflict, the defeat of evil, and the triumph of good that have guided the good sense and artistry of past storytellers and controlled their audience's ability to respond. [9b]

But today the reporter must put the mark of empirical truth on the story—over the whole of his plot, its *dramatis personae*, and its solutions—as if it all really happened. He must believe (or pretend) that the facts, rather than the story, speak for themselves. Although the events of the news story may have all occurred in the form in which they are set forth, the relations of the major and minor characters, the arrangement of the incidents, and the symbols used to refer to them must be part of the storyteller's art. The news report is consequently composed of fact combined with the thematic materials supplied by the reporter and the conventions and traditions of his profession as well as those of his readers and his society. [9a] An exact correspondence between the scientific reality of what has actually happened and the story of what is supposed to have happened is not necessarily a test of the story's capacity to convince its readers. The mask of empirical truth is often present only for the easier acceptance of the non-logical "truths" of contemporary popular arts. The empirical facts of an event for those who write and read may be no more than a passing illustration of the deeper evocative "truths" of the non-logical symbols of our culture. [76a]

Biggy Muldoon and the Mass Media

The symbolic transformation of Biggy began with the paid advertisements he placed in the local paper when he first challenged his enemies to answer his charges of injustice and foul play. He thus unknowingly began his public transformation from the inconsequential boy from the wrong side of the tracks to the American citizen who has not been given a fair chance. In one of his first political ads Biggy told everyone that all he wanted was an opportunity to show his "true worth." Later he said that his enemies, the high and mighty "codfish aristocrats," were conspiring to destroy the rightful chance of every American to be somebody. "There is a little crowd of bankers and aristocrats in this old town," he reiterated throughout the campaign, "who don't want anybody else to have a chance but themselves. They have run this town long enough. They don't want me to have a chance. That's what the row has been. They've ridden me." When he became mayor he added, "Now, I'm going to ride them. I'll repeal their zoning law and go after that permit."

He told the people along the river and anyone who would listen that the zoning law his opponents used to stop him from putting the gas station on Hill Street was a law to protect the people on Hill Street, not the people of Riverbrook. The clammers (almost entirely Yankee and lower-lower-class) were being deprived of their livelihood, he said, because no one had come to their assistance; but he, Biggy, would be their champion, lead them, and force the state to purify the polluted waters of the river and make their clams fit for sale and human consumption.

These efforts were the first suggestion of his transformation into the hero who championed the poor. But as Biggy himself has said, it is doubtful if they would have been sufficient to elect him. Just before the election a further development in his symbolic transformation occurred which lifted him out of himself and made him something more than the man, Biggy Muldoon. This was the story, previously mentioned, which appeared first in the metropolitan press, then in hundreds of other papers, thus beginning the transformation of Biggy into a real public hero. It changed the campaign of local fact and fancy into what was also a battle between positive annd negative national stereotypes, symbols now identified with Biggy which both friends and enemies tried to use to capture the imagination and votes of the people. The story was published in a Boston paper a few days before the election, a two-column, front-page news item with Biggy's picture, recounting the incidents—now dated by a year or so—of the circus posters, the chamber pots, and the house of Hill Street. It will be remembered that outwardly, until the mayoralty election, his acts in themselves, dramatic as they were, had done little to advance Biggy's political aspirations. It is certain that very few persons thought of what he had done on Hill Street as important enough to make him a successful candidate for the highest political position in the community. Yet the emotional foundations for this had been established.

The man who wrote the story, a former resident of Yankee City, having full knowledge of what had happened during the time Biggy had attempted to remove the house and establish his filling station, had considerable insight into the episode.

Biggy Muldoon [the article began], Yankee City's thirty-one-year-old bad boy, perpetual foe of mayors, city councilmen, police chiefs, fire chiefs, judges, and other symbols of law and order, once more threatens the serenity of this quiet old city.

Conservative citizens are just recovering from Biggy's antics of last summer when he entertained motorists along the Yankee City Turnpike with displays of circus posters, imitation gravestones, and genuine old-fashioned chamber pots on the old Sampson property on Constitution and Hill Streets. And now when everything seems set for a long quiet winter Biggy proceeds to furnish these same conservative citizens with material for new nightmares by threatening to get himself elected mayor.

In facing the question of issues that might elect Biggy and capture the votes of the city, the author of the piece found it difficult to formulate a suitable answer.

If someone should ask why Biggy's candidacy is so serious at this time, the only appropriate answer is, ask me another. Perhaps it is because he represents the wild and reckless spirit of youth and has caught this prim city in a moment when she is tempted to do a little high stepping. Perhaps it is because he is a self-confessed grudge candidate and there are so many people in the town who have grudges of their own to work out.

Take, for instance, the clam diggers of Riverbrook. They sit outside their picturesque shanties these sunny autumn days and hurl imprecations at the law which says they shall not dig clams in the Yankee City harbor because its waters are polluted by the waste from the big manufacturing cities up the river. Who wouldn't have a grudge under such circumstances? Well, along comes Biggy Muldoon and he tells them that if he is elected mayor he will build a new sewer at a cost of more millions than Yankee City can raise by taxation in a decade, and that when that is done they can dig their clams. Even though they know the boy is talking through his hat they like his audacity.

The writer retold the story of the Sampson house. He told it dramatically and clearly in a form not uncomplimentary to Biggy, adding that "tearing down the stone wall which flanked the turnpike was a public-spirited act because it improved vision at a dangerous corner." But he went on to say that after these exhibitions Biggy's candidacy was regarded as another joke, that

. . . the citizens laughed when they learned that in a harangue at Smith's Cafe—a speech which was not recorded in the news-papers but which reached every voter nevertheless—he had de-clared that when elected he would commit the police chief to an old man's home and designate the deputy chief official keeper. Biggy despises the fire marshal, too, and another promise was that he would replace that official with a certain business man in whose establishment mysterious fires occur with exasperating regularity. The very efficient policeman who recently arrested Biggy for loitering on the corner was to be assigned to the cemetery beat, "where he will have a lot of other dead ones for company."

It is possible that the story in the Boston paper would not have provoked the developments that rapidly followed had not Biggy responded with an extraordinary advertisement in the local paper. He wrote it—his enemies said with the help of others but Biggy said "with the help of my own pencil"— partly in fear that the irony and gentle leg-pulling of the news story might do him harm. He also believed that such important news coverage indicated that his powerful enemies were responding because he had hit them where it hurt. He addressed himself to "Mr. Voter and Taxpayer."

I have harpooned the whale.

I am using its oil in the machines that will carry you to the polls to vote for me.

Such bombastic fiction brought fame to said Barnum.

As the pup in Aesop's Fables. The codfish aristocrats give way.

They acknowledge they have lost, the substance is grasping at the shadow.

Wake up! Wake up! staid old Yankee City. Defeat the invisible king of Shylocks that has ruled our city the past thirty years. Let the shop whistles blow at seven every morning by casting your vote for Thomas Ignatius Muldoon for Mayor December sixth.

Bring health, prosperity, and employment to all.

THOMAS IGNATIUS MULDOON

The ad aroused everyone. Literary critics who admired Herman Melville and Walt Whitman, historians and writers who knew and loved the culture and lore of the glorious days when Yankee City and other ancient New England towns were great seaports, responded with delight. For everyone who loved New England it stimulated deep feelings about the period when her merchant princes built and sent her ships to trade in the Indies or hunt Moby Dick in distant seas, when her able seamen manned vessels that brought Yankee daring and economic enterprise to the whole earth. No New Englander, particularly a native of Yankee City, could remain indifferent to the impact of its symbols.

Despite their criticisms of the grammar and syntax everyone knew and, better yet, felt what Biggy meant. The metaphors may have been a bit involved, but "harpooning a whale" and "the good old oil," "Shylocks," and "codfish aristocrats" are all solid parts of our traditional equipment.

The attack on Biggy now had to shift, for the drama was no longer confined to the local scene. Immediately following this advertisement his opponent addressed a personal letter to him in the local paper. Unfortunately for the writer, despite the factual points made, its mockery and lofty air were not easily appreciated; it embarrassed more than it pleased.The crude implications of the bad grammar, the joking about "happy laborers," the supercilious air of a superior person addressing his inferiors validated Biggy's contentions as to the common man needing a common man to represent him. The general effect was further to enhance his reputation as champion of the little people.

Dear Thomas [the letter began]:
The Yankee City bad boy write-up you got in the Boston papers was wonderful. You got your picture in and everything. We never did think you was so bad [said the writer invidiously], even after you used your youthful strength in beating up a man of Mr. Flaherty's age. Oh, Thomas, please repeat that ad about the health and happiness you are to bring to us sleepy old residents of Yankee City. Just think of it: that could only be exceeded by the wonderful prosperity that you would bring to our factories. In our fancy we hear the cheerful blowing of the whistles every morning of the year. The happy laborers tripping lightly to their labors with songs of praise of our Biggy on their lips, all the long happy day. After we elect you and make our factories prosperous you must promise not to overlook our clammers. We pray that you give us a mild winter and a nice early spring.

JOHN J. SMITH
Hill Street

The intervention of the Boston and New York and other papers now brought about a drastic change in Biggy's significance and the character of the local political struggle. A vast new national audience suddenly joined the local one. The impact of this force on the community was great, but its effect on Biggy as a public symbol cannot be overemphasized. Biggy the man remained largely the same, but Biggy the symbol rapidly went through mutations and elaborations that made him a national celebrity. Minor aspects of his public personality took new form and grew into dominant themes of the fabricated legend; soon the man Biggy was acting a new role before the new audience the mass authors had created. Although there is only slight evidence of change in his inner world, there is clear proof that the outer man, Biggy's social personality as publicly conceived, changed greatly. New interpreters selected and rejected events in his life and political battles and translated them for national consumption. The camera's eye, the microphone, and the wire services of the news syndicates captured the excitement of the drama and began to recast it into the stereotypes that entertain mass audiences.

As soon as the metropolitan press focused the public's attention on him, Biggy became the "two-fisted, redheaded, hardworking go-getter. He not only calls a spade a spade but he will go farther and identify a pick and shovel for you in a manner that leaves nothing to the imagination.

"But don't get the idea that Mr. Thomas Ignatius Muldoon is a harem-scarem gashouse roughneck. His talk and manners may be a bit rough at times but his mental apparatus works as smoothly as a ball bearing in olive oil."

It was no longer easy for Biggy's enemies to ask rhetorical or satirical questions in the local press about his competence and know that the answers from the electorate would always be the ones they wanted. When his well-placed opponent inquired, "Would you want him for your boss? Would you place him in charge of the city's money? Do you want him to look after the education of your children?" many replied in effect, "Why not? He's a hard-working go-getter, and maybe he didn't go to Harvard but he was educated in our high school and he's smart as hell. Look what he's done to that bunch on Hill Street."

The transfigured, symbolic Biggy and the flesh-and-blood

person became inextricably interwoven in the public mind. The real Biggy acting as hero of the plot—developed sometimes by the press, sometimes by Biggy himself—and the symbolic stereotype became one. Moreover, since the local audience now read about Biggy in the metropolitan press, what people thought and did was now determined somewhat by symbols coming from the outside world as well as from the local group. Perhaps Biggy needed no prompting to do what he did as mayor, but the reporters' early delight and extensive coverage of the first acts of the drama shaped the course of events and helped Biggy, his friends, and his foes alike to learn who they were and to define to themselves what they were doing.

His inaugural speech immediately after election brought to Yankee City still more reporters, cameramen from the motion picture companies, and agents of all America's great mass media to record and report what was said and done by the new mayor and those around him, whether friend or foe. The symbol of Biggy as the untamed man from the wrong part of town, the big tough hero of the multitude, the strong and powerful protector of the weak who had no social pretensions, was further delineated, expanded, made more attractive, more understandable and, for a time, more acceptable to the American public.

Despite the fact that he was a person of considerable substance, to some of these legend-makers and myth-builders he was "the man with only one shirt," the fellow who had "a cheap $25 suit," and "the redhead with the old hat that doesn't fit." These external signs were supposed to represent the inner man and what Biggy was to his community. Such a positive symbolic person, created as a physically powerful man clothed so that he became a person who dressed "just like everyone else only worse," was easy for the masses to understand and someone with whom they could easily identify. "You don't laugh *at* a guy like that," it was said, "you laugh with him, you laugh because you like him. He is the kind of a guy who can take care of himself and he doesn't have to think he is Jesus Christ to do it."

Some news accounts played at length on the relation between Biggy's clothing and his status. Under the heading

MAYOR SAYS HE HAS A SHIRT one reported on the experience of a salesman entering the mayor's office.

The silk-shirt salesman was most confident of them all coming in. Going out, and he went out quickly, he was almost indignant. He let his wrath spill over in the hearing of the usual anteroom crowd.

"The mayor was kidding me," he sputtered.

"What did he say?" asked one of the mayor's friends.

"He said he had a shirt."

"Well," said the mayor's friend unsmilingly, "he has."

When Biggy walked out on the platform to make his inaugural speech to a huge crowd overflowing beyond the auditorium through the corridors and out into the street, one of the great metropolitan dailies having a large circulation in Yankee City reported that

Biggy's football physique didn't squeeze with real dignity into his grand new $25 mayor's suit. Biggy's flaming red mop of hair can't be tamed by even such an afternoon as he spent today in Nick's Nifty Barber Shop. Biggy never made a speech before in his life if you don't count the times that he has told this gang or that gang just where to get off and what to expect. So the "big bunch of fellow citizens" out front thought they saw something funny. Biggy opened his mouth to read and then snapped his jaw shut. He jerked loose a half-dozen buttons of his overcoat with one yank. He bent a steely blue eye on the nearest and huskiest laughter. That gentleman never so much as snickered again all evening. Biggy's eye roved, silence followed his glance.

All the press reported his speech and described everything that Biggy and his audience said with great enthusiasm. All used the same symbol in anecdotes and stories, the only difference being the order or emphasis. All played up the point that Biggy now had control over constituted authority, and all made particular reference to what he had to say about policemen. "And best of all," the American public was told, "were the cops, the cops that have 'hunted' Biggy and have 'pinched' him twice and have treated him like a 'bum.' They were all good cops tonight. They stood respectively at attention. They 'Yes, Mr. Mayored' him, and Patrolman Johnny

Evans, whom Biggy has promised to 'get,' stood by Biggy's side while Biggy spoke and held Biggy's hat. It was a big night."

Under such headlines as NEW MAYOR TO BE FRIEND OF BUMS other reporters said that Biggy had declared he was "going down to the cop station and tell a few flatfeet something for their own good and 'if I ever hear they are getting too high hat to send out word at night for a prisoner who wants to arrange bail, they will be up on charges. That is what they did to me when I was arrested for bouncing my fist off the then mayor's mug.' "

When Biggy Muldoon announced that he would reward his friends the press changed his expression to meet the demands of the symbol they had helped to create, and to satisfy the appetites of their readers. "What the hell," they had him say, "we won, didn't we? Don't the winners deserve the gravy?"

Within a few days following his inauguration Biggy was in a bitter fight with the city council. "This morning," the big dailies announced, "before the smoke of the press photographers' flashlights had cleared away on the inaugural scene, Biggy called his brand new council into his presence and, in the picturesque and often unpublishable language of which Navy forecastles and Yankee City street corners have made him a past master, told 'em straight from the shoulder 'what is what, who is who, and why, from now on in this man's town.' "

The first meeting with the city council, which still prevented him from getting his permit for a filling station, was reported in the *New York Times* under the following heading and lead lines:

NEW MAYOR, EX GOB, SWABS CITY'S DECK. MAYOR TELLS YANKEE CITY COUNCIL WHAT IS WHAT, WHO IS WHO, AND WHY. WILL PAY OFF GRUDGES. MAN WHO HAD HIM "PINCHED" AND ONE WHO CALLED HIM "PUPPY" ARE OUT OF LUCK.

Within two weeks after his election, two classes of functionaries pushed into the drama of Biggy Muldoon: representatives of the stage and entrepreneurs who thought they saw a chance to make some quick money out of the fame of this new celebrity. The Boston papers played up his Yankee shrewdness at bargaining in this new situation. The headline over one of them summarized a long story: BIGGY LISTENS TO SIREN CALL

OF VAUDEVILLE. ISN'T GOING TO GET HIM DIRT CHEAP, HE SAYS, AFTER SEEING AGENT. ANTE MUST BE DOUBLED AT LEAST. Meanwhile the following wire, one of several, came from a motion picture company. "Your colorful career excellent material for motion picture story. Please wire collect if you are interested in starring in this production to be made in Yankee City." Another headline announced: BIGGY GETS $10,000 THEATRICAL OFFER. MAKES ENGAGEMENT TO JUDGE TWO BEAUTY CONTESTS. The story reported a wire from New York offering him a thousand a week for ten weeks.

Biggy signed a contract with one of the great theatrical producers to appear for a week with *The Connecticut Yankee*, at that time playing in Boston. After being introduced by the star, he made a speech each night. He told them, "Mark Twain was considered erratic and a fool in the days gone by. A lot of persons consider me a fool. But let me tell you if I wasn't the mayor I'd still be making a living. I can always buy gas and I can sell it cheap."

A short time later the country's public prints were reporting new developments in Biggy's career under such headings as these from the *New York Herald Tribune:* BIGGY MULDOON SAILS FOR COAST, PERHAPS IN SEARCH OF BRIDE. MAYOR OF YANKEE CITY SEEKS REST AND QUIET AS HE LEAVES FOR THE WEST. PREDICTING REPEAL OF BAY STATE DRY LAW AND THE ELECTION OF A WET GOVERNOR. The American press generally reported: BIGGY MULDOON IN THE WEST TO FIND BRUNETTE OR REDHEADED WIFE. MAYOR DECIDES TO "GIVE BREAK" TO SOME BEAUTIFUL GIRL. BARS BLONDES BECAUSE THEY ARE "NOT SO GOOD AS HOUSEKEEPERS."

All these stories were part of the publicity that ensued when he was asked to judge beauty contests, dance marathons, and similar exhibitions all over the country. He accepted a large number of these invitations. Wherever he went he was warmly received by the press and the people, and spread the story of his mistreatment, telling his audiences how he stood for the common man and for everyone's having more fun out of life.

He became a symbolic figure of pleasure, of permissiveness. With him millions could vicariously rebel against the restraints of their environment and have a good time. Although he did not drink, prohibiting people from having a drink was not to him a "noble experiment"; he was for everyone's drinking as much as he wanted. He swore and enjoyed gambling with his friends. He liked to have fun. For his great audience he was a "good guy" and a "straight-shooter"—not a hypocrite or a stuffed shirt.

Lady's Favorite and Masculine Symbol

As indicated by the references to blondes and redheads, one of the most striking symbolic transformations of Biggy Muldoon, following his recognition by the national mass media, was his masculine role and his relation to women. It will be remembered that at the time of his election his reputation was such that he felt it necessary to declare publicly, "I'm supposed to be a woman-hater, that's the bunk," and that with the Navy in the Caribbean he had been forced to "jump out of a second-story window to keep my independence."

Editors and those who controlled other mass media soon got the feel of Biggy's potentialities as a sexual symbol. Within a month or two he was being played up as a judge of beautiful women, a man in search of a beautiful bride, an authority on female attractiveness. The businessmen who put on such attractions as beauty contests, marathons, and burlesque shows saw in him a figure that would appeal to male and female alike as a man who knew his way around and was attractive to women. He was regarded by both sexes as a he-man, "not a pretty boy you see in the movies, but a two-fisted guy." Biggy became a powerful masculine sexual symbol for many in the great audience. For the women he was something more than the bad boy who said girls were "like puppy dogs"; multitudes of letters, coyly or openly erotic, poured in on him.

In America the cluster of meanings about the big two-fisted, strong young male who knows what he wants and sets out to get it always evokes positive feeling among many as to his sexuality and potency. In the fantasies of his mass audience Biggy was soon transformed and served as symbol of the untamed male, the great muscular "brute." He became still another example of the libidinal male found in the literature of the superior such as *The Hairy Ape, Lady Chatterley's Lover,* and Robinson Jeffers' "Roan Stallion," or in popular novels, movies, and radio as the truck driver and the husky sailor; or in folk myth and ballad as expressed in the powerful sexuality of the subordinate white or Negro male. Symbolically he was to many the anarchal monad, the free man, free from weakening middle-class morality. In fact, even in middle-class terms Biggy was in many respects a well-reared, proper boy; he was not loose sexually any more than he was loose in other areas of his deportment. His mother's training had stayed with him. He did not drink or smoke and, though not ascetic, his conduct with women was scrupulous and careful. But the women who wrote him from all over the United States saw and responded to another Biggy—the symbolic one created by the press. A Missouri young woman wrote him:

I guess you are beginning to wonder who in the world has the boldness to write to you. I am a widow twenty-six years old. I have a daughter two and a half years old. I have said in the last two years that no man was worthy of my respect. But I changed my mind yesterday when I read the article about you. I said to myself, "there's my ideal man, a man that decides what he wants and then gets it . . ." Have you a sweetheart? I hope not, for maybe if you haven't you will write to me . . . P.S. I wonder if you care if I cut your picture and kept it?

A young mother sent him this note: "Dear Mayor: I have a baby son fourteen months old who is a Red Head and a wow. He's bound to have everything he wants and to have his own way, so I hope you won't feel bad if I call him Biggy Muldoon the second." Biggy replied that it was O.K. with him.

A young lady from Mississippi told Biggy that she "loved his picture and admired his taste for beauty." She went on to say,

I'm a perfect brunette, 5 feet, 4 inches, under thirty (unfortunately a widow) but just the age and with enough experience to be the most loveable and devoted companion you could ever dream of.

Why don't you spend your summer vacation in the good old

Dixie state—Mississippi—or Memphis, Tennessee? Sports of all kinds if you like that too. I am anxiously and eagerly waiting for your answer.

Not all Biggy's letters were from women of his own age. Many were from much older women who gave him motherly advice. One began, "Dear Sir: I am an old lady of seventy years and I want to *talk to you* and hope you will take what I say in the same spirit that I mean it, which is very kindly." There followed a long set of moral instructions on how he should act as a man and as a mayor.

On the masculine side there was considerable variety. Although in grammar, punctuation, and spelling the following is not representative of all the letters he received from men, it does indicate some of the interests of a large class who wrote. Mr. Muldoon, Dear Sir:

i have been appointed to see if you could come to speake in this city [an industrial community in New England] in one of the largest hall in the center of the city we have a strick in the cotton mills there are 27,000 on strick and things are bad i thought i would see a good boam to come you might run for governor some day i was one that helped to bring you here to sant Marey smoke talk and we paide you price but that was a church time and the tickets were 75 cents each. you will dou the wright thing if you come remember you are not the only on that wants money just help and you will get used all wright.

hoping to here from you.

Another large group of letters came from people who were asking favors or financial help. Others expressed gratitude for help received. One covered with bright-colored figures of lions and tigers was from the general agent of the wild animal circus whose posters had brought him fame. It began

My dear Sir:

It is my desire first to say, "That's the spirit, Muldoon, and here's wishing you luck and congratulations." As I have just heard your little piece of Oratory over the radio—I am the little fellow that Approached you and asked Your Permission to Tack Cloth Banners on Your Garage for the West Show and you Helped Give me a Reputation by not only letting me tack Your Garage but you also gave me Permission to Tack Our Cloth Banners on Your Residence on the Boston-Portland Highway Which Caused our Show to get a world of Publicity which is a Star in my Crown and practically made me as a circus press representative.

The newspapers shifted Biggy, the symbol, from the man who was calling certain ethnic groups "guys who weren't white people" to a man who said every American was just as good as anybody else. It also seems probable that Biggy himself, in response to his new situation, had modified his position. By the time he got ready to run for president, he declared,

I hope some of this radical hatred may be wiped out. What difference does it make what we are, whether we are black men, white men, red men, or green men? I judge a man as a man if he pays his bills. You know what they used to say about the man from the South of Ireland a few years ago in Yankee City. I hate to tell you. Now they make as good citizens as anybody else. After the Irishers came the Wops, then the Greeks, then the Armenians. And now you can't tell what they are. They became as good Americans as the rest of us. So I say don't hold nothing against no man. Consider yourself as good as anybody else. That is what I do.

A summary review of a few of the comments appearing at that time in newspapers throughout the United States gives an impression of the kind of composite symbol Biggy had become for the American public. The *New York Times* said that "although his theory that 'the winners deserve the gravy' is not new in politics, it at least is refreshingly frank." The *Kansas City Post* said, "As any soldier knows, women are the silly sex as far as gobs are concerned—Mayor Biggy Muldoon's official behavior promises to be deplorable, but he will get away with it. The women of Yankee City like the women of other towns will forgive him on the grounds that he is picturesque." The Lincoln, Nebraska, *Star* characterized him as an "honest, frank, outspoken, two-fisted mayor, much different from most of his contemporaries." The South Bend, Indiana, *Tribune* editorialized, "He occupies a position which many persons at some time or other wish they held. Many a citizen has told himself, 'Now if I were mayor of this town,' when a traffic man gets rough or some ego-ruffling act is committed by a public servant!" The whole situation as far as Biggy's own career is concerned was well summarized by the *New York Herald Tribune:*

The redheaded ex-"gob" has the distinction of having aroused nation-wide interest in an ordinary filling station in Yankee City. What newspaper has not carried accounts of the multitudinous developments centering around the filling station? . . . It is difficult to begrudge him his victory. Granting his comic-strip qualities, his obvious unfitness for the position of mayor of old Yankee City, one cannot but admire his amazing courage and persistence. He has shed a veritable sea of troubles. He has emerged unbowed with unshaken purpose from a thousand contests. And despite everything, his spirits are high, his vocabulary is as untamed as ever. Probably it would be well if the "big bugs" called off their war on the indomitable redhead. Biggy has threatened to run for governor. Given plenty of violent opposition, another fine or two, and a few more jail sentences, and he might be elected.

Biggy the man, living and acting out his life in Yankee City, had largely disappeared in the enlarged and greatly modified heroic mold into which his life had been re-formed by the public press and other mass media. Although each part of the popular figure was founded on elements of fact, the few quotations from the letters of his public make clear that his meanings for them, although intensely personal, express the collective values, the hopes and fears, the wishes and anxieties of the American people. [77]

Martyr and Clown

When Biggy and his mother were put in jail he bitterly resented it. He felt they had been unfairly treated and that the courts were unjust; he publicly stated that he had not been jailed for a crime but for political reasons. At times he felt and acted like a martyr.

As a prisoner in a jail a man's feelings and beliefs about

what he is as a person in our free society are affronted, his freedom is greatly limited, his right to self-initiated action is taken from him, and he is always in the power of, and subordinate to, others. As long as society believes and feels the prisoner has committed a reprehensible act for which he has been justly tried and convicted, the subordinate, slavelike role seems justified. But when, in the thinking of the community, the free citizen loses his freedom because he has been unjustly convicted, his position as prisoner is likely to enhance the regard of the public and increase his personal status. He can, as a man who has sacrificed himself for moral or civic principles, become a martyr.

To gain full recognition from his own group or the whole society, the martyr must sacrifice his liberty, his life, or some precious object for a moral or sacred principle well above the ordinary level of the market place; or he must make this sacrifice for a highly regarded institution that represents great moral worth. He may sometimes achieve martyrdom and become a sacrificial symbol for only a segment of the population, or for those who belong to a particular class level. When this role appears in a society it always means that there are opposing values within the culture and that certain groups are sufficiently differentiated from the rest to use this symbol to strengthen their internal cohesion.

The martyr is the victim who is sacrificed for the good of his group. The group he represents may be a subordinate one, strong in moral power but weak in political and material strength. The perfect substance for fashioning a martyr, however, is the person of superior status who is secure in his own social and political position, yet identifies himself with, and sacrifices himself for, subordinate and socially inferior people by yielding to the moral force of higher spiritual values. Such a person can also be a traitor to his own class. Should the definition of his behavior by the superior class be accepted as official and correct, the martyr may in time become the detested traitor.

Moving to another extreme we have the clown. In ordinary life the man who for his own purposes plays the role of clown plays a very dangerous game. He may find himself confined within a symbolic wall he has built around him in people's attitudes. If the transference from him to the targets he selects is not well directed, the attack may be turned upon him; if people direct their laughter at him rather than at his targets, his aspirations may be destroyed. For such dangerous enterprise the successful performer needs to be very adept and his audience susceptible and ready to be entertained. Biggy's actions aroused laughter at first—at his foes, but also at himself. Although a considerable accomplishment, for one of his aspirations it was not sufficient. His audience "got a laugh out of it," but he did not thereby accumulate enough respect for what he had done. If the fool of convention is to increase his own stature in the eyes of those who laugh, his tricks must direct laughter at others and divert to himself some of the respect usually tendered to the objects of his attack. He must demonstrate that he possesses some of the talents and social strength his fellow men admire.

Biggy's assets were considerable. He was energetic, honest, industrious, courageous, a fighter, and an underdog; yet he obviously lacked many of the necessary attributes of the citizen who is commonly regarded as a fit candidate for high office. Moreover, many who accepted him as mayor found it difficult to conceive of the image he and they had created fitting easily into a governor's chair or a senator's place in Congress.

The traditional clown still carries the aura of his earlier significance. Not only is he the circus buffoon who entertains children by his feigned stupidity and commits offenses against decorum and propriety, but for some he is identified as the low fellow of an earlier day: the ill-bred man, the clod from the backwoods, the hillbilly, or the jerk from the dockyards of Brooklyn. In a radio skit a character with what is called a Brooklyn accent may be identified as funny, often stupid, socially awkward, and by implication from the wrong side of the tracks. He can be the fool whose nonsense is ordered by persistent stupidity; or his behavior may be no more than a mask to fool the proper, the pious, and the hypocritical who wear the social masks of pretended virtues. The mask of the clown for dramatic or social purposes can be worn over the face of anyone or in any role. The wise, the virtuous, the weak and the strong, the good and the wicked, can all be fools in fact or wear this social mask in their social or theatrical environment, either by their own choice or because of the actions of others.

Ordinarily those who laugh at a fool feel superior to him; by their laughter they claim the virtues he lacks. If he can direct the laughter of his audience toward the targets of his attack he can sometimes destroy the superior symbols of convention and increase the self-regard of his audience. Because it is felt that he lacks moral and intellectual sense he is able to release tension in those who laugh by permitting vicarious gratification of pent-up wishes and longings. The much appreciated role of the trickster hero found in many cultures and civilizations is largely founded on release from moral and logical restrictions. [139a] Stories of the trickster's outrageous conduct—upsetting the moral order, shocking the proper, and making fools of the powerful—arouse laughter which allows the story teller's audience to feel gratification through breaking the rules with the transgressor while applying a satiric sanction against the very deeds they vicariously commit. The force of the laughter is directed both outward and inward; it acts as a social and psychological force for maintaining the rules and controls of the moral and social order; within, it functions to free a person from some of his morally disapproved and self-condemnatory wishes.

When the laughter released is *at* the clown who inspires it, the hatred and hostility stored up and thus vented seem to be directed at unconscious figures within the inner life of the individual. They may be figures of authority or unrequited love or, more consciously, the self. Since the emotions have to do with the individual's private world and with the pleasure and pain felt by him, such laughter is purgative, it "makes you feel good," and the symbol which acted as the trigger for its release is treated permissively and sometimes with affection. The outer world becomes "a better place" and more rewarding because the inner world of the individual is "a better place" and less self-punishing. In this symbolic situation the satiric sanction is applied positively and rewardingly. [114d]

The clown may thus explicitly or implicitly direct laughter and hostility against the target of his attack, such as a conventional rule, role, or social institution; or he may stand for something else in the unconscious of the spectator and arouse and direct hostility to the object for which he stands. Children who take such deep pleasure in seeing clowns at the circus in a world of make-believe can also laugh at grown men and women who are as absurd and unworthy as children wish and sometimes know them to be. Adults are less easily able to have this experience.

The shift from fool or villain to sympathetic clown and vice versa is an interesting one. As long as Biggy could be stigmatized as a man from the wrong side of the tracks, either clumsy and unworthy or actually a person of evil intent, he had little chance with the local voters. The "Bad-Boy" label attached to him by mass media helped to change him from a "bad" person to a "bad boy"—a very different thing—and the champion of those who knew what he was doing. This symbolic shift took place in many people. The "Bad-Boy" label changed him from mere clown or "tough guy" to someone whose actions are not only funny but approved. This symbol or label, once applied, was used by all the mass media whenever they referred to Biggy. It is a symbol highly valued in our society. It connotes someone who is indulged and often liked for behavior that is ordinarily disapproved. His infractions of the rules usually take a form which allows those who think of him in this light to identify with him. The ingenuity of the bad boy is usually directed against persons and restrictive rules which the public finds irksome and from which it needs emotional release. His deeds they might easily wish to do, and the consequences are events which they might wish to see happen. Hated but respected objects can be temporarily reduced to insignificance by the pranks of such a youngster.

The bad boy is the rewarded antagonist of all figures who have authority over him—parents, old maids, teachers and preachers, cops, or little girls whose moral authority, when properly applied, subordinates little boys. He is an indulged, immature, small male, not quite grown, over whom society and its members still feel they have ultimate control; yet the very nature of this symbol embodies a high degree of autonomy, more than is possible in ordinary life. His actions in real life or in fiction can be enjoyed and forgiven because he does not outrage conventions to the point where seriously punitive sanctions need be used. Despite the seeming extreme violence of his behavior, there are always limits beyond which it is believed he will not go; usually self-imposed limits are clearly discernible.

The story of *Peck's Bad Boy*, a tale filled with scores of old jokes in which adult authority is successfully flouted, or nostalgic comic strips about the carefree days when boys play hookey, or the escapades of Tom Sawyer and Huckleberry Finn, as well as thousands of stories and jokes told in periodicals, novels, plays, radio, motion pictures, and the anecdotes adult Americans tell each other about their youth—all attest to the power of this symbol. The infractions of propriety by the bad boy of fiction are often much less restrained than those committed in real life. The Katzenjammer Kids play tricks on the captain that would result in punishment for flesh-and-blood boys. Biggy, being removed from the immediate environment of the national audience, although a living man, was for them a fictional boy. He satisfied the basic rules of a good news story: he existed in fact and everything he did could be referred to as such. Thus the mask of reality could be placed over the fictive elements of the story.

One only need put the bad-boy symbol in opposition to the bad-girl symbol to show its significance. As applied to a child, the "bad girl" can be no more than naughty, but when used for a young woman Biggy's age the term carries strong moral connotations which are not likely to lead an audience to expect something innocently funny. Here the symbol, falling in the category of the morally reprehensible, is subject to moral sanctions; it may be "understood and explained," pitied or forgiven, but rarely approved and indulged. The bad-boy symbol, evoking feelings of permissiveness and indulgence, indicates that the preliminary preparations for adult responsibility for the sexual role of the young male are far more flexible than those for a young woman.

When Biggy became the bad boy, the local picture of the "tough boy" who had been arrested for gambling and fighting and the "hobo who associated with jailbirds" shifted. The ready acceptance of the bad boy by "everybody" in the outside world and the continued appearance of the term in the metropolitan papers provided a permissive symbol for accepting and understanding Biggy in Yankee City. It helped to recast the happenings on Hill Street in a context more likely to arouse sympathy and permit identification. When the bad boy of the family is appreciated and liked by outsiders, other members sometimes begin to find what he does not only excusable but amusing, provided they are not laughed at or held responsible for his nuisance value. He cannot break the rules all of the time, but he can do so much of the time; however, he still arouses anxieties lest he go too far and get everyone punished.

Should the audience feel that those responsible punish the boy too severely for behavior that is only amusing, its reaction is always hostile. A bad boy's unmerited punishment inevitably turns sanctioned authorities into disapproved, ridiculous people. When Biggy wore the more pleasing mask of the bad boy, the police, the judges, and the authoritative persons of Yankee City who arrested and jailed him were deemed morally reprehensible. But when the news stories accented the less acceptable symbols of villain and fool his position became increasingly difficult.

The Image of a Villain

Throughout the period of Biggy's first two election campaigns and terms as mayor, his local enemies and those who opposed his political and personal ambitions as well as his business aspirations continued to attack him with symbols expressing their hatred, scorn, and derision. They attempted with considerable success to transform him, in the minds of the electorate, into a villain—one who, for selfish gain, when entrusted with the moral and legal responsibilities of mayor, deliberately smashed the moral order of his city, destroyed its good name and the pride of its citizens, wickedly violated his allegiance to the people, and led them toward destruction; or a fool, a clown, who for private gain and public attention had made Yankee City a joke and its people ridiculous.

He had betrayed the city and its people, it was said, in aiding the evil forces of status and class which can divide the people of a democracy and turn groups of citizens to fratricidal strife—citizens who should be brothers advancing their common interests. While mayor of his community, they said, by a series of violent acts he had violated his oath to uphold the legal and moral order and, arraying class against class, had destroyed the ancient unity.

At the start of his first campaign for the office of mayor, the symbols by which Biggy was cast as a disapproved person among the *dramatis personae* were restrained and tempered. It seemed sufficient then to contrast the characteristics of his opponent, representing the traditional qualities of the long line of public figures who had occupied the mayor's chair, with Biggy's disapproved traits and allow the voters to choose the sort of man they always selected. As a leader of the opposition wrote in a news article,

The good sense and pride of the voters of the city are on trial in this campaign as they have never been before. On the one hand, we have a mayor running for re-election who, though opposed by some elements of the community, is nevertheless a man of standing, a member of the local bar and associate justice of the local court. He has had a university education, experience in municipal life, and a full understanding of the responsibilities of the office of chief executive of the city. His administration of the past few years has been such that no notoriety has been attached to it. Yankee City has not been exploited in the press of other cities as having elected a sensational chief executive. The city business has been cared for with dignity and economy and it will be for the next two years, if the present mayor is re-elected.

The speaker then turned his attention to Biggy.

On the other hand we have a young man we must commend for his ability to do things, and for his persistence in the face of obstacles, even though these obstacles were well-grounded in law and the public welfare. But his experience in business has been but for a short time, under the tutelage of a very shrewd and hard-working mother, who has left him what he has, and his own skill in the management of business affairs has yet to be tested by the passage of years. He has never had any experience in government, even in the most minor positions, and there is no belief that he could qualify for the office of mayor without this experience.

The portraits of the two men are drawn with seeming dispassion, but the intent to show Biggy as a person unqualified for high office is clear. In the light of later events and Biggy's subsequent symbolic development, the mildness and comparative "objectivity" are important—there was no *open* public effort then to put him in a symbolic rogue's gallery. [5*a*]

Gentle mockery was continuously used. Although not always deliberately designed to harm Biggy, it contributed to the "clown" stereotype. John Marquand, then writing for a Boston paper that appealed almost entirely to the New England upper classes, wrote one of the many long stories about Mr. Muldoon. Marquand's family has been in Yankee City almost from its beginning. Its members belong to some of the top families. The author, deeply ambivalent about his city and its people— himself partly a product of its life—wrote a satirical article which drew its immediate inspiration from Biggy's ad about "harpooning the whale." In it Biggy was seen as a contemporary "Lord" Timothy Dexter, a lower-class man of Yankee City who had made money in the early eighteen hundreds and had annoyed and defied the high and mighty of his community, but was thought of as something of a clown and a fool. Marquand, writing with more skill but the same mockery as Biggy's political opponents, saw him as the mobile man from the lower ranks who had refused to follow the ordinary, acceptable routes of the ambitious.

We love to see plain people succeed and [we] help them at the polls. The kid-gloved, white-collar candidate hasn't a China-man's chance with any red-blooded electorate. The remarkable, the unique thing about Yankee City's boy mayor is that for the past three years and more he has been a public nuisance which had degenerated into a jest. Unlike other boys who have succeeded, Thomas has not gone to night school, nor as far as we know has he ever clipped a coupon for a correspondence course nor read a book of etiquette. He has never held an office or shown diligence or merit. Instead, to the casual observer his previous record seems to consist of a two-months' jail sentence for swinging upon the jaw of a previous Yankee City mayor in a most vulgar and reprehensible display of temper, and again in the display of a row of antiquated crockery upon the ridgepole of a dwelling house at the head of Constitution Avenue.

It almost seems as though another Timothy Dexter had arrived in Yankee City, and, better still, it seems as though the

Knowing Ones of Yankee City, those descendants of the other knowing ones who welcomed the other hero, have welcomed Thomas Muldoon and have put him in his place. Dexter rose to fame and fortune and a self-created lordship, but his weaknesses and extravagant misuse of the symbols of the upper class made him the butt of their ridicule even to the present day.

A front-page editorial in the Yankee City *Herald*, written before the second mayoralty election by its influential editor, a highly respected and solid member of the upper-middle class and spokesman for the Levels Above the Common Man, is a good example of how some people transformed Biggy into a villain. Restraint and forbearance are no longer present; deep concern and hostility dominate the symbols used. Under the heading CLASS FEELING RUINS COMMUNITY Mr. Jones spoke to his city:

Any man who, for his own purpose, arouses class feeling in his city is an enemy of his kind. It is not enough to say he is not a good citizen. He is positively a bad influence in a community. Where he ought to have built up community good feeling, he has torn it down. He has aroused unjustified feelings of envy and enmity. He has arrayed the residents of one locality against another or one religion or race against another.

Every class in this city is dependent on the other for success, and the man who tries to create enmity between them should be made an outcast. He is really thrusting a dagger into the side of the city. The man who advances his political fortunes by arousing prejudices based on race, social position, and religion is a traitor to his city's best interests.

In this editorial and many others Biggy was condemned not only as a bad influence in his community, a man who destroyed the good feeling that all people presumably had for each other, arousing enmity and envy, but as a traitor to his city who was trying to destroy it by whipping up class hostility and thereby "thrusting a dagger into its side." There can be no doubt that most people in the classes above the common man and many of the lower-middle class saw Biggy as an evil man who, in arousing the latent hostilities and satiric laughter of the lower classes, threatened their own self-respect, prestige, and power as members of the higher social levels. Although in other contexts they might and did appreciate some of his humor, during the heat of battle it was not easy for them to enjoy Biggy's fighting art. The belief that anyone who mobilized the hostilities of the lower classes against the upper was an enemy of the people as a whole was repeated literally hundreds of times during the first two campaigns in which Biggy was elected, his first two terms in office, and the following election when he was defeated. [76c]

All overt manifestations of class feeling were considered breaches of the moral code and of the basic faith of American life. One of his accusers declared,

This self-appointed defendant of the common people tries to incite his followers against those who are better off in the world's goods. The demagogue tries to make the poor feel that the rich are his enemies. He thrives on propaganda that those who live on the best residential streets are enemies of the poor. Whatever may be the case elsewhere, it is not so here. Rich and poor alike are united by a love of Yankee City. He who incites Riverbrookers against Hill Streeters deceives his hearers and is a public enemy.

It might be supposed that Biggy's immediate activities as a public figure in Yankee City and throughout the United States, making speeches, appearing at public functions, judging beauty contests, and addressing large audiences over the radio as well as appearing in scores of newsreels, would have made it impossible for him to devote much time to being mayor or developing new quarrels with his old enemies. This, of course, is not true, for he soon found himself in his greatest crisis, which resulted in a battle that brought him increasing publicity throughout America and contributed greatly to creation of the public symbols that finally enveloped the real Biggy. We take up the story again shortly after his first election, to see in the varied mirror of the press the incidents already seen from other angles.

Under the headline WILD SCENES AT MEETING OF THE CITY COUNCIL and the subhead DISGRACEFUL ATTACKS MADE ON MEMBERS OF THE BOARD BY THE MAYOR IN CONTROVERSY ON TREE REMOVAL, the Yankee City *Herald* reported: "The City Council last night at its regular meeting before the summer vacation and after wild and stormy scenes in the council chamber voted not to allow the trees in front of the property of Thomas Ignatius Muldoon, at Constitutions and Hill Streets, to be removed." The story reviews the controversy that took place when Biggy once more presented his petition to have the elm trees removed and his permit for a filling station granted. The paper reported,

The mayor said, "There was a time when I used to come here and no attention was paid to me. Now I am boss and I can talk good and plenty. As mayor I say these trees will come down." During the argument one of the older men in the council remonstrated with the mayor for personal remarks about some of Biggy's antagonists. "Sit down," roared the mayor and again he ordered, "Sit down," and after a moment the councilor smilingly did so. "I'm the boss," shouted the mayor, "and I'm going to run this city for two years." The mayor insisted he would cut the trees down to make way for progress.

The following day the same paper reported,

MAYOR SLASHES FINE ELMS DESPITE REFUSAL OF COUNCILORS. TAKES LAW IN HIS OWN DESTRUCTIVE HANDS. OVERSEES THE REMOVAL OF FINE GROWTH LINING HIS PROPERTY. The slaughter of the trees lining the estate of Mayor Muldoon at Hill and Constitution Streets was begun early this morning. The mayor supervised proceedings.

Alongside this news story was a two-column front-page editorial. It bore the caption WHAT ARE YOU GOING TO DO ABOUT IT?

It is almost inconceivable that a mayor of a city, having been refused permission to do something which was only for his personal interest and which was to further his own defiance of the law, which action has been protested by the people in the immediate vicinity of the operation and which further was opposed by public opinion, should go ahead and persistently flaunt the law and public sentiment and insist upon taking action into his own hands.

It is possible that by the time the people of this city finish reading this, these grand old trees of half a century or more of growth will all be laid low by the ruthless axes of the tree department, acting under the orders of the mayor of the city. A more sickening proceeding than this has never been seen in Yankee City.

A few days later the same paper reported, "The zoning law is not one for Hill Street or any class. It is for the protection of all the people." It said that people who have small homes realize the protection the zoning ordinances give them in the enjoyment of their property.

The metropolitan press told the same story but gave it a different accent and tone.

No longer ago than Monday night Biggy put his pride in his pocket and asked the council's permission to remove the trees. The council turned him down by a vote of nine to two. It was plainly up to Biggy to stick up for himself. He acted this morning.

This morning, four lofty elms were nodding their aristocratic heads over the highway edges of Biggy's lot. They weren't at all ugly to the eye, all newly green, but they were unmistakably in the way of the motor traffic which Mayor Muldoon expects to see turning in to his door as soon as he has changed the law a bit and put the city council in its place.

Biggy borrowed a saw and showed 'em how an ex-gob would do a trifling job like that. Those elms never had a chance. Between Biggy and the gang they were down in a couple of hours. Then Biggy rolled his sleeves down, slipped into the coat of what he calls his "$25 mayor's suit," and strode down to his office at City Hall. He found a court summons waiting for him. It was almost like old times. Biggy will be again at the bar of justice Friday morning.

When Biggy was found guilty in the lower courts he appealed and his case went to the higher courts. The gas tanks had meanwhile been installed and he was soon prepared to sell gas. The metropolitan press, the newsreels, and other media once again were on hand to provide publicity for the occasion. They did this, needless to say, without prompting; it may be recorded here that at no time did Biggy hire anyone to exploit his interest in the papers. The out-of-town press continued to deal with his career in a cheerful vein. Under the heading BIGGY GRINS AS JAIL LOOMS the Boston paper which had given him the most space said,

Today was the day Biggy showed the world where it got off. Today was the day when Biggy kept the promise he made as his home-town's "Bad Boy" and ne'er-do-well four years ago. To-day, operating under a permit granted to himself, Thomas Ignatius Muldoon, citizen, by himself, Thomas Ignatius Muldoon, Mayor, "Biggy" sold gasoline from the brand new Biggy Muldoon filling station located at the historical residential square which is formed by Constitution and Hill Streets.

Under a subhead MANY CUSTOMERS the story went on to tell how big machines drove up and their drivers embarrassedly asked for "just a gallon or so." Their tanks were full already but they wanted to say that they had been patrons of the far-famed Muldoon station.

Biggy greeted them all with impartial hospitality. By mid-morning he had doffed his coat and vest. By lunch time he was collarless. And when the afternoon sun got down to duty he shed his blue striped shirt and cranked the pump handles in his sleeveless navy jersey. It was all one to Biggy whether his visitors came to look or came to buy. He sold them gas anyway and grinned as the cash came clanking in.

"You know," he said, "I am quite a well-known guy at that. Imagine those birds from California and South Carolina and Washington and all over coming here just to get a look at Biggy Muldoon. I'm wasting my time at this mayor business."

But in imposing a jail sentence and fine on Biggy for cutting the elms and installing the gas station, Judge Cabot T. Perkins, himself a resident of Hill Street and a member of the old-family class, declared: "This man is an outlaw. Such a man as this can be described only by that term. He seems to forget he is a mayor."

Perhaps the most dramatic effort to cast Biggy in the symbolic mold of a villain and traitor to his community was made by a former mayor who also belonged to the upper levels of Yankee City. This gentleman had held many posts of esteem and power. Mr. O'Connell, one of the very few Irish Catholics who enjoyed an upper-class position in the community, was married to a Protestant and had kinship connections with some of the most highly placed families in the community. His denunciation of Biggy appeared just before the latter's second successful election, in a double column in the center of the front page of the Yankee City *Herald*. It was reinforced by a letter of endorsement signed by five former mayors, all prominent and distinguished, who praised him for his action as a good citizen and for his moral courage. In his letter "To the People of Yankee City" Mr. O'Connell said to them: "I have lived in this beautiful little city of homes and happiness most of my life. It has been good—too good—to me; kind and generous to my faults and feelings, applauding my petty work in the community's daily life with rewards far above my just desserts. I am its debtor without the ability to pay in full."

It is worth noting that Mr. O'Connell had advanced from the lower ranks of the society by using the conventional and highly approved methods of acquiring a higher education and, while working hard and adjusting himself to the conventions, had served the city and himself well.

Yankee City is my home. I love it. I expect, God willing, to live, die, and be buried here. I love its people. They are my people and I am jealous and proud of Yankee City's fair name and fame.

In the recent past my Yankee City has changed. The old friendliness, gentleness, generosity, self-respect, and respect for others have departed. In their place have come with a rush of hatred, roughness, greed, self-assertion, and contempt for others and their rights and their reputations. Rowdyism, rampant and unashamed, has taken the place of respectable, God-fearing behavior. We are living under a reign of petty terror—a reign of profanity, vulgarity, and ignorance.

I appeal to the good, honest people of Yankee City—and there are very few who are not honest and good—to put an end to the whole thing. Think well of your city's honorable history.

The hostile symbols of mockery and derogation which gradually accumulated around Biggy began to appear with increasing frequency in the outside press. There was a tendency to reduce the permissive acceptance of him as champion of the little people and an amusing fellow who turned the high and mighty into targets for his low comedy. He was now shown in a form which more nearly resembled the figure presented by the Yankee City paper. Finally, when he was first defeated after two terms as mayor, *Time Magazine* reported the event. Evidently their files were filled with clippings from the New York and Boston papers.

Just as "Lord" Timothy decorated his home, "Lord" Thomas rigged up a line of oldtime bedroom crockery on the ridgepole of his house, planted a graveyard in the front yard with names of his opponents on the tombstones. Fascinated Yankee City elected him its Mayor. He won a second term. Contrary to Yankee City tradition, he stood for election a third time last week. This time, shocked by his brawling, his publicity junket to the Pacific Coast, his high-handed method of turning the municipal administration over to his cronies, Yankee City did not vote "Lord" Thomas a single ward. Into the quiet hands of Frederick Markham, retired shoe manufacturer, was placed what was left of the city government.

When a public figure loses his heroic stature, his role often shifts to that of fool or villain. It is difficult for him to return to the life of an ordinary man; the people in their myths and legends find it hard to allow him this blessing. This is true partly because hero and villain are clearly interconnected and partly because different social levels use these symbols to express their differences and hostilities. It is always difficult to understand the villain without knowing what a hero is; equally, the role of the hero needs to be delineated by understanding that of a villain. The roles are dualistically conceived in our society, supplying the imaginable limits at the two extremes of moral belief. Each symbolizes in human form the moral code of the group and allows its negative and positive moral beliefs and values to be expressed and continuously recreated to conform to its ever-changing yet forever permanent form.

In the larger sense of the standards or ideals they represent, what one is the other must be, for each is the creature of the same necessities within the individuals and systems of life which hold them together and provide cultural and biological continuity. If perceptible signs are necessary, such as emblems of the totem, the cross of Christianity, or the star of Judaism, to express the love and approval of a people for the beliefs and values of their group, and if these same objects embody the projected moral self-regard of each individual while serving as models to discipline and guide the conduct, then other material objects are necessary to evoke hatred and fear of the forces and things which threaten the existence of the group or the individuals in it. They are also necessary to express the negative values in the ambivalence all humans feel for the controls, disciplines, and frustrations necessary to contain human flesh and emotions within the ordered confines of a social system. The villain, properly drawn, allows an audience to escape vicariously from the domesticating restraints of society and a sense of over-confinement into the primeval, untamed world of the villain. It is evident that each individual often wants, but usually suppresses, his desires to strike and injure any person or social object which interferes with his personal wishes while he struggles egocentrically to achieve his selfish goals. Sometimes gratification may come from a sense of pleasure realized in the fancied or actual injuries he inflicts, often on those most loved. Evil lies here and the symbol of the villain gives it vicarious expression.

The villain in his ideal form must have another characteristic. It is not enough that he embody the evils of the whole people within his person and express them dramatically in crucial situations. Ideally a villain should be a member of the in-group, for then he functions most efficaciously to symbolize and express the ambivalence all individuals feel toward their domestication and the constraints of their membership in the group. Such a villain dramatizes their fears about the disintegration of the group and the punishment suffered by those who, by intent, attack the social order. Obviously Benedict Arnold performs this function admirably for Americans, as does Judas Iscariot as one of the Twelve Apostles for Christians, and Iago for all men when he betrays his friend.

An individual outside the group can be a convenient hated object, but he is rarely an ideal villain since he lacks significant qualities necessary to evoke, direct, and organize certain emotions felt by everyone in our contemporary society. There must be a betrayal of the basic moral order of the group to which he and those who consider him a villain belong. Only a member of the group itself can adequately play such a role. Pilate and the Roman soldiers may be hateful symbols of the outside world which attacked and helped destroy Jesus Christ, but Judas, one of the Twelve, who actually participated in the sacred mysteries of the Last Supper and the First Mass, transcends all such figures in the ideology of Christian villainy. George III, Cornwallis, and the Redcoats, while hated symbols of the founding period of America, can never be such candidates for villainy as the traitor Benedict Arnold.

The problem which revolves about the understanding of the meaning of *betrayal* and of villainy inevitably takes us to the role of a hero and its meaning for human society. In popular myth the hero's role positively reaffirms and strengthens the ideals of the moral structure of the group; the villain's role as the hated betrayer of the group and its moral principles allows moral disapproval of antisocial acts and vicarious satisfaction in them, thus reaffirming and strengthening the private convictions of each member and the moral life of the group.

For many people of Yankee City Biggy Muldoon was a villain who had brought disgrace to them and to their city. Whereas other Americans living beyond the community and not identified with it could view him as an intelligent court jester and laugh with him and get pleasure out of him, many of the people of Yankee City were humiliated because they were made to feel identified with him as a fellow citizen. Consequently, many grew to hate him, and some of these helped to defeat him when he ran for office.

The symbolic design of a villain or a traitor, when fitted to the person of an individual, although composed of immaterial values, signs, and social acts rather than the visible cloth of a costume, nevertheless fashions its materials into significant form to fit the demands of the immediate social stage. It uses whatever stuffs are available to maximize the individual's worst and most condemned qualities and thereby create a symbol capable of arousing the most hostile and sometimes ungovernable responses of those related to it. Such a symbolic garment was made for Biggy by those who feared and hated him. They transformed him in the minds of some people into the kind of person for which they had designed the costume. He was attacked in the local paper in editorials and communications to the press, as well as in speeches and in the informal gossip which spreads and permeates an entire community. [5a]

No doubt a few of those who contributed to the development of his villain and clown roles were filled with malice and had this very purpose in mind, but they were in the minority. These disapproved roles grew out of the values and beliefs of the people, particularly those whose positions impelled opposition to Biggy; they came into being as naturally as did his heroic role. In fact, they were necessary elements of a social drama in which a political champion of the lowly challenges social convention and power. Champions of the people, in the folk values and beliefs of their contemporaries, must also wear the mask of villain and fool. The same conscious and unconscious folk fantasies as are expressed in the heroes, villains, and fools of popular literature transform the ordinary individual into antithetical roles of wise and noble champion who is at the same time the stupid or crazy fool or ignoble villain. Only the paranoid can believe this is always a consciously contrived plot against the hero, designed by the powerful few to defeat the just demands of the many. [71d]

Broadly viewed, Biggy's political career, once it became public property, bears a strong resemblance to the old morality plays. From the moment he first ran for mayor, through his early triumphs, his subsequent defeats and humiliations, and until the present day, a never-ending struggle has gone on between a dual and antithetical set of traditional symbols for control of his significance to the people of Yankee City. Each of the contending forces by symbolic means tried to capture the public personality of Biggy Muldoon and envelop it in a symbolic form which would make him the object either of praise and approval or of condemnation and contempt.

In the morality plays, the whole audience as well as the players knew who was the hero and recognized clearly the persons and forces of good and evil; they knew, therefore, whom to be for or against. But in our society one group's hero is often another group's villain or fool. In the drama of Yankee City the same man is hero and villain. He is both the strong leader of the people and the contemptible clown. It is not the characters of the social drama who are divided and in opposition but their audience. Those who watch hold antithetical views about Biggy; it is they who struggle to capture, if not the soul, at least the meaning of Biggy as a public personality. They cannot settle between them which role he plays.

It must also be added that for many spectators there is a conflict within themselves between the symbols of Biggy the fool, the clown, the man of evil, and those of Biggy, the man of valor who fights for the rights of the people. This last group wavers from year to year, and so do their votes.

Writers and poets who fashion reality into the forms of fantasy, founded more often than not on the deeper traditions of the culture, permit their audiences to express vicariously their private emotions in response to the actions of the characters and plots that draw upon them. [82] Whether the central character becomes and remains a hero, sinks to the level of fool, traitor, or villain, or rises to the spiritual heights of a martyr, may depend on the actual circumstances of his life, on the interpreters of his actions, the communications they transmit to the general public, as well as upon the social and psychological needs of a people in particular periods of their history. A Robin Hood may at first be defined as a robber and destroyer of the social order, but in time may become the symbolic leader of the oppressed, who redresses their wrongs, defeats their enemies, and brings justice to the society. Jesse James, one of the modern American forms of Robin Hood, was for many at first only the merciless killer and train robber, enemy of law and order in the West. But through the years the storytellers, the ballad-singers, and the social themes and values they utilize have transformed him into the champion of the little people of the time: the pioneers and the settlers of the West in their helplessness against the vicious attacks of eastern bankers and giant railway corporations, who, without regard for human rights, took people's property from them and robbed them of their freedom and equality. Jesse James the man, dead and in his grave, is still Jesse James; but his symbolic villain's role has been exchanged for that of the folk hero who championed the oppressed.

The inverse process may also take place, and sometimes both together, in inextricable mixture.

Economic, Social, and Symbolic Factors in a Hero's Career

Biggy fought a successful fight as a common man and an underdog against the highly placed powerful people at the top of the social heap. The figure of little David, champion of the little people, attacking the giant Goliath is but one of thousands of similar symbols that permeate every aspect of our sacred and secular life. From the secular extreme of such recent favorites as Mickey Mouse and the Three Little Pigs and their animated nonsense to that of the sacred Lowly One attacking the power of the highly placed Jews, multitudes of our symbols express the wishes, beliefs, and values of a people hungering for a lowly champion who, as their representative, can treat the high and mighty with the scorn and contempt they are believed to deserve and can righteously defeat or slay these "evil enemies of the people." A champion in America, however, must be forever on his guard to be more the common man than champion, lest his followers look for new Davids to slay him— the old David—who for them has become a new Goliath.

Biggy won his fight to degrade and commercialize the mansion and its environment. He succeeded in translating them from status symbols, which evoked superior feelings related to the way of life of the elite, into purely economic symbols needing only the value of money for their possession. The house was moved to a poor-status area and divided into apartments inappropriate for the superior. Its location and lovely garden became a service station, one in the chain of a great petroleum corporation.

After the place was sold, his violence was no longer so easy to connect with the underdog's attack on his superiors. The sale removed his struggle from the public arena, where he was the little man fighting entrenched wealth and the champion performing extraordinary deeds in the service of his fellows, and reduced it to the level of a private economic transaction. Maybe the spectacle had been fun to watch, but the symbol of the struggle of right and wrong, good and evil, poor and rich, the many versus Hill Street, had been removed. When the house became a large roll of bills in Biggy's pocket, everyone could cheer for his triumph, but the power of the money now became part of Biggy's own meaning. His new position demanded a different style of behavior. In some ways he now dramatically represented some of the very things and values he had assailed. The attack on the mansion implicitly made him one of the people; the translation of it into money made him explicitly a man of wealth.

Muldoon never reached the place where his name stood for legal or political help for the common man. His governmental accomplishments were not great or in any way spectacular except in terms of personal conflict. He was a good businessman in office; he did what he promised, namely, to maintain an honest businessman's administration. He appointed good men and honest men. He demanded that they work hard, and they did. In no way did he institute any kind of reform or change in the government of the city.

Furthermore, in his later political career the great depression changed matters. No longer could local government or private agencies satisfy the needs of the poor in the community. Local charitable organizations and public aid for the needy were abandoned and federal and national aids substituted. The New Deal, a vaster champion of the underdog, came into being at the time Biggy was struggling within himself to understand what had to be done to solve his own and other people's political problems. Many of his political adherents deserted him as they did other Republican leaders to follow Roosevelt. Yet after suffering a few defeats Biggy was re-elected mayor in 1935. Thereafter he was defeated until he ran in the last two elections.

We do not have space to follow him in his later career. The affection of very many of his townsfolk is evident. The whole history of his life would be needed to understand him fully as a political symbol, but the earlier parts of it, including his first two victories and meteoric rise to fame, followed by defeat and failure to achieve his aspirations for higher position, contribute most to our knowledge of the significance of such a symbol in the political life of Americans.

Having achieved economic success, Biggy conformed to the powerful rags-to-riches motif which is a basic tenet of Americans. The myth of ultimate success and the creation of the symbolic role of the successful man who rises from lowly beginnings to greatness and final heights is a necessary part of the apparatus of our social and status system. To live as normal and respected citizens, most Americans must either internalize this myth and make it a part of themselves or in some fashion achieve an acceptable peace with it. Otherwise they face social attack and possible destruction. A man without ambition needs to explain himself.

Biggy was able to translate his own attitudes, intentions, and behavior into simple but highly powerful symbols with which most people in Yankee City (and the United States) could sympathetically identify. They were rudimentary symbols carrying a great emotional impact anyone could understand, symbols that aroused laughter in the electorate rather than anger.

The reasons for his later defeat are numerous, diverse, and difficult to determine; the principal ones, however, can be stated. The signs and symbols of the mass media, unless constantly refreshed with new meanings, rapidly become shopworn and no longer attractive to their audiences. In simple terms, the same man in the same variety act frequently repeated soon becomes tiresome. On radio or television the audience can turn him off or try another station. When a character on a local scene loses his appeal the editors of the press turn the main spotlight elsewhere to another set of fresh events. These factors operated in Biggy's decreasing popularity and the waning use of him as a symbol by the mass media.

But more fundamentally, the role of hero with Biggy in charge as a master of ceremonies who could make fun of his enemies, with the Hill Street mansion as a prop for his public spectacle, had changed for the most part to that of clown or, for those who had learned to hate him, villain, because he had threatened and endangered their self-respect and their position in the community. From the beginning of his rise to fame he was never free from the implication that much of his behavior was funny and he himself ridiculous.

Americans have always appreciated the antics of the low fellow in politics who makes fun of those who believe themselves superior. In his lifetime Abe Lincoln, often humorous, was considered ludicrous by many. Abe's humor, like Biggy's, was at times too broad and earthy for polite society. He came from the bottom of the social heap and his humor expressed his

origins. Lincoln's enemies attacked him partly in the belief
that he was rowdy, crude, vulgar, and lower-class. Editorial and
cartoon depicted him as a buffoon and rustic clod incapable of
the responsibilities of high office. Yet Lincoln rose above the
limits set for him by his enemies. How did he, and others far
less gifted, manage to defeat their foes and escape being permanently branded with the symbols of inferiority?

The factors are multiple, but an important one was their
willingness to play the game of social mobility according to the
traditional rules. When they did so, the values, beliefs, and
themes which permeate the basic structure of our society were
easily attached to them by those who became their followers.
Lincoln rose from the log cabin of a poor white family in a
backwoods state to the White House by playing the game
according to the rules of cultural convention. Each step he
took, occupationally and economically, prepared him for the
one above. Each occupational and economic step was translated
into social advancement. He changed his speech and his dress,
the houses he lived in and their location, modified his manners
and some of his values, as he advanced to higher levels. He
married a woman from a superior class. He took off the coon-
skin cap and put on the silk hat of Springfield and Washington.
He removed the moccasins of the backwoods and pulled on the
shiny, well-cared-for boots of the successful railway lawyer,
intimate of the socially superior. Instead of arousing the enmity of the common people he excited their approbation, for
he always acknowledged his early beginnings and insisted that
he was still one of them, even when, in his later years, he was
on terms of equality with heads of state. His followers could
easily identify themselves with such a symbol and realize their
own wishful fantasies in his reality.

Lincoln never conceived of mobility in purely economic
terms, nor have thousands of other successful Americans. They
have not renounced the symbols of status nor attacked those
who wore them. They have played the game. It is doubtful
whether the Great Emancipator's followers were conscious of
this. They saw him as the man of the people, of lowly origin,
who was smart enough to be a successful lawyer and brilliant
politician, something they might have become themselves had
they had the luck and the will to do it.

Biggy refused to obey the ordinary rules that guide most people in their efforts to advance themselves in the social heap. He believed in middle-class economic values and morality but rebelled against middle- and upper-class social values; yet he still wanted to be mobile and achieve recognition even to being President of the United States. However, he did not want to pay the price of learning how to do it. He attacked the whole system controlling the rise of a successful man, and his attacks created conflicts that could not be resolved within the ordinary functioning of the system.

To be successful in our society a man and his family who are socially mobile must be willing and able to translate their economic gains into status symbols acceptable to the social levels above them. Neither Biggy nor his mother was willing even to attempt to do this. On the contrary, they defined their active goals for advancement in the community in strictly economic terms and violently attacked everyone at the superior levels who was playing the game according to the social rules. Their behavior was too deviant not to arouse the anxieties and hostility of those around them. Had Biggy and his mother been able to introduce their own values, beliefs, and consequent behavior into Yankee City they would have constituted a threat to the whole system, for the basic values on which contemporary society rests run counter to what they attempted to do. Mother and son knew and followed the rules for the economic game as conventionally defined in America: they worked hard, saved and invested their money in property, and as good entrepreneurs they bought cheap and sold dear. They accumulated a small fortune and thus conformed to the traditional rags-to-riches pattern, from immigrant poor to wealthy Americans. But here they stopped. They not only refused to transform their accumulated wealth into symbols of social status and into social status itself, but also refused to make their behavior conform to standards set by those who were placed above them; in fact, they attacked and tried to destroy the symbols of status and, instead of submitting to higher authority, attempted o defeat and subordinate it.

The destruction of the Hill Street mansion and the substitution of a filling station, with all the prior and subsequent behavior related to that hostile act, explicitly expressed this conflict in values. Neither Biggy nor his mother *wanted* to translate their economic rise into social mobility. They usually looked upon the symbols of the superior, the mansion and its gardens, the elm-lined dwelling area of Hill Street, as economic rather than social objects; but whenever they felt them to be something more than objects of trade they deliberately misused them to attack the power and prestige of the upper and upper-middle classes. Clearly, they were aware that these objects represented something more than economic items. Their use of them, although exactly the opposite of that intended, demonstrates that they, too, felt them to be status symbols.

Biggy achieved his immediate goal and realized his intentions partly because neither he nor his mother wanted to do what had to be done if they were to rise socially, and they steadily ridiculed and lampooned the successful Irish who had accepted conventional ways of gaining the respect of their fellows and finding worth in themselves. They called such people by the derogatory term of "lace-curtain Irish" as well as other names less mentionable. The deep hostility of each to authority seemingly made them incapable of accepting the standards of a status society.

When Biggy defeated his enemies in the superior classes he translated his victory into an economic triumph. When he sold his filling station to the Standard Oil Company he detached the controversial symbol of the house and garden from himself and thereby proclaimed himself conqueror of the Hill Streeters, but by the same act transformed the social symbol of the mobile lower-class man's triumph into the cold realities of a financial statement. There can be no doubt that in the values of his lower-class and common-man following he gained a great victory. Many admired and envied his financial achievement and his ability to defeat his tormentors, but once he had attained his goal he separated himself from the powerful symbol that had brought him their attention.

Biggy's continual attacks on political authority and on the status system forced people toward either open revolt against the system—too frightening for most of them to sustain—or annoyance, embarrassment, and finally confusion and weariness. His following changed constantly. At one time some would be close in his counsels, then they would be out and often his enemies. At some moments he would have a tight little clique that would work closely with him, at others no more than two or three people. Essentially he is a very lonely man. People are afraid of him.

Our political order permits ambitious individuals a choice among a number of possible career routes. They can accept the present world for what it is; they can attack its weaknesses and abuses and attempt to improve parts of the structure to conform to the precepts of justice and morality; or they can challenge the whole social and political order and attempt to substitute a new system for the old. This last inevitably incurs the application of violent sanctions against those who lead such revolutionary movements, yet such roles are provided for, recognized, and grudgingly accepted by our society. In the larger sense, they are theoretically necessary for the successful operation of the political community, for our society is built on a premise of free and reasonable individuals making choices for the collectivity. Men who choose the path of revolution reassert the right of others to think and act as individuals free from restraint and demonstrate that our politicial precepts are in fact possible. At the same time, most revolutionaries are object lessons proving that such choice can overreach itself and that there are sensible boundaries beyond which reasonable and patriotic men must not go.

In politics Biggy was a social and not an economic rebel. He was not the conventional political or economic revolutionary. Yet he was attacking one of the foundations of American society, our status order. Psychologically he was always in revolt and consequently found it impossible to adjust himself to a situation where he was the man with authority and political power. While mayor he sometimes confused his following by continuing in revolt against what in fact was his own power. For a while he aroused more anxiety and increased more tension than he could release. After his election his fighting, though still highly regarded by some, embarrassed and frightened many, particularly when he fought some of his own people and created disorder in his own ranks. Many of his followers no longer felt easy with him; their champion had become a potential threat to their sense of security. Increasing fear in Biggy's social group restrained and limited action. This was not necessarily his fault, but possibly a function of the loose social structure of the lower groups and of the aggression of people attracted to his cause. There was also increasing fear of Biggy because of his attack on the moral shortcomings of those he knew. Although supposedly very permissive, he attacked the moral imperfections of those around him, asking embarrassing questions or referring to incidents involving cowardice, drunkenness, infidelity, and other disapproved behavior.

The champion of the people, the martyr, the traitor, the villain, fool, and clown—all roles Biggy played or was forced to play—express in ideal form some of the values and beliefs we have about ourselves. They exaggerate the petty acts, the minor observances and infractions of the rules, which are part of our own behavior. Human conduct and all the values and beliefs which order it are enlarged in such roles to heroic and godlike proportions. These symbolic figures stretch our ordinary feelings about good and evil, impulse and restraint, order and individual freedom, to their ultimate extremes.

The good citizen who becomes the martyr, who sacrifices his life for the moral principles which maintain and sustain a nation, the hero who at great risk and with utter abnegation of self conquers the wicked foes of his country, the evil man who leads his people to destruction or betrays them to an enemy, and the ridiculous impulsive fellow who knocks over the chairs of constituted authority while chasing well-formed blondes through the halls of respectable hotels—all are human figures enlarged beyond life size into symbols which evoke basic feelings about ourselves and our social world. They release and free us, yet bind and control us, for they take us beyond ourselves and permit us to identify with the ideals of our culture. The sacred ideals of godhood are never more than one step beyond; sometimes they are immediate and present, for in human history heroes often become gods.

The cultural values of a people themselves supply the powerful symbols which, properly molded, become the plot and story of a life or mystic hero, a villain or a fool. The cultural hero is an attractive and powerful symbol with which to identify; he easily arouses those who listen. To outsiders who are not personally concerned his story is only a story, but to those involved the drama of a champion struggling against his and their antagonists is not a story but "reality." The most fantastic legends, the most curious fables, can be believed once the "reality" of the political hero has been established in the feelings and beliefs of his followers, while—equally true—the most scurrilous and impossible tales of iniquity are faithfully credited by those who feel the "reality" of his reported evil acts.

Villain and hero, idealizations of the interdependent, dual forces of good and evil, make vice and virtue manifest in sensuous, perceptible human form. When this happens fantasy reshapes reality, the non-rational, mythic symbols dominate the logical and empirical ones, and the semi- and unconscious inward images emotionally control the outer concepts of empirical fact. Men can hate and love, and take pleasure in doing it. It's holiday time for everyone. If actual holidays are not publicly declared and real processions formed to celebrate the love of a hero, they take place in the informal actions, beliefs, and excitement of the people. Sometimes a generation later those who were not originally present, in their effort to recapture and participate in the emotional excitement of yesterday, formally declare a holiday dedicated to the dead hero. But the intense pleasures experienced in worshiping him usually remain as dead as he is; only the feeling of moral worth can be revived when they celebrate his birthday. Now and then the work of a great artist, poet, or dramatist, or the folk drama of a people, succeeds momentarily in helping a new generation to experience the excitement felt by an older one when their hero walked on earth.

In the heat of political battle Biggy Muldoon, Huey Long, Al Smith, Senator McCarthy, Franklin Roosevelt and, in generations past, Andrew Jackson, Abraham Lincoln, and others, each to his own degree has captured the imagination of the people and in his own time has been transfigured into the human symbols of good or evil, sainthood or villainy. The cold propositions of reason can prevail only when the myths of today's heroes no longer arouse the wishes and fears of those who love and hate them; even then their legends become the canonized myths and moral representations necessary for the persistence and cultural continuity of their society. The symbols of Abraham Lincoln as clown and villain are dead with the fears and hatreds of the past, but the sanctified myth of Old Abe, whose wit defeated his enemies, whose laughter carried him and his nation through the bitter and fearful hours of defeat and impending disaster, lives on in the lives of all Americans, and with it the folk legends of the powerful body which out-wrestled the town bully—the big and humble man who rose from the backwoods and the river bottoms to greatness, yet stayed common just like everybody else. The evidence and reasoned propositions composing the most objective research are easily fitted into the moral assumptions and values, the social logics, of the Lincoln myth.

Biggy Muldoon is not, nor does he claim to be, an Abraham Lincoln or an Andrew Jackson. But he and other Americans who have enjoyed and suffered transfiguration by mass media into symbols with power to evoke hatred and love share the necessary psychological and social attributes which are the materials needed by their countrymen for the substance of their collective myths.

To understand Biggy, it helps to view him as if he were the hero of a tragic drama who had the power, because of the precepts and underlying assumptions of the social context where he strove for success, to achieve partial, but never complete, victory. There were always present the latent but well-established factors which would defeat his aspirations for greater achievement and ultimate triumph. Although "time desireless" had shown him to be a courageous man who fought without fear, Fate, in the form of social reality and the inner world of his personality, temporarily at least defeated his aspirations. The strong man of classical drama, believing he is unjustly treated, pursues the dictates of his own ego, but in doing so finds he has violated part of the code of his group. Muldoon, the strong man, knowing he was a good man unjustly treated, following the urge of his ego, strove for success using some of the accepted rules of his society; but he, too, violated some of the basic rules of his group.

Perhaps such a man as Biggy Muldoon will never again appear in Yankee City or even in America, but others will come forward to play the role of hero or champion of the down-trodden, or the comomn man who challenges the select few and slays the dragon. Some of these will rise to national positions, but they will achieve the highest levels only when they learn how to conform to the basic beliefs and values of the group. When they fail, sometimes it will be caused by their inability to adjust their basic beliefs and values to those that govern American society.

PART II

THE SYMBOLS OF HISTORY

INTRODUCTION

The chapters of Part I presented a sequence of developing political events occurring in the immediate present to learn their symbolic significance in the actions of the community. Those of Part II examine historical concepts, the beliefs and values the people hold about their immediate and ancient past, to learn from their view of the past how they presently see themselves. The symbols used to evoke the past and their meanings are thus analyzed. History as fact and history as symbol, as they were used in the celebration of the city's three-hundredth birthday, are compared and questions raised about the validity of each. Time is investigated as a product of collective life.

Within the polar dichotomies of secular and sacred, the behavior analyzed here and in Part I belongs largely to the former category. But as we enter Part III the interest is increasingly with "sacred" behavior until in Part IV all chapters are devoted to the meanings and functions of sacred symbols.

Most of the evidence for the three chapters on the historical Procession with which Part II is concerned was gathered from the following sources:

1. The official files of the Tercentenary Committee which planned and organized the celebration of Yankee City's history. They were full and ample and contained a day-by-day account of all meetings, activities, participants, and events from the period of planning until the celebration was over. The files also contained newspaper clippings from the local and Boston papers, the sermons of ministers for the occasion, the historical chapters about each episode portrayed in the Procession, the official guides, the titles and descriptions of the floats as well as a great variety of other materials fully used in Part II.

103

2. Interviews with the principal participants and organizers, particularly the chairman, who also provided a running commentary on the materials in the files.

3. The Procession itself. Only one member of the research staff saw the parade. It took place when Yankee City was one of several places then being surveyed and before it was finally selected for intensive study.

4. Several local histories and many historical documents. These provided rich materials, but since this volume attempts to maintain anonymity for the community and its people as in previous volumes of the series, we cannot give them the credit they deserve (see Warner and Lunt [139c], p. 127).

5. Standard economic and social histories and other standard sources such as the publications of the United States Bureau of the Census.

Among the somewhat special terms that recur frequently in Part II are: *collective representation, collective ritual* or *rite,* and *sign.* We shall see still more of them in later sections of the book, but they will perhaps be clearer to the reader if noted here. A *sign,* in the language of symbolism, is any form of perceptible token whatever—word, gesture, painted signal, complex composition in any medium, ritual acted out, even silence on occasion—that is made, and/or accepted, to stand for a meaning beyond just what it physically is. I.e., a *sign* is something that points to a meaning. A *symbol* is the complete unit or combination of sign and meaning. Experience of a symbol means the recognition of meaning from the sign. Although either term, *sign* or *symbol,* may be used in discussing man's symbolic experience, the distinction holds and should not confuse.

A *collective representation* is a symbol developed by the group, expressing the significance of the group.

The terms *ritual* and *rite* are not used here in their narrow meaning of the formal motions of a church service or Masonic ceremony, although these would be included; they carry rather the broader sense of any social behavior performed for the sake of expressing a certain meaning or meanings of importance to the group concerned.

Masculine and *feminine* elements, mentioned in Part I, are more extensively noted in this section and again in Part IV.

Also expanded is the *non-logical* motivation of many symbols, and the distinctive experience of the *ethnic*, or person whose family is of direct or fairly recent foreign origin. Here, too, we begin to use the term *species*—speaking of *species* condition, or *species* events, etc.—for the aspect of man's life determined by his nature as a complex animal, with all the faculties and "instincts" to which he is born, rather than by the cultural habits or patterns handed down to him through tradition, from older persons and the society around him. The distinction will be increasingly observed and its interweaving elements noted as the study proceeds.

The term *species* emphasizes the group character of man's animal nature and behavior rather than the individual. It emphasizes the unconscious, non-rational and adaptive aspects of human thought, emotion and behavior rather than the irrational. A principal distinction between non-rational and irrational behavior is that the former is adaptive and the latter is not. The first holds human beings together and is creative; the latter pulls them apart.

CHAPTER 4

THE RITUALIZATION OF THE PAST

The Citizens of Yankee City Collectively State What They Believe Themselves to Be

During the early period of our research, Yankee City celebrated the three-hundredth anniversary of its existence. Forty thousand people came from all over the country to be a part of the historic event. Natives gone to the West and to the great metropolitan cities returned home and others born elsewhere came there for this historic moment, many seeking ancestors and hoping to identify with a known and desirable past. The people of Yankee City had spent the major part of a year carefully preparing for this tercentenary celebration. Everyone was involved: the aristocracy of Hill Street, the clam-diggers of the river flats; Protestants, Catholics, and Jews; recent immigrants and the lineal descendants of the Puritan founders. Fine old houses and other places of prestige and pride throughout the city were selected and marked with permanent signs which told of their importance and significance.

Five days were devoted to historical processions and parades, to games, religious ceremonies, and sermons and speeches by the great and near great. At the grand climax a huge audience assembled to watch the townsmen march together "as one people" in a grand historical procession. This secular rite, through the presentation of concrete historical incidents, stated symbolically what the collectivity believed and wanted itself to be. Those who watched saw past events portrayed with symbolic choice and emphasis in the dramatic scenes of the tableaux which passed before them. At that moment in their long history the people of Yankee City as a collectivity asked and answered these questions: Who are we? How do we feel about ourselves? Why are we what we are? Through the symbols publicly displayed at this time when near and distant kin collected, the city told its story.

Forty-two dramatic scenes representing over three hundred

years of history (1630–1930), beginning with an idyllic view
of the continental wilderness—"the forest primeval, before man
came"—and concluding with a war scene from contemporary
times, passed before the official reviewing stand and the vast
audience. Among the scenes were Governor Winthrop bringing
the Charter of the colony, the landing of the founding fathers
of Yankee City on the banks of the river, a local witch trial, as
well as episodes from the French, Indian, Revolutionary, and
other wars of American history (see Table 1, p. 131, for the
entire list). All had immediate significance for Yankee City,
and most of the scenes were important in the history of the
nation. Among the personages portrayed were Lafayette,
George Washington, Benjamin Franklin, and William Lloyd
Garrison.

Extraordinary care had been taken to make each scene historically correct. Local, state, and national histories were consulted by an expert committee to be sure that each occasion,
each character, the actions depicted, the clothes worn, and the
stage settings were authentic. The Boston Museum of Fine Arts
supervised the production of most of the floats, constructing
authentic models of the historical characters and incidents.

The total sign context of the parade from the beginning
"Before Man Came" until now, the very movement of the trucks
that carried the floats, each vividly portraying things past, all
showed time going by. "Events" from the distant but diminish-
ing past moved toward the present in preordained "inevitabil-
ity," supposedly bound to the imposed irreversibility of chronology. They came into the eyes and present worlds of the audience, then once more disappeared into the past like the
historic events they represented. What was put in and left out,
selected and rejected, became symbols which revealed something
of the inner world of those involved and the present beliefs and
values of the collectivity.

The great Procession passed before the dignitaries of an
official reviewing stand who were the city's official representatives. Then, in effect, the collectivity officially accepted the
significance of the signs that it had fashioned and now offered
publicly to its ceremonial leaders: the sign-maker accepted his
own signs in self-communion. On such a memorable occasion
what meanings flowed from the past to be again part of the

present? At the particular moment in time and place when the group see the symbols they have made and chosen, what are they saying to themselves? And to whom, other than themselves, are they speaking? This question is necessary, since what they say about themselves will be partly determined by the audience to whom they communicate it. The city's Tercentenary Committee made all this quite evident. On several occasions the chairman and others declared that the Procession would help to establish "understanding among citizens of diverse racial origins and points of view" and "teach our children the importance of our city's past." It was clear they were also talking to themselves, for they said, "We will learn of our own greatness and the important part we have played in this country's history."

Despite the successful use of expert knowledge, the authentic reconstruction of each event, and the overriding emphasis on evidence and fact, the significance of each event selected (and rejected) was not a matter of reference and rational sign behavior but of collective emotion and evocative symbolism. The story's plot, its characters, actions, minor and major episodes and their development, as well as the opinions and attitudes of the audience and the producers, were significant symbolic evidence which could be collected and analyzed. Each dramatic episode and the entire procession were examples of pure symbol. They were fabricated signs whose present meanings referred overtly and explicitly to past events in the life of the community and the nation. But beyond this, they were evocations and present products of the past emotional life of the group *as presently felt*. As symbols they were collective representations which conformed to Durkheim's classical definition of collective rites. Collective representations, he has said, are signs which express how "the group conceives itself in its relations with objects which affect it." Within their meanings is collective power individually felt, the condensation of the "innumerable individual" mentalities of past generations whose social interactions produced and maintained them. All societies uphold and reaffirm "at regular intervals the collective sentiments and collective ideas" which help to maintain their unity. They achieve this unity at times by means "of reunions, assemblies and meetings where individuals being closely united

to one another reaffirm in common their common sentiments." [42a]

More important than the rational and scientific, not to say
Puritan, moral resolve to "create understanding" and teach by
"learning of their own greatness," the people of the community unknowingly revealed their non-rational, unconscious
feelings and beliefs about themselves. In talking to themselves,
in presenting their own signs to themselves, with their own
meanings given to these signs as they were offered and accepted, revalued and reconceptualized, they were dealing with
George Mead's "significant symbol." They were saying not
only what history is objectively, but what they now *wished*
it all were and what they wished it were not. They ignored this
or that difficult period of time or unpleasant occurrence or
embarrassing group of men and women; they left out awkward
political passions; they selected small items out of large time
contexts, seizing them to express today's values. Thus, at times
they denied or contradicted the larger flow of history and the
intentions of yesterday's understanding, often repudiating beliefs and values that were once sanctioned or honored.

In wish and fear, in guilt and hidden emotion, they were
using the unconscious symbols of Freud or perhaps Jung.
But since the individual concepts of Freud do not fit the group
phenomenon present, and Jung's "*racial* unconscious" although
collectively founded carries false implications, we must examine these signs of meaning as the expression of the unconscious emotional group-life of the species, given cultural form
in the experience of each individual (see Chapter 16).

The condensation of collective experience expressed in the
forty-two tableaux was much greater than the condensation
of an individual's dream, for the latter at best reflects only one
lifetime, whereas the images of this procession dealt with a
span of time which covered the total meaning of the lives of
tens of thousands of individuals who had lived, died, and passed
on their collective and individual significance to those now living. The forty-two dramatic scenes were intended to represent
historical truth and recreate the past for three hundred years
of experience—for the actions of thousands of men and women
who had once lived, their accumulated total being many times
the city's present census. This represents an incalculable num-

ber of events, of comings and goings, deaths and births, failures and triumphs, beginnings, endings, and continuities, which make up the lives of individuals who compose the living history of the group. Any one of these events, any one of the forgotten thousands, had a significant story whose meanings, properly unraveled and told, could inform today's people of their beginnings and their past. Yet most of them, both events and individuals, have disappeared without identifying trace. They have not been "forgotten," for most of them were never remembered. Yet they were woven into the fabric of group life.

During the three hundred years of its history thousands of families, each biologically and socially founded, emerged, matured, and dissolved in death. They were the solid foundation on which the generations of Yankee City built and maintained community life. Which were remembered, and their presence and significance celebrated, when Yankee City "took stock"? The solid superstructure of institutional life, the church, the school, and the government—town, state, and national—each during these three hundred years had its own continuing life, changed its meanings and forms or held firmly to its way. What of them and their past? What is their significance to the present collectivity? What influence did the economic life of Yankee City exert, with its old and new forms, with inventions and new technologies supplanting older ones and new economic institutions taking the place of, or reordering, those that had gone before? What were the meanings of the economy in the great collective rite?

Finally, not only had these countless events flowed continually through three hundred years—not only had individuals lived their collective lives in the institutional and economic matrix—but the events, the individual lives, and the social relations of the community had been evaluated at the time of their existence and later reevaluated. Individuals had felt these social beliefs and values as joy and sorrow, pain and pleasure, triumph and despair. As a collectivity at various times they had felt them as the upward swing of well-being and high hope or as despair and suffering, accordingly as life moved quietly or convulsively along. Such emotions had also been expressed in the collective symbols and life of the time. Are they, like those who felt them, dead? And if still active—

as I believe they are—how are these collective memories stored and expressed in the signs and meanings of today? What has happened to these "delayed" communications from the past as they are transmitted and transformed through the generations, and learned and re-expressed today? How do contemporary members of Yankee City publicly recognize and evaluate them in a collective ritual designed for such a purpose? What does the community's "available past" signify to the interested or apathetic present?

In brief, what is remembered of things past? Which of past beginnings, endings, and continuities are marked with significance? Which have mental and emotional signs placed upon them saying in effect: "Look at these objects. Understand and feel again through them what was once true and what, when you recognize and value its significance, will be true again."

Despite the careful historical research of specialists in the fine arts and the social sciences and the knowledge of local antiquarians to insure that the events depicted and the objects marked were historically correct and individual characters properly portrayed, the whole at certain levels of understanding was like a dream, perhaps a collective fantasy. Tableau after tableau moved dreamlike across the minds of the beholders. External and fixed, they moved out of the past across the reviewing eyes of present beholders in exactly fixed time relations, yet their deeper meanings disregarded time. They told a moving, non-rational story of how things should have been, while giving moral approval to what a God-fearing community should approve; or covertly nudged the audience to enjoy, perhaps unconsciously and vicariously, some of the same forbidden pleasures their ancestors experienced more directly and consciously.

For the investigator these symbols of things past provide a long shaft sunk deep into the dark interior of the mental life of Yankee City, and in this symbolic "stocktaking" the non-rational levels were tapped and brought into view. The unconscious world of the species living out its existence within moral and intellectual forms is present and active. In what ways did it find cultural expression? What parts of its meaning gained access to these rigidly controlled symbols? These answers found, what new knowledge can they give us about the moral forms which constitute the structure of social life in Yankee City and America? To begin to answer these questions, we must guide our search with an explicitly understood procedure.

Theory, Method, and Evidence

The Tercentenary had three phases: its early planning, organization, and assignment of authority; the activation and ritualization of the community as a whole in preparation; and the celebration itself. Each is important for understanding the significance of the entirety. Based on larger theory and method, each demands its own techniques of inquiry. In the opening phase the major committees were selected which organized, planned, and directed the entire proceeding. A brief examination of their membership is necessary to learn what kinds of persons and social attitudes and values were involved in the community's conceptualization of what Yankee City is or should be to its people. It will answer such questions as: What ethnic and class levels were represented? How did their beliefs and values influence the dramatic ceremonies? What kinds of significant or insignificant tasks were assigned to representatives of the various social groups? How did the lower-class levels and the various ethnic and religious groups share the responsibilities of the production with the higher classes and the descendants of Puritan ancestors? Who controlled the celebration and had the power to choose the symbols? What effect did these persons or groups have on the kinds of symbol selected and how were they defined and presented to the public?

The second phase consisted in activating and organizing all the people of Yankee City to make them integral and active participants in the preparations and the celebration itself. This was done partly by organizing further committees and enlisting the aid of the city government, schools, churches, men's and women's organizations, and also civic, business, and industrial organizations throughout the city to sponsor the floats. Sponsorship involved some degree of congruence or relation between the social meaning of the sponsoring group and the meanings of the symbols they selected.

After the preparatory phases the celebration opened on a

Sunday with sermons by the clergy, a showing of ship models and pictures by the local historical society, and visits to a Navy cruiser anchored in the harbor. This was followed on Monday by the Washington parade, when the first part of the two-day Procession took place; on Tuesday by garden displays, sports, and other activities; and on Wednesday by the second part of the great Procession, when the other forty-two tableaux were shown. The festival ended the following Sunday with a service on Old Town Hill. The three aspects of the celebration that proved of greatest public interest were the two parades and the historical markers visible throughout the city.

During the second phase the latter had been placed about town on objects of "historic" interest. These were signs of collective concern and social value and contributed an important part to the ritualization of the community. For example, before a private dwelling and its gardens this sign appeared:

LOWELL-JOHNSON HOUSE

Built 1771 by Judge John Lowell, author of the clause in the state constitution which abolished slavery in Massachusetts.

Approximately a hundred objects were so marked, indicating their special significance to the collectivity. About half were dwellings, all occupied; the others included public buildings, churches, graveyards, bridges, and historic locations on roads, rivers, and the harbor. The sign itself, designed for the occasion, carried the name of the city and of the Tercentenary and the name and date of the object. An official guide book, a handsome and dignified brochure illustrated with a clipper ship, Georgian houses, and an ancient church, listed all the objects marked for ritual attention, described them, and showed their location on a map.

All these objects were chosen by the central committee and are subject in our inquiry to the same theoretical questions as those for the Procession. What periods were favored, and why? The questions previously raised about the floats are of significance here in helping us to understand what signs "the City" selected to provide images of its self-regard.

A member of the central controlling committee was assigned

to write a series of connected historical sketches, more than forty in all, each a little chapter which dramatized the local importance of a national hero or event and, in so doing, traced chronologically the history of the community. During the months before the Procession these sketches were published at regular intervals in the local paper, which had a large circulation among all groups and classes.[1] They were further used in the public and parochial schools for history and civics courses and as texts for little plays the grade-school children wrote and produced for their own entertainment. The public response to the published articles was highly favorable; their topics became subjects of ordinary conversation among old and young. Letters to the press by the older inhabitants about the various episodes, discussions at home and at social gatherings, public congratulations of the committee and the author of the series, demonstrated the broad appeal of the articles and the response to them. We learned by interview that a large number of local people had clipped and mailed them to distant friends and kindred.

Most of the local audience on the day of the Procession carried some of this knowledge with them in viewing the floats. Much of what they "saw" had been learned or brought back into memory by reading and talking about the series of stories. For the Tercentenary the most important function of the little vignettes was that each was designed to provide the background for a float in the Procession. It functioned as the text and authentic source from which a small physical model was first prepared by museum specialists and a tableau of living actors in a dramatic scene, sponsored and prepared under supervision by a local organization, was later presented to the audience. The whole series of scenes, properly known and understood, thus became living chapters of the Yankee City Book of History made manifest in the Procession.

This arrangement of story and dramatic ceremony is of methodological importance to our study, for fundamentally it is a close analogue to the historical myths and rites of primitive society. It proved possible to study the collective rites of Yankee City by some of the same procedures used successfully

1. Fifty-two per cent of all newspaper subscribers in Yankee City, including substantial numbers from all class levels, took this paper.

on primitive peoples.[2] The origin myths of primitive groups and their legendary accounts of how and why contemporary man came to be, each portrayed symbolically in great totemic rites that tell those who produce or see them the meanings of life and the significance of the collectivity, were almost exactly paralleled by the historical stories of Yankee City and the related dramatic ceremonies of the Procession. The parallel is in fact even closer than this suggests. Myths in primitive Australia and elsewhere are socially sanctioned by tradition and belief, and their ceremonies informally "supervised" and sponsored by the old men who control the necessary knowledge and social and sacred power. This was also true in Yankee City. All floats chosen by religious, ethnic, and civic sponsoring groups had to be selected from the "official" history of the community set forth by the central committee. Each had to follow the "authentic design" established by the story and the sculptured model. All this for purposes of "historic accuracy," to maintain a "dignified and trustworthy" presentation of the city's past. Such stipulations made it possible for a consistent story to be told; the official "myth" and its control made certain that various ethnic, religious, and other status groups could not insert discrepant versions of historic truth.

The oral (non-literate) traditions of a simple society are more easily maintained and transmitted by its responsible members than those of a complex culture, partly because the undifferentiated social system is slow to change and produces a symbol system which expresses meanings that all can feel and appreciate. There are few variant values or ways of knowing and believing. For the investigator the relation of the primitive social structure, of family, clan, of age and sex, to the collective representations which express present realities as well as past significance raises many basic questions about the relation of symbol and sign to social structure; but such theoretical problems are simple compared to those which must be answered for a complex modern society.

Although legends and myths of simple cultures are often historical in the sense that they purport to deal with past time and tell the official history of the group, they are all oral

2. Warner [138a], pp. 244–411.

products of non-literate peoples who do not have the control of written documentation from the past to help them recall their history. The significance of this "delayed communication" of written history will be treated in a later section. Here we will deal only with some of its methodological and technical aspects in our treatment of the evidence and its effect on our interpretations. The crucial effect of the background of a written culture on method in this case is that it allows comparisons to be made between the historical facts of historians and the historical symbols of the Procession and its stories. This permits a search for divergences and conformities, and the reasons for de-emphasis and over-emphasis of given periods, appearing both in the symbols of the parade and among the symbolic objects marked throughout the community because of their asserted historical importance.

We need to know what history we are talking about. To do this we must know what *the* people considered to be *their* history. We must learn what broad principles of inclusion and exclusion were used by the committee to determine what men and events should be part of the collective ritual. In the symbols of the Procession the people of Yankee City, as we shall see, felt themselves to be in several historical universes. The meaning of people and what they do within the context of the city itself was of great significance to them. Its citizens identified themselves closely with Massachusetts and New England, particularly seaboard New England, and thereafter, in an ever-widening circle, with the United States, Western culture, and the rest of the world.

Scrutiny of the subjects of the floats shows that, after the founding of the city, all were representations of events taking place in the community or of those beyond it where its citizens were present (this was perhaps dictated by the terms of the celebration) ; local men and women were favored. The events and persons chosen were preferably of national consequence or part of a national historic development; the history of Yankee City, while conceived within its own limits, was placed within the larger context of national and even world events. Consequently that part of our own analysis which has to do with comparing historical *symbols* with the *events* of history must include the broad relations between local and national histories.

Since methodologically it was necessary to compare the events of various periods with the symbols of the Procession and the objects marked for historical significance, it was fortunate that several excellent histories and commentaries had been written at various times in the city's life, two of them by such distinguished men as John Quincy Adams and Caleb Cushing. Further, the archives of the city and county historical societies, as well as histories of the various churches, associations, and other institutions, were available, along with invaluable documentary materials from the libraries. Also used were histories of Massachusetts, New England, and the United States. [2b] It will be only too evident to scholars in that field that the author is not a trained historian; yet for our purpose it was necessary to consult and use historical documents, not so much to reconstruct history as to throw light on the symbolic process (this enterprise I should think might be of some interest to scientists involved in historical reconstruction).

During the early months of the second phase, when the stories were being published and models constructed, various groups chose their subjects for the Procession. The requests for certain subjects and not others throw considerable light on the problem of the relation of collective symbols to the complex structure of contemporary society. The sponsorship of an historical episode has to do with the theoretical problem of structural, status, and symbolic congruence and the clusters of social meaning which can relate a group to some but not to other symbols. For example, it is obvious that the Canadians of French culture found it emotionally easy to commemorate and sponsor collectively the ceremonial visit of the Marquis de Lafayette to Yankee City, when the great Revolutionary hero was received by the important people of the community at a time when the whole United States was paying him honor. The French Canadians could thus be treated, and act as part of, the continental French tradition made one with the history of the city and the nation. They were separate, yet united with the social life of America and the city by the symbol of Lafayette, the Frenchman, who played such an important military and political role and who participated on a level of equality with the ancestors of today's birth aristocracy.

Other sponsorships were less happy. One historical story for the Tercentenary gave an account of Benedict Arnold's important expedition through Yankee City to secure Canada for the United States. There is a monument on the Old Town Green commemorating his army's departure for Canada. All this, of course, before he betrayed his country. Who could choose or be given such an equivocal hero? It is clear that a perfectly secure group—the D.A.R., let us say—might have sponsored without embarrassment this valid episode involving a figure which later became ambiguous. But the most awkward and unpleasant moment in the production of the Procession occurred when it was announced in the local paper, the official voice of the Tercentenary Committee, that the Jewish community wished to sponsor this tableau. The sponsorship was later withdrawn. The question of congruence becomes an integral part of the problem of symbol, status, and structure. The question of prior rights to certain symbols also enters.

To eliminate unnecessary complications and reduce our inquiry as a whole to manageable proportions, we must use simple procedures with such a complex and difficult subject. One of the two chief questions we must answer is: What was the chronological distribution of events in the Procession and the objects (houses, etc.) within the community marked for symbolic reverence? Was there social distortion of chronological time? Were the events spread evenly, or did they cluster at one or more historic periods? And this known, what do these oversimplified numerical answers tell of the larger theoretical problem of the city's collective regard for "itself" and its people?

The second major question we must ask is: What are the meanings and functions of this very great emphasis on historic accuracy and realism? In terms of the development of the argument this last question must be dealt with first.

The Period of Preparation: the Secular Rites of Legitimation

The meanings and functions of (symbolic) drama, as everyone knows, range from the most sacred rituals of an established religion to those which are purely secular in character. The drama of the Mass at the altar of a Christ crucified, sacred processions on public streets, the tragedy and comedy of the theater, the celebrational themes of thousands of festivals and fiestas, among them stern morality stories or those evoking licentious abandon, as well as the skits and trivialities of vaudeville, radio, and television, are among the many varieties. In each a story is dramatically portrayed, where the actions of a hero and other characters embody the values and beliefs communicated.

In the Yankee City celebration, to make the symbols chosen for the Procession perform the function of evoking the past—to make them believable and manifest to a diverse audience—was a most difficult task. How were the signs to be fashioned and presented so that they would mean something real and legitimate? It is our thesis that most of the period of preparation immediately preceding the Procession was itself an unintentional, informal, secular ritual of consecration. Supposedly entirely devoted to the examination and selection of historical facts referring to the past of Yankee City, and their transformation into authentic concrete form, the preparatory activities served primarily to perform this function in such a way that the audience could make the mental acts of affirmation necessary to accept the symbols as true. Faith in their scientific truth had to be established.

One may note in passing that because science has been wrongly viewed as founded only on skepticism it is too rarely recognized that those who practice or believe in it must found their skeptical search for truth on an ultimate faith in its modes of mental activity. Science, too, has its own values and unprovable beliefs. Like religion, it must have its acts of unreasoned assumption about, and acceptance of, the unknown; in brief, it must have its own myths.

There was a variety of ways theoretically available to those who produced the Procession to establish its symbols as real and legitimate. [140] Taking in the broad possibilities of cultures in general, the symbols used might have been consecrated by religious leaders invested with the power to mysteriously transmute them from ordinary into supernatural ones through rituals of sacred legitimation. Or at the secular level the belief system of the community might have been such that the organizers of the Tercentenary could have been invested with political power from an ultimate Leader, endowing them with this ability to establish faith; or with a political or economic doctrine, conformance to which would establish a sense of reality in the symbols. The symbols of the Procession might conceivably have involved belief in the conversion of ordinary men into extraordinary ones—for example, returned soldiers whose extraordinary courage, valor, and good luck in the face of death as champions of the people, or as defenders of the faith against the infidel, had changed them into heroes or martyrs whose meanings could be infused with the collectivity's values about its own survival.

To an extent this was true of the Procession; but its symbols and objects did not intrinsically carry *their own* proofs of validity. To evoke such meanings it was necessary to use and manipulate modern values and beliefs—to utilize "scientific" means. In a social world founded on Protestantism, the usages of sacred investment fail and the usual mystical ritual methods cannot accomplish such ends. The belief in the efficacy of the power of words and acts of ritual such as those of the Mass, which transform modern objects not only into transcendant signs of godhead but into God Himself, cannot be used. There can be no sacred icons, images of sacred investment, to speak the truths that need to be expressed. Nor is there a divinely or politically appointed authority capable of performing such acts of ritual consecration. No one would believe what he did. The souls of the ancestors cannot be called up ritually from the past to live in the present as they are in the totemic rites of simpler peoples. Something else needs to be done. The people of Yankee City, mostly Protestants and all skeptics in that they live in a modern science-based civilization, must settle for less—if not the souls of ancestors, then at least images that evoke for the living the spirit that animated the generations that embodied the power and glory of yesterday.

The techniques and authority of scientific reconstruction provided signs—incidents, costumes, settings, etc.—which supposedly referred to real things and happenings of the historical past. This faith established and the proper preparatory activities performed according to prescribed standards, the symbols —the accepted combinations of sign and meaning—could be and were legitimated. To the audience (since the signs could be believed) their meanings were true, and this being so, all or

many of the evaluations and interpretations of events portrayed could also be accepted and believed. To understand this,
let us begin our analysis of the preliminary (second) period
to present the evidence.

The first official announcement by the Tercentenary Committee to arouse public interest and launch the collective activity which culminated in the great celebration eight months
later, appeared in a front page story in the local paper. "The
people of Yankee City are to have an opportunity," it said,
"to hear Professor Albert Bushnell Hart of Harvard College,
who will come here to speak of the significance of the Tercentenary Celebration and what other cities and towns are doing
to observe the great event. All persons residing in Yankee City
are invited to attend and get the advantage of Professor Hart's
learning, as he is an historian of national reputation." It said
further that he had written "a special article on the subject"
in which he declared that the occasion "will be the greatest
opportunity in 300 years for the people of Massachusetts *to
take account of stock, to sum up what they have been doing
and to set it forth* [italics mine]."

This first document in the official files kept by the chairman
of the committee and used as evidence in our study also told
the people of the city (as mentioned above) that a "proper
observation" of the Tercentenary would not only be "worth
while in showing the development of 300 years, but it will also
have a valuable effect in *establishing understanding among our
own citizens of diverse racial origins and points of view and
demonstrate their relationship and importance to community
progress* [italics mine]."

To all races of traders, whether merchant princes of seagoing
fifteenth-century Venice, eighteenth-century Yankee City, or
their modern successors, taking stock and setting forth their
wares to the customers has always been an exciting exercise.
Balancing the books to show a profit and demonstrating the
success of an enterprise to others as well as to those engaged
in it, in fact and symbol, lie at the heart of their economies
and moralities. Selling historic objects and symbolic events to
tourist pilgrims seeking "culture" or to nostalgic natives returned to reinvest themselves and some of their money in the
world which first made them is even more worth-while and ex-

citing to these men. "Establishing understanding" in this kind of customer is doubly worth-while, for it brings additional profits while teaching buyers of "diverse racial origins and points of view" the importance of the stock and their need to have it when it is set forth.

Two weeks after this announcement the elder statesman and keeper of the tribal knowledge came forth from Harvard and made his appearance in Yankee City. The great authority on American history reviewed the great events and "paid a noble and well deserved tribute to the Massachusetts character and mentality which sent so many famous men to the presidency, to the Senate and House of Representatives and to all parts of the country." He left his paper with the committee. For Yankee City and other Bay State communities it became a guide and source book for their programs. From its ultimate authority of science and learning first flowed the ability to believe.

Interestingly enough, considering the official desire to demonstrate the "relationship and importance" to the community's past of its ethnic citizens (almost half of the Yankee City population, most being Catholic), he did not speak at City Hall or a similar non-sectarian place but at Unitarian Hall, the meeting place of a very small, yet powerful, New England Protestant sect. With few exceptions those who attended were Unitarians, Episcopalians, Presbyterians, or Congregationalists. The executive committee of the Tercentenary was entirely so composed. The members of the subcommittee that selected the subjects for symbolic display and decided on the models for the floats and their suitability were entirely from the old-family aristocracy. Later, after these important decisions had been made, various groups chose the episodes they wished to sponsor. Included among sponsoring groups were "the citizens of French descent," "the Polish people," and "the Jewish community." Then came such sponsors as lodges, secret societies, and churches which represented citizens of "diverse racial origin," many from social ranks far below those who made the conceptual decisions. Only then was the committee greatly expanded to be sure "everyone is included," as everyone ultimately was, to guarantee the popular success of the collective rites.

After Professor Hart's departure the local historical author-

ities took over. Authenticity and exact reproduction of the
events of history were the ideals dominating their efforts and
purpose. The symbols had to be as objective and reliable as
expert historical authorities and institutions could make them.
The committee to select the events and choose the markers of
historical sites included local historical authorities but consulted other authorities as well as local and national histories.
These and other sources, such as the local historical societies,
helped to ensure authenticity. Genealogical experts were employed; to increase the feeling of historic reality, descendants
of original participants in the great events were interviewed
and encouraged to re-enact the roles of their ancestors.

The Tercentenary stories appearing serially were written
by a local citizen, as we have seen. The writer's family name was
greatly respected by everyone; the family lineage went back
to Yankee City's period of renown and was connected with important events portrayed in the Procession. The artist who
directed the construction of most of the models was himself an
authority on the history of the town and of New England and
a member of the Boston Museum of Fine Arts. Moreover, he
was a son of one of the aristocratic families of the city. Thus
the directors strove for historical validity and reliability. In
the rational aspect they were scientists, in spirit seeking to
establish secular rather than sacred realities; non-rationally
they were ritual functionaries consecrating and legitimizing a
secular rite.

When the Washington parade occurred, initiating the Procession, it was in "exact" accordance with the preserved full
account of this event. "Washington" came from Ipswich attended by people playing the roles of those who originally
accompanied him. He was met on the steps of the great mansion
where he had originally been received. The same speeches—
fortunately preserved—were given and replied to in the words
originally spoken.

Each float in the main procession was heralded by a placard
with its date and description prosaically and rationally set
down (see Chapter 5, pp. 130 to 132). Immediately following
came the historic tableau, played by living men and women each
costumed according to the period. At one level of understanding they were, except for their movement, display cases in a

modern scientific museum—well-labeled, authentic representations of ethnological reality. Behind them was authority expressed in expert design and workmanship.

Clearly this almost obsessive effort for scientific realism was an exemplification of the mentality of the people and a need to satisfy some vitally important demand for certainty. They did not look for sacred authority, as did their ancestors, to prove whatever they were trying to demonstrate, but for secular authority. Although they spoke as heirs of their forebears, and Yankee and Puritan values were everywhere being expressed— in their manner of "taking stock," "summing up and setting forth," as well as in professions of scientific purpose—the emotionally symbolic factors operating were of greater significance.

From the learned essay of Professor Hart and the study and efforts of those who followed him flowed the prestige of higher learning and the power to capture popular contemporary faith in modern science. From the authority of the latter's signs and facts came the ability to believe that the committee and their experts on local history could re-create the past and make it manifest in the signs displayed in the Procession and on the highly valued objects of the community. The physical presence of the "high priest" himself among them, giving a "noble and well deserved tribute to the Massachusetts character and mentality" while telling them what they must do to praise themselves by telling nothing but the truth, increased their desire and their will to believe. The facts of history, symbolically re-created through scholarly knowledge and the skills of the arts, were the ultimate and absolute sources of belief. Those who knew them were sufficiently authoritative to make their symbols of history legitimate and believable. To themselves and to others the search for, and emphasis upon, scientific fact and its reproduction in authentic representations were, as we have said, in effect a modern scientific ritual of consecration.

For this ritual to be efficacious in legitimizing the endeavor and thus establishing faith in it, the action system involved had to conform to standards of objectivity, reliability, validity, and such other tests and judgments as will create in the minds of those concerned the feeling that they are in the presence of facts. The authority of "facts" could not be disregarded; their meanings had to be sought and understood. Once understood, they must carry ultimate weight. Thus the empirical symbols, in this case those of history, which refer to, and stand for, objective facts command very great respect in our society. The methods used to find and establish facts, and the outward signs necessary to create and reliably communicate their meanings, accumulate their own social power. Those who can manipulate these skills and whose delphic voices speak for facts and their meanings, once believed by their audience, possess a secular form of absolute power. At this moment in Yankee City, because the audience believed in scientific fact and skill and the authority of those who use them, they could identify with the images of what purported to be their individual and collective past and reaffirm their feelings and beliefs about what they were by faith in selected facts of history. Thus the whole period of preparation was a secular ritual of scientific consecration. Like priests at the altar, the members of the committee took ordinary things and, by the authority vested in them, transformed them into symbols of ultimate significance. The differences between priestly and "scientific" power are notable here because they throw further light on the problem of how the symbols of the Tercentenary were legitimized and made believable. The Christian priest, for example, performs a sacred ritual under the mystical power of God, and as his agent transforms ordinary things into elements of ritual significance which become, among other things, the symbols of an historic sacred event. He represents, and is authorized by, a church to perform this act. Ultimately he represents a community of men who believe in Christ. The ritual of the priest by intent and official pronouncement functions to make this transformation possible.

Secular rituals of consecration, although habitually functioning in our society, are not publicly recognized or authorized as such. If those engaged in the preparatory activities in Yankee City had believed that their intent was primarily to establish belief in their symbols—or, putting it speculatively, had their audience believed this was their primary purpose— it could not have succeeded. They needed to believe in the intrinsic power of historic fact and their ability to represent it. Their audience also needed to believe that the symbols of the Procession were invested with this ultimate factual authority.

Then the ritual drama of the Procession could be accepted, because the creation of its symbols was *not* recognized as a form of secular consecration.

To see clearly that the symbolic function of this period of preparation was not so much historical reconstruction as ritual consecration to establish belief in the values of the symbols chosen one need only think what might have happened had Professor Hart—from Harvard and Cambridge, in Massachusetts—not been invited to establish the ideology and voice the values and beliefs of the Tercentenary. Suppose Professor Charles Beard of Columbia and New York City, author of the *Economic Interpretation of the Constitution*, had been requested to write the founding document for the Procession. Let us suppose he had made his own kind of speech, with his characteristic values and beliefs, to launch the celebration. It seems unlikely that the historical facts as he would see them could have become effective symbols in the Procession. The preparatory ritual of consecration would not have achieved its end, for the community could not have identified with it; or, having admitted his facts as true, could hardly have incorporated them into its system of beliefs and values as symbols of its faith. Moreover, what he and Hart as *persons* stood for, as well as their places of origin, would give the latter the mark of approval and acceptance and the former probable doubt and disapproval.

Further, a committee composed, let us say, of third-generation Irish Catholics, all of Yankee City, all rightly respected professional historians, and all devoted to their home town, could not have hoped to establish the faith necessary to make the symbols of the Procession carry authority. In brief, while scientific processes were part of, and necessary to, the preparation, and historic facts were indeed collected and arranged in symbolic form, they were the lesser part of the enterprise and perhaps necessary only because they successfully disguised its real nature.

We have given our attention only to the Procession signs; we must also examine the problem of the ritualization of the objects of the community. Later we shall give a full description of the objects marked throughout the city, their chronological distribution, and their factual and symbolic significance. Here we must hold to the problem of their ritual consecration and the differences involved between their legitimation and that of the signs of the Procession.

The same careful procedure was used to determine the dates and history of the various things marked; the dates when houses were built, the time of their occupancy by distinguished families, and their association with important happenings were all traced. The houses and other historic objects were surviving facts of a living past; the people, their activities, and the historic events were gone and could only be represented by descriptive signs in the Procession, but the dwellings and public places where persons or families had lived and great events had taken place were a part of contemporary Yankee City. The problem was to turn them into objects of special regard and ritual significance.

The historical markers placed before the houses were signs, as were those that accompanied the floats. But, supported by the authority of the Tercentenary, they changed objects of present utility into those of ritual significance. In terms of the broader theory which we shall examine in Chapter 14, they moved from objects and facts into "intermediate signs" standing for something else and expressing values other than what they were unto themselves. The markers were needed to make them historically legitimate. Those who now viewed them knew that they came from, and were authoritatively blessed by, their intimate association with the ancestors. But to accomplish this transformation so that the meanings attributed would turn them from present objects into signs of past significance, their historical contexts needed to be known and verified to permit confident acceptance. They could then evoke the proper feelings about the glories of the past. These authoritative signs allowed everyone to share in the investiture of significance put upon them by the Tercentenary ritual.

CHAPTER 5

THE PAST AS HISTORY—
SYMBOL AND FACT

The Procession: Social Time and Its Measurement

The problem of using the general methodology (see Part V) to analyze the variety of collective symbols in such an occasion as the Yankee City Procession is, on the one hand, to avoid erring on the side of sheer theory and speculation to the point where fact is lost and evidence not sufficiently used to found our conclusions securely—or, contrariwise, to refuse to go beyond factual descriptions and simple generalizations on what occurred and not learn the deeper meanings of this great collective symbolic act. I shall not try to steer safely between these two extremes, but rather push our interpretation far over to the extreme of theory and speculation, at the same time, where possible, using empirical evidence fully, counting its units, and pressing the results against overexpansion of theory.

In terms of general theory and method, the problem is to relate the signs of the Procession to the "facts" of history to which they refer and to establish their meanings in the mental life of the people. To solve this problem, after identifying the parade placards and examining their chronological distribution, we shall in this chapter examine briefly the social and economic history of the community. In the chapter following, the meaning of the signs belonging to each period will be established by relating them to the past history and present life of the community and by drawing the necessary inferences.

The forty-three floats of the Procession (including that of Washington's Visit) were spread throughout the three hundred years being officially celebrated. A few represented the period before settlement. An overview of the grand design shows that the tableaux can be divided into several major periods which express the conception its producers had of the city's past. Further inspection demonstrates that chronologically they are not spread equally throughout the three centuries. There are sharp divergencies between the social time of the Procession and the chronology of objective time. The values and beliefs of the history of the Procession conform only outwardly to the measurements of objective time. A major problem confronting us is the nature and meaning of time in this culture. Other references of the signs of social time do not necessarily coincide with those of objective time; rather, they conform to the collectivity's feelings and beliefs about itself (see Chapters 8, 12, and 16). They arrange logical and objective constructs and verifiable events according to the non-logical values of the collectivity. As such they are expressions of men's relations to each other and not to the objective world of nature.

Since three hundred years were being celebrated, if only the statistical probability of pure chance were at work each century would receive a third of the scenes displayed and each half- and quarter-century be given its proportion of symbolic events. The criteria of objective time and "probability" would both be served. But in fact, one brief period of little more than a decade received as much attention as the previous hundred years. One full quarter-century was not represented at all. The time chosen to celebrate a great man's relations to the city's history was often arbitrary, certain times being favored more than others.

Such an uneven distribution demands explanation. What does it mean? Does it reflect the importance of events in the historical and objective sense of the dispassionate historian? Or the symbolic importance of events to those now living in contemporary Yankee City?

The forty-two floats in the sequence that appeared before the reviewing stand during one day in the great parade are listed in Table 1 (this does not include the forty-third, Washington's Visit, which was given a separate day). It will be noted that all but a very few carry a date and appear in their chronological order. Short descriptions of the scenes also appeared on the placards preceding the floats. This material was condensed from the histories previously published. It constitutes some of our raw evidence—part of what the audience actually saw and read—and of course indicates what the audience looked at as each dramatic episode was presented. Reports on the texts of the stories, necessary for full analysis, will appear

TABLE 1. The Procession (Floats)

Period I. The Creation: Before Man came

The Forest Primeval: Before Man Came
The First American: The Red Man in the Wilderness
1492. Columbus Lands in the New World and Is Met by Indians
1614. Captain John Smith Sails along Our Coast

Period II. The Beginnings of Life on the New Earth

1630. Governor John Winthrop Brings the Charter
1635. Yankee City Is Settled

Period III. The Early Fathers

1642. The First Class of Harvard
1647. Aquilla Chase, Pilot and Fisherman
1663. John Emery, a Tolerant Puritan
1679. Curzon's Mill at the Mouth of the River for Grinding Corn
1679. The Trial of Goody Morse, the Witch
1690. Early Silversmithing
1695. Indian Raid at Turkey Hill
1697. Judge Samuel Sewall Repents after the Witch Panic Subsided

Period IV. The New Nation

1745. Yankee City Man at the Seige of Louisburg
1754. Benjamin Franklin in Market Square
1756. Beginning of the Comb Industry
1762. Governor William Dummer Makes His Will To Found Dummer Academy
1770. Whitefield, the Great Evangelist
1773. Yankee City Tea Party
1775. Col. Moses Little Leaves for Lexington
Old Time Shoe Making

Period V. Climax: the Power and the Glory

Bishop Bass. In 1797 Made First Bishop of Massachusetts
1786. Westward Ho! The Search for New Lands
1789. Theophilus Parsons' Law Office. John Quincy Adams Studies Law
1792. French Refugees from Guadeloupe from the French Revolution
1794. Hon. William Bartlet, Driving to His Byfield Mills
1794. The First Water Line Model [ship]
1795. Timothy Dexter, a Famous Eccentric Yankee City Character
1796–1823. Bishop Cheverus, First Catholic Bishop in Massachusetts

Period VI. The Aftermath to Greatness

1821. Joshua Coffin and the Boy Whittier
1824. Lafayette Visits Yankee City
1830. Garrison, the Liberator, Born in Yankee City
1843. First High School for Girls
1843. Caleb Cushing in China
1849. The Forty-niners. Many Vessels Sailed from Yankee City
1853. The Dreadnought, "the Fastest Thing Afloat," Built in Yankee City
1861. Civil War
1884. The Greely Expedition, the Search for the Furthest North

Period VII. We Endure

1898. A Camp in Cuba
1917. The World War

in sections devoted to interpretation of the separate floats. I have divided the scenes for purposes of clarity and later analysis into seven grand periods.

"The Creation: Before Man Came" (Period I) covers the time before settlement and before the three hundred years being celebrated. It tells of the unspoiled "forest primeval" before man's appearance, presents an idyllic view of the "Red Man in the Wilderness," and ends with the period of discovery. The second major period, "The Beginnings of Life on the New Earth," tells of the bringing of the Charter, the establishment of the legal foundations of the social order, and the landing of the founding fathers of Yankee City. The third, "The Early Fathers," presents scenes having to do with men and events that symbolize the beginnings of things as they now are. They vary from the beginning of shipping and fishing to the witch trials and religious problems of theocratic New England.

The fourth period, "The New Nation," celebrated such incidents of the Revolutionary War as Lexington, Concord, and Bunker Hill, and such themes as Benjamin Franklin's gathering of evidence as to the nature of lightning. "Climax: the Power and the Glory," covering little more than the last decade of the eighteenth century, has some nine events—if Washington's visit is included, ten. They cover such diverse subjects as John Quincy Adams and Senator Tristram Dalton, with references to the signing and adoption of the Constitution and the institutions of the new government, the great westward migration, the beginnings of the Catholic and Episcopal hierarchies in Massachusetts, and the triumph of Yankee ship builders through their inventive, technical, and organizing skills.

"The Aftermath to Greatness" (Period VI) tells the story of the time when Yankee City's fortunes had not so much declined as failed to keep pace with the rapid development and expansion of the rest of the country. Period VII, "We Endure," brings to a conclusion the themes of the previous one. Yankee City is no longer an important center of activity; the important events occur far beyond her borders. The participants are no longer names of heroes but anonymous depersonalized roles in mass undertakings. Yankee City is now but one of hundreds of cities of like size in this country and is outranked by many more. For those who rate communities by population and by economic and political power, it is insignificant. But self-respect is still present and vital, and the knowledge of past greatness makes the modern city important to itself and to the whole society.

The symbols at the beginning of the Procession show the virgin land to which history comes. Subsequent ones depict the city's rise to national significance. Still later, others show that the power and glory are gone, have moved out to the prairie states, to the Far West, and to the great modern metropolises of a mass society. Through it all—the coming, the settling, and the going—Yankee City continues and endures.

We can now examine the chronological distribution of the symbolic events portrayed to determine what periods of history were considered important. Chart 1 shows how the events of the Procession were distributed over the three hundred years. The chart is divided into quarter-centuries.

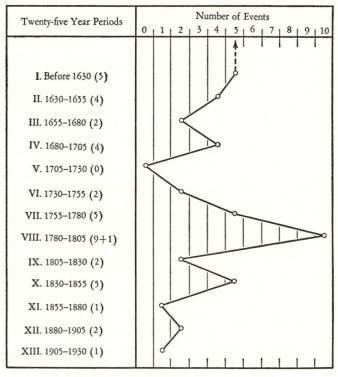

CHART 1. Social Time and Chronology

Although the great ceremony celebrated the three-hundredth anniversary of the founding of the Massachusetts Bay Colony and served as an historical rite signalizing the founding of Yankee City itself, and the establishment of the present order and early growth of American culture on the new continent, few of the events of the Procession were devoted to this early period.

The division by quarter-centuries shows that the time from 1780 to 1805 was given 10 events, twice as many as any other span of twenty-five years. Of the 43 events, 5 were before 1630 and 1 was not dated (early shoemaking) ; the 37 dated events gave an average expectancy of 3 for each quarter-century, but five periods were over- and seven underrepresented. The period 1705–30 had none.

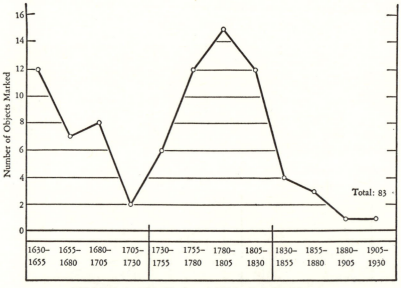

CHART 2. The Marks of Historical Significance

The dates of the markers on Chart 2 are distributed by quarter-, half-, and full centuries. Over half of them (54 per cent) were devoted to the period from 1730 to 1830, more than a third (35 per cent) to the previous century, and only 11 per cent to the century preceding the celebration.

The quarter-century with highest representation in the markers is 1780–1804, the same period as was given most attention and the largest number of scenes in the Procession. The first quarter of the first century starts with considerable attention, then less interest is shown until 1705–29, the lowest of the eight periods in the first two centuries. This is the only period that received no attention in the Procession. From this low there is a steady rise to the great period of 1780–1804, followed by a rapid fall, until by the middle of the nineteenth century very few historic signs are found.

The clusters of signs, for both events and objects, which occur at the close of the eighteenth and in the first decade and a half of the nineteenth century appear to indicate that this era ranked highest in Yankee City's self-regard. Then the collective symbols which represent the community's positive values and beliefs about itself are most displayed for the respect and admiration of the world and for themselves. The signs of *events* cluster at the end of the eighteenth century; those for *objects,* in the first years of the nineteenth.

Some of our questions can now become more specific: Why is this period favored more than all others? What constitutes its high significance to contemporary Yankee City? Was it in fact the historic time celebrated? If so, what is involved that impressed its forms upon the symbolic life of today? Is it the present meaning of past events? Are the symbols of this greatest of all periods significant because of the needs of the social life and structure of contemporary beliefs and values among all, or only some, of the more powerful groups in the life of the community? Or are there other formative considerations to be noted?

To answer these questions we must first examine the "facts" of history so that we can relate symbolic meaning to historic fact, and then take account of the attribution of present rational and non-rational meanings to past facts and present signs.

Space, Time, and Population

Seen from the broad view of the human geographer or ethnologist, the history of the United States, its several regions, and its many communities, including Yankee City, is a movement of huge populations from the European land mass westward across a great barrier of water to another part of the earth's land surface. [110] It began in the random efforts of the period of discovery, in the trial and error of exploration. The first phase of the mass migration was from the extreme limits of the Euro-Asian land mass to the coastal periphery of the North American continent. A second phase consisted of at least three aspects, all significant to Yankee City and the historic movement of which she was a part. There was the continuing movement of people across the water to the little coastal cities; and an advance by some of them into the new land, which coincided with the settling of others on the coast. [2b] Meanwhile, economic and social interaction was maintained among old and new communities on this and the other side of the Atlantic. Yankee City, from its beginnings, received new settlers from England, some remaining, others leaving for the new frontiers that continually formed with the movement westward. The migrants coming into and going out of this and other settlements of the seaboard carried diverse technical, moral, and spiritual equipment which they modified to adjust to the influences of the new regions. Meanwhile the culture and the general technology differentiated and developed. Greater and greater power for satisfying man's creative needs was exerted over the natural environment.

The history of those who settled on the seaboard involved the establishment and consolidation of new social forms and the remodeling of the older ones brought with them to fit the new physical and human conditions. The history of the migratory peoples who pushed inland beyond the permanent settlements to the new peripheries emphasized random experiment, the need for adaptive responses by each individual and family to immediate conditions for survival, with consequent emphasis on individual autonomy, freedom of choice in action, and the need to share and communicate what was learned. [153]

The moving frontier was a continuous process, a mass advance into a continent, but there were rhythms of comparative quiet and settlement followed by surges of population into and beyond the natural barriers of mountains and deserts and the human ones established by colonizing powers or hostile Indians. [135] As the established order of the older settlements on the seaboard continued to give birth to new western frontiers, the values and beliefs of the new and old conditions influenced each other. From these influences many of the events of history were made, some few of which survive in professional histories and in the memories of the inhabitants, but all *felt* in the mental life of each generation which gives literal embodiment to them. The symbols of the Procession reflected these influences.

The conservative and traditional tendencies of the older settlements like Yankee City meant a steady increase in the ordering of the relations of community life, greater control over the human and natural environment, and an increasing appeal to the established order of the past to govern present choices and solve present dilemmas, rather than to the present or future. Political, economic, and moral values and judgments were apt to be conservative in the sense of conserving the past and resisting changes that eliminate it. Furthermore, it meant in fact that those at the top in the community, whose way of life, security, prestige and power were derived from established forms, were likely to be political, economic, and social conservatives.

When Yankee City began, the local historians all tell us, twenty-two men and their wives and children landed on the Parker River with a general grant in hand to the land, heads of families receiving title in fee simple to a few acres of land and the rights to common pasturage. It may be observed parenthetically that the records show even at this early stage that some men received very small grants and others very large ones. It may be presumed that degree of skill and number of able-bodied persons in the family, as well as status in the group, influenced the distribution. Among those receiving large grants, it is interesting to note, were two families who received prominent mention in the floats of the Procession.

We shall start with the population figures as a rough measurement of the city's growth. [98] Increase in population is an expression not only in fact—of the developing strength and power of the community—but in American thought and values: of being "bigger and better" and as something positive and good.

Although in the beginning, before Yankee City was founded, Massachusetts as represented by the Separatists at Plymouth grew very slowly, the colony of Massachusetts Bay immediately prospered economically and socially as well as in numbers, partly because of the great Puritan exodus from England. According to reliable local histories, some 2,000 were present by 1630 and by 1640 over 20,000 persons inhabited the small cities, which included such places as Salem, Boston, Ipswich, and the town we have called Yankee City. The twenty-two founding families of Yankee City contributed their bit to this total. By 1760 there were approximately 1,600,000 individuals in the thirteen colonies, one-fourth of them Negro slaves. By 1765 the population of Yankee City, by the computations of the province of Massachusetts Bay, had grown to 2,882. Massachusetts was second only to Virginia in population, and Philadelphia was America's largest city. By the time of the Revolution Yankee City had grown to 3,700, and in 1790, in the first U.S. census, it was 4,800. Ten years later it had grown to almost 6,000. In the census just before the beginning of the War of 1812 it reached a grand total of 7,600, but immediately thereafter dropped considerably, to 6,850 in 1820 and 6,375 in 1830. These increases and decreases, we shall see, are directly related to the economic and social development of the community and to the estimations of it by those who lived and wrote during the times. [97]

After 1830 the population began to rise again, from approximately 7,000 in 1840 to over 13,000 in the 1860's (part of the last ten-year increase was produced by annexation of an urban area). In the seventies it dropped slightly, and thereafter at ten-year intervals increased to reach 14,500 by the turn of the century and 15,000 in 1930.

Since Yankee City has not recently lost population and is still important economically and an autonomous, self-run community, the town in one sense remains the important city she once was. Absolutely speaking, this is true; relatively, it is not. In the difference we find the story of her rise to greatness and the long aftermath when the rapid pace of changing times and the development of a vast continental United States left her behind and greatness went elsewhere.

The population of the United States in 1790 was almost entirely east of the Alleghenies (95 per cent of the approximate four million total). By 1850 only 55 per cent resided east of these mountains, New England's rate of growth being but

10 per cent, whereas that of the new Northwest had been a 75 per cent increase. At the close of the Revolution there were only five cities with over 8,000 population. Yankee City then, with approximately 4,000 population, ranked as one of the largest in Massachusetts, and in size and economic development an important one in the nation. By 1850, although more than double in population, it was only one of more than a hundred cities of its size or larger; no longer one of the few but far behind the great centers of the eastern seaboard and western prairie. It had come down to a small place in the reckoning of those who count importance in terms of bigness. [123*b*]

The relative shrinkage of Yankee City was not only in numbers but in physical space. At the end of the Revolutionary War the United States extended, politically speaking, to the east bank of the Mississippi. Thomas Jefferson, the agrarian, the Southern equalitarian disciple of Rousseau and a hater of cities, in 1803 purchased the Louisiana Territory and more than doubled the land surface of the United States. Soon after followed the annexation of Texas, the land taken by the Mexican War, and the Oregon Treaty, so that by 1850 more land had been added to the great continental nation than was its total possession at the close of the Revolution. The nation now stretched all the way from the Atlantic to the Pacific and from what is present-day Canada to modern Mexico. By the middle of the twentieth century Yankee City was a small town in one of the smaller states at one extreme corner of a continental nation. Furthermore, it was in a nation that was turning its attention from New England and the Atlantic seaboard toward the great prairies and beginning to look at the far distances of the Pacific. [8]

The great increase in territory and population, as everyone knows, was accompanied by tremendous movements of people across the Alleghenies immediately after the Revolutionary War, and thence gradually on to the Pacific coast. In 1700 the frontier for Yankee City and the United States was little more than a few miles up "the river" and other coastal rivers. But shortly before the Revolution the early pioneers started across the Alleghenies. Immediately after, some migrants from Yankee City joined the others in the great march into and across the prairies. States soon appeared that became powerful political rivals of Massachusetts and her New England cousins. Kentucky, with 70,000 people, was admitted into the Union in 1792; Tennessee in 1796. Then in rapid succession sovereign prairie states—as sovereign and powerful in Congress as the Bay State herself—were created and rapidly settled, to become heavy competitors in the struggle to settle the economic and political destinies of the United States. While Yankee City after the War of 1812 suffered its first major decline, such rapidly growing states as Indiana, Mississippi, Illinois, and Alabama were sending their senators and congressmen to the national capital. Meanwhile, on the eastern seaboard itself, migration had spread northward into Maine; in 1820 that state left Massachusetts and joined the Union. Some of its coastal cities became competitors for Yankee City's maritime and inland trade. [1]

In brief, although from the beginning the Puritan inhabitants of Yankee City obeyed the Lord's command and were fruitful and multiplied exceedingly, and for nearly two centuries Yankee City grew to become a city of size, prominence, and power, not long thereafter the rapid westward spread of United States territory and the huge increases of the nation's population left her behind, reduced (in these respects) to a community of no more than ordinary importance. Instead of a young city with a great future she had become an old city with a great past.

The Social and Economic Foundations of the City's History

The early settlers of Yankee City were farmers, but not long after their arrival they began the enterprises that in time made them largely a seafaring people. According to local records the first wharf was built in 1655. By 1700 interest in commercial enterprises had grown to such an extent that the land along the river, hitherto held in common, was divided into river lots. "For two hundred years," says Samuel Eliot Morison, "the Bible was the spiritual, the sea the material sustenance of Massachusetts . . . For two centuries and more, the tidal waters [of the river] . . . midwifed hundreds of noble vessels; and Yankee City was the mart for a goodly portion of interior New England . . . [As early as] 1660 ship-

building had become a leading industry in Yankee City . . ."
By the time the Constitution was signed, "the lower river from
Haverhill to Yankee City was undoubtedly the greatest shipbuilding center of New England, at this period as in colonial
days." [1]

Following a brief depression after the Revolution, the people of Yankee City quickly regained the prosperity they had
enjoyed before the war. They continued to harvest great oak
logs from up the river and turn them into ships, the cordage
industries flourished, fishing prospered, the distillation of rum
and the rum trade yielded splendid profits. Capitalistic enterprises such as building bridges across the river and canals
around the falls, and trade in lumber, farm, and manufactured
produce with the populations of the interior, contributed their
portions to the renewed prosperity. A class of powerful merchant princes had firmly established their dynasties.

From 1790 to 1812 the mouth of the river harbored the
greatest shipbuilding center in New England and the United
States. At the same time the sea industry was led by some of
the most astute men in the country. Yankee City supplied
many—some say most—of the great names among merchant
princes of the time. We have noted that the population almost
doubled from the Revolutionary War through the period up
to the census of 1810. From 1790 to 1806 the duties collected
on imports tripled, while the sea-carrying trade in general
grew enormously.

A high civilization had been established and a powerful economy founded which poured great wealth into the city and the
rest of maritime New England. A great war had been won and
a vigorous new nation established. A powerful party, the Federalists, dominated by the wealthy merchants of New England
and the southern planters, through the instrument of the Constitution was running the country. Here Yankee City reached
her greatest moment.

Some of the great names associated with the mercantile em-
pires centered in Yankee City were the Lowells, the Jacksons,
and the Tracys, as well as the more lately arrived Bartlets and
Browns. In Yankee City as elsewhere in the harbor towns of
Massachusetts, says Morison, "there was a distinct class of

1. Morison [98], pp. 101–2.

merchant princes who lived in magnificent style, surrounded
by suggestions of oriental opulence." After the Revolution and
up to the War of 1812, "they clung to the ways and fashions
of colonial days or of 1790 at the latest, unwilling to admit even
by the cut of a waistcoat that Robespierre could change the
world." (This was the period from which an overwhelmingly
disproportionate number of the floats in the Procession were
taken.)

With their wealth the great merchants first built elegant
mansions, such as the Dalton and Tracy houses, in the center
of town and established country estates a few miles distant.
Just before the turn of the century they started building along
Hill Street, using the craftsmen whose competence had bested
Europe in the building of ships. They surrounded their homes
with gardens, filled them with furnishings and the other facts
and symbols of European civilization. "Federalist architecture
has here left perhaps her finest permanent trace. Hill Street,"
Morison remarks, "winding along a ridge commanding the
river, rivals Chestnut Street of Salem, despite hideous inter-
polations of the late nineteenth century. The gambrel-roofed
type lasted into the seventeen-nineties, when the Yankee City
merchants began to build square, three-storied, hip-roofed
houses of brick, surrounded with ample grounds, gardens, and
'housins.' . . ." [2]

Within these houses, dressed in the "small clothes" and "tie
wigs" of court life of the eighteenth century, the great families
accumulated the wealth, prestige, and power that ruled Yankee
City and soon, with families from similar cities such as Salem
and Boston, dominated the life of New England. [108] Speaking of this period, Morison states,

Yankee City boasted a society inferior to that of no other town
on the continent. Most of the leading families were but one
generation removed from the plough or the forecastle; but they
had acquired wealth before the Revolution, and conducted social matters with the grace and dignity of an old regime . . .
We read of weekly balls and routs, of wedding coaches drawn
by six white horses with liveried footmen, in this town of less
than eight thousand inhabitants. When personal property was

2. *Ibid.,* p. 153.

assessed, several Yankee City merchants reported from one thousand to twelve hundred gallons of wine in their cellars.[3]

In each of the colonies, later states, there was antagonism between the wealthy cultured towns and the new farming communities spread along the western frontiers as they moved to the prairie and then to the Far West. The people of Yankee City shared this feeling of hostility. True, merchants and financiers were economically interested in developing the back country. Moses Titcomb was one of the important men in Yankee City who helped to develop and settle "the wild country in the interior." Many others could be mentioned—for example, Samuel Parsons, a son of a Yankee City minister, who led the expeditions and pioneers into Ohio when the Northwest Territory was opened. This, too, was a great land speculation. [48]

But men in the back country were often in debt to those in the cities. Much of their land was owned and controlled by absentee landlords, some in Yankee City. The legislature of Massachusetts clearly reflected the differences between the two areas. Its members from the interior were radical and liberal; those from the sea communities, conservative and often reactionary. During the period following the Revolution, at the time of the Articles of Confederation and later during the deliberations which resulted in the new Constitution, men of the back country were for fiat money; those from the cities stood for "sound money." Local histories tell us that Yankee City, like the older cities of the seacoast, enjoyed a larger representation in the state legislative halls in proportion to its population than those in the interior.

The dissension between the frontier and the sea towns was brought to a climax and open conflict in Shays' Rebellion. Yankee City sent an entire regiment under command of one of its prominent citizens to put down this insurrection. At the same time, during the unsettled period between the end of the war and the establishment of the new government under the Constitution, the great merchants and other men of property, as well as those engaged in the scores of industries connected with shipping and trade, were disturbed by the continuing

3. *Ibid.*, p. 190.

spirit of rebellion. Their distress and the similar feelings of others of their kind in the other twelve colonies undoubtedly were directly related to the movement which resulted in the Constitution. The men who appear in the floats—Rufus King, Theophilus Parsons, Tristram Dalton—are not the small, valiant Revolutionary heroes we sometimes think of as our founding fathers; they are the men who prevented the western revolutionaries from taking power and ruling in a fashion which, it was feared, would in violence and disorder be similar to that of revolutionary France. [123*b*]

Once the Constitution was adopted and the strong new central government under Washington and the Federalists established, the city and its merchants prospered enormously. Some of the leading merchants, along with John Hancock, speculated in Continental money and, through their perspicacity and Hamilton's Federalist benevolence, accumulated fortunes. Meanwhile, the Federalist Party policy of neutrality in the wars between France and England had given most of the carrying trade and much of the shipbuilding of the time to the sea cities of Massachusetts—communities near the mouth of this river receiving the largest share. All classes benefited. Despite official neutrality, the Federalists maintained close relations with England and expressed hostility to Republican France. Among other things, they favored the rule of the few; their principles and programs embodied the aristocratic ideals of maritime New England. Their opponents under Jefferson and Madison represented those who advocated expansion into the interior, philosophers of equalitarian agrarianism and political champions of revolutionary France. They were not popular in Yankee City. The economic classes of all levels earned their living, and a good one, from the sea and the older way of life. They were Federalists. [84]

When Tristram Dalton (depicted in the Procession) set forth from his Yankee City mansion as one of the two senators who first sat for Massachusetts, he came as a representative not only of the state but of his conservative, aristocratic class. When George Washington made his grand presidential tour of the new nation, recently established by the Constitution, he came not only as the Father of his Country and leader of all his people, but as a visiting Virginia aristocrat, a Federalist, and one of the wealthiest men in the land. When he arrived he was entertained in the great houses of the town by people who knew him as an equal and were ardent members of his party. The requirements of *political* history would make it highly probable that both Dalton and Washington should appear in the Procession; but the values associated with the highly regarded old-family status and the prominent place of its members on the committees would make it even more likely. Thus the democratic ideals of the greatest good for the greatest number and the aristocratic ones of recognition of the high worth of the few were combined and expressed in the symbols of the pageant.

The citizens of the town itself at the time of Washington's visit recognized that its social and economic life was built upon the strong economic foundations of the sea and the power of the new central government under the Federalist Party. They recognized Washington not only as "first in their hearts" as a countryman, but as first among those beyond New England who understood them and were willing and able to help those who were helping themselves. This recognition of class position and interests extended beyond the borders of the United States even to Canada and England. Moreover, they recognized revolutionary France clearly as an enemy and by the same token found themselves in sympathy with the unhappy French aristocracy. Since Longfellow is the best known and most quoted of all New England poets—since his ancestors were among the original people who settled Yankee City and the opening lines of his *Evangeline* were quoted in the first scene of the Procession, while many of the unfortunate Acadians once actually lived in Yankee City, their activities being well reported in the histories—it might be supposed that these figures of romance and tragic injustice would be selected, both for dramatic and historical reasons, for representation in the Procession. They were rejected in favor of a float devoted to the French aristocratic refugees from Guadeloupe. The full title of the float itself provides eloquent and sufficient evidence of some of the important reasons for its inclusion: "Following the French Revolution many French aristocrats fled from the West Indies to the United States . . ." Thus the strong positive feeling of the time in Yankee City for the French monarchy and aristocracy, and the hostility to the revolutionaries and fear of them, were re-expressed in the symbols of the Procession.

The great climax of Yankee City's economic and social history came immediately after the Revolutionary War and continued until the War of 1812. Before the Revolution there had been opulence, beautiful houses, and a gentle way of life; the merchant princes had already established themselves; but it was in the period after the war that the city flowered and the wealth of the sea was turned into a socially recognized superior status. The great merchants, certain lawyers, clergy, and other professional men were a confident, powerful prestige group who dominated the life of the town. Their class sentiments prompted them to marry into similar families, and they gave their own women in marriage to men like themselves. Their sons and daughters inherited the legacies and great houses after being trained to maintain their economic competence and social graces, and the continuation of the family, its name and status. In short, in this brief euphoric period, well prepared by two hundred years of economic and social growth, the society produced as part of its social structure a superior status whose members, by their political, economic, and social achievements, validated in their own minds and those of others their superior position. It was sanctioned by social approval and deference given to it. Marriage within the group and descent from it as the generations went by established it as a birth aristocracy, the superior old-family part of the upper class.

Although later generations strengthened the lineage of the old families and wove a newer one by marriage and achievement, the classic period, as it were, is the moment of history in which present-day Yankee City can return to greatness. When it does so, the city legitimizes the status of the old-family class. This was the time when Yankee City and New England were at the zenith of their power and glory. When the city looks back to this period as the time of greatness, families of the birth elite who can trace their position through a superior lineage to the great men and families of that high period automatically legitimize their superior status, for it was then that the upper-upper-class status itself, as a recognized position, was securely established. Once lineage is given superior place in the status hierarchy, birth into a family with such lineage is sufficient for membership in the superior class. It cannot be a matter for surprise that the custodians of tradition in Yankee City who determined what symbols and periods of history would receive particular attention were members of the old-family class. That they favored the "great" period and their own ancestors more than others and that the town approved is even less surprising. Their lineal ancestors and the town's social ancestors are often the same.

The embargo and catastrophic War of 1812 ended this period. [32] Yankee City did not recover from the destruction of her shipping and commerce, not only by the war itself but by the government policies of the southern and western agrarians, first under the leadership of Jefferson and Madison and later under new men from the western states. Other cities in Massachusetts—though not all—did retrieve the places they once held. Boston rapidly rose to be the great metropolis of New England. Evidence of the decline of Yankee City and the end of the period of power and glory was fully summarized at the time (1825–26) by Caleb Cushing, able son of a prominent local family. After speaking of the embargo and the war he declares: "During that calamitous period, our seamen were thrown out of employment; our traders lost their customers; the farmers, who had looked to us for foreign commodities, and of whom we had purchased lumber, and provisions, left our market,—and our merchants were compelled to sit down idly and see their ships rotting in the docks."

Having summarized the melancholy state of Yankee City's commerce and her decline and noted the development of Boston, he asked himself why Yankee City did not "resume its prosperity, and continue to Rise." His explanation was not the embargo, or the war, or the recent fire that had ravaged the town. While conditions of trade now required ships of larger draft, the sandbar at the mouth of the river impeded navigation and confined it to the smaller vessels. Rapids and falls only a short distance inland prevented river navigation into the rich interior of farms and forest. A canal, built by the enterprise of local capitalists in 1792, did not permit transportation of "heavy goods" from and to the market of Yankee City. Meanwhile, at the very falls that had prevented the city's growth as a great river port, the manufacturing community of Lowell had grown up and the Middlesex Canal routed inland trade away from Yankee City into Boston.

The name Lowell, city and family, is connected with the rise and loss of place of Yankee City. The Lowell family is a good example of what happened to it. They had a part in building the city into a maritime and mercantile power. Yet it was Francis Lowell, born to the same great family while it was contributing to the intelligence, energy, and prestige of the local merchant princes, who helped to establish power manufacturing in America. The city of Lowell not only in fact dimmed Yankee City's greatness but is a symbol of the inland movement of glory away from the coast to the great industrial and manufacturing communities of the interior. These in turn were expressions of the change from a technology of the sea to the new industrial technology of the land. They were developments, also, of the new relation of the eastern seaboard to the great populations of the West as contrasted to those along the American and European borders of the Atlantic.

Francis Lowell and other members of the merchant families of Yankee City had been instrumental in establishing the new manufactories that were growing up throughout New England. His uncle, John Lowell (son of the minister whose church had been struck by the bolt of lightning Benjamin Franklin earlier investigated in Yankee City), had preceded him among the earlier emigrés to Boston. While visiting in England, Francis had seen the great textile mills and machinery that had led to rapid advances there. He and others copied and improved the English machines and, soon after, started great mills in New England. After his early death, the textile mills at Lowell were established and given his name in recognition of his industrial pioneering.

Within a few years Lowell and other inland metropolitan towns drew the population of the towns of the sea to them. While this was occurring, Boston became the financial center toward which many of the great families of Salem, Yankee City, and elsewhere migrated. There they reinvested their wealth in the industry of Lowell and similar inland cities that were to supply the needs of the agrarian millions who were rapidly settling the prairie and southern states. Southern cotton increasingly filled the New England mills. Yankee manufactured goods, carried westward by Yankee traders, were sold to the pioneers of the great land empire in the West. Meanwhile Yankee money was invested in land and other speculations that were part of the migration and settlement of the West. From these investments great fortunes were developed. It is often thought that this change from the mercantile and marine period to that of manufacturing and land trading meant that the old maritime families lost their controls and their place in the society and the economy, and that new people and new families succeeded them. While some great merchants and shipbuilders were ruined, and some new families did rise to power and place, the change from sea to land was not accompanied by an entire change of personnel. Rather—like the Lowells—many if not most of those who once had power reinvested their money, brains, and energy in their new enterprises and maintained their economic dominance and social position.

Caleb Cushing, writing at the time, recognized this change and the meaning of it to investors and families such as his own. He declares in his history of Yankee City,

. . . The most efficient and comprehensive reason of the decline of the town is, in truth, the immense alteration of the general condition of business during the last fifteen years. The whole of Europe, with the exception of its extreme eastern regions, is in a state of peace. We are no longer the carriers for its many nations. The sphere of our commercial enterprise is wonderfully narrowed. Our capital is now driven into new channels, and the entire circle of the relations of business and trade has undergone a radical revolution. Foreign commerce now requires a larger capital than formerly, and the profits on it are less. We are beginning to perceive and appreciate the importance of encouraging and protecting domestic industry, for the most substantial reasons; and if we did not, the impossibility of employing all the resources of the country in commerce would force open our eyes to see the necessity of investing a portion of it in manufactures. Here, then, we lose our population whilst other towns gain it.

Morison, commenting on these conditions says,

. . . Just before the war ended, two scions of shipbuilding families, Francis C. Lowell and Patrick Jackson [also from a great house on Hill Street] prepared against peace by setting up power looms at Waltham, in the first complete American factory. . . . On a social pinnacle of their own making [in Boston and New England] were the mercantile emigres from Essex County . . . the Lowells, the Higginsons, and the Jacksons, who (according to Colonel Henry Lee) "came up from Yankee City to Boston, social and kindly people, inclined to make acquaintances and mingle with the world pleasantly, but they got some Cabot wives who shut them up." . . . *Despite the rise of manufacturing, merchants continued to dominate the social life of Boston* [italics mine].[4]

The author might have added Yankee City and all the cities and towns of Massachusetts that changed from the sea to the land for their living. Socially as well as economically speaking, his statement means that the old-family status continued and that many if not most of the families of prestige maintained the continuity of a birth elite, even though they had changed the sources of their income. Prestige now came not only from the power of their present economic position but from the great past they had established from the sea, and also socially as part of the high culture of western Europe, by now well founded on the shores of both sides of the Atlantic.

It is small wonder that in 1812, with ruin about them—a disaster of federal policy—many contemplated what the rest of the United States has called treason and plotted among themselves to join Canada and once more become a part of the political union of British peoples; or considered secession, a movement that culminated in the notorious Hartford Convention. During the transition from the sea to the land they saw their respectable and profitable way of life being destroyed by the agrarian South and the West, and by the forces of democracy that came from revolutionary France as well as from the new frontier states which espoused the cause of France against that of Britain. Once the transition had been made, all New England learned what Francis Lowell and others had quickly understood, and they too became integral parts of a continental United States and were able to continue in the great traditions established by their fathers.

4. *Ibid.,* p. 129. See also pp. 213–14.

In the Yankee City celebration, their descendants and those successfully incorporated into this superior status dominated the organizing committees; they conceived, presented, and controlled the great Procession which expressed for all their contemporaries the history of the town. Their sources of income and economic power have changed, but the roots of their social prestige lie deep within the living traditions which took form and became a way and style of life in the decades before the Revolution and until the War of 1812. After a brief return in the days of the clipper ships (1850–60), the sea culture disappeared forever. Reluctantly Yankee City returned to the land and in time built factories for textiles, transformed her comb and silverware arts from hand to machine manufacturing, and, with the aid of "the new shoe people" from outside, built the great shoe industry that now supports her people.[5] A large proportion of the people are now ethnic, including Catholic Irish, Jews, French-Canadians, Greeks, Poles, and others.[6]

Houses and History

Before concluding this chapter we must examine the history of the objects which received ritual consecration for the Tercentenary and relate them to the present part of our discussion. Over half were dwellings, all occupied. Let us observe these family residences in the light of the discussion in this chapter concerning the town's periods of affluence and greatness, its relative loss of position, and the creation of an old-family class through lineage. We may ask which houses were chosen. What kind of people live in them now? Who built them? What kind of people have lived in them during the interim? And how do the answers to these questions relate to the larger problems of the historic periods and the meaning of the symbols of the Tercentenary.

The official guide of the Tercentenary gave a special section to the "Homes" of Yankee City and the list of houses honored by markers.

5. For a history of manufacturing, particularly of the shoe industry, see Warner and Low [139*e*].
6. See Warner and Srole [139*d*]. Only a few of "the new people" have been rewarded by achieving a secure status at the top social level of the society.

Like other seaport towns of New England [it declared], Yankee City has many excellent homes of 17th, 18th and early 19th Centuries. In the beginning, these buildings were simple farm houses, generally with one huge chimney in the middle of the house, with the stairway in front and rooms on either two or three sides. . . . As time went on, the Colonies grew prosperous and larger houses were necessary. The Short House, No. 6 Hill Street, with a chimney at either end, was built in 1720. It is a fine example of early 18th Century architecture. About the middle of the Century, comes the Dalton House on State Street with its fine panelled rooms and elaborate stair rail with intricate spiral newel post. . . .

Yankee City is especially rich in three-story houses. Two of these were built in 1771—the Lowell-Johnson House, 203 Hill Street, built by John Lowell, and the Dexter house, 201 Hill Street, built by Jonathan Jackson. The former of these is one of the best existing examples of its type and, with its towering and symmetrical chimneys and handsomely detailed porch and windows, is a splendid picture of the dignified and stately life immediately preceding the Revolution.

In the short space of this article, it is impossible to do justice to the great number of interesting houses with which Yankee City abounds. It was a shipbuilding community and that industry developed splendid craftsmen whose work may be seen in countless cornices, doorways and window heads on almost every street of the city.

These brief sketches tell us in a general way about the houses and some of the interests and values of those who created them. With notable exceptions, such as the small home of William Lloyd Garrison, most of the houses listed were identified and categorized in our study of all the houses in the community as large and in good or medium condition. Less than 6 per cent of the people of Yankee City lived in such houses.[7] Two-thirds of the houses marked with signs within the incorporated city belonged to this superior category. The present people who occupy them belong largely to the upper class; most are owned and occupied by the old-family aristocracy.

There is considerable historical evidence to help us learn the

7. Warner and Lunt [139c], pp. 239–46.

past meaning of the houses to those who built and later lived in them and what they meant in the social setting of their time. Timothy Dwight during his great tour of the New England states visited the city at the turn of the eighteenth century. Dwight, former president of Yale, conservative Calvinist and aristocrat whose words were often not commendatory, declared,

Hill Street, which lies . . . almost on the summit of the acclivity, is remarkably handsome; and commands a noble prospect.

. . . The houses, taken collectively, make a better appearance than those of any other town in New-England. Many of them are particularly handsome. Their appendages, also, are unusually neat. Indeed, an air of wealth, taste and elegance, is spread over this beautiful spot with a cheerfulness and brilliancy, to which I know no rival. . . .

The wealth of this town is every where visible in the buildings and their appurtenances. Several of the inhabitants are possessed of large fortunes. You will remember, that two of the associate founders of the Theological seminary at Andover, Moses Brown, and William Bartlett, Esqrs. are citizens of Yankee City.

The manners of the inhabitants are, I think, unusually agreeable. They are easy, unaffected, graceful, yet marked with simplicity, and on that account peculiarly pleasing. They are also distinguished for their hospitality; and in a public, liberal spirit are not exceeded.

Their morals and religion, there is reason to believe, are on a higher scale, than those of most other towns in New England, of the same size. Upon the whole, few places, probably, in the world, furnish more means of a delightful residence than Yankee City.[8]

We have examined the high period of the past when the symbolic objects were built. We have ascertained the present position of the houses in Yankee City. We have not yet attempted to determine what the position of the houses was in the social status structures of the intervening years. The answer to this question is of considerable theoretical importance for a number of reasons. It will illuminate our understanding of the relation of these symbols to the social structure through time.

8. Dwight [43], pp. 439–40.

For those interested in problems of status and social class it will throw further light on the legitimation of the aristocracy's social "right" to their high position.

The committee for the Procession and the historical markers utilized several local histories and a number of more general ones to guide them. One of the local sources was a book on *Old Yankee City Houses* written by the owner and occupant of one of them. The book has a brief preface, then presents a "collection of views . . . intended to show some specimens of the houses built in Yankee City during the period when it ranked as one of the principal shipping and commercial centers of the country—near the time of the American Revolution and during the early part of the nineteenth century . . ." A picture of each house is usually given a full page, with the chronology of owners on the facing page. The list of owners is a "lineage" for the house and—for those in Yankee City conversant with the meaning of the times—the claims of the house and its occupants to high status. The vast majority of the houses listed are among those marked for the Tercentenary. Approximately 90 per cent are in the Hill Street area. Of these, two-thirds are on Hill Street itself. Six out of ten were built in the period following the signing of the Constitution through the War of 1812; a few before, and a very few after that time.

A fourth of the houses are now owned and occupied by those who trace family ownership back to the Great Period; some to an earlier period, the seventeenth century. Many have changed hands only once in the last hundred years. The houses not only are symbols of the upper class but in fact gave shelter and grace to generations of families whose parents and children with marriages into similar families transmitted the values and beliefs and other products and symbols of superior status down through the years.

We know enough about the past owners to say that most were in the upper class at all periods of the history of the houses; some were moving hopefully into that class when they purchased or built them; a few occupants, present and past, have not achieved upper-class position. The houses as cultural products and symbols of high position were from the beginning in the custody of high-status people. As such and as symbols they accumulated and held the social power and prestige of that high level. What they are and stand for as a style of life and a social class has been held together by a system whose nuclear structure is the family, and by the interconnected generations who have inherited or acquired positions in the system.

Further examination of the lineage of the great houses shows that very few were built after the War of 1812. The criterion "old" in Yankee City houses means mansions built before the end of the War of 1812—well over half in the quarter-century from 1790 to 1815. Not only were great names created in this period and great families founded to which future generations could trace their lineage, but the old-family status itself then became a superior point of reference, so that those who hold high status now feel that they do in fact embody the virtues of a superior class. In brief, the great period was when the highest status in Yankee City and New England was established and in fact and symbol legitimated.

With the factual outlines of the history of the city traced and broadly related to the periods of the Procession, we can examine the symbols for each period to learn their meanings and functions in the life of the society. We shall start with the images of sexuality in the Period of Creation—when, for Yankee City, the world began.

CHAPTER 6

THE PAST MADE PRESENT

AND PERFECT

The Period of Creation: Sexuality and the Images of Males and Females

Those in the reviewing stand, the Mayor and other dignitaries, saw the first float preceded by a sign announcing "The Forest Primeval." They saw a "maiden" standing "on the land of Massachusetts once covered with forests, where rivers, ponds, and damp marshes made open places." Under the titles, "Massachusetts' Great Birthday" and "The Wilderness," the two introductory historical sketches had said, "This year Massachusetts will celebrate its 300th Birthday." During the period "Before Man Came" the wilderness was untouched: "there was no government. There were no roads, no towns or cities, no churches, no schools or colleges."

The Forest Primeval of course came directly from Longfellow and the romantic conception of the wilderness. It is the world God called good before he created man. The place—the land, harbor, and river—are clearly marked as female. Nature is conceived as feminine. It is both pure and wild in its untouched state. By implication the masculine society later dominates and controls it. The men who farm the fields, who sail the boats, the technology that masters the wilderness and builds the roads, the towns, and the cities—they and their technical, moral, and sacred order are felt as masculine. This impression in the first scene is further substantiated by a later tableau called "1647. Aquilla Chase, Pilot and Fisherman. The first white man to cross the bar at the mouth of the river." The scene is preceded by those showing dominant male symbols, Columbus and Captain John Smith, related to subordinate feminine ones, the Indian "maidens" associated with the fruitful land. All these scenes show powerful males controlling and ordering the natural environment. The virgin wilderness, the land, New England,

156

wild and dangerous yet pure, fruitful, and bountiful, yields to the strong masculine society and shares in the creation of contemporary Yankee City.

Although the minister of the First Church of Yankee City (Unitarian, and prominent in the Tercentenary) surely did not consciously have such an interpretation in mind when he preached the first sermon on the subject of the Tercentenary, his words give support to this interpretation. He told those principally involved in the celebration, as preparation for understanding their task, that "the masculinity, the strength and ruggedness in the Puritanism which formed us are the absolutely essential ingredients of any religion which is worth while." "Our fathers did what they did," he said, "because, banked up in them by their strength of spirit was a strong, explosive vigor."

This theme of the "Great Birthday," when elements of femininity, nature, and fruitfulness cluster closely together in interaction with the explosive masculine vigor of the dominant Puritan civilization, was related to another which needs to be examined. Many of the scenes in the Procession represented the beginnings of things, when a given activity or institution had its inception. Only two, however, depicted the settling of new earth, the first being "1635. Yankee City Is Settled," followed many scenes later by "1786. Westward Ho! The Search for New Lands." These were the only two where women shared the primary roles with men. Where we find a creation period, of land being settled by man, telling of the formation of things as they are now, female and feminine symbols are emphasized. When the city and the West begin, women are the principal symbols. Women's organizations selected and sponsored these scenes, thus giving them public meaning for others to understand what Yankee City is and what they themselves are.

There was only one scene and one moment in the Procession when women were not in the custody of men. In the beginning, "Before Man Came," the female "Spirit of the Wilderness" was free—extricated from the social consequences of her species condition. But she was also outside the human world and the reproductive cycle. In its time mythology the forest primeval was a symbol of quiet, tranquility, eternal timelessness, when nothing happened and all was still. Femininity, inactivity, virginity, and timelessness are clusters of meaning expressed by the "Spirit of the River and the Wilderness," while after "her" contact with the dominant male civilization of the West she becomes the "mother" out of whom a great nation sprang. When man is not, time does not exist, for the symbols of time on which it depends are not there and the measurement of it and its human significance are lacking. For understanding the non-rational thought expressed by the forest primeval it is significant that as the "mother" *out* of whom all men come, "she" herself, eternally fruitful, remains the creative womb where there is no time. From her, by male contact, are born the generations of time-bound man whose linear events, arranged visibly in the moving line of the Procession, give spatial representation to the line of time moving from the past ever onward into the present.

The Yankee City of the Procession is masculine-dominated, its culture is masculine, and its significance and notable achievements are masculine.

Sexuality as a powerful driving force operating importantly in the lives of men and women and events of the time is nowhere depicted or consciously expressed in any of the forty-two scenes of the Procession or the Washington visit, nor is it present in the text of the supporting historical stories. Passion is not in them. In none of them is the passionate love of a man for a woman the dominant theme. Although female abstractions are used to express the meanings of the natural world, in none is woman symbolized by means of classical or romantic imagery as an embodiment of transcendant feminine ideals to which men subordinate themselves and their activities. Romantic love as a primary or secondary theme was not expressed in any of the scenes. Youthful beauty and sexual glamour as attributes of Yankee City girls were not there; there was no Juliet with her Romeo, no Isolde and Tristan dominating a scene. Present were costume displays and aristocratic elegance, with mature but unimportant ladies who served as period pieces and as supernumeraries for men of high position. Their presence often places the appropriate status accent on a context for an important male. The place of women is subordinate and, while respected and often represented, is not important in the dramatic developments of history.

Before further comment the research methods used to

verify these and other generalizations must be presented. In the signs of the Procession the facts of history become symbolic products of present meanings. In our research techniques we treated the forty-odd scenes as "stories" told by those who presented them. Loosely structured and unmanageable history had been in these stories compactly re-formed into the symbolic scenes. Heroes with their secondary characters were found acting out a plot, usually with dramatic outcome. The meaning of each dramatic scene supported by the historical story and comments from some of those who viewed the Procession made it possible to develop an analytical procedure for establishing symbolic units that could be identified and their meanings ascertained.

The procedure was as follows: The story line of the plot was identified, the central character or hero determined, and secondary and supernumerary characters identified and their symbolic functions so far as possible ascertained. The negative and positive feelings attributed to the characters, particularly the hero, as the principal center of interest and identification were established through the treatment of the figures in the Procession and the historical stories told about them. [6] In addition, the various symbolic elements of all the scenes could be counted to determine major themes and the overall grand design of the Procession. [61b]

There were forty-six leading roles or "heroes" among the dramatis personae; forty-one were male and five female. In four scenes a woman played the principal part; in thirty-eight, males were the principals; and in one scene there were two leads, divided between the sexes.

Among the five principal feminine roles two were wives and mothers of early pioneers and settlers; one was a victim of tragedy, member of a family in an Indian raid; one a "persecuted" old woman (and wife) charged and convicted of witchcraft; and one an abstract figure played by a young unmarried woman representing "the Spirit of the River," who was also the "Spirit of the Wilderness." In leading roles all the female figures representing human beings were subordinate to superordinate males; the female symbol of nature was alone on stage.

There were fifty-five secondary characters (not including the supernumerary "walk-on" parts), of which women played thirty-two. Twenty-two of these were Americans; seven were foreign or dark-skinned, including Cuban and Spanish señoritas, Indian girls—maidens and squaws—and three mythical symbolic figures: a Chinese moon goddess, the Winds of the Earth, and Columbia. Twelve of the twenty-two Americans were wives and mothers of prominent men, the remainder being customers in shops run by males, female congregations dominated by famous preachers, passengers on a famous clipper ship built by a great Yankee City inventor, and female high school students presided over by a famous male educator. Only one had an occupational role: a Red Cross nurse in World War I.

In sharp contrast, the male roles were most diverse and powerful, with marked prestige. All the principal male characters were superordinate and dominant. Along with the secondary ones, they covered the whole complex division of labor portrayed, though usually from the higher reaches of the society. Among them were presidents, admirals, generals and other high military officers, senators, signers of the Constitution, merchant princes and philanthropists, professors, famous lawyers, manufacturers; as well as sailors, soldiers, mechanics, and others on the less highly placed rungs of the occupational ladder. Great names were frequent.

From masculinity, presented as powerful and full of prestige, flowed the significant events that molded the life of the society; in it were contained the superior and authoritative virtues. Femininity was conceived as subordinate, and if superior socially, then because of a father or husband whose status established the position. In general, woman's position was dependent and given little interest or attention. In this collective rite there was little excitement in seeing or being a woman of Yankee City. The audience was meant to attribute its feelings of value to male, not female, images.

However, sex and sex attraction in women were not entirely absent. The sexually appealing woman, to whom direct sexual interest might be given by the audience, was placed in entirely secondary roles. All women whose sexual life was committed to a particular male and conventional custody were defined as American; however, around the edge of some contexts appeared several attractive women in secondary roles whose positions were sexually ambiguous—all exotic foreigners and racially different, outside Yankee City and American culture: for example, the Indian "maidens" and "squaws," attractive Cuban girls and Spanish señoritas. Although not in the same category, the Chinese moon goddess, in exotic and appealing surroundings, was an attractive female. The males with these ambiguously placed women were sailors, soldiers, and traveling salesmen, all occupations to which clichés are attached about unconventional sexual relations. Sex as a compelling force giving women power and esteem was not for these Yankee women. It was the sexually attractive Latins and the women of other races who were found with American males. The expression of impulse life is highly constricted and rational. The images of the Yankee women floated by in the Procession like the set pieces of a dream collected and recollected with the rational detachment of a scientific instrument. In this dramatic ritual the life of the species and the passionate and exciting events of three hundred years seemed to flow placidly through the cold chambers of the rational mind, not those of the passionate or overburdened human heart.

Such easy acceptance of this feminine role is surprising, for the committee in charge, which created the artistic conceptions for each tableau and passed on the fitness of each, was composed mostly of upper-class women. All could trace their ancestry back to colonial times. Several were, or had been, professionally trained and employed.

A closer inspection of the several contexts they created reveals something more than rational acceptance of the subordinate role of the mother and wife. Interpretation and content analysis are now necessary, for we do not have the necessary "psychological" materials or records of how decisions were made to relate the symbols presented to the actual historic processes which determined their presence. Two of the three most dramatic and emotional scenes had to do with a violent male attack on defenseless women and children and the persecution of Puritan women. These need more detailed analysis.

The twelfth float, "1679. The Trial of Goody Morse," was sponsored by the Yankee City Woman's Club. Those who played the roles were at the superior levels of Yankee City. All were of old Yankee stock. The float was designed by an older woman, the unmarried daughter of an old family. Perhaps the meaning

of the subordinate role of women and possibly the guilt of contemporary man for their subordination is brought out by the
sponsorship of the Woman's Club. The women perhaps publicly
displayed their hostility for their unfair treatment and yet
appear to forgive the men for what they do. The men who
played the roles of "persecutors" acted out the guilt and possibly, it might be guessed, some of the satisfactions of being
in such a dominant and superior position.

The sign which preceded the float gave the date and title
with the explanation: "She was accused, tried, and condemned
to death on the charge of witchcraft but subsequently released
by the trial judge, thanks to her husband's persistent efforts.
This was Yankee City's one witch trial." And, incidentally, the
only scene with married devotion as one of its themes.

The heroine is clearly Goody Morse, the hero her husband;
the "villain" is equally clearly the male magistrate and the
theocratic law of the times. Although a female is mistreated by
men and unjustly punished by the male law of the clergy and
magistrates, the outcome is favorable. The magistrate turns
from being a bad to a good man, her husband stands loyally beside her, making it possible to condemn masculine dominance
while at the same time defending it. Three scenes later in
the Procession the theme is repeated. The tableau follows a
placard entitled "1697. Judge Samuel Sewall Repents," with
the subscript, "After the witch panic subsided Judge Sewall,
who presided over the witch trials realized the absurdity of the
charges and did penance for his part in the persecutions by a
confession in the Old South Church, Boston."

The story, one of the newspaper histories, declared:

Samuel Sewall was the son of one of the first settlers of Yankee
City. . . . He went to Harvard College and was graduated high-
est in his class of eleven. . . . became Chief Justice of the Bay
Colony.

Soon after he was made a judge some persons were accused of
witchcraft. At that time almost everybody believed there were
witches who did evil things. When it became his duty, with other
judges, to try these persons in Salem he condemned to death
those whom he thought guilty.

A few years later he realized that there were no witches. So he wrote a letter saying he had made a mistake and was sorry. While it was being read to all the people in the meeting house he stood up so all could see him and bowed his head. He never ceased to be sorry that he had condemned innocent people to death.

The outcome of the "plot" of this drama implies that the women who were the objects of the attack of the masculine clergy and magistrates were the victims of the evil ones who condemned them to death. The public confession and penance of the judge bring about a favorable outcome: rationality triumphs and the slaying of the innocent is condemned. Meanwhile male authority is both attacked and defended. The ambivalence felt for the male ancestors, the founders and fathers of the tribe, is also expressed; they were good despite their evil, misguided act. There is pride in the judge as an ancestor. In him rationality and masculinity triumph, the past is absolved of its crimes and the present dominance of males forgiven. Still there is protest; the judge, symbol of masculine law and authority, is publicly humiliated in the confession of his guilt, recognizing the validity of the moral charges against him. In this masculine society the victims, by their involuntary sacrifices, are the moral agents who symbolize his guilt and its public recognition.

Early Fathers and Villains

The period of the Early Fathers and the seventeenth century as a whole were given eight scenes in the Procession. [2c] Although outwardly all were presented positively and had such outcomes as befit the public stock-taking of the community, several attacked the traditional authorities. But they also defended them, for this was a family affair, to praise, not condemn; to display white linen, clean and freshly laundered for company. Yet the complaints of the subordinated and persecuted women, Goody Morse, the persecution of the Quakers, the felt guilt for the massacre of the Indians and the taking of their lands were all covertly present and occasionally openly expressed by these contemporary sons of the Early Fathers, inheritors of those who found and captured the promised land.

Like their prototypes in Palestine they, too, found the deeds and words of their first ancestors not entirely tolerable.[108] Still, if they were to maintain their own legitimacy it was mandatory for them to trace their ancestry to the very beginnings. Consequently, for the maintenance of their position it was necessary to invent new myths and new expressive rituals to hold the power of the ancestors, maintain it within the confines of the modern Christian ethic, and express all of the changes that occurred in the mental life of the group during three hundred years. The powerful influences of Channing, Emerson, the Unitarian movement, the New England renaissance in the arts and literature, as well as what was in fact the beginning of the Puritan Counter Reformation, combining with the influence of the scientific and rational enlightenment, made the invention of new myths necessary. [96]

Throughout our discussion of the symbols of the Procession we have dealt largely with heroes and the supporting secondary characters. Since all the scenes are dramatic episodes, and drama inherently has its heroes opposed by its villains, the question arises whether villains were present or in some way implied in the various floats from the several periods. In the minds of those who composed, presented, and produced the pageant, the villains were no longer the hated Redcoats or the greatly feared British regulars who, by historical account, sometimes threw the city's inhabitants into a state of hysteria. There was no scene depicting the "Boston Massacre," so popular in earlier community celebrations. There were only two floats devoted to the Revolutionary War. Colonel Little and his Yankee City Men now set quietly off to Lexington, but there was no visible or implied symbol indicating a hated antagonist.

Nor did the Red Indian, despite the bloody history in which Yankee City spent her men and money, play such a role. Yet this was a considerable phase of the city's experience. The early accounts tell us that "at the disastrous battle of Bloody Brook, September eighteenth, 1675 at South Deerfield during King Philip's War 'the flower of the population of Essex' [the county in which Yankee City is located] were massacred. There were thirty men from the single town of Yankee City." They were part of the company that marched to Deerfield. By January 1676 "sixty eight men" had joined the local company. "The

ratable polls at this time were only one hundred and fifty nine."
During the earlier Pequot War in 1637, immediately after the
city's founding with but twenty-two families, eight men were
raised in Yankee City.

No villainy is found in the once despised and greatly feared
French whose Catholic "idolatry" was considered "an abomina-
tion" by the Puritan iconoclasts, constantly under threat of
bloody attack during the French and Indian wars. In fact,
only one float was devoted to this long period of rivalry and warfare which finally resulted in the destruction of the French
empire and the triumph of English culture. In the placard,
the text for the tableau, and the float itself we see the attack on
the great fortress of Louisburg that once menaced the peace
and safety of Yankee City and New England. The text, while
telling of the heroism of the men from Yankee City who were
part of the expedition, makes quiet fun of the early beliefs about
Catholic idolatry. In the scene devoted to the Spanish-American
War, where Yankee City forces are depicted in a camp in Cuba,
the Spanish do not appear as villains; nor do the southern rebels
or the Germans in the other war scenes. All these onetime
enemies are no longer villains; but the men of Yankee City who
fought them are heroes. Villains, as properly defined, were
present and part of the history of the city. Although Benedict
Arnold and Aaron Burr, traditional American villains and
traitors, were once actually present in Yankee City, Arnold
himself in a very prominent and powerful role, neither appears
in the pageant (see pages 200 to 203 for why Arnold did not).
Each of course would have made an excellent villain for the
Procession.

Since this great public ceremony was a "stock-taking," and
since merchants of history are likely to put the things of
positive worth in their windows and ledgers for public inspection and quietly forget awkward items of the past, it might
be argued that the hunt for a villain is futile and that the transformation of former villains into ordinary men who are not
objects of hatred or contempt presents no problem. Closer inspection of the principal and secondary characters and their
actions and the implied outcomes of their stories leads one to
the same conclusion. No villain is explicitly presented, and
there appear to be none off stage. Although this conclusion is

justified as regards the spirit which animated those who composed the drama, further inspection shows that there are villains and that deep hostilities are expressed and projected on them. On some of these figures not only hatred but love is focused, but always in such a form that a second inspection is necessary to learn the full significance of the signs for such a tableau. Sometimes known names of prominent men—some historians would say great men—are quietly dropped and a scene becomes anonymous and depersonalized, their figures thus losing their individual meaning and becoming the targets of new meaning attributed to them by contemporary feeling in the community.

We will begin our analysis of these signs of villains and the present hostility to certain symbols of early history with one of the more explicit accounts. Early in the Procession appeared the fourth scene having to do directly with the history of Yankee City, entitled "1663. John Emery . . . a tolerant Puritan who defied the authorities by entertaining Quakers in his house at a time when they were outlawed." The tableau depicted Emery and his wife, ancestors of prominent families, and two itinerant Quakers standing before two stern magistrates who were the secular enforcers of the theocratic law of early New England. The sympathy of the audience for the Quakers is clearly bid for. Their local identification with John Emery would also cause a positive response for Emery and the Quakers and arouse opposition to the magistrates. The names of the magistrates are not given. They have become the representatives of an anonymous status and of the early Christian fathers who founded New England.

When it was announced that the Loyal Order of Moose would present the float of the "Tolerant Puritan," a quotation about him was given from one of the local histories.

In 1663 John Emery was presented to the court at Ipswich for entertaining travellers and Quakers. From evidence sworn to by several witnesses, it appeared that two men, Quakers, were entertained very kindly to bed and table and John Emery shook them by the hand and bid them welcome. Also that witnesses heard John Emery and his wife say that they had entertained Quakers and that they would not put them from their house and used arguments for the lawfulness of it.

The story of the float is based on this historical text. It indicates who the implied "villains" are, but does not publicly name them. It says,

Just for this act of kindness some stupid persons of the town had him taken before the court where he was actually fined, because at that time Quakers were not allowed to stay in the colony. Nevertheless, John Emery refused to say he was sorry, although he was obliged to pay the fine. He and others like him kept refusing to obey such cruel orders and after a time most people came to think as he did, and the Quakers were left in peace.

The language remains vague but, as we shall see shortly, there can be no question that those who designed the float knew exactly and specifically the names of some of the local persons who had been involved and to whom the symbols refer.

Before we can say specifically who these men were and by their identification get at some of the basic changes that have occurred in the collective meanings and representations in the mental life of Yankee City, we need to examine the symbols of the first tableau having to do with this land and its new people. It was preceded by the title "1635. Yankee City Is Settled." "Twenty-two men and their wives and children came up the Parker River in the spring of 1635 and encamped on its banks. They were the founders of the community." The float was sponsored by the Sons and Daughters of the First Settlers of Yankee City. The float of the "Tolerant Puritan" sponsored by the Loyal Order of Moose, which emphasized of course the belief that all religions must be respected and recognized, was a perfect symbolic fit for the membership of that group. The organization was composed primarily of ethnic peoples, of very diverse denominations and even religions, many of whom had only recently arrived in Yankee City. The Sons and Daughters of the First Settlers, on the other hand, were composed of the oldest Yankee and Protestant families. Yet both groups sponsored symbols expressing not only respect for the past but, as we shall show, hostility to the authorities and important men of the time.

The overwhelming majority of the scenes of the Procession dramatized actual persons whose names were given on the placards and further amplified by other names and descriptions of them in the text. This was particularly true for the earlier ones. With the exception of those having to do with early shoemakers, all, beginning with Columbus in 1492 up through the seventeenth and eighteenth centuries to the Revolutionary War, used a named hero, sometimes with several named subsidiary characters; yet this most important scene, the actual landing of the founders of Yankee City, remains anonymous and its people unidentified.

Once again it might be conjectured that their names were lost or not validated by historians. Such is not the case. The names of the leaders and many of the followers are well known. The small river they first landed on, the Parker, bears the name of the clergyman who led the band. The present real name of Yankee City was given it by this leader, calling it after his home town in England. One of the important houses marked by the Tercentenary bears the name of another clergyman, the Reverend Mr. Noyes, who was his cousin and second in command of the landing party. The two were constant companions and protagonists in the theological warfare that took place among these contentious Puritans; yet neither is mentioned in the scene or text—only the name of young Nicholas Noyes, the immature son of the second leader, appears. The Yankee City histories carry long stories about both of these men. The local town and parish histories are filled with pages of references to the first leader; the *Dictionary of American Biography* has a long article on his life demonstrating his worth, power, and great influence on the development of the city. Samuel Eliot Morison also devotes an article to Mr. Parker and his theological activities.

A brief examination of the latter's influence and the historic role he played will provide us with further clues to the astonishing refusal to give him recognition and identification in the float. Thomas Parker (1595–1677) was born in Wiltshire, England and received his advanced education at Magdalen College, Oxford, and later on the Continent. [39] He obtained a grant to the land which became the present township of Yankee City and with his cousin, James Noyes—both properly sponsored by the Puritan authorities—founded and established Yankee City. Although trained as a Congregationalist, we are told, he believed in the Presbyterian doctrine of the clerical control of the laiety. He favored the theocratic principles of the rule of the few over the many, of the sacred elect over the unredeemed. He spent his life in controversy with various members of his flock, trying to "restrain the democratic pretensions" of the congregation. Historians of Yankee City and New England tell us he "hounded the Quakers" with their individualistic doctrine of inner illumination and grace. In short, in fact and sign he personified the masculine, authoritarian, theocratic, Calvinist values of the ascetic Puritan society that founded New England. They had banished Ann Hutchinson and her brother-in-law to the "wild country" across the river for her belief in spiritual love. Parker belonged to the conservative clergy who brought the strongest pressure on Governor Winthrop and the magistrates to protect the "New Jerusalem" from the forces of the Devil and the promptings of the flesh and the "unredeemed."

The Quaker doctrine of the inner light, emphasizing individual autonomy and love, struck at the very foundations of the Calvinist legal and absolutistic control of the totalitarian state ruled by magistrate and clergy. Quakers accordingly were whipped, mutilated, and imprisoned at first (1656) and later sent to the gallows (1659). Although the more severe clergy and the magistrates approved such barbarities as well within the rights and duties of a government founded on the divine law of the Old Testament and the Hebraic code, many if not most of the laiety did not. John Emery, the Tolerant Puritan, hero of our scene, was directly or indirectly opposing Parker, the unnamed villain in both scenes and the first father of Yankee City. The latter's symbolic emissaries in the Quaker scene, called "magistrates" in the official cast of characters—in fact the judges who enforced Puritanic, theocratic law—were the symbolic villains whose anonymity was substituted for the name of Parker. This was made abundantly clear by reference to the actual incident of Emery's arrest. The account comes from a respected local historian whose writings were used by those who composed the texts and prepared the floats, and was thus perfectly familiar to them.

Two of the Quakers visited Yankee City on their way to Dover, and were then entertained by John Emery, as appears from the following statement:

Edward and George Preston, and Mary Tompkins and Alice
Ambrose, alias Gary, passed eastward to visit the seed of God
in those parts, and in their way through Yankee City, they
went into the house of one John Emery, (a friendly man,) who
with his wife seemed glad to receive them, at whose house they
found freedom to stay all night, and when the next morning
came, the priest, Thomas Parker, and many of his followers
came to the man's house, and much reasoning and dispute
there was about truth; but the priest's and many of the people's ears were shut against the truth. . . .

After a while the priest perceiving that the battle might be
too hard for him, rose up and took the man of the house and
his wife out of doors with him and began to deal with them
for entertaining such dangerous people. They replied they
were required to entertain strangers. The priest said it was
dangerous entertaining such as had plague sores upon them.
Which the woman hearing began to take the priest to do for
saying such false, wicked and malicious words but he hasted
away. Mary Tompkins called him to come back again and not
to show himself to be one of those hirelings that flee and leave
their flocks behind them, but he would not turn: and a while
after most of the People departed: and when Ipswich Court
came thither he was had and fined for Entertaining the
Quakers.

Thus the symbol changes not only its meaning but its form
as a sign. The Rev. Mr. Parker disappears as a visible form
and the magistrates take his place before the audience. The
highly respected and highly regarded Mr. Parker, an Early
Father and leader of the founding fathers, becomes an anonymous sign on which contemporary hostilities are projected and
by which derogatory meanings are evoked. The audience saw
his substitutes less as magistrates than as persecutors. In fact,
the local newspaper's full account of each scene in the parade,
on the day following, refers to them as "two persecutors," thus
indicating the meaning of the symbols of the Early Fathers to
the audience of the Procession.

Other floats for this period express the same hostility to
these founders of Puritan New England and to the authority
and power of the seventeenth-century church and state. The

"Trial of Goody Morse" was followed by a depiction of the famous confession of Judge Samuel Sewall, "who did penance for his part in the persecution," said the placard of the Procession, "by a confession." As a judge, Sewall was a hard, not to say cruel, person. As a man he was said to be gentle, warm, and kind. His famous diary and his love of the land of his youth in Yankee City seem to verify these statements about his humanness. [35]

The scene having to do with Sewall's confession, dated 1697, is the last presented for the seventeenth century and the time of the Early Fathers; it is not until about fifty years later (1745) that the next scene takes place. A whole new era, "The New Nation," had succeeded the old. This concluding scene of the Early Fathers, Sewall's confession, where one of the great men of Yankee City and New England "repents" and openly confesses his guilt in the socially approved auspices of the Old South Church of Boston, may well be symbolically the open confession of the ancestors put in the mouth of one of their most prominent representatives by the people of today. Through him, in the modern symbolism of the Procession, they are made to say that they felt and knew the deep guilt of their violence, hatred, and destruction of those who could love. The several scenes of the period of the Early Fathers, when examined as parts of a total symbolic mosaic clearly indicate that, while the fathers were respected and sometimes honored, there is beneath it all a strong feeling of hostility. Contemporary Yankee City is ambivalent in its feelings about them. The victims who were attacked by these authorities— the Emerys, the Goody Morses, and many others—and those who gave shelter and comfort to the believers in the inner light and a loving God, have superseded the stern fathers in the affections and values of the community.

Perhaps even the stern elders of the tribe of Calvin, among whom was Thomas Parker, felt this ever-present and often suppressed antagonism and fought those among their followers who expressed it. They who believed themselves to be the Moses and Aaron of the new Canaan—these fathers of the new kingdom of God on earth who banished, whipped, imprisoned, and occasionally killed their living sons and daughters—were not unlike the harsh God they worshiped, who allowed men to scourge and crucify His own Son that all might benefit by His suffering. Cruelty sanctioned by sacred authority can and must be forgiven; human cruelty, whether sacred in New England or secular in other totalitarian states, ultimately must find its judges who condemn and repudiate it. Inevitably, no matter how great their virtues otherwise, such men become candidates for the role of villain; or when grudgingly accepted, are given obscure places when the people gather to celebrate their humanity.

In our search for villains we need to examine the relations of the early Puritans to the Indians. We have noted elsewhere that in history the Indians were portrayed as bloodthirsty savages who wantonly killed the innocent Puritans. There were four scenes in the Procession in which Indians appeared and several texts which defined what contemporary Yankee City thought and felt about the red and white men of earlier times and the outcome of their relations. In the second scene, "The First American," Indians were identified as part of the context of the "Wilderness." Here they are noble savages after the manner of Rousseau. In the scenes of Columbus and Captain John Smith they are friendly children of nature, young and attractive females more often than males. In "1695. The Indian Raid on Turkey Hill," a farmhouse is attacked and "the women and children were carried off." However, the placard insists that "all but one of them were subsequently found alive" and then, sympathetically, that "this was the only raid in Yankee City." This scene is the last in which Indians appear.

The texts for the several stories about Indians provide further insight. We learn from them that the Indians "lived a happy and idyllic life" and that they were "kind and hospitable to the first settlers." From these accounts it might be supposed that the relations of local whites and Indians were undisturbed by warfare. Yet a brief scrutiny of early histories indicates that, while peace sometimes characterized relations between the two races, many of the ancestors of Yankee City believed that the Indians were "children of evil and of outer darkness." Though little difficulty was experienced by the community itself, few Indians being in the close neighborhood, almost from the beginning members were engaged in hostilities on a broader field. We have seen that men from Yankee City fought in the Pequot and King Philip wars; money was also collected from heads of families in the town to support the latter enterprise. In the Pequot Wars, four hundred Pequots were burned. William Bradford's descriptions of the massacre of the Pequots by the whites, quoted in local documents, help us to understand some of the present symbolic changes and re-evaluations of the Indians and the white ancestors. He says, "It was a fearful sight to see them [the Indians] thus frying in the fire and the streams of blood quenching the sand, and horrible was the stink and scent thereof." Bradford, however, evaluates this "fearful sight," giving not only the facts that went into the relation of whites and Indians in which Yankee City was involved but the feelings and beliefs that came from them and became part of the collective life. "The victory," Bradford's piety led him to believe, "seemed a sweet sacrifice and they [the whites] gave praise thereof to God who wrought so wonderfully for them, thus to enclose their enemies in their hands, and give them so speedy a victory over so proud and insulting an enemy."

The shifting images of the Puritan ancestors and their relation to the men of today may also be illustrated by brief quotes from the Tercentenary sermons preached at the opening of the celebration. The pastor of the First Church of Old City, whose history began with the founders and whose pastorate went back to the original Puritan divines and their theocracy, obliquely protested against the rejection of the Early Fathers and the rising secularism of the city. In his sermon called "The Soul of History," printed in the local paper, he told his congregation,

History means absolutely nothing of any lasting worth save as it is interpreted in human life. And not the lives of men, even the best of the race, as they have lived in the past, but of the immediate generation. *What good is there to be gained from a sort of half-apologetic holding up of the life of the Pilgrim or the Puritan?* [Italics mine.] For example, acknowledging their cold, repellant, conceited, self-righteous bigotry, but pointing to some praiseworthy acts and a few principles that might be worthy of emulation, when the truth is that his life was but the interpretation of a man's conception of the Divine revelation.

His character was the soul of the religious life of his day; and its true worth all depended upon his, and his generation's ability to read the story of the past aright.

This is the great Book of Life that lies open before our generation today. All the stirring events which we may crowd into the next few days; the scenes we may try to reproduce, and notable characters who shall again seem to walk our streets, will leave nothing of lasting worth for us to build into our lives, save as we find their contribution to the great revelation of God, as through the succeeding generations of men.

The minister of St. Paul's Episcopal Church, where many of those in charge of the Procession were parishioners, fashioned quite a different image of Puritan ancestors for the members of his congregation, whose forebears once listened to the elegant Bishop Bass. He emphasized the original unity and oneness of the Puritans with the Anglican Church from which the present Episcopal Church emerged.

While yet in the harbor of Yarmouth, England, the Puritans who left England in 1630 wrote an affectionate letter directed "to the rest of our brethren in and of the Church of England" themselves avowing their continued attachment to "our dear Mother Church." The realization that their convictions would lead them out of the arms of their "dear Mother Church" came over them very gradually. In fact it was not until after a conference with members of the Pilgrim colony that they saw their destiny at the time to be that of separation from the church by the founding of a new one.

The pastor of the fashionable Unitarian Church, present product of the early nineteenth century revolt against the rigid ascetism of the earlier Puritan theocracy, in a sermon likewise printed in the local paper spoke of the "outward lack of grace in the speech, manners and religion of our ancestors, and the much greater and proper sense of joy in life and beauty that we have today. The reason for the difference is that the Puritans were specialists, and, like all specialists, hard and narrow, able to see only the things with which they were preoccupied. The life of God is properly held· by us as something meant to permeate all existence."

The Symbols of Power and Glory

The first of the nine floats in the period of greatness carried the announcement, "Bishop Bass." With it was the explanation, "In 1797, made first Bishop of Massachusetts; minister of St. Paul's Church, Yankee City, in 1752." Its sponsor was the Episcopal Church itself. The present membership of the church is still one of the most aristocratic in Yankee City, leading all others in the number of parishioners belonging to the old-family class.

From the histories of the time it appears that the bishop, a lineal descendant of the daughter of John and Priscilla Alden, started his ambitious career as a Congregationalist, but soon found the aristocratic Anglican Church more in keeping with his spiritual needs and earthly ambitions. After he graduated from Harvard, followed by a period in England where he was ordained to the priesthood by the Bishop of London, he returned to Yankee City and was installed as the pastor of St. Paul's. During the Revolution, historical reports inform us, he was at best "lukewarm" to the American cause, being in constant touch with those in the church who maintained allegiance to the throne. Following the troublesome times that came after the defeat of the British, when the Anglican church was in the greatest disorder, its leaders reorganized and strengthened it to make it a purely American institution. When the Constitution became the fundamental law of the land and Yankee City began to prosper, at the time when the great houses were being constructed on Hill Street, all those who had once been British Anglican became American Episcopalian, and many others among the wealthy upper class, then laying the foundations for its later acceptance as the old-family status, moved over to what a noted local writer has called "the aristocratic Anglican church of St. Paul." Most of their descendants are still there.

The mitred bishop, splendid and at the very pinnacle of the sophisticated church whose elaborate rituals offered spiritual and aesthetic grace to the worldly elegance of the families of Hill Street, was in his time their *man*. The splendor which surrounded his office and the very structure of his church's organization were in every way contrary to the Puritan and pietistic simplicity which motivated the spiritual life of the early fathers who had founded Yankee City. Yet it was in turning against these very aristocratic, hierarchic forms and their outward symbols that the early fathers had migrated and come to found New England. But in the Procession the bishop and his mitre were symbols which expressed the aristocratic values not only of his contemporaries but of their descendants who now trace their origins and legitimacy to the period in which this class established itself. Bishop Bass, as a symbol, is not the sacred representation of a saint often found in the community processions of Catholic Europe and Latin America, where they are offered to the faithful for their adoration and spiritual respect, but the image of a community ancestor whose presence today speaks of the power and glory of the period of greatness when the mercantile economic class and the social old-family class became the functional leaders and models for the whole society.

Eight floats later, ending this historical period in the Procession which started with Bishop Bass, came Bishop Cheverus, first Catholic bishop in Massachusetts. The text tells us, "He often visited Yankee City," later returned to France "and was made a Cardinal." In this same text Bishop Cheverus is closely linked with the superior Protestant society of the time.

In Boston, a Protestant and Puritan city, his noble character and winning manners, his learning and his eagerness to be a good citizen of the community where he lived, soon made him friends of all creeds. When the little Catholic chapel became too small for the growing congregation, there were as many Protestant as Catholic names on the subscription list for a new church, and at the head stood that of John Adams of Boston, then President of the United States. Father Cheverus often spoke in Protestant churches, often addressed learned societies and helped found the Boston Athenaeum.

The Holy Name Society of the Immaculate Conception Church in Yankee City—the "Irish church" in popular parlance— sponsored the float which displayed the bishop's image. All the sponsoring committee had Irish names. Only the designer, a functionary of the central committee, had an old Yankee name.

When the bishop rode forth among the people he must be regarded not as one immersed in the close and intimate sacred
mysteries that unite God and man and celebrate His eternal
timelessness, but as a *man* who wore the proud regalia of a
bishop and later the red robes of a cardinal—a dignitary whose
high position at the time of greatness was recognized not only
by the Church but by the superior Protestant society which he
frequented. To those who sponsored him and to those who designed and fitted the symbol of the bishop into the Procession,
his first duty as a sign was to give secular status and high
place in the community to the Irish, primarily, but also to
other and later Catholic Americans whose cultural traditions,
like the Irish, were not sufficiently anchored in the early tradition of the town. From the point of view of both the Yankees
who designed the Procession and those who accepted and sponsored the design, this superior symbol nicely fitted their needs
and was most convenient to have. The bishop had been around
at the right time.

In the same year as Tristram Dalton's leaving Dalton House
as a first senator in the new national government, and immediately following in the Procession, came a placard saying,
"1789. John Quincy Adams studies law in Theophilus Parsons'
law office in Yankee City. John Quincy Adams, Rufus King,
and Robert Treat Paine studied law under Judge Parsons."
The setting showed the future President of the United States
with King, a man who later signed the Constitution, ran un-
successfully for the presidency but successfully for the Senate
as a member of the right wing of the Federalist Party, and
became Ambassador to the Court of St. James. With them was
Robert Treat Paine, a son of one of the signers of the Declara-
tion of Independence and a writer who was the most noted
literary figure in Massachusetts. They sat as scholars before
the great lawyer, Theophilus Parsons, who later became Chief
Justice of the Supreme Court of Massachusetts.

Judge Parsons, who came from a noted family and whose
father was a famous clergyman of Yankee City, was then at the
height of his power. His fame was so great that he commanded
large fees, which helped to make his fortune, from wealthy
clients from "all over the Union, particularly New York." The
newspaper accounts of this float reported the dramatis personae

somewhat differently from the text: "Theophilus Parsons, John Quincy Adams and two students." (Alas for the permanency of fame and glory, Rufus King and Robert Treat Paine.) All these men were active members of the sophisticated society of that time and added their own personal contributions to its prestige and power. Their own activities, as well as those displayed in other floats, demonstrate that, although these communities were isolated, the members of the top levels were in close contact with each other. Boston, Salem, New York, as well as cities farther south, were well aware of what the members of the great families were doing and what was occurring in their lives. All four of the men whose figures appear on this float were rigidly and proudly conservative. All had an aristocratic outlook on life. Each feared the leveling revolutionary influence of the Republicans and of the "ignorant and vulgar" pressures of Demos. Rufus King said it in so many words. Adams' father, a President of the United States and the last of the Federalists so honored, was a man greatly admired in Yankee City and one who fully reciprocated their feeling. His son John Quincy had recently graduated from Harvard. Following extended visits to many of the capitals of Europe, where as his father's companion he met the great and powerful and found time to study in European universities, the latter set down a very lively volume about the social life of the superior class of Yankee City in which he participated.

Theophilus Parsons graduated from Dummer Academy and then from Harvard. He married the daughter of a well-known and highly placed Yankee City family—was born to the elite and married there. He was influential in the convention which wrote a constitution for the State of Massachusetts and later collaborated closely with Rufus King in the state convention which ratified the federal Constitution. His leadership and that of two or three others, it is reported, were largely responsible for defeating the equalitarian demands of the farmers of western Massachusetts in their efforts to prevent ratification. He fought the back-country counties, forcing them to accept the Constitution, dear to the hearts of the maritime communities, and with Rufus King, recently returned from the Constitutional Convention in Philadelphia, outmaneuvered the more numerous antagonists of this new form of government and beat them.

During the entire deliberations he was for a strong central government, a powerful executive, property qualifications for political candidates, and for what amounted to establishment of the Congregational church as the state religion. In brief, he believed in authority and in the authority of the few rather than the many.

Rufus King, son of a successful merchant, was also a graduate of Dummer Academy (see float on that subject) and Harvard, and, as we know, studied law with Parsons. In 1780 he opened a law office in Yankee City. Throughout his life, one of his biographers says, "he was thought to be haughty and austere." After the state and national constitutional conventions he was an eloquent advocate of the strong central government and a noted conservative in the Federalist Party. He helped to revise the final draft of the Constitution before it was submitted to the states for ratification. Somewhat later he moved to New York, married the daughter of a wealthy New York merchant, was elected to the United States Senate, and there ably supported the strong central government and the financial policies of Alexander Hamilton. It will be recalled that he ran for the vice-presidency on the Federalist ticket with Timothy Pickering, candidate for the presidency, one of the leaders who advocated secession and worked diligently to prevent the Louisiana Purchase—that great addition of land whose development threatened the primacy of maritime New England and the mercantile class. Near the end of the then reactionary Federalist Party's power, King himself ran as its candidate for President. Three states voted for him, one of them Massachusetts, where most of the vote came not from the farming west but from the mercantile and financial cities of the eastern seaboard. The image of King fits well into the tight little mosaic composed of the figures of Theophilus Parsons' law office and into the larger one of the floats representing the few years so highly favored by those who designed and sponsored the Procession.

Robert Treat Paine, the poet—christened Thomas—had changed his name because he felt the indignity of being too often identified as the author of such revolutionary documents as *The Rights of Man* and *The Age of Reason*. He was of old colonial stock, his father the lifelong friend of Governor John

Hancock. Young Paine graduated from Harvard, studied law
with Parsons, and was admitted to the bar in 1802. "In temper
and manners he belonged wholly to the Tie Wig School," says
Parrington, who devotes a considerable part of one chapter
of his *Main Currents of American Thought* to him, "that
swaggered until the War of 1812 and then became obsolete
overnight." Mr. Parrington, brilliant and admirable, was a
devotedly biased Jeffersonian; democratic Tom rather than
aristocratic Robert was to his agrarian taste. "As a young man
about town" and as a "most dashing product," young Robert,
Parrington says, "showed himself most elegantly in the latest
London clothes. . . ." He clung to small clothes and like an
honest Federalist refused to adopt the Jacobin trousers. He
was a bon vivant, drank, gambled, and loved the theater. He
spoke publicly of "the vandal spirit of Puritanism," his politics were Federalist, he announced that he "understood the
Constitution as Washington administered and Hamilton ex-
pounded it." [108] In an oration on republican France and
democracy to "the young men of Boston," quoted by Parrington, he told his audience that

. . . the worshippers of democracy, though their altars are
thrown down, are not yet converted from their devotions. The
frozen snake has still some sparks of animation; and, if placed
by compassion near your hospitable fires, he will revive with
exasperated venom, and sting the hardy fool that fostered him.
Deal therefore with these ferocious demoralizers, as our crafty
mariners trade with the savages of the Indian ocean—with your
men at their posts, your guns loaded, and your slow matches
burning.[1]

John Quincy Adams, the gay blade who studied law in
Yankee City and left a vivid account of his observations there,
seems almost another person from the image of the President
of the United States who filled his later journals with somewhat austere political observations. Here his social world was
full of gaiety, excitement, and personal interest; love, emotion, fun, and flirtation were major parts of it, though not
represented in the Procession. Adams boarded at the home of
a widow in Market Square. When he walked from her house

1. *Works*, p. 319; see Parrington [108], pp. 285–6.

past the great mansions that excited the pleased comment of visiting Europeans, up to Hill Street, he often stopped at the elegant house and garden of Tristram Dalton and at many of the other great houses of the community. Adams and his companions on the float were the social equals, but certainly not the betters, of a distinguished society. His diary tells the story of a young man who was at that time fresh from Harvard. Quotations from it in one of the local histories reveal that John Quincy attended "brilliant gatherings and dancing parties." These notes also appear:

October 15, 1787. . . . from seven 'till three and four in the morning we were continually dancing— I never saw a collection of ladies when there was comparatively so much beauty. Two or three gentlemen got rather over the bay . . .

December 27, 1787. We had this evening a good dance. There were only thirteen gentlemen and fifteen ladies . . . the company [was] spirited . . . One gentleman [a captain] who had the generosity of his heart at dinner, rather than the reflections of prudence did not lay any illiberal restraints upon himself in the evening . . . In general I was much pleased. It was between four and five in the morning before we broke up.

The society he frequented and the style of life that composed its existence had come a long distance since the time of the Rev. Thomas Parker; in truth, despite the marks of Puritan ancestry, it was nearer Elizabeth than Cromwell.

From the time of young Adams' arrival the young ladies of the great houses were "forever" attracting the young man's attention, each consciously or not being "looked over" as a possible mate. It is noteworthy that shortly thereafter he married (1797). The serious law student, fearful that as the son of old John he might not make the proper mark of a true Adams, was being pulled away from his studies by feminine attractions and the gay society of the town. Perhaps to maintain his critical faculties and partly to express his romantic interest, the young man wrote a long poem addressed to "Some of the Young Ladies Prominent in the Social Life of Yankee City." These were the reigning belles of the town. Though the names were fictive and the manuscript was at first privately circulated (now available in a local historical document), the

excitement caused was so great and the actual families so prominent in New England and elsewhere that each was soon identified to the satisfaction of those who knew them. Later the
poem was published in a weekly issue of the *New York Tattler*
(cited in a local history). We will examine part of it to learn
something of the social and family life of the community of the
period which was so highly regarded by those who presented
and produced the Procession.

Falling asleep, the young man had a "vision" in which (he
declares) Cupid, bow in hand, appeared and with "a feathered
dart prepared his bow and leveled at my heart." The dreamer,
attempting to divert the attention of the god of love to others,
then cried out:

> Behold around you swarms of youthful swains
> The blood of passion boiling in their veins
> 'Tis theirs from love to gather perfect bliss
> On beauty's lip to print the burning kiss.

Thus the young Adams, who has been called by historians
"the stern Puritan," reveals more than a thrifty Yankee's
search for a fitting mate, judged by the standards of financial
convenience and Puritan distaste for romantic allurement.

With Freudian simplicity, in John Quincy's poem, the god
"waved his potent wand" and a "virgin throng arose at his
command, unnumbered beauties stood before [his] view." Ro-
mantically strengthened by the god's potent wand, yet fearful
of "the power of the wanton god," the youth stood before the
"virgin throng" listening to the counsels of love and wondering,

> Shouldst [he] prefer the beauties of the face
> Or in the form admire peculiar grace
>
> .   .   .   .
>
> . . . [or perhaps] in the search we possibly may find
> Some who possess the beauties of the mind.

Then one by one the virgins "blooming" or "withered, pale
and lean" pass in review before the warm but fearful and critical eye of the male dreamer. They represented the flower of
fashionable Hill Street. Their fathers were great merchants,
eminent judges and lawyers, statesmen, and other men of re-

nown. In a few years all the young ladies had married men of the same high status and borne children.

We can only give brief attention to Adams' stanzas devoted to some of the ladies, but it is hoped enough to communicate something of the way of life of the times and the warmth and gaiety and love of fun of the young people whose activities were important parts of the life of the town. When Yankee City presented the society of the turn of the eighteenth century in its Procession it was talking about much more than public lives embalmed in political histories. We tend to remember "the stern Puritan,"—the older Adams who wrote volume after volume of comment on the politics of the United States—and to forget this other man, young scion of the Adams family, who knew a pretty face and could "admire" a form of "peculiar grace."

> . . . the fair Narcissa smiled
> Her winning softness all my soul beguiled
> My heart with rapture dwelt upon her charms
> And hoped to clasp her beauties in my arms.

From local historical sources we learn that Narcissa was the fictive name given by Adams to Miss Mary Newhall, daughter of Captain Samuel and Elizabeth Newhall. We are further informed that she married on October 17, 1793 the Rev. Ebenezer Coffin of Yankee City, an ordained Congregational minister. It seems doubtful that Mary in later years, sitting securely in her pew listening to her husband's scholarly sermon, was ever looked upon by the devout as one who had "beguiled" the soul or enraptured the heart of a fearful young man; or that still later her husband, turned schoolmaster, could believe that she would have used:

> Cunning art to raise a lover's sigh—
> Then view his woes with a disdainful eye.

We have seen that one of the most majestic and imposing scenes to move by the reviewing stands displayed Bishop Bass, first bishop of Massachusetts. The date assigned to Adams' float was 1789. The Rev. Edward Bass, not yet a bishop, in November of this year married Miss Mercy Phillips. His first wife, a local document tells us, had died "six months previous to that date." Elsewhere in an historical document we learn from a dry comment, in vast understatement, of the displeasure felt by some of his parishioners when after this very brief period he took his new bride. At the time of the private circulation of Adams' diary Mercy was in her early thirties. When she married she was thirty-four years old, long since as an old maid the easy target of the wits. Edward Bass was many years older. This lady, called in Adams' poem Statira, was easily identified.

> Behold Statira's ancient beauties rise
> With conscious wit and wisdom's glancy eyes
> . . . autumnal roses she alone admires
> And gray-haired charms excite her warmest fires.

After a number of others had stood before the poet, Corinna appeared.

> With intimate warmth of constitution blessed
> Her greatest pleasure is to be caressed
> Her lips sip rapture from an amorous kiss
> Viewed as a pledge of more enduring bliss.

Corinna was the daughter of the famed and powerful Theophilus Bradbury and belonged to one of the great families of New England. Bradbury was a highly respected lawyer and United States congressman; he had taught Theophilus Parsons his law. Two or three years after the poem was written Corinna married Thomas Woodbridge Hooper, grandson of Robert Hooper, "King Hooper of Marblehead," one of the wealthiest merchants in New England. Robert Hooper had been a loyalist during the Revolution. His daughter Ruth married the Tristram Dalton who appears in one of the floats reviewed earlier as a senator leaving his mansion for Congress. Hooper's son Stephen moved to Yankee City and married Sarah Woodbridge, and their son Stephen in turn married Susan Coffin Marquand, of one of the great merchant families of Yankee City.

The descendants of many of these families are scattered throughout New England and the United States, but a significant proportion of them still reside in the city; some were active members of the committee which selected the symbols and proposed the floats representing the glories of the community.

We must examine the images of two other tableaux which were important presentations of the period. Following the float showing the French aristocrats fleeing the egalitarian wrath of the revolutionaries and finding safe haven among their friends and peers of Yankee City came one whose placard said, "1794. Honorable William Bartlet," and two tableaux later, "1795. Timothy Dexter." The descriptions of the two reveal very different personalities, quite differently regarded in the Procession as indeed by their contemporaries. Timothy Dexter, often disliked and always disapproved of, was treated then and now with contemptuous amusement; William Bartlet, highly respected, with honor and esteem. Despite their different evaluations for their time and for history, they share many of the same social characteristics and each is the symbolic hero of the same morality tale, viewed as part of the status and social structure.

The placard of the Honorable Wm. Bartlet told his audience that he was a "Public Benefactor." He was shown driving to his woollen mills, which were built "to utilize the falls in Byfield for the manufacture of woollen cloth, one of the first factories in the United States. William Bartlet, of Yankee City, was one of the proprietors." Dexter is dismissed in the description on his placard as "a famous eccentric Yankee City character, reputed to have made his fortune by shipping warming pans and mittens to the West Indies." The text further emphasizes this derogation. As a symbol, Dexter—although grudgingly appreciated as a figure of fun—is no hero to his designer, nor was he meant to be more than amusing to the audience.

For the purposes of the Procession and the need to represent the once very significant local textile industry, Bartlet appears as a financier of the beginnings of a new industry. He was much more than "a proprietor," just as Dexter was much more than an "eccentric merchant" who allegedly sold warming pans in the tropics. The *Dictionary of American Biography* and local historical documents inform us that Bartlet was born in Yankee City, a descendant of one of the original families. All the other men whose images appeared on floats or their names on placards or in the text for the period were sons and usually descendants of two or more generations of high position. Tristram Dalton was the son of a great merchant and born in a mansion. The French refugees were "birth aristocrats and planters." John Quincy Adams was a New England Adams, while Paine, no more than a minor figure on one of the floats, was born to high position. But William Bartlet, despite his descent from an original settler, came from the lower ranks. He had to quit school when very young and learn the shoemaking trade to support himself—a profession, by the way, which was the object of scornful contempt in a poem by Robert Treat Paine.

But Bartlet, by his intelligence and wit and his great energy and desire to succeed, was soon in commerce and by the end of the Revolutionary War had become a merchant prince with a great fortune invested in all variety of capitalistic enterprise and in a large fleet of trading vessels. His name appears as the owner of privateers that sailed from Yankee City to bring back fortunes to their owners and sometimes to those who sailed in them. Soon Bartlet's ships were anchoring at his "numerous wharves and warehouses." It was only after he had accumulated a great fortune from the sea that, along with others, he invested in the textile mill.

Meanwhile, not being born to position but knowing what merchant princes must possess to be properly equipped, he built a great mansion, and later two more for his sons. Two of these houses are still the pride of Yankee City.

In short, he was the eighteenth-century model for the oil baron, the automobile, rail, and steel kings of the twentieth century. He was widely accepted in the society of his time, and his sons moved securely in the social life of the community. He was a mobile man who, born to low position, made his way by thoroughly approved means to high position and there conformed to the role assigned to men who accumulate money and desire social position for their families. The name of Bartlet, to those who designed the float, was a solid sign of the strength, vitality, and social worth of those who compose the Yankee City elite.

Timothy Dexter, a figure of caricature and scorn, also rose from low beginnings to a position of wealth. He, too, occupied two of the great houses of Yankee City. He, too, surrounded himself with the purchasable symbols of the high-born. Yet as a symbol himself he evokes laughter and ridicule rather than respect. Since there are a number of biographies of him by local men, it is not difficult to obtain the evidence necessary for understanding his function as a contemporary symbol and man of his times.

Dexter, like Biggy Muldoon, refused to obey the basic rules of social climbing. Having arrived in town on foot with two loaves of bread under his arms, he rose from the lowly trade of a leather-dresser to the position of merchant prince and shipowner. Following a marriage to a lady of some substance and an investment in the "worthless" Continental currency which Hamilton's Federalist Party redeemed and established as sound federal money, Dexter bought the mansion of another wealthy merchant and surrounded himself with the bought symbols of affluence and position. Beyond that he would not or could not go. John Marquand's biography of him tells the story of his rise and the derogatory values attached to him, his efforts and accomplishments.

. . . A leather dresser had bought Nathaniel Tracy's house, not for speculation, but as his own dwelling. Timothy Dexter of the Wooden Glove was coming to live beneath the roof which had sheltered Washington, bringing with him his plainly nurtured wife, and his two grown and noisy children. He had not even waited for a decent time to elapse. He had snapped vulgarly at his opportunity. A scant two days after Nathaniel Tracy had relinquished his rights, Timothy Dexter was in possession . . .

. . . .

. . . No common, humdrum, climbing obsequious bourgeois had sullied the Tracy threshold, but a man with the strength to sell a freedom suit . . .

. . . Without any visible effort, or any awkward transient stage, he stepped from his leather ship blandly upstairs into the world where houses were large and square, and silks and lace were prevalent—and immediately assumed the role of an established gentleman! . . . Dexter became a gentleman without self-consciousness in naive and complete entirety . . .

. . . He could assume the clothes of a federalist gentleman, and also all the appurtenances and responsibilities which went with that estate; and immediately he did so. He purchased a coach of his own, and a pair of horses, and employed a coachman . . . He acquired a complete service of silver, and finally a stock of wines and liquors which called for comment even in a period of precocious and exacting palates . . .

. . . Only a few, if any, caught the magnificence and shackle-breaking freedom of the gesture—others saw only a clumsy man playing the idle fool.

The welcome given to the first President of the United States when he visited Yankee City six months after taking office under the new Constitution was supposed in the Tercentenary to be exactly re-enacted. The Washington scene was expanded into a half-day procession and treated separately. The speech of welcome, of which John Quincy Adams was said to be the author, was repeated by "Theophilus Parsons," as he had originally delivered it. "George Washington" replied in the words used in 1789. He and his presidential party were met and escorted with great pomp by "an imposing procession" of the citizens of the town. Notables of the town such as Tristram Dalton "and other gentlemen from Yankee City" met and entertained him in their homes.

A comparison of the original "order of the procession" preserved in a handbill of the Historical Society of Yankee City along with the "order of position" of the Tercentenary Procession—supposed to be a replica of the former—is more than suggestive of the changes that have taken place at least in outward recognition of the occupational hierarchy. The former lists the important and superior political, professional, and economic statuses first, followed in decreasing levels of importance by lesser occupations until the status of "seamen" ends them, to be followed by the more subordinate one of school children. In the original procession were

The Selectmen	Strangers, etc.
Overseers of poor	Bakers
Town Treasurer	Blacksmiths
Magistrates	Block makers
Reverend Clergy	Boat makers
Physicians	Cabinet makers
Lawyers	Coopers
Merchants and traders	Cordwainers
Marine society	Distillers
Masters of vessels	Goldsmiths and jewellers

Hairdressers	Saddlers
Hatters	Sail-makers
House carpenters	Shiprights, to include calkers,
Masons	shipjoiners, etc.
Mastmakers	Taylors
Painters	Truckmen
Riggers	Seamen
Rope makers	School-masters, their scholars

The half-day ceremony devoted to Washington's welcome, which for dramatic and ceremonial reasons might have used an elaborate list of dramatis personae, reduced the forty roles of the original to nine positions. They were

Cavalry	Coach
Artillery	Citizens
Music	Ode singers
Militia	Scholars
Washington and suite	

The military roles remain, the scholars are present, but all individual occupational distinctions are subsumed under the title "citizens." It seems probable that the principles of covert recognition of high and low status and the rejection of official and explicit recognition of them operated to reduce all differences to this equalitarian term.

The power of the symbols of the Period of Glory originated within the processes which validated and made legitimate the status of an American birth aristocracy. The period of consolidation following the adoption of the Constitution, when wealth accumulated and was translated into an upper-class style of life and families of high social position were leaders of the economic and political life of the community, was the time when all Yankee City felt its greatest sense of well-being. The great families were integral parts of the great period and leaders of it. By informal approval they assumed and were then granted their high position.

Once single families and individuals had attained a recognized high position for themselves and were able to pass this status on to the generation which followed, a birth elite was socially established. The facts of its way of life could and did become symbols representing it as the superior part of the status heirarchy. Families and men who rose not long before that time, or during it, do not come under definition as mobile or climbers in the status system of Yankee City. In the status of the (upper-upper) birth elite are embodied the superior virtues of the past. They belong to the whole society, for like the houses and other social objects which are "permanent"—*enduring*—signs of collective prestige and power, they represent social values in which everyone in varying ways shares. The *ancestor period* when the power and the glory were common to the group and when Yankee City as a collective unity not only came into being but rose to fame and prestige in which all feel a common pride, was the collective moment when the aristocratic status of a birth elite was founded. Families which possessed the greatest prestige and power when the society was at its peak of glory established the social position which is now the source of prestige and social superiority. Within very broad limits, how they got their money, their economic, political, and social power, does not matter. [137]

The mobile man, as now understood and socially defined, arrived after the investiture of an era, its objects, and its whole way of life with social authority and grace. From then on, families with lineage possessed the certain heritage of those who belong. Since the status system is open and people move up and down the social ladder, it has been possible for ambitious "new families" to move into it.

War and Peace

The Procession devoted seven scenes to symbols of war and military conflict. The early Indian wars were reduced to one scene. The whole long period of French conflict for the conquest and settlement of North America was represented in but one scene; since a number of highly important wars were involved, all of them concerned with the destiny of English culture and the continuation of the present way of life in the United States, this reduction is in itself of considerable importance. The Revolutionary War had only two scenes—the local tea party and one depicting the departure of a local hero and his troops for Lexington—and thus, in its larger context, the joining of Yankee City with the larger efforts of the colonies under Washington and their rebellion against England. Washington himself, although given a half-day in the collective symbols celebrating the past, was not depicted as first in war and as the leader of his people but rather as the first President and a man who stood for solid, conservative government. The Civil and Spanish-American wars and World War I each had one scene.

Every war except two, the War of 1812 and the Mexican War, was represented (perhaps "type of war" might be more nearly correct, since the French wars were all subsumed under one type). Symbolic representation sometimes more effectively states its meaning and speaks loudest when the items of a given context, in this case major wars, are eliminated and absent. The question immediately arises, Were they deliberately rejected; were they ignored for reasons of expediency or because of their unimportance in the history of the town; or were perhaps other reasons, not immediately apparent, responsible for their exclusion?

It was not because of lack of heroes for the two conflicts. Each produced figures who have a conspicuous place in local histories and, for that matter, in the histories of the nation. At least one of these wars was of the greatest importance in its effect on Yankee City, in making it the kind of community it now is.

Why were they not presented in the Procession? It was not because they are ranked as comparatively minor struggles and, to Yankee City, of less concern, for the Spanish-American War was of much less magnitude, yet it was one of the few events given place in the last hundred years of the city's history. It might be supposed that the two conflicts, when they happened, did not stir the deep emotions of the people and thereby failed to contribute enough emotional power to the community's mental life to insure their later symbolic significance. Local and national histories, as we shall see, fully testify to the opposite: the city was much stirred and its people deeply involved. Vital meanings of history flowed from these conflicts. Their confluence with the flow of the mental life of the community decisively and deeply affected it; but, as we shall demonstrate, they decisively affected the Procession itself in a negative sense. To prepare ourselves for a proper analysis of why these wars were not among the symbols of the celebration we must briefly inspect the presentation of the other wars to learn their common meanings and to find out how they fitted into the total design.

The local Indian wars, as we have seen, were greatly reduced in importance. The Indian raid was included almost as a necessary period piece to prove that Yankee City, like all self-respecting colonial towns that appear in the school histories of our nation, could demonstrate her historical worth according to the standards of the old third grade reader—as well as by contemporary criteria set up by the movies—with a local Indian fight and white massacre.

The wars with the French, symbolized in the seige of the great fortress of Louisburg, validate the city's place in that dramatic struggle where the names of Montcalm, Wolfe, and others cluster symbolically in a romantic aura, now that the bitterness of history and the earlier fears and anxieties have been dissipated and lost. Louisburg was also a period piece that served a symbolic function, very like certain ecclesiastical holy days in a liturgical season. When it appeared and passed the reviewing stand, the ancient past came to an end; it brought to a close the symbolism of a long historical epoch. With the figure of Benjamin Franklin studying the causes of lightning in the Yankee City market place the new nation begins.

The Revolutionary War was also invested with adventure and romance, its people being regarded with the respect and reverence that ancestors must receive if the present is publicly to preserve its self-esteem.

The Civil War, of the greatest emotional importance, has been thematically and symbolically transfigured in the life of Yankee City, for the purposes of the Procession, from the images of life to those of death. Memorial Day and the graveyard; Lincoln, the sacrificed hero on the altar of democracy, and the multitude of dead anonymously lying about him, are the principal symbols that have emerged from that war (see Chapter 8). The Tercentenary was a symbolic expression of the *life* of the community; past life is brought into the present, never in the form of death but always in the form of the living. Consequently, despite the enormous importance and great effect of the Civil War on the symbols of community life in Yankee City, this important aspect of the meaning of the Civil War and other wars had no place in the Procession. One scene showing the intimate life of Yankee City soldiers without their names, although these were well known, was sufficient for the symbolic needs of the Procession.

The Spanish-American War and World War I were represented, but again by anonymous and depersonalized beings, there to occupy status roles in a military setting. They are called "officers and men, guards and nurses" and the like—all stock figures with the costumes and stage properties that are always present in the storerooms of theatrical warehouses.

The War of 1812 and the Mexican War, it is hypothecated here, were not included in the great Procession because in economic and political fact the outcome of these wars could not be positively evaluated, but led to loss of power and prestige for the community. And they are now so defined. Their emotional impact at the time was also so great that, despite the sincere and intelligent efforts of the community to reproduce the facts of history in this "stock-taking of the three hundred years of our history," those responsible found the two conflicts either too punishing or too unpleasant to regard them as valuable items in the symbolic showcase of the Procession. When efforts were made to present one of the local heroes of the War of 1812, even though the great power of the sea culture of Yankee City was directly related to romantic battles in which he engaged, he was not included.

Euphoria and well-being for the collectivity came out of the other wars; their symbols easily elicited the positive responses, not only of the producers of the Procession but of the audience. The emotional impact of the facts of these two less fortunate conflicts resulted in dysphoria and loss of self-regard by the community. The War of 1812 suddenly and violently brought the period of power and glory to a tragic end. The Mexican War further reduced the significance of the city and the seaboard as a whole by adding huge blocks of territory to finish what Jefferson's purchase of the Louisiana Territory had begun. By making America a vast continental nation, the results of the Mexican War further contributed to the early feelings of disquiet and frustration that had evoked the plottings of New England's dispirited Federalists at the time of the Louisiana Purchase. The remembrance of these bitter feelings of the time is related to a growing sense of guilt as well as of loss.

This became more poignant when the westward expansion of the United States led to a positive outcome and high feeling of euphoria as America became a great nation.

We must look briefly at the evidence from a reliable local history to determine how Yankee City felt at the time of the two wars—to learn how events affected the community and how they were then evaluated and conceptualized. One of the local historians, writing of the period after Jefferson's Embargo Act, notes,

Items like the following were frequently published in the newspapers of the day:

[July 12, 1808] There are now collected in our harbor 24 ships 28 brigs and 27 schooners—this is the first six months product of farmer Jefferson's embargo.

[July 15, 1808] Our wharves have now the stillness of the grave,— indeed nothing flourishes on them but vegetation.

The War of 1812 aroused even greater hostility. After a town meeting in February 1814, a memorial was composed and forwarded to "the Honorable Senate and the Honorable House of Representatives of the Commonwealth of Massachusetts; we the inhabitants of Yankee City, in the county of Essex, qualified to vote in public affairs in town meeting assembled, on Monday, February 7, 1814, respectfully represent,

. . . We are called in common with our fellow citizens of the Eastern States to consider whether the Republick still exists, or whether in the government under whose oppression we now suffer we have any rights, priviledges and interests worth a struggle to maintain. It is not our intention to enumerate in detail the parts of that system of infatuated national policy which, in so short a period, has wasted the substance and prostrated the character of the nation; which has paralized the hand of labor and industry, and converted into a theatre of crime and wickedness, a country which lately was, and still might be, the most prosperous and happy portion of the globe.

The Hartford Convention, which threatened the existence of the union, was held in December 1814. On January 16, 1815 "the inhabitants of Yankee City in town meeting assembled sent a spirited memorial" to the Senate and House of the Commonwealth of Massachusetts. In it we read,

Peace itself could not heal the wounds which they [Madison's Democrats and the western agrarian pro-war administration] have inflicted on their country, or atone for their sins, nor can we hope for a lasting peace while corruption is seated in our high places, and the stain of blood, wickedly and wantonly shed, is crying to heaven for vengeance. . . .

It was with feelings of unqualified approbation that we witnessed the appointment by your honorable body of delegates to a New England Convention [the Hartford Convention]. . . .

And it is for the purpose of expressing our assent to all its doctrines and our willingness to support to the last hazard and extremity the measures which it proposes, that we now approach you, . . . we have no hesitation in saying that we shall consider our State Legislature as the sole, rightful and bounden judge of the course which our safety may require, *without any regard to the persons still assuming to be the National Government,* nor have we a doubt that the citizens of the Northern States, . . . *would declare that our own resources shall be appropriated to our own defence, that the laws of the United States shall be temporarily suspended in their operation in our territory, and that hostilities shall cease towards Great Britain on the part of the free, sovereign and independent states of New England* [italics mine].

Not only had the city's sources of prosperity and well-being been destroyed, but the economic life which literally fed, clothed, and sheltered its people had been taken from them by the new western states and by the action of the South, led by Virginia. New England's proud position and great political power were reduced to impotence and frustration. Small wonder that its people could be roused to mutiny! However, today's remembrance of the "incipient rebellion" of 1814, though the city's own people were the rebels, does not make these events of history easy to celebrate or to present publicly as part of its moral position. The problem becomes more awkward when the moral position of Yankee City and the North in defending the Union against the rebellion of the South must necessarily be presented as part of a critical later time in the history of the nation. The rebels of the southern states seceded because their own economic and political position and way of life were threatened by a coalition of the West with the North. Now that self-esteem is no longer dependent on the rigid moral code and culture of theocratic Puritanism, Judge Sewall can symbolically repent for the misdeeds of the Early Fathers and thereby absolve the group from tribal errors. All that belonged to the first period of creation and growth. But who is there among the honored ancestors to confess or make a bold front out of the threatened rebellion of New England? Moreover, who wants to, when the outcome was so tragic? At the very climax of power, the War of 1812 plunged Yankee City to the lowest moment in its entire history. Objective history or not—stocktaking of actual events or not—this is too much to ask of any people celebrating the glories of their past.

Still, they attempted it. The committee wrote a text and designed a float that symbolically referred to this period; its close reading discovers embarrassment and hostility. Despite the fact that the privateer and its men are positively evaluated and the sea thought of as the "great mother" from which most earthly good things flowed, the privateers and the *Wasp*, noted locally as well as nationally as "an heroic vessel," failed to find a sponsor. Perhaps, like the tableau of Benedict Arnold, when compared with the others it did not seem attractive. The story itself reveals present feelings far more explicitly than did the one written for Arnold, who became the traitor.

The Mexican War, unlike the War of 1812, was not in the front yard of Yankee City and did not have a direct and immediate effect on the lives of its people. [125] Yet many Yankee City men were in it. The most prominent local leader of the time, the historian Caleb Cushing, took a most active role in encouraging the community to fight. He contributed financially, urged young men to volunteer, and became an active participant in the war. He led a regiment, including Yankee City soldiers, to Mexico and in time was raised to the rank of general. Despite his efforts, the war was not popular and was morally condemned in his native city and New England. The aggrandizement of southern and agrarian power was also feared. Perhaps the contemporary emotional effects of the war can be most succinctly set forth by a quotation from a local history:

"May 11, 1846, congress declared, the American army on the Rio Grande having been attacked, 'that war existed between the United States and Mexico,' and the president, James K. Polk, was authorized to arm and equip fifty thousand volunteers to re-inforce the regular army. The pulpit and the press in New England opposed the war and only a few men volunteered to enter the service."

All in all, one may see clearly that while the facts of the past leave their impress on the symbols of the present, the emotions of an earlier time, when in congruence with the values and beliefs of the present social structure, will carry through into the present far more effectively.

Benedict Arnold and the Image of the Ethnic

From the earliest stages of their planning, those responsible for the success of the Yankee City Tercentenary were conscious of the need for obtaining the wholehearted collaboration of the organizations and churches of ethnic and religious groups. Since almost half the community was of ethnic origin and consciously participated in groups which identified their members with minority subsystems, and since it was hoped to induce the whole community to participate, the leaders of the celebration, recognizing their problem, were anxious to do everything possible to obtain full cooperation from the various cultural and religious minorities.

Since these groups, including Jews, Poles, Greeks, French Canadians, and others, were all of comparatively recent origin, none being older than about the fourth decade of the nineteenth century, when the Catholic Irish first appeared, to select appropriate symbols for sponsoring ethnic groups and to make assignment of them was a difficult problem for the central committee. Since the interest and main emphasis of those responsible for the subjects chosen was upon periods before the arrival of the new migrant groups, the problem was even more thorny. The conception of the celebration and the pageant had to do with the Puritan ancestors and the flowering of New England culture; the themes of the great ethnic migrations and their assimilation—the melting pot, the Promised Land, and the goddess of Liberty welcoming them—democracy for all and every kind of race and creed—such themes were nowhere present. Indeed, those who conceived and presented the pageant saw themselves as teachers initiating the new peoples into the true significance of the nation.

Symbols such as Bishop Cheverus, first Catholic Bishop of Massachusetts, present at the end of the eighteenth century; the Marquis de Lafayette, heir of the American Revolution; the aristocratic French Catholic refugees; and Columbus and others provided symbolic representations from which many of the groups could choose. The problem of sponsorship progressed smoothly until the leaders of the Jewish community selected (and were granted by the central committee) Benedict Arnold to be their group's symbol in the Procession. This was publicly announced by the local paper. The next day the chairman of the central committee issued a statement to the effect that there had been a mistake and the Jewish group had yet to choose their symbol.

How could such a situation have arisen? Why did it occur? And what is its significance symbolically?

We shall attempt to provide probable answers. To understand the immediate problem, we must first take up the whole question of symbolic congruence, the identification of the symbol with its sponsor, not only in the case of the Jews and other ethnic and religious groups, but with all the symbols developed in the pageant and their corresponding sponsoring groups.

The problem of sponsorship, of a collective symbol—the rejection of all other representations and the selection and acceptance of one to stand for the meaning of the group before the community—of course involves the question of the degree of identification with the symbol, what the group's aspirations are, and what the symbol means to the larger collectivity. Such identification with the meaning of a sign to members of the group and to those outside it depends on several factors: the group's structural place in the community, its status and rank, and the symbolic congruences of its own meanings to itself and to others. The identification also involves historical factors: the present and past historical significance of the object or event that has become a collective symbol, the historical significance of the group which selects it for sponsorship, and the historical meanings which the larger group, in this case Yankee City, attributes to itself.

We will examine the problem of sign and group identification by first reviewing a few of the more obvious sponsorships and analyzing them in the terms just given. The float for Columbus, a Catholic, was sponsored by the Catholic Knights of Columbus; the "First Class at Harvard" by the local Harvard Club; the landing of the first settlers by an historical association composed of lineal descendants; old-time shoemaking and early silversmiths, by those industries.

The choice of the Knights of Columbus was multi-determined by several identifications. The identity of name, of group and hero, and the Catholic religion as well as other factors were primarily involved. But there was no direct connection of the local association with the person for which the symbol stood, such as descendants of the first settlers had with the "Landing of the Founders." Still, Columbus was the "first" European to land in America and is credited by history with the first beginnings of this society, even preceding the Puritans and the Founders; as such his symbol had prestige and was popular and clothed its sponsors with a great variety of significant meanings. The criteria of structural place, symbolic congruence of group, and the meaning of a symbol to the sponsor and others, were well cared for by this choice. The prestige of this highly rated Catholic club and the prestige of the Catholic discoverer took care of problems of the group's status and all those having to do with history.

But although of probable significance in the meaning of the community, Columbus was not of the group that was celebrating its *own* history; his activities were but a distant aspect of the settlement of a huge continent. He and his sponsoring group—highly valued and respected—were identified, but not completely, with the whole life of the community. The symbol of Columbus in the pageant conveyed among other meanings that old and new Americans were integral parts of a larger whole; that they were inextricably intertwined, yet that differences were present and distinguishable. In terms of ultimate identifications and belongingness, the Sons and Daughters of the First Settlers of Old Yankee City who sponsored their own ancestors, the first founders, had a collective symbol to represent them to the whole collectivity which satisfied all the criteria. It said—and they and the community said—that they completely belonged, and they were so identified.

Coming now to the problem of selecting an appropriate symbol for the Jewish group; this proved more difficult and awkward. "The Chairman of the Tercentenary Committee," a brief paragraph in the Yankee City *Herald* said, "wishes to state that an error was made in the announcement of the assignment of the float to the Jewish citizens. The design of the historical event their citizens will portray has as yet not been made by the artist." The "error" was of major magnitude, the only apparent one committed by the committee in planning and arranging the delicate matter of "fitting" the themes of the floats to the sponsoring groups. The event apparently first assigned to the Jewish community, or requested by it, was the encampment of Arnold's troops in Yankee City before embarking for his Quebec expedition. The official announcement on the previous afternoon had said that "the Jewish citizens of the city have notified the Tercentenary Committee that they will enter a float in the parade which will be a feature of the celebration. The subject assigned to them is the expedition of Benedict Arnold to Quebec." Following was a description of the event.

On September 15 and 16, 1775, nearly 1000 soldiers under the command of Arnold arrived in Yankee City on their way to Quebec. . . . In this regiment was one company composed largely of Yankee City men commanded by Captain Ward. Rev. Samuel Spring was chaplain of this regiment. He preached to a large congregation at the First Presbyterian church on Sunday, September 17 and he later became pastor of the North Congregational Church.

How this embarrassing public situation could have happened under such carefully controlled conditions clearly has much to do with symbolism. Benedict Arnold, the great villain for Americans, is consciously and unconsciously identified with Judas Iscariot, the betrayer of Christ. The Jews in the minds of the ordinary, or higher, classes of Yankee City are not fully and completely identified with the rest of the community. They are a people who are not Christian, often believed to be hostile, or worse, by those who are anti-Semitic; thought of as the betrayers of Christ and responsible, through Judas, for his crucifixion. It was the Jews who were publicly accepting the symbol of the traitor and betrayer of the republic, Benedict Arnold.

The problem becomes more perplexing when it is realized that one of the active members of the committee which decided upon the historical events and heroes to be depicted and how each event would be shown by the sponsor, was a member of a highly aristocratic family which in cultural background had once been Jewish. She and her friends, all of the upper-upper class, had been responsible for preparing the Tercentenary story which placed Benedict Arnold and his expedition in the symbolic showcase of historic personages from which the sponsors chose their symbols.

An analysis of this occasion and its outcome will permit us to understand something of the symbolic position of this ethnic people and their position in American life. It was established that the agreement which became an "error" had taken place, but since the field research started sometime after the occurrence, we were unable to elicit reliable evidence about all the circumstances. Such possible factors as initial ignorance of Arnold's full significance could not be ascertained. In general we were told by everyone, still with embarrassment, "It was a mistake." Everyone preferred to remember that the Jews had sponsored "that wonderful float" of Captain John Smith "which came almost at the beginning of the parade."

Since it is abundantly clear that the members of the committee had every reason to avoid unpleasantness and were anxious for the ethnic groups to be smoothly incorporated into their enterprise, and since it is equally certain the Jews did not want to be identified with disloyalty and the symbol of a traitor, how was it possible for this event to occur?

Interviewing after the event clearly indicated that the selection and assignment had indeed been made and that the "error" announced was but a face-saving politeness. This is further validated by the later selection, with no further awkwardness, of the symbol of Captain John Smith.

For our first approach an examination of the larger symbolic context is helpful. We have been asking the question, why did the Jews select, or why were they given, Arnold? But the more general and significant question, which goes to the fundamentals of the symbol system of the collective rite and on which the Jewish selection is merely dependent, is this: Why was the symbol of Arnold included at all by those who planned the floats to which the religious, civic, and other social groups were limited? Three hundred years of history made the problem of selecting historic episodes difficult; why, then, was the theme of Arnold, awkward to handle and to sponsor, included among the select and significant few? The question now is not why the Jews first sponsored him, but why the committee itself should put the mark of approval on him and sponsor him as a fitting hero of its history.

Liberal quotes of the text are necessary to understand its significance to those who wrote it and to anyone, including the members of the Jewish community, who selected it.

September 15, 1775 was one of Yankee City's great days. War had been declared between England and America. The Battle of Bunker Hill had been fought, and now General Washington was besieging Boston which was occupied by British soldiers.

Canada was called the back door of America, and Washington feared the British might attack our frontier settlements from the North, or even march upon Boston or New York. He decided to make the first move himself, and so on this September day Yankee City saw Colonel Benedict Arnold at the head of eleven hundred troops, march briskly into town, ready to embark on a campaign against Quebec.

In this account Colonel Arnold, the trusted representative of George Washington, is a hero. There is no mention of his villainy. He was leading a powerful group of men, many of whom were Yankee City soldiers, on the famous Quebec expedition. He was an officer and a gentleman, entertained by the Tracy family in the mansion that still stands as a monument to them. Many can trace their ancestry to the men who were in his expedition. A prominent historical spot on the Old Town Green is a monument to them and to the event.

To the upper-class committee he was a hero, and he was presented as such, later historical and symbolic events notwithstanding. The importance of the expedition to Quebec, its identification with the birth of the nation and with Washington, the land and sea aspects of it, all identified with Yankee City, made it for that city the most important military event of the war. Arnold was its leader.

Had one of the old Yankee organizations or one from the old-family upper class sponsored the float, the meaning of the *expedition* would have become paramount in the symbol and the meaning of Arnold, while prominent, would have been absorbed in the larger context. His villainy would not have been forgotten, but its significance in the pageant would have been unimportant. The congruence of sponsor and sign would have emphasized the story's text.

But when the Jewish connection was made, the ambiguous history of the relation between the Jewish and Christian groups and the present secular group's separation from full integration into the larger community were brought into focus. All the deep anxieties and concerns of both groups about their relations to each other and among themselves were mobilized. The Jews could not really afford to sponsor such a symbol; their own self-regard and the respect and esteem they needed from others would not permit it. Whoever may have been responsible for the suggestion, the success of the celebration itself made it impossible for either of the parties involved in the sponsorship to allow it.

Symbolic congruence is here something more than the fit of a symbol, along with others, into an approved form; it also includes the relation of the group to the symbol and other groups' relations to the sponsoring one and to their own symbols. The Jewish community and the central committee in seeking to represent the power and prestige of a great event failed to realize that one person in the event had his own—and the most powerful—symbolic significance, deeply involved in the connotations of betrayal. They failed to see this soon enough. From one point of view it speaks well for the place of this ethnic group in the community that the committee regarded their place in the city as being such that they could afford the sponsorship, heedless of any symbolic risk.

The Aftermath of Glory

When the last of the scenes of the Period of Climax passed the reviewing stand closing the eighteenth century, eleven more followed, spread through the whole nineteenth century and thirty years of the twentieth. These ended the Procession. Instead of an average of one float a year, as for the great period, there was only one for every twelve. Perhaps less happened in this hundred-odd years; yet four wars were fought in which Yankee City men participated, the industrial revolution came to the city and to America, large industries grew on the eastern seaboard and in the city, America became a world power, and the great migrations westward took Yankee City people as far as San Francisco, where a street was named in its honor. The exciting clipper ship era came and quickly departed; the tremendous migrations of the peoples of Europe—Irish, Jews, Poles, and many others—poured into America and radically changed the cultural and religious composition of Yankee City. The great surge of technological invention and application—railroads, canals, the telegraph, the automobile, the airplane, radio, and hundreds of others—grew and accelerated.

Yankee City was an integral and active part of all these changes. Yet the whole time of more than a century received no more representation than did the last fifteen years of the eighteenth century. Clearly the city, for the purposes of the Procession, was less interested in this final period, which apparently had for it less meaning than the previous ones. Yet considered in other light—that of economic or political history, for instance—the more recent period is of the greatest significance.

We have summarized what the larger movements of history have done to the pride and power of this once important city, and the part they played in its descent from the heights of greatness to the comparative anonymity of a little city fighting to survive and maintain its small place in a continental culture with mass production and an industrial economy. Now we must examine the Procession's symbolic interpretations of these movements of history and the changes in Yankee City to learn something of their meaning in the mental life of its people. Certain themes will become evident, and these and their symbols will be analyzed. From this analysis we shall derive not only interpretations and theories as to the meaning of the period and the effects of history on the minds of present-day men, but, it is hoped, also certain broader generalizations about man's mental life.

When the princely robes of Cardinal Cheverus moved by in the Procession, the pageantry of the eighteenth century closed. The opening of the nineteenth began with Joshua Coffin and the boy Whittier. These were followed by scenes of Lafayette's visit to Yankee City and William Lloyd Garrison, the liberator, who was born there. Then in 1843 came the first public high school for girls and Caleb Cushing negotiating a treaty with the Chinese. Two more tableaux appear before the Civil War: that of the Forty-niners, who left by vessel from Yankee City to sail around the Horn or cross over the Isthmus of Panama, and the building in local yards of the great *Dreadnought* to represent the brief clipper ship era. Three scenes more and the pageant ended: in 1884 the Arctic expedition of Adolphus Greely, a local hero; the war against Spain in Cuba; and World War I.

Six of the eleven scenes and their subjects were treated anonymously. No great names were mentioned. They were no more than type characters, the named heroes who once played the leads had become the nameless supernumeraries; the third-string characters who played "walk-on" parts beside the great heroes of former times were now themselves the heroes. The actors in the Spanish-American and World wars were not the Colonel Moses Littles and Washingtons of past glory, but "sailors," "soldiers," "nurses," "officers," and others named by military occupation. Those who are given names stand for a different set of social values and individual self-regard from those viewed in the previous period. Joshua Coffin and the boy Whittier, "Schoolmaster and Poet," are present first for the reasons indicated in the title: these two joined Garrison in the struggle for the abolition of slavery and in general fought for the equality of the masses. Whittier was the poet of the common man, Coffin his advocate on the lecture platform. In the text for the scene about "old time shoe making" a selection from Whittier's poem praising the shoe worker was presented. The poet himself was of modest origin. Two floats later "Garrison the Liberator" appears with "citizens" and slaves. He, too, came from the "side streets" and began his printer's career as the young impecunious boy employed for a time on the local paper.

All these were representations of the common man, of the average American, of equality and democracy. As such they were symbols of the leveling tendencies of the twentieth century, of the anonymous many, not the individuated few. They were moral figures fighting for justice and democratic equality for all men, the nameless little men of the mass who are recognized in sociologists' statistics and in type parts of pageants founded on aristocratic values and beliefs. They show up, for example, in a scene from the Civil War, "Tenting Tonight on the Old Camp Ground"—the logical and symbolically expected progeny of the values of an industrial democracy, common men fighting a common cause against the aristocracy of the South and the fixed status of its Negro slaves. No individual hero leads them; they are all heroes. Moreover, they too are symbols of the men of today; the relation to the sponsor makes this clear. The sponsor was the local "camp" of the Sons of Union Veterans, a group of citizens whose status was no more than average in the community—respected and valued, but not aristocratic.

Whereas these several scenes represented moral issues involving the equality of races and of *men*, the one on the girls' high school was also a "protest." The problem here was essentially a moral one, having to do with the equality of the sexes and the rights of women to a superior education. The text for this float declares:

Harvard College, as we remember, was established six years after Boston was settled, but it was twelve years before measures were taken by the Bay Colony to provide an education for the younger children. Even then, although children was the word used, it really was the boys who were meant.

Yankee City did little for its girls.

Then Yankee City took a long and important step ahead. It established a "Female High School" which was believed to be the first girls' high school in the whole United States.

This new school was opened in 1843 with 78 pupils . . .

The other scenes in which named heroes appear, show ing the Marquis de Lafayette, Caleb Cushing and Adolphus Greely, and possibly a fourth, "The Clipper Ship," are quite different by intent and symbolic significance. In one sense they are a symbolic aftermath of the period of greatness and the age of heroes. Lafayette's actual visit to Yankee City was a ritual act recognizing the historical significance of the city. Caleb Cushing, a great son of a great and important old family, negotiating the first treaty with the noble families of the reigning Chinese dynasty, clearly is of the genre of the earlier period, where he might well have appeared. General Adolphus Greely, the leader of an Arctic exploration and a son of Yankee City, was a military hero continuing the exploits of adventure and exploration of former times.

Although these figures and their settings appear to be like the others, and in some senses are, still they are sufficiently different to need further analysis. Lafayette's visit to the city in 1824 was at the nadir of her prestige and prosperity. At this very moment Caleb Cushing was writing his history, after the disasters of 1812 and the rise of industry and manufacturing in New England. Lafayette was there not because of the City's present glories, but because of the past. He was there, too, because some of the great families who had brought him there and entertained him earlier still persisted, their fortunes diminished and their futures uncertain. His presence as a young man grown old was a return to the past both for him and for the town. Having fallen on evil days, he was visiting America at the invitation of Congress to receive present homage for past glorious achievements. The city that received him found in him the perfect symbol to express and parallel its own bad fortunes. Whereas Judge Sewall with symbolic effect looked back on the age of the Early Fathers and confessed that its ancient virtues were present vices, Lafayette returned to Yankee City in the Age of Machinery to testify to her past greatness.

Caleb Cushing, who lived long and had a most varied career, might have been fitted into several places in the pageant's chronology (see p. 196 for his part in the Mexican War). He, too, came from a time of early greatness. His family, even now a powerful one in the Hill Street society, took prominent parts in the Procession and are judged people of great (inherited) wealth. But the story text about him indicates ambivalence and conflict in the evaluation of his career. Cushing, those interested in the abolition movement will recall, was against the anti-slavery cause. He and other great merchants and cotton manufacturers in the North favored the politics of let-well-enough-alone. When Cushing is placed today with Whittier and Garrison in a pageant, his moral position is not easily defended. The text indicates all this and more:

Caleb always wished to serve his country, even when he differed from men whom we now believe to have been right when he was mistaken. He so feared the break-up of the Union of States over the question of slavery that he opposed the fight made against it by the Abolitionists—such men as William Lloyd Garrison and the poet Whittier—and worked for a compromise that would prevent war.

The famous *Dreadnought* and General Greely are the two clear cases of present glory for the nineteenth century. The *Dreadnought* symbolized the magnificent though short period of the clipper ship, when Yankee City shipyards and builders again distinguished themselves; Greely's exploits, the advance of human society and Western civilization into Arctic waters, the present equivalents of the "trackless wilderness" of earlier centuries of discovery and exploration.

But time in the aftermath of glory has run down; it is a period of diminution, of loss of meaning, when life is less vital, men are less significant, and heroes harder to find. Symbolically, Yankee City has changed her image of herself. She has become another symbolic collectivity, with new collective representations to tell her what she is and express what she is to others. New themes have emerged, with their new configurations of value, to go below the mental surface into some of the covert and hidden significances of the non-rational life of the collectivity.

There are a number of interrelated thematic clusters whose configurations of meaning and value we can examine and analyze. These are the theme of the Enduring City and the Moving Frontier—of the ever-enlarging world stretching into an ever-expanding distance, and the ever-decreasing size of the city in this expanding space, together with the official and overt theme of the values of progress and their most doubtful, covertly contradicted significance. The theme of the purity and idyllic state of nature, the Garden of Eden before man came, is posed against the present good and evil consequences of his arrival. These, with motifs of aristocracy and commoner, of rank against equality, of the old and the new, of ascetism and luxury, all contribute their meanings to the last period and to the entire pageant. Let us examine some of them.

We will use the theme of the Permanent City and the Moving Frontier and, since the others are related to it, try to see how they fit into the non-rational feelings evoked and expressed by the symbols of the Procession. The non-rational meanings, values, and images of Yankee City's later development are clearly interrelated with the underlying themes of the wild and ever-moving frontier and the sophisticated and eternally placed city. The several interrelated themes of the composed city, unordered progress, technological and cultural advancement, the wilderness and the untouched world, all are part of the city's feeling toward the frontier. Where nature and the frontier meet and join, man pushes forward and beyond, producing new cities and towns. The frontier in fact and symbol is where the powerful forces of nature, untamed by man, and the strength of civilized man meet. Civilization and the forms of civilized life, its laws and order, are shaken and sometimes shattered; then order reasserts itself. The disciplines and conventions of society appear, and the American frontier once again moves west. In this theme, before the frontier comes the "forest primeval" of the wilderness; man arrives, with order and society governing his actions, and. the frontier is established.

The frontier was depicted in a dozen or more of the tableaux of the pageant. In some it was the dominant and principal theme; in others, secondary or implicit. "In March, 1786, an Ohio Company was formed in Boston, Westward Ho!" A story of the float informed its readers that General Samuel Parsons was one of the chief men.

In March, 1786, an Ohio Company was formed in Boston, and the son of a Yankee City clergyman, General Samuel Holden Parsons, was one of the chief men. Another winter a little company started for the new land, in order to be ready to plant their crops in the spring. Men, women and children went over the mountains in sleds and wagons.

.   .   .   .

The pioneers went further and further West. People from Yankee City helped to settle Illinois, Lewis and Clark showed the way to the Rockies.

General Samuel Holden Parsons, son of a local clergyman in Yankee City, was a great speculator in lands. His adventures as such earned him a rather dubious reputation, which is not mentioned in the text for "Westward Ho!" His important family name gives him the right to appear in the story, but possibly the facts of history prevented him from becoming its heroic leader in the Procession. The near frontier— just beyond the backdoor of onmarching civilization—has always been a real estate development for Americans. Here the "boomer" of yesterday and the "broker" of today in new cities and regions speculate and risk their word and occasionally their capital to make a profit. The land speculator has always had ample precedent in American history. The very legal foundations of the Massachusetts Bay Colony, as well as many others, were built on risk-taking for profit and were speculative enterprises. The Charter itself, the occasion for the celebration, was a businessman's document, drawn up with stipulations about profit-making and how such an enterprise was to be run and organized. The colonizing pioneers, as well as the adventurous discoverers and explorers, have always been accompanied by, or themselves were, land speculators willing to risk their lives and money (often helped by liberal use of political influence) to get rich quick. For reasons of historical accuracy, and for symbolically expressing a fundamental, though often disguised, value of American history, it was most fitting that General Parsons should be tucked inconspicuously and without unnecessary comment into the text of "Westward Ho!" with the pioneers and other frontiersmen.

This float was followed by that of the forty-niners who sailed out of the harbor. Earlier, from the story of the Indian raid in Yankee City, we learn that "almost from the first the settlers moved west." Their precursors in the pageant were Captain John Smith and Columbus who, belonging to the age of discovery and passing by, left no permanent settlement and did no more than establish the social preconditions that make a frontier. These two floats were continuations of the first two: "The Forest Primeval" and "The First Americans, the Red Indians." Thus wilderness, frontier, and city are found symbolically throughout the pageant.

Symbolically the frontier moves from the settlement itself and the seaboard a few miles inland to its immediate backyard, where at first danger and fear were and where the Indians attacked the land's new people, then onward across the Appalachians to Ohio and, with the forty-niners, to the Pacific. The frontier is not only a place; it is motion, symbolically and chronologically, present in the symbolism of the floats from the beginning until the last period.[2] As a changing symbol it goes from the sea into the forest primeval, stops momentarily in Yankee City, then moves away from it. The frontier is a symbol representing not only space, as location, men, and historic contexts change, but a time concept. At a more primitive and less rational level, it is a feeling of incoming and outgoing to and from Yankee City, coupled with permanency, continuingness, and stability—a syncretistic melange of Yankee City as a physical place of rocks and rivers, of land and water, that is changing yet eternal. Movement and permanence: some who came stayed and built a proud city, filled with the virtues of New England civilization; the others, who became the human frontier, went on to found a vast continental nation of which Yankee City is proud to be a part. Yet this is not New England, nor is it Massachusetts; most importantly, it is not seaboard Massachusetts or Yankee City.

Furthermore, we in Yankee City who speak in the symbols of the pageant are still here. The great deeds and the men of valor and fame were also here and, in the meanings of the Procession, remain with us. Others have moved or died but we endure, we and our kind, despite everything. The frontier

2. Nowhere is the frontier as movement and change more clearly felt and expressed than by Francis Parkman in his personal account [107] of the masses of moving people going from the settled regions of the East through the Rockies and on to the Pacific Coast. It will be remembered that this was written at the time of the Mexican War. He and his companion, Shaw, were Boston aristocrats.

came and went and in great strides marched into the distances over the mountains and far away. With it, following it, went the new power and the new prestige. In the remote lands and distant places the political and economic expansion of the United States and the development of new kinds of power came to their own greatness. Not only have power, prestige, and wealth spread more widely and more abundantly elsewhere, but they are no longer here, by the sea and the river.

In the period of creation when the forest primeval and the feminine spirit of the river yielded to the technical and masculine moral power of those who brought us into existence, there was born a new society which, nurtured by sea and river, grew to greatness and fulfillment in the age of glory. Then came the great exodus of those who went west to found new worlds, went north to establish a new state, or, being highly placed like the Lowells and the Jacksons, migrated to the great cities of Boston and New York. They went on, but we stayed. Out of our strength they went on to greatness and new power.

None of these statements is consciously or explicitly made, yet the symbols of the pageant, it seems possible to discern, express such feelings. The evidence at very best is no more than suggestive and any conclusions must be pushed beyond induction and inference to speculation. Yet such feelings and thoughts are present in the non-rational world of the groups and individuals of Yankee City, proud of its own past—proud, too, of the advances of a nation that grew to greatness as the moving frontier went on to the Pacific and to world power, leaving Yankee City and her glory far back in time and far distant from present world events. Only the rational ordering of the symbols of place and time could here loosen non-rational feelings about today and tomorrow to make a distant yesterday come true today and continental distances shrink to the limits of a city.

The Autonomous Word and the Autonomous Individual

In the collective rite celebrating three centuries of its life, the Yankee City that was symbolically presented to the world and for its own people's self-regard and esteem was a secular, not a sacred, society. When descendants of the Puritan ancestors who founded a theocracy repudiated the authority of the early fathers, they also renounced the spiritual primacy and ultimate authority of what was once a sacred order. The established church and the sacred mythology of the ancestors did not have symbols in the celebration which related men to God's authority on earth or to his mysteries in heaven. Bishops, evangelists, and divines were displayed, but as jewels to adorn the robes of a secular order. They were the "facts" of history, conceived within the secular matrix of values and beliefs from which historians bring their presentations about the truth of past time. The symbols, officially and in fact, were referential; their signs were marks that pointed to events of the Puritan past. But nowhere in the entire pageant was there any sacred sign which demanded an act of faith about a sacred world of the past, through the holy men of Puritan history connecting men of today with the mysteries of the supernatural and Christian deity. The whole celebration was cast in rationalistic terms; all supernaturalism was suppressed. In its symbols the Puritans were no longer God's men; no miraculous intervention was celebrated; it was all secularly determined. Each great event in the symbols of the Procession was earthbound and morally determined by men. If God was present he was remote. If the Puritans of the past saw themselves as the children of Israel and their fate the working out of God's will, their descendants did not view them or themselves in this image.

It is significant that the event celebrated by Yankee City and the other seaboard towns to mark their "birthday" was Governor John Winthrop bringing the Charter to the Massachusetts Bay Colony; Winthrop, the bringer of the word "in the beginning" of the Procession, did not come with the Sacred Book. The word he brought was the Charter, an economic and political agreement among men.

More significantly, the Charter with its controlling words was meaningful in the Procession and the whole celebration because it was *moved* from England and brought to America where, being controlled by the ruling theocrats and magistrates and clergy, it was considered, then and now, as the symbolic source of the collectivity's autonomy. Still more significantly for purposes of symbolic theory, the word issued by royal authority to set up the legal conditions of the religious and economic experiment could be moved. By nature, in the beliefs of those who used it, the word, as it once had been in the early history of man, was no longer inherently one with the speaker and his context. The symbol as a written sign system could itself be moved and not lose its meaning (significance and power). It, too, could adventure beyond the confines of its physical place of origin.

Not only was the individual developing autonomy, but symbols themselves were becoming free and more autonomous. The autonomous symbol, made possible partly by the less perishable and more permanent marks of writing and partly by the attitudes of increasing acceptance of its validity in meaning and power beyond the place of its origin, once "turned loose" could ultimately go elsewhere. Its only boundaries, under ideal conditions, are the total environment of human interpreters. The symbols of oral speech and human gesture tend to be fixed and stationary; those outside man, beginning with writing and continuing in many of the new mass media, tend to be autonomous and to move with a life of their own.

Their autonomy may reach the point where the communication they carry may be directly received from a sender of three hundred or three thousand years ago. Delayed communication is a necessary characteristic of permanent signs. The effect of such communication on holding the generations of men together is immeasurable. Furthermore, if words and other such signs are free and capable of movement, then presumably each man is free to choose among them for their significances of his life, and each generation is partly liberated from the thralldom and absolute authority of the preceding generation, who alone once possessed the symbols of oral tradition. The contemporary generations of each society become the human environments to which the moving, autonomous signs of meaning have migrated—these, too, like their human counterparts, to be assimilated or to remain impervious to the influence of their most recent setting. These sacred or secular objective symbols of the past or present, free from the control of their creators and their contexts of origin, as they move may radically change their meanings and the manner of their acceptance; the sacred word may become secular, or the secular marks of the economic and political agreement of the Charter become semisacred. The Puritan children of Israel coming to the Promised Land of New England in their own self-conceptions were a holy people directed by God and his Word, the Bible, and by Governor Winthrop who, like Moses, also had the Charter of Law on which the laws of men were founded. The words of the Charter, the symbol of free men and their symbol of autonomy, in the Procession also represented the beginnings of things as they now are and marked the change from a world without form to one of order.

The Bible, whose words carry different meanings for each of the churches, had no part in the general collectivity's pageant rites. Only in the sermons of the churches and a brief collective ceremony at a hill beyond the dwellings of the town after the celebration was over were the Bible and the sacred world allowed to enter the symbolism of the Tercentenary. As in life, the need for unity and agreement and the evolutions of history which had produced the religious diversity of the town, drove the marks and meanings of sacred life into the confined contexts of each church, and for some to the brief, unimportant ceremony on the hill.

We must return to our consideration of the *delayed, indirect,* and unintentional use of signs. In the literature the economic, political, and religious aspects of autonomous men have been stressed. [110a, 110d] This is not enough. Above everything else this shift in the Western world's culture was related to the release of secular and sacred words from oral control and from the face-to-face control of their meaning and overwhelming power to influence action and behavior. When they were freed from the bodies of the users and were no longer bound by the necessities of direct action, in which mouths and ears create and consume perishable sounds and signs, a whole set of new possibilities developed. If men can symbolize saying-what-they-mean so that it is no longer a momentary act of attribution but something that persists in time, the possibilities are limitless for extending the number and kind of people to whom signs can be "sent" and who may be influenced *indirectly* by the sender.

In the simpler stages of man's life, for words and other objective signs to continue circulating in the limited environment of those who create and maintain them, it is of course necessary that individuals of each generation relearn and refashion them as signs of communal agreement as to what they mean and are signs of. It is said that words are exchanged in communication between the sender and receiver. More correctly, sender and receiver, when conversing, stimulate themselves with *socially selected sounds and silences*. As long as this verbal stimulation is labial and auditory and strengthened with the auxiliary gestures of an interpersonal and immediate context, those who know what the words are meant to convey and who choose to speak, or choose not to, are in positions of great strength. They have control over these vehicles of collective knowledge, which can be, and often are, of incalculable power. When they speak, those who cannot understand what is told them may be placed fortuitously in positions of helplessness. They do not have some of the tools necessary to control their environment; the others do. The control of the use of words demands that their meanings be known by the user, and he can choose to speak or not speak, hear or refuse to hear.

When words are written, being no longer dependent on the *immediate* organic environment where sounds and silences stimulate meaning in live organisms, several powerful new factors enter. Freed from immediacy, words can now go elsewhere, beyond the interpersonal context. The secret intimate written words of two people—for example, a love letter—freed from sound, may leave their first context and move into a space limited only by human environment and into a time limited only by mankind's survival. Those who use words in the present or future by the use of the written form of delayed communication may "converse" with the past. Delayed communication, which at times may be more accurately called continuing communication, between individuals of generations widely separated in time and space, is one of the important ways in which words are freed from their immediate controls and, thus circulating, become autonomous—move beyond the bounds of mortality (where to live they must be consumed) toward immortality.

Being still dependent as signs on human beings, they must be protected to attain full autonomy. The autonomy of each individual person is dependent on a social structure with values and beliefs which do not fix his position but allow him freedom to move from one social place to another, from one social context to others. So it is with words. When the morality which controls their proper use defines them autonomously, they can move more easily from context to context, from B.C. to A.D. In oral tradition, their meanings can move through time in a chain of live interaction from mouth to ear, from ear to mouth, within the continuing flow of human tissue, but un-broken generational continuity must be present.

The written word, an object whose form is an agreed-upon sign, is by nature so constituted that the objective part of the sign—the material object—does not need to be refashioned or recreated each time a new individual or a new generation uses it. If used, however, the meaning must be under the influence of intervening generations. The archaeologist may unearth unused inscribed tablets whose signs belong to a culture long forgotten and never before known to this civilization. Al-though the signs remain the same and the meanings intended have not passed through any transformation of changing be-lief and value, the receivers of this delayed communication have been influenced by the flux of cultural transition of per-haps a hundred generations. What they know and feel cannot be what those who invented the delayed message could have meant, even though the message comes directly from the for-gotten source. In this sense the sign is autonomous—depend-ent, like the autonomous individual, on the values and beliefs of society for its freedom of movement. So long as its existence in the human mind is important, involving the value of wanting to find out what it meant to those who sent it, then within the human limits of such a term it has sign autonomy. And as such it is both free and bound—free to move within the limits of human mentality; bound to serve the meanings attributed by those who use it.

As such it also acts both as a conservative force, strengthen-ing the hold of the past on the changing present, and as a liberalizing one, freeing the present generation from depend-ence upon oral transmission of the immediate older genera-tion's interpretations of the sacred tradition. Not one, but a hundred generations are now sending their own delayed inter-pretations of what both they and we are. If a written sign like the Massachusetts Bay Charter or the Constitution of the

United States has passed through continuing generations of interlocked interpreters, then not only is the original sign present as a whole, but the inscribed meanings are also directly sent to help distant ancestors communicate with their present "contemporaries." This is in fact the purpose of such a document as the Constitution, with its effort at "wise provision" for the future. The written sign loosens the control of time and modifies its effect upon us, for as we can now send words to the present and future, those in the past have been able to send directly these same signs of meaning to those born long after them. The signs of delayed communication have a quality of simultaneity about them—they "speak," we "listen," in the same moment of interpretation, as it were. Like receiving a telegram sent across the distances of a continent, to be read a brief moment later, reading these signs of distant meaning changes the significance of space and time. Through the unity of meaning between sender and receiver, the realities of time and space are transformed into *social* realities of meaningful nearness. "The" meaning that was "instantaneously" "put into" the signs which is the Charter, three centuries ago and a continent away, by the sign-maker, in the receiver's act of interpretation today in Yankee City can be "instantly" and "immediately" shared.

Thus the autonomous word, for instance, within the guarantees of freedom of speech and press to tell the truth, has a variety of meanings in Yankee City which have clashed. All played vital roles in the symbols of the Procession and in the historical events symbolized in the signs of this collective rite. The Word of the first settlers was in two forms: the Sacred Book which put them in direct communication with God through the literal signs of his Truth, and the secular Charter which Winthrop and the proprietors of the Massachusetts Bay Colony brought with them. Those early ancestors thus had the absolute power of the Word of God and the great but less powerful word of the secular covenant in their hands. As such, the Bible, the Holy Word, was the ultimate source of all authority; its truth was absolute. Those who controlled the interpretation of the scripture could be—and some were—theocratic tyrants, but since the truth was believed to be in the Word, directly communicated by God to those who were the

instruments of his communication, this infallible Book, freed
from the controls of an ecclesiastical hierarchy, potentially
gave to each man who could read absolute autonomy and
power. For there he could find the truth and, thus informed, be
not only free to know it but duty bound to tell it to others.
Each man might become his own private sect, at peace or war
with all others.

Since it was believed that it was each man's duty to learn
the truth and read the Scriptures, it was necessary that he
learn to read and have immediate access to the Holy Word.
From the very beginning, Massachusetts and Yankee City
taught their young to read. Public schools were believed necessary, and they were publicly supported. Private academies were
endowed and Harvard College founded, all primarily because
of implicit faith in the written word, particularly the Sacred
Word. The second float after Winthrop and his Charter was
"The First Class at Harvard. Benjamin Woodbridge of Yankee
City ranked highest in this class of nine . . ."

The social and symbolic processes which, through time,
formed the symbols in the minds and hands of the modern
symbol-makers to create the signs of the Procession representing things past and evoking and expressing contemporary
beliefs and values about them, emerged from the most diverse
sources. As such these signs of the past were given *delayed
attribution of meaning*. The action of meaning took place over
hundreds of years rather than in the immediacy of a moment.
Meanings deriving from three hundred years, tens of thousands
of hours, and millions upon millions of past words and events
were condensed into a few brief hours and forty-two passing
symbols. The condensation of the meanings of experience
stored in the unconscious of one individual is slight compared
to the condensation of social significance in the symbolic equipment of each generation and the special signs of historical
works or rites used by collectivities to speak to themselves about
their past.

Necessarily in such signs there is *displacement* of significance; necessarily many of the older meanings are no longer
allowed explicit expression. Unconscious meanings, never permitted open expression even during the occurrence of an
event, still seek and find covert acknowledgment. The older

meanings of signs, implicit or explicit, rational or non-rational, also change their accent. Some retreat into somber obscurity, not being publicly acknowledged and celebrated; others once not publicly admitted come from their closets and parade before an approving multitude. Through time, as everyone knows, signs and symbols stand for something more—something less—something quite different—or cease to exist. New signs stand for old meanings, old ones for new—sometimes the opposite of what they once meant.

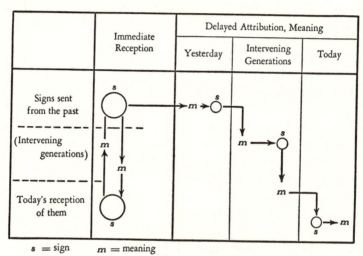

s = sign   m = meaning

CHART 3. The Delayed Attribution of Meaning

Chart 3, "The Delayed Attribution of Meaning," depicts the major outline of this process. At the upper left are the signs sent from the past; below, in the same column, today's reception. At the top of the left-hand column the label "Immediate Reception" shows the situation when today's generation receives its signs directly from the long dead past. In this vertical column the circles representing signs are *directly* connected by two vertical arrows, the one pointing from the past to the present circle, indicating that the sign has been conveyed directly from the past without passing through the minds of intervening generations; the other pointing upward from present to past, indicating no more than past signs presently interpreted.

Beyond this column are the vertical columns from left to

right: Yesterday, Intervening Generations, and Today. The circles and labels *m* and *s*, connected by arrows, depict no more than the passage of meaning *m* through the mental life of the generations.

The flow of signs, events, and their meanings depicted by the chart takes place, of course, in the interconnected organisms and species events which have composed the collectivity during the span involved. The flow of events through the social and status structures influences the content of each symbolic form. The continuing interpretation and reinterpretation of the events and the society in which they occur contribute an important share to the significance of symbols of the past wherever they are being used by the collectivity. The conceptualizations of what man is, what the world is, and what the supernatural is, flow through the social and status structure, influencing and being influenced by its changing values and stream of events. All of these—status and social structure, values and beliefs, and the events of time—persist and change and add to and subtract from the meanings of the past as they are caught and momentarily held in today's symbols. Logical or non-logical, rational or irrational, conscious or buried far below in the organic life of the species, adequately or not, they find expression in man's collective symbols. [42b]

The Non-logical Time and Space of the Species

The meanings of life were represented in the non-rational symbols of the Procession as events of ordered time which, moving out of the unknown toward, and into, a timeless region of earth and water, became the living time and space of Yankee City. There resting briefly, the significance of time developed into enduring importance in the recorded activities of the community. Then, at an ever-accelerated speed, we see the significant present move out beyond the city to the vast western distances, to the great metropolises, to the more important economic and social life of a powerful nation. The importance of time in Yankee City is not in the here and now but as it once was, in an enduring yesterday that has remained while present time has gone elsewhere. Since the end of the nineteenth century events are felt to be "too recent" and, while important, lack significance. They are not invested with the full social power of the mental life of the group. Yankee City is now enmeshed in the huge, dull world beyond it. Recent time in the meanings of the Procession lies sprawled and mired in the ordinary rounds of unimportant events. The splendor is gone; the power and the glory are elsewhere. Yankee City must go to them; they no longer come to Yankee City.

Within the non-rational feelings of today, time has run down. [10a] The spiritual and absolute certainty of the Protestant faith of the early fathers has been drained from the people, the great period has gone and only a diminished secular prestige remains. Yet as the nation grows into world greatness we, the people of Yankee City (the symbols of the Procession seem to say), who started and established things as they are, possess a unique kind of prestige shared only with those who were present when the Great Society came into being. Our present power is relatively weak, our contemporary prestige not conspicuous, but properly viewed in the context of the past we are identified with the most powerful symbols of the Great Society. To establish their claims as legitimate heirs and present holders of the great tradition, they who live elsewhere—the hundred-odd million—must come to us. In us the great tradition lives and our symbols legitimately express it.

Analysis of the forty-two scenes of the several time periods demonstrates that, although the whole Procession is a representation of the passage of time, and time as movement and change, in these same symbols there is also present a nonrational eternal finality. This static, unchanging, eternal quality has to do with the ultimate nature of man; it is in the fixedforever of the species group. The eternal verities of the drama were in the unconscious assumptions that created it. By their sequential movement before the stationary reviewing stand, the scenes of the great Procession, precisely following each other chronologically, stressed the rational and linear qualities of time. But the symbolic conventions of such dramatic processions demand that the reviewing stand, those in it, and the public they represent, be still and rest in one place.

For that moment the lives of those who viewed the spectacle were suspended and timeless. In them the meanings of the Eternal City of St. Augustine were present. Coming from the past, time moved by them. The time-ordered events of the parade moved from the starting place in Yankee City through the streets of the city as *one* thing. The Procession itself, while trying to emphasize the rationality of time, played havoc with it. The meanings of objective time were non-rationally contradicted. Although first things came symbolically and logically first and the beginnings of history were spatially and logically at the beginning of the Procession, while last things appeared at the end, to those in the stationary reviewing stand their own time stood still. All the scenes were parts of one timeless thing.

In the feelings of the people, past and present life were one. Governor Winthrop and his Charter were of a piece with Greely, the ancient living hero, for they were of one substance. [151a] In this symbolic unity the simultaneity of 1630 and 1930 was non-rationally stressed. The great past of the ancestors was evoked and symbolically lived in the present. Many sensed this. On the first day of the celebration the minister of the oldest church, which traced its being to the beginnings, said to his congregation, "The Great Book of Life lies open before our generation; today, in the scenes we produce [its] notable characters seem again to walk our streets . . ." Those in the reviewing stand saw the forty-two scenes move as the "one Book of Life" across their vision, and pass on through the spaces of the city. In their diversity there was logical empirical time; within the non-rational meanings of their unity was the static, fixed quality of being. The timeless sense of species existence, felt as eternity, was present. The rationality of Durkheim's "Chart" depicting the points of time, and the deeply felt unconscious sense of total existence where, in Freud's findings, there is no time, were both present.

Despite the prevailing and perhaps necessary belief in the unitary character of time held by members of our culture, there are nevertheless many kinds of time. For our purposes we can divide them into what some philosophers have called objective and subjective time, forgetting their quarrels about one or the other being true, or all time being one or the other.

Objective time, as we said earlier, supposedly has to do with the world beyond man, particularly the movements of the earth, stars, and planets. Objective time is numbered and measured. [56] We think we take account of it by the clock, calendar, and the instruments of the physicists and astronomers. We relate objective time to our social life and regulate much of our existence by clock and calendar. Events are accordingly timed and regulated. The individual, being part of this action context, learns and internalizes it and makes it part of himself. Such "objective" time concepts are then applied to social age status, to biological change, and to the transitional activities of the individual through the age statuses and the events of his life history. Days, weeks, months, and years, anchored to a birthday, produce a person forever measured by "objective" time, but by a time to which he and others also attribute human values. By this means the time of the individual and the society can be named and numbered.

The time symbols of the Procession were multiple and diverse. There was the objective time of chronology and verifiable historical references. Events of men and the chronology of the planets were synchronized. Such references can be validated by many people and the self-correcting devices and criteria of science. Then there were the subjective levels in which the individuals involved possessed non-rational beliefs and feelings about time. Rational concepts were rearranged in a non-logical manner. These were systems of feeling non-rationally organized. Ideas were syncretistically arranged.

The symbols of non-logical or subjective time, on the other hand, are laden with affect. These non-logical feeling systems are not necessarily individual; more often they are social. The vast world of feelings and the images which express them are passed on from generation to generation and change as experience affects them. The subjective, non-logical (social) time of Yankee City can compress the objective time of half-centuries into nothingness and extend a mere ten years into what, measured by objective time, would be a century.

The symbols of time (and of space and all other meanings) are not only signs of constructs and logical thinking, but are available and used by the non-logical feeling systems of a people and their culture. Moreover, they are subject to the needs and demands of a still deeper level of being and understanding. The non-logical meanings of our mental life are products of the species group in interaction with its environments; meanings accumulate in, and are reordered by, the organisms that compose the species. The limitations of the species, and the actual extension of its capabilities into experience and environment (accepting or not accepting available stimuli), provide the limits of knowing. For time, and indeed all knowing, cannot go beyond the nature of species being. The turtle, the chimpanzee, the firefly, and the angleworm, as species, by their own nature and being have their inherent limitations and extensions of understanding. So it is with man. That which makes the human species different from all others makes its knowledge different.

The logical objective categories of time and space, the non-logical affective systems, and the species sensations constitute three levels of understanding. Each refers to worlds of reality. They refer to the physical objective world beyond man, to the ongoing organismic world of the species, and to what the individual experiences when he experiences himself. In terms of time, physical time is the sequence of events (which may or may not have the form it is believed to have) that occurs in the world beyond man. Social time is beyond the self; it is a sequence of happenings, with or without form, which take place in the world of social relations. Self time is a sequence of events, with or without form, having to do with what it is I am and do.

We thus have three broad categories referring to the several realities: objective time and space references to physical, social, and self phenomena; non-logical systems of feeling, which refer to the same three; and species sensations, which order experience about the objective world, beyond other organisms as they are socially related to each other, and the self as a being apart.

These phases will be re-examined in the chapters on the symbolic structure of the sacred year and the character of non-rational thought. Now we must turn to the other symbol system forming part of that whole which is the mental life of Yankee City.

PART III

SYMBOLS BOTH SECULAR
AND SACRED

INTRODUCTION

The interlocked memberships of the various types of American association penetrate and are influenced by every aspect of our social and status structures: the top, the middle, and the bottom; the old and new Americans; our economic, political, and religious systems. Accordingly their symbolic life is diverse and the manifestations most numerous and frequent. In the next chapter we analyze, classify, and interpret the thousands of activities which compose the symbolic life of associations. In the two following, the symbolic relations of the dead and the living as expressed in the rituals of the Memorial Day cult of the dead and in cemeteries are explored to begin to learn some of the ultimate meanings life has for Americans. The influences of death and other life crises on the prestige and power of doctors, clergymen, and undertakers are studied and interpreted.

Rituals, whether they be formal and explicit or informal and implicit in human behavior, symbolically state the meanings and social values of some part of the world in which the group is involved. What is concerned may be an object in the natural environment, such as water or food; some part of the social order, such as the family; a status, such as that of a ruler; or at the supernatural level the meanings and values attributed to a god. Sacred rituals may combine all three at once; for example, a sacred ceremony of totemism expresses the meanings and values of the animals of the natural environment, the significance of the family and clan, as well as the values and meanings attributed to the totemic deities. *Rites de passage* are transition rituals, which are given particular attention in Part III. They mark the critical moments in the life career of the individual, particularly those of birth, puberty, marriage, and death. Those of birth, puberty, and marriage are likely to give more emphasis to the here and now, those of death to the spiritual significance of eternity.

With the completion of this part of the book our view of American symbolic life will have spread across many of its diversities and uniformities. We will have moved from the action systems of the present, where politics included everyone and all forms of communication, across the many class, ethnic, and other variations of our culture back through time to the ancient past; we will have watched the living with their dead, and through their relations approach the threshold of ultimate beliefs, values, and symbols of divinity. In Part IV we will extend our analysis to include the sacred symbols of Christianity.

CHAPTER 7

THE SYMBOLIC LIFE

OF ASSOCIATIONS

Structural Complexity and Symbolic Diversity

In Yankee City as in other American communities certain symbol systems organize the participants into segmentary groups, temporarily separating them from the rest of the community; other symbol systems function to unite all the people of diverse segments into a common group. The first serve such semi-autonomous and diverse structures as churches, associations, and ethnic groups; the second, such as those of the Tercentenary celebration, contribute to the integration of all the citizenry for enterprises common and important to the total community. The two types of symbol system are present and necessary wherever societies are differentiated. Segmentary systems provide the symbolic means to express the sentiments of members within the limited solidarity of autonomous structures; the integrative systems allow common sentiments present in everyone to be expressed, giving participants the necessary symbols to express the unity felt by all members of the community. At different times certain symbol systems can be used for either purpose.

To take an example from a simpler culture, in most of the communities of Melanesia there are numerous autonomous secret societies which include some of the men but not all, thus emphasizing exclusiveness and separateness from the common group. These societies have secret rituals which express, and function to maintain, the autonomy of their organizations. On the other hand, there is an organization called the *sukwe* which includes all the men of the village. Its rituals unite all men of diverse age, wealth, and status in the community into a common whole. The functioning of the symbol systems is related to and expresses the structural forms.

The great diversity of American symbol systems is related

231

to the high division of labor and extreme complexity of the social structure. Two contrary tendencies operate in the symbolic behavior of contemporary America. Since early settlement there has been increasing diversity, heterogeneity, and exclusiveness, now to the point of individuation. Very small groups, for example, take a proud delight in being the only ones who understand certain esoteric poetry. The groups in which various kinds of scientific languages are known and understood are necessarily small, for expert knowledge of terminology requires a long training and the interest of particular kinds of personalities.

The small groups characteristic of a high division of social labor in complex societies, such as lodges, secret societies, civic groups, and other associations, are not only "interest" groups, held together by sharing common values, but also symbol-sharing groups. [124a] They can communicate with each other as they cannot with any other group. The reciprocal exchange of symbols which have a common referent for each member involved in the exchange holds the groups together, but the fact that they share these symbols only among themselves and cannot do so with others creates at once an exclusiveness and an inclusiveness that strengthen the solidarity of the group. Since this is true of each symbol-sharing group it clearly contributes not only to each group's solidarity but to the maintenance of heterogeneity within the culture. Such diversity demands the successful articulation of the separate symbol systems to each other and to the common language of the whole group—otherwise they cannot be used as an effective part of the division of labor.

As the societies of America and Yankee City grow more complex and the symbol systems more diverse, a second tendency, an opposing but necessary one, has operated. There is increasing generalization and standardization of public symbols understood by all levels of the society and by every kind of person. Some of these public symbols, such as the communications of certain mass media, are highly stereotyped and, as their name suggests, have common acceptance among the diverse groups within the masses of the people. Whereas the segmenting symbolic process is related to the diverse structural units, social differentiation, and the increasing tendency of American society to form each individual into a semiautonomous unit and private social system of his own, the second, or unifying, tendency is directly related to the social need to maintain minimum cohesion and the larger solidarity. Over-all integrative symbol systems which everyone understands and which evoke common sentiments, values, and beliefs in all members of the society are expressions of this second tendency. They provide the symbols which are exchanged by everyone in the group and are the materials most fitted for the daily newspapers, radio, and motion pictures. Although there may be variation in the form in which they are expressed (print in newspapers and magazines as compared with pictures in television and the movies), they have a common unity in the beliefs they represent and the emotions they arouse.

Complex societies must have a common core of basic understanding known and used by everyone or their complex and diverse symbolic superstructures will not stand. They need general symbol systems that everyone not only knows but *feels*. The increasing structural diversity and social complexity of contemporary society, the greater development of individual autonomy, the proliferation of specialized symbol systems— these and many other factors raise serious difficulties for communication and collaboration. If more and more problems are to be solved and greater and greater areas of reality comprehended and conquered, the social labor of a society must be increasingly divided and the advance in symbols must keep pace with technical and social achievement. And advance in symbols, as we have previously seen, requires not only the invention of new special systems but the development of new forms of discourse containing the old core of general meanings common to the whole group.

The problems of general communication, crucial for survival in complex societies, are partly solved by use of certain of the traditional institutions such as schools to train all children from every background in the rudiments and core meanings of symbols that must be used feelingly as well as knowingly by everyone. Common social conditioning creates common ways of response. As we turn again to Yankee City, we see that the learning experiences of the several social levels and of the numerous ethnic and other groups take place in a social maze so constructed that all groups have certain experiences in common and some have other experiences as special groups.

We will see how American society has developed new general public symbol systems, often of a hallowed character, such as Memorial Day, and has created heroic myths such as those of Lincoln and Washington, which have common core meanings for the diverse subcultures. We will examine, in this and the following chapter, how these devices of symbolism are used by a complex society either to achieve communication with common meanings permitting ideational and emotional collaboration for common ends, or to maintain the exclusiveness and separate values and beliefs of a high division of social labor.

In Yankee City the vast majority of the symbol systems are segmentary, most of them related to associations. The whole social life of the town is permeated by the activities of social, civic, and other associational groupings. These numerous organizations function to maintain the solidarity of the whole, yet help to maintain the autonomy of separate groups. It would be expected that their symbolic activities would exhibit these opposing structural functions. Our essential problem is to learn how the "infinite variety" of symbolic activity is related to the structure of the associations.

Social anthropologists have always considered Melanesian and West African societies as the outstanding examples of organized groups with a large proliferation of associations, yet Yankee City exceeded them. Through the period of the research, 357 associations continued as permanent organizations, but this figure was augmented by less permanent groups, organized usually for specific purposes, which at one time brought the total to 899. The formal association, such as civic and fraternal groups, has explicit and definite rules (usually written) of entrance, membership, and exit as well as those governing payment of fees and ritual procedure. It derives its authority, ultimately, from the members themselves rather than accepting it as handed down from a permanent control group, as in the usual economic organizations such as factories and similar productive units.

Types of Symbolic Activity

The activities of associations provide rich material for symbolic and functional analysis. Much, if not all, of their behavior is directly or indirectly, consciously or unconsciously, symbolic, since what they say and do in a given activity usually stands for something else and thus conforms to our definition of symbolic activity. The full meaning of an associational activity is found not only by treating it in the light of what the members of the association say it is, but by studying the activity and its implications and meanings in terms of the structure itself and the satisfactions which the members receive from what they do. [145] Associational activities are valuable for symbolic analysis because they enter into every part of the American social structure and reflect the variety of sentiments, attitudes, and values of every part of American society.

Before continuing, let us define what an "activity" is to the observer. An activity such as a parade or an installation of officers is a recognized and socially defined public use of symbols in a set of formal or informal social relations. An activity is recognized as such by those who participate in it and by those who study it at the explicit and open level of social behavior (it is not something they do unconsciously). Each activity occurs in a situation which involves the relations of the members alone, or the members of the association in relation to the rest of the community. Each activity includes a symbolic situation in which the members exchange symbols among themselves or with other members of the society, according to the nature of the relationship. For example, the members may belong to a secret society such as the Masons, where they perform rituals known and participated in only by members of their own group. On the other hand, these same members might join in an interfraternity activity where all are involved in a ritual whose successful performance demands that they exchange symbolic objects between them or cooperate in some community activity, such as fund-raising.

To gather representative data from the complex variety and large number of associations involved here, we systematically studied them for a period of two years. We attended meetings, collected records on activities, and carefully followed the detailed reports in the local newspaper. Since most of the news stories were provided by the members themselves, and since we were able to check them by our own observations, we learned to accept what was said as reliable evidence.

Five thousand eight hundred events or activities were recorded. We observed these during the two-year period and were able to classify them into 284 forms (subtypes) and then into 19 types. (Table 2 lists the 19 types.) For example, a boys'

TABLE 2. Events, Forms, and Types of Activity

Rank Order of Events	Type of Activity	Number of Events	Per Cent	Number of Forms (Subtypes)
1	Drama and talent exhibitions	828	14.28	41
2	Speeches	744	12.83	1
3	Organization	567	9.78	13
4–5	Eating	499	8.60	24
4–5	Fund-raising	499	8.60	22
6	Ritual, secular-external	335	5.78	30
7	Ritual, sacred	333	6.74	23
8	Ritual, secular-internal	306	5.28	21
9	Gifts	291	5.02	14
10	Sedentary games	214	3.69	15
11	Hospitality	198	3.41	8
12	Contests	158	2.72	8
13	Athletic games	157	2.71	23
14	Crafts and skills	126	2.17	8
15	Ritual, secular-sacred	123	2.12	8
16	Socials	119	2.05	2
17	Outings	118	2.03	10
18	Teaching and learning	99	1.71	7
19	Dancing	86	1.48	6
Total		5,800	100.00	284

club might play a baseball game with another team. The particular game was counted as an event and listed under type of activity as an athletic game, while the form (subtype) of activity was listed under the heading "Baseball."

The activities recorded covered everything from the most sacred to the most profane and secular, from extreme forms of competition and opposition to the most intense cooperative efforts, from the polar extremes of utility and Yankee hardheadedness to the ultimate in philanthropy and good will. They also ranged from the most reasonable and sensible behavior to the ultimate in triviality and nonsense. We shall be concerned here only with their public meanings, and we are going to be concerned less with the interpretation of their meaning than with pointing out the multitude and variety of activities of American associations and drawing certain conclusions by using our knowledge of their functional significance.

The social scientist can recognize four types of public ritual among the activities of these associations. The four include only forms which are consciously used by the association for ritualistic purposes. As such, they are pure forms of symbolic behavior. All the other types of activity have varying degrees of ritual, but they are not designed primarily for ritual ends; that is, their ritual significance, when present, is secondary and often not recognized by the participants. The four forms of ritual are: sacred ritual; ritual which combines sacred and secular elements; and secular ritual—this latter being concerned (a) largely with the community beyond the association or (b) wholly or almost completely with its own inner world. As used here the term "ritual" means that the members of the association express in overt symbolic acts the meanings which socially evaluated objects or relationships have for them, and at the same time also state in symbols what their relations are with such objects. The devout Christian, for example, does this in the rite of Communion, as does the patriotic American in some of the exercises customary on Lincoln's birthday.

Sacred ritual symbolically relates the participants to sacred things—Deity, the spiritual dead, and such things as emblems which represent God and the sacred dead. Secular ritual expresses the values and attitudes of the daily round of life in the community and gives symbolic form to the importance of ordinary things that compose the lives of most people. Certain secular rituals—adopting and maintaining a European war orphan, for instance—symbolize along with other purposes the American alliance with certain European countries and the present feeling of unity with these countries. At the same time, they serve to relate the members of the association to the larger community beyond the association itself. Others, such as celebrating Lincoln's Birthday, flag ceremonies, and similar patriotic rituals, relate the association to the whole community. Still others tie the association symbolically to the families, schools, and the local community. There are thirty forms of these secular rituals.

Twenty-one forms of ritual activity concerned with internal relations are largely composed of symbolic elements which have been created by the members of the associations. Their function is to tie the participants more closely together, emphasize their unity, and indirectly maintain in the feelings of the members their separateness from the larger society.

The several types of ritual, combined, compose about one-fifth of all the activities of the associations of Yankee City; the other four-fifths of association activities were divided among fifteen other categories (see Table 2).

Where combinations of ritual are not involved, drama and talent exhibitions are the most popular type of activity. Dramatic exhibitions include everything from classical and contemporary plays to tap dancing and jazz band concerts. Generally they are expressions of the talent of the local people; but what is said and done on the stage is usually pure symbolic communication. Many people in the community, particularly those in the lower classes, use talent to help improve their stations in life and gain social recognition. If they are successful, two developments may follow. They may be recognized economically and advance themselves accordingly, or—and what is more likely—they may be recognized socially by more highly placed persons and participate at a higher level in the social system. Very often, to the observer, the efforts are pathetic, since they accomplish nothing for the participant and even evoke ridicule—the ever-present risk which mobile people must take. The plays vary from classical and modern, which present rigorous and almost scientific representations of modern life and employ the skill and dexterity of first-rate artists, to those which are little more than an opportunity for the participant to exhibit himself in a public place. There were 41 subcategories and 828 events of this sort, composing over one-seventh of the total.

The members of associations of Yankee City and, in fact, those throughout America seem never to tire of listening to speeches. The unfriendly critic or field worker who must attend many of these functions might well say that many of them are dreary, uninformative, and filled with wind. But speeches, even when not listened to by the members, are felt to be necessary and are appreciated as part of what should happen when members meet. Analysis indicates that a considerable proportion of them, when stated in propositional form, are composed of ritual rather than reason. Some of the "best speakers" freely avail themselves of well-tried symbolic and ritual materials and resort to reason only when it is necessary to disguise what they are saying. One-eighth of the many thousands of activities we observed were speeches. Speeches, unlike talent presentations, are usually given by outsiders; the association members merely listen. Like the social set-up for dramatic activities, the amount of participation of most people tends to be minimal. We were unable to classify the speeches into types of subject matter, but our list of subjects indicates clearly that they ranged over every variety of topic.

An activity of associations to which a great amount of time is devoted, ranking third in importance, is organizational work. This includes "reading the minutes," "new business," "making new rules," "voting," etc., and is largely concerned with maintaining the formal organization of the association by expressing the rules in group action and emphasizing the social autonomy of associations, as well as that of the members, by making new rules or rescinding old ones. Usually to the observer, and often to some of us who participate in such organizational forms, what is done seems dull and unimportant; but the prosaic outward forms themselves must be given further examination, for their meaning is of great importance.

For example, long, boring discussions take place over the rules of order, which give opportunities to define the status of members and their officers and, above all, permit the organizational activities of members to express—i.e., symbolize in social form—the democratic character of the association and of the society generally. Criticism of an association's chairman or president, heated reference to "railroading," and declarations about one man's vote being as good as another's are all recognitions of how organizational activity very often voices something more than the "business of the day" or rules of conduct governing the actions of the members. The critical observer, however, leaves with a feeling of futility, for he sees "more time wasted in the discussion of the rules than in action." No doubt this is sometimes true, but more often than not what is being observed and defined as not important is of the utmost significance because of its meaning to those who participate and the emotions which these activities arouse. Ten per cent of the activities were concerned with rules and organization.

Eating, although a biological act, in its social form consists in the sharing of food at a common meal. As Robertson Smith and Ernest Crawley pointed out long ago, it is one of the strongest ways to engender sentiments of oneness among participants while they share group attitudes. Eating is an activity used in the greatest variety of ways to promote solidarity or separate the members of a particular association from all others. Sometimes the participants themselves recognize the unity that the function of "breaking bread together" implies. Their behavior always expresses this significance. A great variety of ways of eating were collected. They range all the way from the utmost formality, etiquette, and prestige, through varying shades of formality to informal basket lunches and suppers. The various forms of eating communal meals comprise about 9 per cent of the activities.

Fund-raising ranks with eating in importance. Twenty-two ways of collecting funds were observed. They included everything from benefit shows and suppers to tag days, auction sales, rummage sales, campaigning, and bazaars. Thus an activity was identified as belonging to the general category of "fund-raising" if one of its immediate explicit purposes was to increase the amount of money in the association's treasury. If another element such as eating—as in the case of a fund-raising supper—was present, this element was also counted under its appropriate category.

The process of fund-raising includes getting money from both within and outside the membership of the organization. Women's organizations show much more ingenuity and diversity in their fund-raising enterprises than do the men's groups, often disguising or de-emphasizing the purpose. Members and outsiders are invited to play at benefit card parties, eat a benefit lunch, or buy a piece of bric-à-brac at a bazaar and, accordingly, are often doubly rewarded by getting an object of utility and having the moral satisfaction of making a contribution to a worthy cause.

Patterns of mutual obligation are often established between associations, for the members of one organization feel obligated to attend a fund-raising card party or supper of another because their own has just had a similar event. The exchange of services and money, usually in the pleasant context of entertainment, constitutes one of the great contributions of the associations to the social unity of the community, for it knits diverse groups tightly together.

Fund-raising may not be easily viewed as of symbolic significance. There can be no question that part of its ultimate use is purely utilitarian and technical. However, the giving and taking of money in such a context and in the set of relations usually established for such an activity symbolically define what the set of relations is or what it should be. Very frequently it is little more than a gift exchange, sometimes with overtones of competition in it, that looks very much like some of the competitive and cooperative elements of the potlatch of the northwest coast Indians. It will be recalled that these Indians made elaborate and very expensive gifts to each other at public ceremonies; the unfortunate recipient, to save face and protect his status, was forced to return an even more elaborate gift or conspicuously to destroy a highly valued object. Thorstein Veblen did not find it difficult to transfer Franz Boas' account of the potlatch among the Indians of the Canadian Pacific coast to his own theory of conspicuous expenditure in contemporary America.

Explicit gift-making and taking occupy an important part in the life of the associations. The gifts are made between members, or given to, and accepted from, other associations. Examples are ceremonial presents to a retiring officer and gifts to churches or to worthy philanthropies. There are some fourteen ways listed as proper for giving and receiving gifts. The presents which are supposedly given voluntarily and graciously by one association to another without thought of compensation, like all gifts set up obligations for a return of goods and services in the future or imply repayment for something done in the past. This exchange pattern organizes most of the associations into a system of interaction which emphasizes reciprocity. The goods and services are given as free-will offerings and are returned as such, with no hint of a commercial transaction; yet informal judgments are constantly being made which determine the sequence of such gift-making and the quality of the objects exchanged.

When it is realized that gift-making is one of the many ways of symbolically stating the relations among people and establishing an equilibrium between organizations, its importance to the associations and to the stability of the community can be understood. Such types of activity as fund-raising, various forms of secular and sacred rituals, games, contests, hospitality, outings, dancing, as well as most of the other nineteen types, contribute their share to the interactive cooperation and help to organize the competition and subordinate the hostilities that exist between the various social levels, ethnic groups, economic interests, and religious faiths. Although rather obvious, it cannot be too strongly stressed that most of the activities—particularly gift-making—are ways which increase, by act and symbol, the basic integration of the community and help to maintain its present form.

The gifts between two associations may have little value, yet they are visible emblems of social solidarity, and the act of giving evokes latent feelings of solidarity, unity, and interdependence. This cohesiveness is further related to the interconnections established by the interlocking memberships of related associations. This intricate web, when first viewed, is almost overwhelming.

Structural and membership interconnections, our interviews and observations tell us, organize and express some of the feelings, attitudes, and values of the people who belong to the various associations. The activities among these associations express both the structural connections and the membership interconnections. When two or more associations possess a common core of membership, the members often bring them together for common enterprises which are frequently joint actions or symbolic statements of common membership structure and social values. For example, members of the exclusive dining clubs belong to the less exclusive Rotary Club; their wives, who are members of the Garden Club and other exclusive associations, also belong to the more open Woman's Club. The core of the more highly placed men in Rotary and high-status women in the Woman's Club carry the influence of their other associations

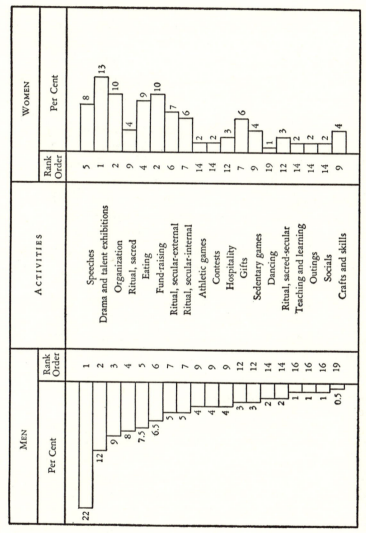

CHART 4. Male and Female Activities

243

into the life of these two clubs. To a lesser extent they take back the effect of some of their experience in Rotary and the Woman's Club to their more highly valued associations. Thus the web of associations functions to draw status distinctions while at the same time pulling the several social levels together.

Symbolic activities favored by men in disproportion to the interest shown by women were: listening to speeches; participating in sacred rituals, particularly those having to do with death (see the following chapter on Memorial Day); and engaging in athletic games and other contests. The ritual participation is partly accounted for by veterans and patriotic organizations. Chart 4 gives the percentages of male and female associations. The activities in the chart are arranged, beginning with the speeches and ending with skills and crafts, according to their proportionate use by men's organizations. The bar diagrams of the chart tell the story quickly; the percentages of the table are for closer inspection.

Women as compared with men show a notable interest in the use and display of skills, in informal social hours, outings, teaching and learning, gift-making and fund-raising. Their disproportionate participation in such events displays a nice balance between informal and formal activities. Five of the first six activities favored by men are also among those selected by women (See Chart 4 where all the activities of the two sexes are compared).

Activities of the Social Classes

Although class differences among all types of activity are quite marked and reveal themselves immediately to the observer, they are difficult to demonstrate in quantitative terms. For example, a comparison of lower- and upper-class associations shows that there is only a small difference in the percentage of total activities devoted to eating (8 per cent for the upper class and 7 for the lower); yet scrutiny of the forms of eating and, of course, actual observation of the style tell quite another story. It was impossible to develop a method which would permit recording of stylistic differences which could be easily counted, but the ordinary procedure previously described of classifying events under their *forms* and *types* did reveal decided differences. Although a comparison of the 284 forms would bring out all the significant differences, we must be content with only an example: a comparison of some of the types of activity of associations composed of members from the three upper (upper-upper to upper-middle) and three lower levels (lower-middle to lower-lower). Certain tendencies, often masked as types by the more general classification, are sufficiently revealed to bring out some of the significant similarities and differences.

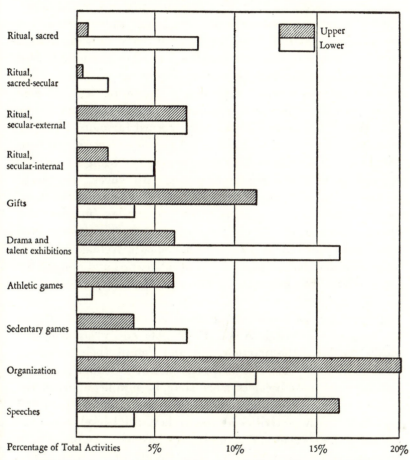

Percentage of Total Activities   5%   10%   15%   20%

CHART 5. The Activities of Lower- and Upper-Class Associations

Well over a third (38 per cent) of all the activities of the lower group involved purely evocative symbolic behavior—in drama (16 per cent) and ritual (22 per cent)—where symbols are used as symbols of symbols and are designed to evoke emotions rather than refer the attention to objects and things (see Chart 5). Less than a sixth of the activities of upper-level associations were devoted to evocative symbolic behavior (drama, 6 per cent; ritual, 10 per cent). Closer inspection of the two categories tells a significant story. It will be recalled that there were four types of ritual, ranging from sacred to secular and from the secret and private to rituals which directly functioned to relate the members to the community. The lower associations were many times more active in sacred rituals than the upper, and two and a half more in those that combined the sacred with the secular (see Chart 5). Furthermore, whereas in the lower-class associations there were two and a half times more occurrences of secular rituals concerned exclusively with the private world, secular rituals relating to the general community showed no difference in percentage between the two levels.

The statistics made it apparent, and interviewing and field observations verified these conclusions, that organized public activities of the lower classes are concerned far more with religious observance and with the use of sacred collective representations which give the feeling of belonging and being related "to the things of the world that matter." Moreover, the use of rituals which relate the associations only to their own members, paradoxically enough, seems to have a similar function; for they, too, encourage the exchange of symbols only among those who belong, and thereby encourage the twin feelings of exclusiveness and belongingness, the mutual regard and respect for the symbols used giving them importance and significance for each participant.

It must not be overlooked that symbols which evoke emotion rather than referring to specific objects and ideas are more easily used by the participants and retain their attention through longer periods. This preference of the lower levels for evocative symbols becomes more sharply significant when the preferences of the higher levels are known. Over a third (37 per cent) of the activities at the higher social level were concerned with speeches and organization business, compared with slightly more than a seventh (15 per cent) at the lower level. Both these activities demand quite different kinds of participation from ritual and drama. Granted that many of the speeches were designed to arouse the emotions and that some of the business had elements of ritual in it, each of these activities tends to be more directly concerned with reality than the other two. The words of speeches have to be placed in propositional and logical form; their meanings are more often concerned with ideas and things than those of drama and ritual. Since members of upper-class associations have had considerable training in school, with a higher education than members of the lower associations, the preference is not surprising. Business activities demand similar interests and, in general, the more precise relating of people to one another. Furthermore, authority and superordination are more easily maintained by their proper exercise.

·Twelve of the nineteen types of activity showed considerable difference as between the two groups. Some of these differences are graphically displayed in Chart 5. Those favored by the lower levels are drama, the rituals mentioned above, sedentary games, "social hours," crafts, and teaching and learning. The preferences of the higher levels were for speeches, business and organization, the exchange of gifts, and athletics. There were only minor differences in the occurrence of the other types of activities.

Although many changes are taking place in the associational life of America in preference for certain types of activity, rejection of others, and the relinquishment of older activities to accept new ones, the basic structure and function of these institutions in the society have fundamentally changed very little. It seems likely that they will continue important in the lives of Americans, for they serve their members well and conform to the way Americans do things. George Babbitt, busy with his real estate, Martin Arrowsmith in his scientific laboratory, and Pulham, Esq. in Brahmin Boston will always pay their dues and remain "members in good standing."

A good example of how the symbolic activities of associations function to maintain their structural separateness while combining to express the feelings and beliefs of the whole community about "itself" will be found in the next chapter, on Memorial Day, although here we shall be chiefly concerned with the meaning of its symbols as a cult of the dead. The Tercentenary, functioning in the same way to organize the sentiments felt by the community about its living past, related the living of today with those of yesterday. Memorial Day ritually unites the living with the dead.

CHAPTER 8

THE SYMBOLIC RELATIONS OF

THE DEAD AND THE LIVING

Cult of the Dead

Every year in the springtime the citizens of Yankee City celebrate Memorial Day. Over most of the United States it is a legal holiday. Being a holy day as well as a holiday, it is celebrated accordingly. For some it is part of a long weekend of pleasure, extended outings, and athletic events; for others it is a hallowed day when the dead are mourned and religious ceremonies held to express sorrow. But for most Americans, especially in the smaller cities, it is both sacred and secular. They feel the sacred importance of the day when they, or members of their family, participate in the ceremonies, but they also enjoy going for an automobile trip or seeing or reading about some important athletic event staged on Memorial Day weekend. This chapter will be devoted to the symbolic analysis and interpretation of Memorial Day to learn its meanings as an American sacred ceremony: a rite that evolved in this country and is indigenous to it.

It is the thesis of this chapter that the Memorial Day ceremonies, and subsidiary rites such as those of Armistice (or Veterans') Day, are rituals comprising a sacred symbol system which functions periodically to integrate the whole community with its conflicting symbols and its opposing, autonomous churches and associations. It is contended here that in the Memorial Day ceremonies the anxieties man has about death are confronted with a system of sacred beliefs about death which give the individuals involved and the collectivity of individuals a feeling of well-being. Further, the feeling of triumph over death by collective action is made possible in the Memorial Day parade by recreating the feeling of euphoria and the sense of group strength and individual strength in the

248

group power which is felt so intensely in time of war, when the veterans' associations are created and the feeling so necessary for the Memorial Day's symbol system is originally experienced.

Memorial Day is a cult of the dead which organizes and integrates the various faiths and ethnic and class groups into a sacred unity. It is a cult of the dead organized around the community cemeteries. Its principal themes are those of the sacrifice of the soldier dead for the living and the obligation of the living to sacrifice their individual purposes for the good of the group so that they, too, can perform their spiritual obligations.

Before proceeding to our analysis, let us say that the material for it was obtained by careful observation of the Memorial Day celebrations in Yankee City. A number of field people covered all aspects of the first ceremony studied. Participants were interviewed before, during, and after the ceremonies. What was said and done was observed and written down at the time the observations were made. Documents, including manuals of ritual, announcements of proceedings, and newspaper accounts were gathered.

The field work of the second year needed fewer observers, since it was used to check on the first year, fill in gaps, and determine how much the ceremony and the separate rites varied. While there were minor differences, they were of no significance —even the scores of speeches made during the two ceremonies varied so little that it would be difficult to distinguish parts of them. In other words, the form of the ritual was standardized and set for both the dramatic and oral rites.

World War II materials on Memorial Day have since been collected on several occasions and show little difference. New names have been added, minor changes in the procedure occur, the organizations vary slightly, but the basic form is the same. The same sentiments, values, beliefs, and rituals are presented. Perhaps the brief inclusion of women as *objects* of the ritual is the most marked difference. They, too, have their place in contemporary warfare.

The sacred symbolic behavior of Memorial Day in Yankee City, in which the whole town and scores of its organizations are involved, is ordinarily divided into four periods. During the year, in the first phase separate rituals are held by many of the associations for their dead, and many of these activities are connected with later Memorial Day events. In the second phase preparations are made during the last three or four weeks for the ceremony itself, and some of the associations perform public rituals. The third phase consists of the scores of rituals held in all the cemeteries, churches, and the halls of the various associations just before the final joint celebration of the entire city. These rituals consist of speeches and highly ceremonialized behavior. They last for two days and are climaxed by the fourth and last phase, in which all the celebrants gather in the center of the business district on the afternoon of Memorial Day. The separate organizations, with their members in uniform or with fitting insignia, march through the town, visit the shrines and monuments of the hero dead, and finally enter the cemetery. Here numbers of ceremonies are held, most of them highly symbolic and formalized.

The two or three weeks before the Memorial Day ceremonies are filled with elaborate preparations by each participating group. Meetings are held and patriotic pronouncements are sent to the local paper by the various organizations which announce what part the organization is to play in the total celebration. Some of the associations have Memorial Day processions, memorial services are conducted, the schools have patriotic programs, and the cemeteries are cleaned and repaired, graves are decorated by families and associations, and new gravestones erected. The merchants put up flags before their establishments and residents raise flags above their houses. Advertisements for wreaths, flowers, flags, and gravestones are prominently displayed in the paper. Some of the shop windows are filled with war relics connected with the experiences of local men and their families.

All these events are recorded in the local paper and most of them discussed by the town. The preparation of public opinion for an awareness of the importance of Memorial Day and the rehearsal of what is expected from each section of the community is carried out fully and in great detail. The latent sentiments of each individual, each family, each church, school, and association for its own dead are thereby stimulated and related to the sentiments for the dead of the nation.

A number of important events in all the ceremonies observed

occurred shortly before the Memorial Day ceremony. The John Cabot – Antony Cellini Post of the Veterans of Foreign Fields met to prepare for the ceremony. This organization, named for two Yankee City men killed in action, was composed of soldiers of World War I. Next day the local paper published an announcement by the officers to the men of this organization: "Veterans of Foreign Fields: The time has again come when every veteran should pause for a day to pay tribute to those men who, in serving our great republic, gave their lives in her defense. To this end you will assemble . . ." There followed instructions for the Memorial Day activities of the association's members. When the commander of the John Lathrop camp of the Sons of Union Veterans, an organization which also had a name of a local hero, issued "orders of the day" he said, "Brothers, you may neglect your duties to your organization for ordinary meetings, but Memorial Day is a holy day."

Meanwhile "six out of thirteen surviving members of the W. L. Robinson Post, 94, Grand Army of the Republic, were given a rousing welcome by the Rotarians at the customary pre-Memorial Day luncheon." The G.A.R. were symbols of a past and a crisis of the United States which everyone knew and felt, but no member of the audience had experienced. The chairman of the day told how Yankee City responded to Lincoln's call and of the "hundreds of thousands who had died as a living sacrifice for their country." He appealed to the members of Rotary to do their share "to make Memorial Day a holy day given over to things patriotic."

The members of the G.A.R., the youngest eighty-five and the oldest ninety-six, replied. One of them, Comrade Smith, spoke of "the stirring times following the firing upon Fort Sumter." He said he became acquainted with President Lincoln while stationed in Arlington as a colonel's orderly. "When the President called on the colonel it was my duty as orderly to escort the President inside. Lincoln was very democratic and did not think it beneath his dignity to shake hands with an ordinary private. I often shook the hand of the President."

The greatest symbol of the solidarity of the American Union, "the martyred President of that great crisis in American life," was thus made to seem near to Mr. Smith's listeners. The old man and his words were living symbols connecting the Rotarians to the dead past.

Another veteran of the Grand Army declared that it "would be a good thing if children in the schools today could be taught to remember love of country and obedience to law." He praised organizations such as the Rotary Club and said "it would be ideal if a committee was appointed to interview the school authorities with the view of stressing the need of patriotic teachings."

Meanwhile members of the American Legion had anticipated this suggestion, for they had made arrangements for members of their organization to give patriotic addresses the day before Poppy Day to all the public and parochial schools "to instruct the children in the principles of patriotism and to indoctrinate them with Good Americanism." Their speeches, too, referred to "our sacred dead and their sacrifice."

Numerous "memorial services" were conducted by men's and women's associations. The Yankee City *News* announced a few days previous to Poppy Day that "the annual memorial services of Michael Collins Circle, Daughters of Isabella, were held yesterday afternoon at three o'clock at St. Mary's cemetery. After the names of twenty-six deceased members were called by the chancellor a wreath was placed on each grave. Reverend John O'Malley, chaplain of the circle, offered prayer. There was a large gathering of members present at the services."

Several days before Poppy Day the former war mayor wrote to the *News*. He had a city-wide reputation for patriotism and for his unselfish services to the city and its soldiers in 1917–18. The letter, addressed to the commander of the local American Legion Post, was printed in the most prominent part of the front page:

Dear Commander:

The approaching Poppy Day brings to my mind a visit to the war zone in France on Memorial Day, 1925, reaching Belleau Wood at about eleven o'clock. On this sacred spot we left floral tributes in memory of our Yankee City boys—Jonathan Dexter and John Smith, who here had made the supreme sacrifice, that the principle that "might makes right" should not prevail.

At Hill 108 we picked the poppy I am sending you. At this

scene of desolation, poppies were growing as plentifully as daisies in New England and one could feel with McCrea the inspiration that caused him to write his famous lines.

With the memory of this visit, each recurring Poppy Day has a deeper significance to us.

I feel sure that our citizens will purchase poppies freely on Saturday of this week and that many will make generous cash contributions to the welfare fund of the post.

Three days later the newspaper in a front page editorial told its readers, "Next Saturday is the annual Poppy Day of the American Legion. Everybody responds cheerfully to this appeal . . . We ask for a generous response to this appeal." The editor concluded:

Everybody should wear a poppy on Poppy Day. Think back to those terrible days when the red poppy on Flanders fields symbolized the blood of our boys slaughtered for democracy. Remember Dexter and Smith killed at Belleau Wood. Remember O'Flaherty killed near Chateau Thierry, Stulavitz killed in the Bois d'Ormont, Kelley killed at Hill 288, Cote de Chatillon, Jones near the Bois de Montrebeaux, Kolnikap in the St. Mihiel offensive and the other brave boys who died in camp or on stricken fields. Remember the living boys of the Legion on Saturday.

The names of those killed represented most of the ethnic and religious groups of the community and all class levels. They included Polish, Russian, Irish, French Canadian, Italian, and Yankee names. The use of such names in this context emphasized the fact that the voluntary sacrifice of a citizen's life was equalitarian. They covered the top, middle, and bottom of the several classes. A front page appeal on the day following, signed by a committee of citizens, included names from all six classes, from all religious faiths, and from nine ethnic groups. Again no explicit reference was made to the selection of names, but the names were felt to be "representative," which meant that they represented the segmentary ethnic groups, all creeds and status levels of the community. The people were appealed to as "citizens," the most equalitarian of Yankee City terms—the democratic status from which men are taken to be transformed to the equally democratic status of soldier.

Poppy Day came the day after this appeal, on the Saturday

preceding Memorial Day Sunday. At that time red poppies are sold to the citizens by the American Legion. As everyone knows, the red poppy symbol is taken from John McCrea's poem, "In Flanders Fields." In this poem the author, a Canadian soldier who lost his life on the western front, first made the red poppy a symbol of the "blood sacrifice" made by the Allied soldiers in France. The poem, first published in *Punch*, gained immediate popularity. Now every Yankee City boy knows it and many have memorized it. It appears in most patriotic exercises in the schools.

The patriotic societies have taken over the symbol of the poppy for their own uses, but its significance is still dependent upon the poem. The cluster of contemporary meaning deeply embedded in the life of this society is found

> In Flanders fields [where] the poppies blow
> Between the crosses, row on row,
> That mark our place . . .
>
> We are the Dead. Short days ago
> We lived, felt dawn, saw sunset glow,
> Loved and were loved, and now we lie,
> In Flanders fields.
>
> Take up our quarrel with the foe:
> To you from failing hands we throw
> The torch; be yours to hold it high.
> If ye break faith with us who die
> We shall not sleep, though poppies grow
> In Flanders fields.

Many of the Legion in uniform, assisted by Boy Scouts and a corps of women aids, sold artificial poppies on the streets and in the business houses of the town. When interviewed, some of the Legionnaires expressed strong feelings of self-sacrifice and of obligation to help less fortunate comrades; some revived memories of former days; others regretted that the people too quickly forget their responsibilities to their soldiers. Unconsciously they all complained that the Yankee City people failed to respect them as soldiers as they once did during the war.

Significant selections from two interviews follow: "Sure, these poppies are for a very fine cause," one said, "you know all the money will be used for Yankee City disabled veterans. Why, I've been here since 5:30 this morning. Last year wasn't so good as the year before. People are beginning to forget, the public doesn't remember things very long. They ought to go into one of them hospitals and then they wouldn't forget so quick."

In the next interview we see the same emphasis on sacrifice expressed somewhat differently. "You see that big fellow across the street with all the medals on?" another inquired. "Well, he was hurt during the war, and he's in pretty bad state; he ought to be in a hospital himself. Last year in the parade he refused to stay at home and insisted on coming out and carrying the colors. In the middle of the parade he just fell down flat from sheer exhaustion. Luckily someone rushed out and just got the colors in time before they touched the ground, but you can't keep that fellow back."

About half the people purchased poppies, and almost all those who did wore them. Each thereby symbolically reminded all who passed of the impending Memorial Day ceremony and of its reference to the dead of the last and previous wars.

The Church and the Military Altars of Sacrifice

The topic for Sunday morning services was the meaning of Memorial Day to the people of Yankee City, as citizens and Christians. We can present excerpts from the sermons of only one Memorial Day to show their main themes, but recorded observations of sermons and other Memorial Day behavior before and since World War II show no differences in the principal themes expressed. Indeed, although twenty years have passed some of these words seem interchangeable. The Reverend Hugh McKellar chose as his text "Be thou faithful until death."

He said,

Memorial Day is a day of sentiment, and when it loses that it loses all its value. We are all conscious of the danger of losing that sentiment. It was that spirit which led the Pilgrims to suffer that a nation might be born, and it led the boys in blue and gray to suffer that a nation might be kept together.

What we need today is more sacrifice, for there can be no progress or achievement without sacrifice. There are too many out today preaching selfishness. The boys of '61 and '65 had the spirit of sacrifice, sacrifice is necessary to a noble living. In the words of Our Lord, "Whosoever shall save his life shall lose it and whosoever shall lose his life in My name, shall save it." It is only those who sacrifice personal gain and will to power and personal ambition who ever accomplish anything for their nation. Those who expect to save the nation will not get wealth and power for themselves.

Memorial Day is a religious day, the day of sweetest memories. It is a day when we get a vision of the unbreakable brotherhood and unity of spirit which exists and still exists no matter what race or creed or color, in a country where all men have equal rights.

It is better to let the soldiers' graves go unnoticed rather than scatter them with flowers of hypocrisy, for the only way to venerate them is to imitate them. [Here he quoted from the end of the Gettysburg Address.] We too must rededicate ourselves to the high ideals for which they died; that is the spiritual test for us today. Memorial Day is above all a spiritual day. We must acquire the devotion of the boys of the Blue and the boys of the Gray.[1]

The field worker filed out with the rest of the congregation. An old gentleman told him that attendance at church was falling off. "Yes," he said, "there are not so many of the old New Englanders. It's these new foreigners who have come in that have spoiled it. That's what cuts down our church attendance. But there are some good foreigners. It's good once in a while to get a mixture of good fine stock, especially from northern Europe, especially from Scotland. You know Scotland is the place where John Knox came from, who started Presbyterianism."

The minister of the Congregational Church spoke with the voice of the Unknown Soldier to emphasize his message of sacrifice. After the congregation sang "Faith of Our Fathers

---

1. Quotations of sermons and speeches in this section are from notes taken on the scene by a field staff of seventeen persons, also written materials supplied in some instances by the participants.

Living Still" the minister preached his sermon, entitled "The Voice of the Unknown Soldier."

It brings tears to our eyes when we see the groups of the Grand Army of the Republic as they decorate the graves of their comrades for it brings to our memory those who gave full measure of life as a sacrifice to preserve the Union. All those who died for liberty and democracy in '61 and '17 speak to us on this day of memory, and of all these nothing speaks as loud as the voice of the Unknown Soldier.

If the spirit of the Unknown Soldier should speak, what would be his message? What would be the message of a youth I knew myself who might be one of the unknown dead? He didn't want to go. He had a home and family, good position, happy prospects, and a sweetheart. I married him on the day he left. A few weeks later he was sent to France. No news for months and then a returned officer told how the youth had just delivered a message under fire and had not stopped to rest when he was struck by a shell. If he could be that Unknown Soldier in Arlington Cemetery I wonder what he would say. I believe he would speak as follows: "It is well to remember us today, who gave our lives that democracy might live. We know something of the sacrifice." If we, the living, only knew the meaning of that blood-washed word "sacrifice" we would use it less freely.

A quotation from the Unitarian minister will be sufficient to introduce the other theme stressed in the Sunday church services. The subject, "Patriotism and Religion," was attacked in a scholarly manner. "The purpose of this sermon is to discover if religion and patriotism conflict. The text of the sermon is 'Render unto Caesar that which is Caesar's and unto God the things that are God's.' " This minister concluded that "religion and patriotism do not conflict when there is real patriotism."

The first two ministers in different language express the same theme of sacrifice of the individual for national and democratic principles. One introduces Divine sanction for this sacrificial belief and thereby succeeds in emphasizing the theme that the loss of an individual's life rewards him with life eternal. The other uses one of our greatest and most hallowed symbols of democracy and the only very powerful one to come out of World War I: the Unknown Soldier. The American Unknown Soldier is Everyman of the mystery plays. He is the perfect symbol of equalitarianism. The third minister showed that there is no difference between true patriotism and true religion. There were many more Memorial Sunday sermons, most of which had these same themes. Many of them added the point that Christ had given his life for all (see chapter 13, "Sacrifice, Suicide, and Tragedy").

That afternoon in the cemeteries, at the memorial stones named for Yankee City dead and in the lodge halls and churches, a large number of rites were celebrated. One was held at a memorial monument on Newtown Common. It was supervised by the Sons of Union Veterans. Another, led by one of the Catholic orders, was in the Catholic cemetery. Two others were in the Homeville Graveyard, one held by the United Spanish War Veterans, the other by the Elks for their dead.

The Newtown monument consists of a gateway and two marble walls with the names of all the Union veterans from Yankee City written in bronze on the walls. Over the names is the legend, "Soldiers and Sailors of Yankee City." Near by is a statue of the "Returned Soldier." The speaker took his position in front of the gateway. To his right men in the uniforms of several associations stood with their guns at rest; to the speaker's left, facing the men, were uniformed women with the flags of their various women's organizations. At the extreme left and in the roadway in front of the tablet two G.A.R. veterans in uniform sat in a closed car with a son of a veteran as driver. The commander of the Sons of Union Veterans started the ceremony. He said, "This service here today is in memory of the G.A.R. We have it every year."

He was followed by a local minister.

We are gathered at this shrine today in memory of the Grand Army. As we come here to these tablets with the quota from Yankee City inscribed upon them, it is a privilege and a fitting thing to do to recall the significance of the names here and what our forefathers did.

There is one underlying principle more responsible for war than anything else. It was this that killed so many men, wounded so many others. It is in three letters, sin, an inevitable principle that never can be evaded. Within sin lies its own punishment. Every sin must be atoned for. The nation had been sinning. Since the nation had sinned it was inevitable that sin must be atoned for.

Lincoln recognized the sin of the nation. Lincoln was one of the greatest men who ever lived. He said that if God so willed, if the war lasted until every cent of money had been spent and every drop of blood in the veins of the people within the nation were shed, yet the judgments of the Lord were trüe and righteous altogether.

We come to these tablets with the names of the men who went forth from Yankee City, those who were with God and who believed in the sovereignty of the nation. God intended the nation to be preserved for greater things, for the Spanish War, for the World War.

If we could all visit the battlefields where men died for their country, we would see for ourselves the scenes of their great deeds. If, like me, you could go to Gettysburg, where men have died and where I went and where my father's battery smashed the flower of the Confederacy, then as I did, you would know about the carrying on of those men, how they fought and bled and died. The deeds of our forefathers are a legacy bequeathed to the community. Memorial Day commemorates what has been done so that the peace of God and righteousness shall triumph.

A prayer addressed to "Our Father" followed: "We thank thee for our fathers, for all they did and wrought. We must accept the legacy from their bleeding hands, not for war but for peace and so these organizations gathered here dedicated to the service of those men will work together for love and country.

A squad of four with a man in charge stopped in front of the statue of the Civil War veteran and fired three volleys. The women placed wreaths and flowers over the tablets. Taps were blown by a Boy Scout and answered from the woods by another Boy Scout. The chaplain pronounced benediction.

The Elks' ceremony presents ample evidence that the Memorial Day ceremony has ceased to be Decoration Day to recognize the soldier dead of the Civil War and has become the sacred day for all the dead. The Elks' service clearly indicates the fear that death obliterates the individual. It also shows how some Yankee City people reassure themselves.

The Elks' memorial service was held at Elks Rest at the Homeville Cemetery. In the center of a group were two standards, one bearing a purple flag with the name and number of the Yankee City lodge and the other the lodge insignia. In line with these two standards stood a flag-bearer with the American flag. Attention was given to the graves of all deceased members.

The speaker was an Elk from a nearby town.

Ladies and gentlemen, we are gathered here today at a hallowed spot in what has often been termed God's Acre. Elkdom, my friends, is the fairest flower that blooms in the gardens of fraternalism. The Elk who lives his Elkdom is bound to be a good man, he cannot be otherwise. Elks being human stumble along through life about like other folks, and when an Elk falls down he usually falls uphill. When he gets up he is on higher ground than before.

Savant and savage are equally dumb before the question: If a man die, shall he live again? No traveller has ever returned with maps or field notes of a life beyond the grave. The marvelous thing about it is that, despite the fact, all of us or almost all of us believe in the life hereafter. It is the universal belief of mankind, a belief that never had to be taught us, we just naturally believe it.

We have every reason to believe that we will see and know our dear dead brothers again. The extinction of the psychic entities is unthinkable, unbelievable, unnatural.

Wreaths were ceremoniously placed on the graves within the Elks Post enclosure.

While the Elks' ritual was being conducted, members of the Homeville United Spanish War Veterans gathered at the entrance of the cemetery waiting for the rest of their group to join them. They marched in parade from the gate of St. Joseph's Cemetery to a ceremonial grave where the veterans and women gathered. The ceremony that took place was in part read from the ritual book of the Spanish War Veterans. The speaker said,

The purpose of this ceremony is to honor those who preceded us to the land of the dead. This is the true patriotic day of the nation when the children of these men honor their fathers, the flag, and all for which the flag stands—bravery, glory, courage of people. It is fitting that the men who sleep beneath the flag of the Union should have graves decked with flowers in remembrance of this trying period of suffering and sorrow which molded this nation. This was in the cause of liberty and of God. It is only right that we quicken the memories of the dead. It is our purpose to preserve and protect Memorial Day. In times of peace it is the duty of us as citizens to defend the flag and fulfill the patriotism of those who preceded us.

This was followed by an order from the post commander to stand at attention. Lincoln's Gettysburg Address was read. This rite and all others in the Memorial Day ceremonies seemed to strive for the perfection of feeling they believed Lincoln expressed when he dedicated the Gettysburg cemetery as a national monument. The speaker intoned Lincoln's words as if they were a religious chant.

After the ceremony this group joined others at the Baptist Church for the Vacant Chair ceremony, which took place late Sunday afternoon. The chief participants, including men of the G.A.R., the minister, and representatives of the Sons of Union Veterans, were on the platform, which was decorated with Memorial Day flowers. The commander of the G.A.R. was escorted to his place of honor.

There were four vacant chairs in a line at the front of the altar. Each had an American flag with a card on which was written the name of the G.A.R. veteran who had died during the year. Flags or banners of the several associations were displayed. At the center in front of the altar was a bivouac of four guns, each representing one of the dead. The pastor, as a son of a veteran, wore a medal. A woman played sacred music; the commander came forward and asked the women representatives of auxiliary organizations to rise and grasp their flags in their right hands. General John A. Logan's General Orders No. 11, which initiated Memorial Day, were read.

The 30th day of May, 1868, is designated for the purpose of strewing with flowers or otherwise decorating the graves of comrades who died in defense of their country during the late rebellion, and whose bodies now lie in almost every city, village, hamlet, and church-yard in the land. . . .

We are organized, comrades, as our regulations tell us, for the purpose, among other things, "of preserving and strengthening those kind and fraternal feelings which have bound together the soldiers, sailors, and marines who united together to suppress the late rebellion." What can aid more to assure this result than by cherishing tenderly the memory of our heroic dead. . . . We should guard their graves with sacred vigilance. . . .

Let us, then, at the time appointed, gather around their sacred remains, and garland the passionless mounds above them with the choicest flowers of spring-time; let us raise above them the dear old flag they saved from dishonor; let us, in this solemn presence, renew our pledges to aid and assist those whom they have left among us. . . .

The Vacant Chair ceremony was an imitation of military exercises. When the minister prayed, both hands were placed on the Bible, his eyes were closed, and the audience lowered their heads in reverent attitudes. Everything was said in a ceremonial tone. A woman cried quietly. The minister prayed,

Father, we bow before Thee in this sacred place, sacred because of dedication and because Thou art here. We come to this service not with cheer and joy but because chairs once occupied are now vacant. We come today honoring those who lived valiantly, to take notice of their service and now that the ranks are thinned by death, bless those that remain with us. Thy blessing on the remnants of the Grand Army of the Republic. Bless those organizations that tomorrow will be decorating the last resting-places of their comrades who have passed.

The commander announced the Gettysburg Address. The brother introduced his reading by saying, "We have present today here on the platform one who has seen and talked as a great friend with Lincoln. I wish I could bring to your minds a greater vision of that great man who saved the Union, as he stood on that battlefield and made that great though short speech, it was only 264 words." He quoted the Gettysburg Address in full ceremonial tone. His voice filled with emotion when he said,

It is for us the living, . . . to be here dedicated to the great task remaining before us—that from these honored dead we take increased devotion to that cause for which they gave the last full measure of devotion—that we here highly resolve that these dead shall not have died in vain—that this nation, under God, shall have a new birth of freedom—and that government of the people, by the people, for the people, shall not perish from the earth.

When the speaker reached the phrase "from these honored dead" he spread his arms out to include the four vacant chairs before him, making his words immediate and personal for the group. After completing Lincoln's address he asked, "Is patriotism dead? Why aren't these pews all filled?" He turned to the minister and said, "A few years ago there would have been crowds here and now there are few. Isn't that right, Mr. Commander? Is patriotism dead? No, it isn't dead, it is sleeping. May we promise Thee, our Country, that our youth will not be exposed to pernicious influences, that the present evils will be overcome. Grant, oh God, that we may perform our duty. Amen."

When he had finished, the commander addressed the adjutant and said, "Adjutant, for what purpose is this meeting called?" "For faith and to respect the honored dead." He was asked whether he had records of the men. The names and the complete records of the soldiers who had died were read. As soon as the name of a dead veteran was called a little girl put a wreath and a bouquet of white flowers over the flag on the chair. A Boy Scout "rolled" the drum three times after each record had been read. At the end the commander said, "The records are honorable and there is a place for the record in the archives of the Post."

Then the commander said, "We will now hear a few words from the Commander of the G.A.R." The old man was helped to the front of the stage. He grasped the pulpit firmly to support himself.

I'm not much of a public speaker. I'm just a veteran. I consider Lincoln the greatest man the world has ever produced. I met him and became quite familiar with him, even shook hands with him. He was a very common man, not too proud to meet and know any one. Very plain, not what the ladies call a handsome man. I'm ninety-one, and I'm not feeling very well. I lost two of my closest friends the last year. Ralph Aiken was a good friend of mine, he was the best natured man in town, always good natured, Tom Alison was a very old friend. I remember them. I have no more to say.

After a song entitled "The Vacant Chair" an address by the Reverend James was announced.

We come to pay tribute to these men whose chairs are vacant, not because they were eminent men, as many soldiers were not, but the tribute we pay is to their attachment to the great cause. We are living in the most magnificent country on the face of the globe, a country planted and fertilized by a Great Power, a power not political or economic but religious and educational, especially in the North. In the South they had settlers who were there in pursuit of gold, in search of El Dorado, but the North was settled by people seeking religious principles and education.

Our grandfathers held united and inviolate a great nation so our duty is to perpetuate the great religious forces of the world. Those who delve into the philosophy of history, as Lincoln did in the Gettysburg Address, discover that God has maintained this nation to be the prophet of the world.

Throughout all the ceremonies held in Yankee City on Memorial Day the survivors of the G.A.R. were treated as spiritual beings and there was definite pressure on them to fit into a spiritual setting as symbols, rather than representing their ordinary lives. When the commander of the G.A.R. spoke he was introduced, not so much as a G.A.R. man or the commander of the Post, but as one who had known Lincoln, a man who had a very high spiritual place because he was identified with the great symbol, Lincoln; the relationship with the "martyred President" was stressed rather than that with the President or the man Lincoln.

On Monday morning, Memorial Day, further ceremonies were held in the graveyards, around war relics and other symbols of death in war and battle. These ceremonies took place in the cemeteries and before monuments to the soldier dead.

At one of them the principal speaker, standing before a tablet covered with the names of war dead, declared that when "things are going to pieces, in these days when the grafter is honored, it is heartening to know that eternal values are still reverenced." He then talked about Washington and Lincoln and their greatness. "Our great institutions of learning would not have let them in because they did not possess the proper qualifications, and yet we know now that Washington and Lincoln had acquired something that made them great." He said no character except the Carpenter of Nazareth had ever been honored the way Washington had been in New England. Virtue, freedom from sin, and righteousness were qualities possessed by Washing and Lincoln, and in possessing these characteristics both were true Americans, and "as Sons of Union Veterans we would do well to emulate them. Let us first be true Americans. From these our friends beneath the sod we receive their message, 'Carry on.' Men may come and go but the cause will live; though the speaker will die the fire and spark will carry on. Thou are not conqueror, Death, and thy pale flag is not advancing."

In all the services of the third phase the same themes were used in the speeches—most of them in ritualized, oratorical language—or in the ceremonials themselves. Washington, the father of his country, first in war and peace, had devoted his life not to himself but to his country. Lincoln (the most important symbol) had given his own life, sacrificed on the altar of his country. Most of the speeches implied or explicitly stated that Divine guidance was involved and that these mundane affairs had supernatural implications. They stated that the revered dead had given the last ounce of devotion in following the ideals of Lincoln and the Unknown Soldier. They declared these same principles must guide us, the living; that we too must sacrifice ourselves to these same ideals.

The beliefs and values of which they spoke referred to a world beyond the natural. Their references were to the supernatural.

The Parade: Ritual Link between the Dead and the Living

The parade, the fourth and final phase of the Memorial Day celebration, formed near the river in the business district. Hundreds of people gathered to watch the various uniformed groups march to their positions. They were dressed in their best. Crowds were along the whole route. The cemeteries were carefully prepared for the event.

The cemeteries had been repaired, cleaned, and decorated for

Memorial Day. The grass was cut, the weeds burned, the hedges and bushes trimmed and shaped. Thousands of people had placed their flowers on "the graves of loved ones" and departed; others were continually coming and going to decorate the graves. Yellow flags with a green wreath had been placed on members' graves by the Yankee City Knights of Columbus. American flags with a star indicated the post of the Grand Army of the Republic. The Elks had blue and white flags in a round plaque. American flags in oval plaques had been placed by the Massachusetts State Guard. A St. Andrews cross was on the graves of the Massachusetts Catholic Order of Foresters. The Yankee City Fire Department also had a St. Andrews cross, with an iron base. The Ladies of the G.A.R. had placed an American flag with a plaque; the Women's Relief Corps a St. Andrews cross with a bow of red, white, and blue ribbon. A gilt crown and cross marked the Daughters of Isabella. The American flag and cross marked "U.S.A. and Cuba" with a red and yellow ribbon marked the graves of members of the camp of United Spanish War Veterans. The Moose had plaques; the American Legion had American flags with decorated plaques.

For one day the cemeteries were a place for all the living and all the dead, and for this one day the bright-colored flowers and gaudy flags gave them almost a gay appearance. Death declared a holiday, not for itself but for the living, when together they could experience it and momentarily challenge its ultimate power.

The people marched through the town to the cemeteries. The various organizations spread throughout the several sections of the graveyards and rites were performed. In the Greek quarter ceremonies were held; others were performed in the Polish and Russian sections; the Boy Scouts held a memorial rite for their departed; the Sons and Daughters of Union Veterans went through a ritual, as did the other men's and women's organizations. All this was part of the parade in which everyone from all parts of the community could and did participate.

The Veterans of Foreign Fields, led by their drum corps, marched through the cemetery to the farther end to the "Greek quarter." The bands played until all the organizations were in the cemetery; then the drum beat. The Legion stood at attention by the grave of "an unknown soldier" while it played "Nearer My God to Thee." A large memorial stone said "The unknown of '61 and '65; W.R.C. of 1909."

Near the end of the day all the men's and women's organizations assembled about the roped-off grave of General Fredericks. The Legion band played. A minister prayed. The ceremonial leader of the Sons of Union Veterans spoke.

We meet to honor those who fought, but in so doing we honor ourselves. From them we learn a lesson of sacrifice and devotion and of accountability to God and honor. We have an inspiration for the future today—our character is strengthened—this day speaks of a better and greater devotion to our country and to all that our flag represents.

Our flag, may we see thee, love thee, and live thee. Our country, may we see thee, love thee, and live thee. Let the flag be an inspiration that our youth may not be subject to pernicious influences. Washington and Betsy Ross created our flag out of a few strips of cloth. May we honor it as the emblem of our country.

A member of the Ladies of the G.A.R. laid a wreath on General Fredericks' grave, speaking of the "undying devotion of General Fredericks, from the Ladies of the G.A.R." Directly after this she bent down and untied a basket she had been carrying and gave it to a child. The child recited a short poem about peace, beauty, and devotion. She opened the basket, releasing a snow-white dove which flew directly across the grave into a tall tree. This, according to the child speaker, symbolized peace and duty; others said it was the spirit of the dead. The band played and a benediction was given by a minister.

After the several ceremonies in the Elm Hill cemetery the parade re-formed and marched back to town, where it broke up. The firing squad of the Legion stopped at the front entrance of the cemetery and fired three salutes and a bugler blew taps. This was "a general salute for all the dead in the cemetery." The Auxiliary of the Legion gave a luncheon for the Legion and the W.R.C. and the Women of the G.A.R. had a lunch prepared for the G.A.R. and the Boy Scouts. At the luncheons the conversation was about "old times," and memories of men long dead were revived. The band played "old-time favorites."

A brief resume of the principal points stressed in the several phases of the ceremony brings out some basic facts to be remembered before we begin the interpretation.

The most widely used symbols, which appeared in many of the rites, were: Washington, Lincoln, his Gettysburg speech, McCrae's "Flanders Fields," the Unknown Soldier, the Gettysburg and Arlington cemeteries, the local cemeteries, and the dead themselves.

The dedication speech of the Gettysburg battlefield as a national cemetery supplies a prototype for all Memorial Day rites held throughout the country. Excerpts from it occur in many of the addresses. Lincoln and Washington have become national symbols which embody the values, virtues, and ideals of American democracy. The Unknown Soldier in Arlington Cemetery is a symbol referring to all soldiers who are dead. McCrae's poem states in symbolic language what the people feel about the war deaths of 1917–18. As a principal symbol of that war it bears many resemblances to Lincoln's Gettysburg speech. Each was written by a man who died for his country. Each stresses the sacrifice of the dead for the living. Each declares that the living must rededicate themselves to the principles for which the dead gave their lives.

The symbolic acts and ceremonial speeches which compose the ceremony have a number of fundamental themes, chief of which is that the soldier dead sacrificed their lives for their country. The dead are all one and equal before the eyes of men and God. They voluntarily offered their lives that their country might live, and in so doing they did not lose their lives but saved them forever. The principles for which they died must be defended by those now living, and the sacrifices of the soldiers oblige everyone to remember these sacred principles by embodying them in deed and thought and by performing the Memorial Day rites as a visible testimonial of their significance to the living.

Throughout the Memorial Day rites we see people who are religiously divided as Protestant, Catholic, Jewish, and Greek Orthodox participating in a common ritual in a graveyard with their common dead. Their sense of autonomy was present and expressed in the separate ceremonies, but the parade and unity of doing everything at one time emphasized the oneness of the total group.

The full significance of the unifying and integrative character of the Memorial Day ceremony and the increasing convergence of the multiple and diverse events through the several stages into a single unit, where the many become one and all the living participants unite in the one community of the dead, is best seen in Chart 6. It will be noticed at the top of the figure that the horizontal extension represents space and the vertical dimension time. The four stages of the ceremony are listed on the left side, the arrows at the bottom converging and ending in the cemetery. The longer and wider area at the top with the several well-scattered rectangles represents the time and space diversities of Stage I; the closely connected

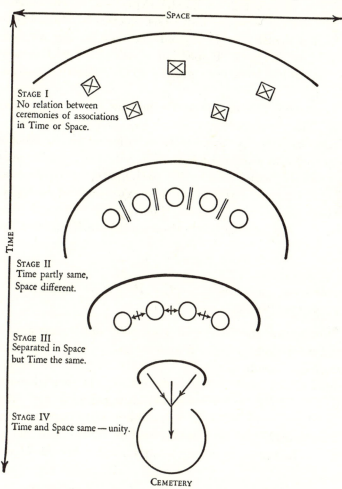

CHART 6. Progress of the Memorial Day Ceremony

circles in Stage III show the greater integration achieved by this time.

During Stage I, in the earlier part of the year, it will be recalled that there is no synchronization of rituals. They occur in each association without reference to each other. All are separate and diverse in time and space. The symbolic references of the ceremonies emphasize their separateness. In general, this stage is characterized by high diversity and there is little unity in purpose, time, or space.

Although the ceremonies of the organizations in Stage II, shortly before Memorial Day, are still separate, they are felt to be within the bounds of the general community organization. There is still the symbolic expression of diversity, but now diversity in a larger unity (see chart). In Stage III there are still separate ceremonies but the time during which they are held is the same. Inspection of the chart will show that time and space have been greatly limited since the period of Stage I.

The ceremonies in Stage IV become one in time and in space. The representatives of all groups are unified into one procession. Thereby organizational diversity is symbolically integrated into a unified whole. This is not necessarily realized in a conscious way by those who participate, but they certainly feel it. This period is the symbolic expression of diversity integrated into a unified whole. The chart is designed to symbolize the progressive integration and symbolic unification of the group.

Lincoln—an American Collective Representation Made by and for the People

Throughout the Memorial Day ceremony there were continual references to Lincoln and his Gettysburg Address. The symbol of Lincoln obviously was of deep significance in the various rituals and to the participants. He loomed over the memorial rituals like some great demigod over the rites of classical antiquity. What is the meaning of the myth of Lincoln to Americans? Why does his life and death as conceived in the myth of Lincoln play such a prominent part in Memorial Day?

Some of the answers are obvious. He was a great war President. He was President of the United States and was assassinated during the Civil War. Memorial Day grew out of this war. A number of other facts about his life might be added, but for our present purposes the meaning of Lincoln the myth is more important than the objective facts of his life career.

Lincoln, product of the American prairies, sacred symbol of idealism in the United States, myth more real than the man himself—symbol and fact—was formed in the flow of events which composed the changing cultures of the Middle West. He is the symbolic culmination of America. To understand him is to know much of what America means. [121]

In 1858, when Lincoln ran against Stephen Douglas for the United States Senate, he was Abraham Lincoln the successful lawyer, the railroad attorney noted throughout the State of Illinois as a man above common ability and of more than common importance. He was an ex-congressman. He was earning a substantial income. He had married a daughter of the upper class from Kentucky. His friends were W. D. Green, the president of a railway, a man of wealth; David Davis, a representative of wealthy eastern investors in western property, who was on his way to becoming a millionaire; Jesse Fell, railway promoter; and other men of prominence and prestige in the state. Lincoln dressed like them; he had unlearned many of the habits acquired in childhood and had learned most of the ways of the highly placed men who were now his friends. After the Lincoln-Douglas debates his place as a man of prestige and power was as high as anyone's in the whole state.

Yet in 1860 when he was nominated on the Republican ticket for the presidency of the United States, he suddenly became "Abe Lincoln, the rail-splitter," "the rude man from the prairie and the river-bottoms." To this was soon added "Honest Abe," and finally in death "the martyred leader" who gave his life that "a nation dedicated to the proposition that all men are created equal" might long endure.

What can be the meaning of this strange transformation?

When Richard Oglesby arrived at the Republican Convention in 1860 he cast about for a slogan that would bring his friend Lincoln favorable recognition from the shrewd politicians of New York, Pennsylvania, and Ohio. He heard from

Jim Hanks, who knew Lincoln as a boy, that Lincoln had once split fence rails. Dick Oglesby, knowing what appeals were most potent in getting the support of politicians and in bringing out a favorable vote, dubbed Lincoln "the rail-splitter." Fence rails were prominently displayed at the convention to symbolize Lincoln's lowly beginnings. Politicians, remembering the great popular appeal of "Old Hickory," "Tippecanoe and Tyler too," and the "log cabin and cider jug" of former elections, realized this slogan would be enormously effective in a national election. Lincoln the rail-splitter was reborn in Chicago in 1860; and the Lincoln who had become the successful lawyer, intimate of wealthy men, husband of a well-born wife, and man of status was conveniently forgotten.

Three dominant symbolic themes compose the Lincoln image. The first, the theme of the common man, was fashioned in a form pre-established by the equalitarian ideals of a new democracy; to common men there could be no argument about what kind of a man a rail-splitter is.

"From log cabin to the White House" succinctly symbolizes the second theme of the triad which composes Lincoln, the most powerful of American collective representations. This phrase epitomizes the American success story, the rags-to-riches *motif*, and the ideals of the ambitious. As the equal of all men, Lincoln was the representative of the common man, both as his spokesman and his kind; now, as the man who had gone "from the log cabin to the White House," he became the superior man, who had not inherited but earned that superior status and thereby proved to everyone that all men could do as he had. Lincoln thereby symbolized the two great collective but antithetical ideals of American democracy.

When he was assassinated a third powerful theme of our Christian society was added to the symbol here being created by Americans to strengthen and adorn the keystone of their national symbol structure. Lincoln's life lay sacrificed on the altar of unity, climaxing a deadly war which by its successful termination pronounced that the country was one and that all men are created equal. From the day of his death thousands of sermons and speeches have demonstrated that Lincoln, like Christ, died that all men might live and be as one in the sight of God and man. Christ died that this might be true forever here and beyond the earth; Lincoln sacrificed his life that this might be true forever on this earth.

When Lincoln died, the imaginations of the people of the eastern seaboard cherished him as the man of the new West and translated him into their hopes for tomorrow—for to them the West was tomorrow. The defeated people of the South, during and after the Reconstruction period, fitted him into their dark reveries of what might have been, had this man lived who loved all men. In their bright fantasies, the people of the West, young and believing only in the tomorrow they meant to create, knew Lincoln for what they wanted themselves to be. Lincoln, symbol of equalitarianism, of the social striving of men who live in a social hierarchy—the human leader sacrificed for all men—expresses all the basic values and beliefs of Yankee City and of the United States of America.

Lincoln, the superior man, above all men, yet equal to each, is a mystery beyond the logic of individual calculators. He belongs to the culture and to the social logics of the people for whom contradiction is unimportant and for whom the ultimate tests of truth are in the social structure in which, and for which, they live. Through the passing generations of our Christian culture the Man of the Prairies, formed in the mold of the God-man of Galilee and apotheosized into the man-god of the American people, each year less profane and more sacred, moves securely toward identification with deity and ultimate godhood. In him Americans realize themselves.

A problem of even greater difficulty confronts us in why war provides such a powerful context for the creation of powerful national symbols such as Lincoln, Washington, or Memorial Day. Durkheim gives us a first important theoretical lead. He believes that the members of the tribe felt and became aware of their own group identity when they gathered periodically during times of plenty. It was then that social interaction was most intense and these feelings most stimulated.

In modern society interaction, social solidarity, and intensity of feeling ordinarily are greatest in times of war. It would seem likely that such periods might well produce new sacred forms built, of course, on the foundations of old beliefs. Let us examine the life of American communities in wartime as possible matrices for such developments.

The Effect of War on the Community

The most casual survey supplies ample evidence that the effects of war are most varied and diverse as reflected in the life of American towns. The immediate effect is very great on some towns and very minor on others.

In the average town the institutional life is modified, new experiences are felt by the people, and the townsmen repeatedly modify their behavior to adapt to new circumstances brought them by the events of a war. These modifications do not cause social breakdown; the contrary is true. War activities strengthen the integration of many small communities. The people are more systematically organized into groups where everyone is involved and in which there is an intense awareness of oneness. A town's unity and feeling of autonomy are strengthened by competition in war activities with neighboring communities.

It is in time of war that the average American living in small cities and towns gets his deepest satisfactions as a member of his society. Despite the disheartening events of 1917, the year when the United States entered World War I, the people derived deep satisfaction from it, just as they did from the last war. It is a mistake to believe that the American people, particularly small-towners, hate war to such an extent that they derive no satisfaction from it. Verbally and superficially they disapprove of war, but at best this only partly reveals their deeper feelings. In simpler terms, their observed behavior reveals that most of them had more real satisfaction out of World War II, just as in the previous one, than in any other period of their lives. The various men's and women's organizations, instead of inventing things to do to keep busy, could choose among activities which they knew were vital both to them and to others.

The small-towner then had a sense of significance about himself, about those around him, and about events, in a way that he never felt before (the same was true in 1917–18). The young man who quit high school during the depression to lounge on the street corner and who was known to be of no consequence to himself or to anyone else in the community became a seasoned veteran fighting somewhere in the South Pacific—a man obviously with the qualities of a hero (it was believed), willing to give up his life for his country, since he was in its military forces. He and everyone else were playing, and knew they were playing, a significant role in the crisis. Everyone was in it. There was a feeling of unconscious well-being—a euphoria—because everyone was doing something to help in the common desperate enterprise in a cooperative rather than in a private spirit. This feeling is often the unconscious equivalent of what people mean when they gather to celebrate and sing "Hail, Hail, the Gang's All Here." It also has something of the deep significance that enters into people's lives only in moments of tragedy.

The strong belief that everyone must sacrifice to win a war greatly strengthens people's sense of their significance. Everyone gives up something for the common good—money, food, tires, scrap, automobiles, or blood for blood banks. All is contributed under the basic ideology of common sacrifice for the good of the country. These simple acts of giving by all individuals in the town, by all families, associations, schools, churches, and factories, are given strong additional emotional support by the common knowledge that some of the local young men are representing the town in the military forces of the country. It is known that some of them may be killed. They are sacrificing their lives, it is believed, that their country may live. Therefore, all acts of individual giving to help win the war, no matter how small, are made socially significant and add to the strength of the social structure by being treated as sacrifices. The collective effect of these small renunciations, in general belief, is to lessen the number of those who must die on the altars of their country.

Another very strong integrative factor that strengthens the social structure of the small town and city is that petty internal antagonisms are drained out of the group onto the common enemy. The local antagonisms which customarily divide and separate people are largely suppressed. The feelings and psychic energies involved, normally expended in local feuds, are vented on the hated symbols of the enemy. The local ethnic groups, often excluded from participation in community affairs, are given an honored place in the war effort, and symbols of unity are stressed rather than separating differences. The religious groups and churches tend to emphasize the oneness of the common striving rather than allowing their differing theologies and competitive financing to keep them in opposing groups. The strongest pressure to compose their differences is applied to management and labor (the small number of strikes is eloquent proof of the effectiveness of such pressure). A common hate of a common enemy, when organized in community activities to express this basic emotion, provides the most powerful mechanism to energize the lives of the towns and to strengthen their feelings of unity. Those who believe that a war's hatreds can bring only evil to psychic life might well ponder the therapeutic and satisfying effects on the minds of people who turn their once private hatreds into social ones and join their townsmen and countrymen in the feeling of sharing this basic emotion in common symbols. Enemies as well as friends should be well chosen, for they must serve as objects for the expression of two emotions basic to man and his social system—hatred and love.

The American Legion and other patriotic organizations give form to the effort to recapture the feelings of well-being when the society was most integrated and feelings of unity most intense. The membership comes from every class, creed, and nationality, for the soldiers came from all of them.

Only an infinitesimal number of associations is sufficiently large and democratic in action to include in their membership men or women from all class levels, all religious faiths, and most, if not all, ethnic groups. Their number could easily be counted on the fingers of one hand. Most prominent among them are the patriotic associations, all of them structural developments from wars which involved the United States. The American Legion is a typical example of the patriotic type. Less than 6 per cent of the several hundred associations include members from all classes. Of the remaining 94 per cent, approximately half have representatives from only three classes or less than three. Although the associations which include members from all levels of the community are surprisingly few, those which stress in action as well as in words such other principles of democracy as the equality of races, nationalities, and religions are even fewer. Only 5 per cent of the associations are composed of members from the four religious faiths—Protestant, Catholic, Jewish, and Greek Orthodox—and most of their members came from the lower ranks of the society.

Most prominent among them was the American Legion. Why should this organization, sometimes accused of being intolerant and hostile to the opinions of variant groups, occupy this democratic position? The answer lies in the social context in which it was created. The American Legion, born of the experiences of the soldiers of World War I, is an organized effort to maintain "for all time" the values experienced by those who have participated in war. The G.A.R., the Sons of Union Veterans, and the Spanish War Veterans are similar products of earlier wars. The Sons of Union Veterans, a nonmilitary group, testifies to the fact that war experiences are not just those of soldiers but of everyone in the community.

Furthermore, in functioning to maintain the values of a war experienced in battle by very few of its members, the Legion demonstrates, as does the whole system of the cult, that something more is involved than the formation of an organization of soldiers.

The intense feeling of belonging, the satisfaction of facing death collectively and conquering its fear, and the sense of well-being and euphoria which war engenders contribute to the wish to maintain its effects in peacetime. In our efforts to accomplish this we organize associations which emphasize the democratic dogmas and create cults which dramatically re-express the feeling of past wars.

Just as the totemic symbol system of the Australians represents the idealized clan, and the African ancestral worship symbolizes the family and state, so Memorial Day rites symbolize and express the sentiments of the people for the total community and the state. But in so doing, the separate values and ideas of various parts of the community are also portrayed. The ideas and values of several religions, ethnic groups, classes, associations, and other groupings are symbolically expressed and their place within the social structure of the community clearly indicated.

Lincoln and Washington and lesser ritual figures, and ceremonies such as those of Memorial Day, are the symbolic equivalent of such social institutions as our patriotic societies. They express the same values, satisfy the same social needs, and perform similar functions. All increase the social solidarity of a complex and heterogeneous society.

The Function of Memorial Day

The Memorial Day rites of Yankee City and hundreds of other American towns, we said earlier, are a modern cult of the dead and conform to Durkheim's definition of sacred collective representations. They are a cult because they consist of a system of sacred beliefs and dramatic rituals held by a group of people who, when they congregate, represent the whole community. They are sacred because they ritually relate the living to sacred things. They are a cult because the members have not been formally organized into an institutionalized church with a defined theology, but depend on informal organization to order their sacred activities. They are called a cult here because this term, though more narrowly used in common parlance, accurately places them in a class of social phenomena clearly identified in the sacred behavior of other societies.

The cult system of sacred belief conceptualizes in organized form sentiments common to everyone in the community about death. These sentiments are composed of fears of death which conflict with the social reassurances our culture provides us to combat such anxieties. These assurances, usually acquired in childhood and thereby carrying some of the authority of the adults who provided them, are a composite of theology and folk belief. The deep anxieties to which we refer include anticipation of our own deaths, of the deaths or possible deaths of loved ones, and—less powerfully—of the deaths or possible deaths of the wise of our generation—those who have taught us—and of men in general.

Each man's church provides him and those of his faith with a set of beliefs and a mode of action to face these problems, but his church and those of other men do not equip their respective members with a common set of social beliefs and rituals which permit them to unite with all their fellows to confront this common and most feared of all enemies. The Memorial Day rite and other subsidiary rituals connected with it form a cult which partially satisfies this need for common action on a common problem. It dramatically expresses the sentiments of unity of all the living among themselves, of all the living with all the dead, and of all the living and dead as a group with God. God, as worshiped by Catholic, Protestant, and Jew, loses sectarian definition, limitations, and foreignness as between different customs and becomes the common object of worship for the whole group and the protector of everyone.

The unifying and integrating symbols of this cult are the dead. The graves of the dead are the most powerful of the visible emblems which unify all the activities of the separate groups of the community. The cemetery and its graves become the objects of sacred rituals which permit opposing organizations, often in conflict, to subordinate their ordinary opposition and cooperate in collectively expressing the larger unity of the total community. The rites show extraordinary respect for all the dead, but they pay particular honor to those who were killed in battle "fighting for their country." The death of a soldier in battle is believed to be a "voluntary sacrifice" by him on the altar of his country. To be understood, this belief in the sacrifice of a man's life for his country must be judged first with our general scientific knowledge on the nature of all forms of sacrifice. It must then be subjected to the principles which explain human sacrifice whenever and wherever found. More particularly, this belief must be examined with the realization that these sacrifices occur in a society whose Deity was once incarnate as a man who voluntarily sacrificed his life for all men.

The Memorial Day rite is a cult of the dead but not just of the dead as such, since by symbolically elaborating sacrifice of human life for the country through, or identifying it with, the Christian Church's sacred sacrifice of the incarnate God, the deaths of such men also become powerful sacred symbols which organize, direct, and constantly revive the collective ideals of the community and the nation.

CHAPTER 9

THE CITY OF THE DEAD

The Cemetery

Yankee City cemeteries are collective representations which reflect and express many of the community's basic beliefs and values about what kind of society it is, what the persons of men are, and where each fits into the secular world of the living and the spiritual society of the dead. [42a] Whenever the living think about the deaths of others they necessarily express some of their own concern about their own extinction. The cemetery provides them with enduring, visible symbols which help them to contemplate man's fate and their own separate destinies. The cemetery and its gravestones are the hard, enduring signs which anchor each man's projections of his innermost fantasies and private fears about the certainty of his own death—and the uncertainty of his ultimate future—on an external symbolic object made safe by tradition and the sanctions of religion.

The social boundaries of the sacred dead and the secular world of the profane living are set apart and joined *materially* in Yankee City by clearly defined physical limits marked by ordinary walls, fences, and hedges. The living and the dead are *spiritually* joined and divided by ceremonies for the dead,— among them funerals which occur daily, Memorial Day rites, and the dedication and consecration of burial ground—which separate the sacred and profane realms by use of these symbolic methods. All are founded on, and give expression to, the feelings and beliefs of the people of Yankee City. Rituals of consecration have transformed a small part of the common soil of the town into a sacred place and dedicated this land of the dead to God, to the sacred souls of the departed, and to the souls of the living whose bodies are destined for such an end. The rituals which establish graveyards tacitly imply formal rules and precepts which define the relations of the profane and sacred worlds of the living and the dead. The funeral—a formal rite of separation of the recently dead from the living—

is, broadly speaking, an unending ritual, for although funerals are separate rites, they occur with such continuing frequency that they maintain a constant stream of ritual connection between the dead and the living. Once a year the cult of the dead in the Memorial Day rites for the whole community strengthens and re-expresses what the chain of separate funerals accomplishes throughout the year.

The funeral symbolically removes the *time*-bound individual from control by the forward direction of human time. He no longer moves from the past towards the future, for now (in the minds of the living) he is in the unmoving, sanctified stillness of an ever-present eternity. At death the ageing process, conceptually a form of human time existing in the nature of things, loses its control of the individual. The march of events no longer has meaning for what he has become. His timeless ("eternal") soul is in a sacred realm where human and social time lose most of their meanings; his dead, ephemeral body becomes part of a process where human time has little significance. The time of the living as the society conceives it cannot be understood without knowledge of "dead" time. In many ways the two are contrary to each other. As opposites, dead and live time express the duality of existence, the sacred and the profane, the "controlled" and the "uncontrollable." The ephemeral and the eternal, activity and inertness, are all part of the meaning of the duality of live and dead time. The popularity of the play and motion picture "Death takes a Holiday" was built largely on the symbolic point that human time no longer had control over human destiny; events were timeless because the *time of death* was no longer in opposition to the *time of life*. Rather the "holiday" of death meant that the sacred time of eternity had been substituted for the secular time of man. Holidays and holy days are moments in the calendar where ordinary time is flouted. The author of the play, however, also made another point when he used the term "holiday" (rather than "holy day"); he allowed his audience to gratify their longing to translate into the sacred, eternal time of the dead the pleasant, sensuous world of the living.

The cemetery, separate and distinct from the living, yet forever a material part of Yankee City's cultural equipment, bridges these two times, ending the one and beginning the other. As man changes physically, the "conveyor belt" of social time redefines his changing place in the community and moves him onward until finally, at death, it ceremonially dumps him into a new set of meanings where human time no longer defines his existence. The cemetery's several material symbols play their part in relating the time of eternity to human time. Man's fate, as Yankee City conceives it, can be found in these signs. Let us examine them.

The cemeteries in Yankee City are divided into lots of varying sizes which are ordinarily the property of particular families, occasionally of associations. The burial plots are referred to by the surnames of the families who own them. The individual graves, with their individual stone markers, are arranged within the limits of the lots—more often than not according to the status of the dead individuals within the family and the dictates of mortuary style prevailing at the time of their deaths.

The emotions and thoughts of the living about their dead always express the antithetical elements that enter into the placement of the dead. Human time continually makes its demands for controlling eternity; maintenance of the identity of the dead is partly dependent on placing them in living time and space. Human space concepts continue to be used to locate the dead. Location of the dead in time and space helps to maintain their reality to those who wish to continue their relations with them. The cemetery contributes its material signs to help maintain this system of meanings and feelings.

The cemetery as a collective representation is both a city and a garden of the dead. The two symbols fuse and merge in the collective thinking of the people of Yankee City. The most modern cemetery in the community, well over a hundred years in age, accents its natural surroundings and emphasizes the symbols of nature, but only as they are fashioned and expressed within the limits and control of men and society in the design of a formal garden. It is a miniature, symbolic replica of the gardenlike dwelling area of a better-class suburb, or an elaboration of the formal gardens of aristocratic families. It is a symbolic city built in the form of a garden of the dead.

"Garden" and "city" are both feminine images in our culture, the former a dependent symbol of the more ancient Mother Earth. The garden is also a symbol of both life and death. As a *place* it symbolizes life, vitality, growth, and the fertility of the earth. As a symbol of the *processes* occurring there it expresses feelings about man's involvement in the eternal cycle of life and death, its shrubs and flowers come and go and are born again, its life dies, decays, and enriches the soil where new plants and shrubs are reborn and flower again. Summer and winter, life and death, eternally repeat themselves in the processes of the garden—an artifact formed by, and subject to, the will of man.

Elm Highlands, the most modern cemetery of Yankee City, was consecrated in the first half of the last century as a "rural burial place" where landscape gardening united "the beautiful in nature with sculptural art, thereby creating a garden cemetery." The citizens composed two original hymns for its consecration. Both explicitly use maternal and female symbols to refer to the cemetery and the return of the living to a maternal and female resting place. The one from which the following quote was taken also recognizes the cemetery as a "City of Our Dead" and refers to the common fate of the living and the dead and their mutual hope for immortality through their relations with the supernatural power of Christ.

· · ·

We here appoint, by solemn rite,
On this sequestered, peaceful site,
With flowery grass and shadowy tree,
The City of Our Dead to be.

Though this now sacred turf must break
Our dearest forms of life to take;
On Nature's calm, maternal breast
'Tis meet her weary children rest.

May He, who, pitying, "touched the bier,"
Console each future mourner here;
And all the dead at last arise
With joy to meet Him in the skies!

The author of the hymn explicitly speaks of the return of the "weary children" to the "maternal breast" of Nature where they find eternal "rest." The more obvious female symbolism involved with the insertion of the body into the open grave which then encloses it in the "body of Mother Earth" is not acceptable at the conscious level to members of our culture. Unconsciously, the open grave and the uterus are compatible; they also fit the social assumptions of our rites of passage. The rite and facts of birth separate the new individual from the womb of the mother and, following the events between the rites and facts of death, complete the life cycle by returning the human body to the maternal body of Nature. The Christian rites of baptism and those surrounding death symbolically recognize the meanings assigned to these facts. In the Catholic Church, for example, the liturgy of Holy Saturday explicitly views baptism as both a birth and a death rite while bringing to the manifest level of understanding the vaginal significance of the "immersion" in the water of the font. On the other hand, Extreme Unction and Christian funerals non-logically—but with great effectiveness—symbolically state the meanings of death as both an ending and a beginning, as a rite of death and a rite of birth.

The author of the sacred poem, in speaking of the "weary children" finding "rest," puts the fixed eternal world of sacred time in opposition to the weariness of those *moving* through human time. The return of the "children" to the breast of the mother, back to the beginning of time for them where the beginning and the ending are one, touches and may evoke powerful yet unsatisfied human feelings and use them positively to reduce anxiety about death. Whether the "peaceful" equilibrium and quiet of prenatal existence influence the postnatal meaning of experience is debatable, but the strong desire to maintain close and unchanging relations with the mother and the infantile need to possess her are well documented human longings. These feelings (see pages 496 to 498), morally stated in the sacred symbols of consecration, non-morally felt in the unconscious longings of men, are bound to the female symbol of Nature, the beginning and ending of human time. The cemetery as an object dedicated to God and man and consecrated to "our dead to be," its graves, and the cemetery as a city and garden, are all culturally controlled female symbols. One must suspect that their significance not only derives from the logical and non-logical meanings of culture but lies deeply rooted in the life of the human animal.

The fundamental *sacred* problem of the graveyard is to provide suitable symbols to refer to and express man's hope of immortality through the sacred belief and ritual of Christianity, and to reduce his anxiety and fear about death as marking the obliteration of his personality—the end of life for himself and for those he loves. The assurance of life hereafter for the dead already in the cemetery and for those being buried is an assurance of life hereafter for the living. Maintaining the dead as members of society maintains the continuing life of the living. The living's assurance of life everlasting is dependent on their keeping the dead alive. Should the dead really die, in the belief of those who put them to rest, then they, too, must die. The cemetery is an enduring physical emblem, a substantial and visible symbol of this agreement among men that they will not let each other die. For a very few, it is a sacred or sometimes an open admission that the power of tradition and convention is greater than the strength of their own rational convictions.

The fundamental *secular* problem the graveyard solves is to rid the living of the decaying corpse, thus freeing them from the nauseous smells of corruption and from the horror of seeing the natural decomposition of a human body, thereby helping to maintain the satisfying images of themselves as persistent and immortal beings. Another social function of the graveyard is to provide a firm and fixed social place, ritually consecrated for this purpose, where the disturbed sentiments of human beings about their loved dead can settle and find peace and certainty. Death destroys the equilibrium of the family and other intimate groups in which the deceased participated during his life. When it comes, the interaction and exchange of intimate gestures and symbols, resulting in each individual's personality internalizing part of the person of the other with whom he intimately interacts, ceases. This process no longer provides a mirror, however opaque and distorted, in which the individual may feel he sees his own reflection and thus realize himself as a social being. The belief in immortality, strengthened and reinforced by the funeral rite, helps correct some of the feeling in the survivor of loss of self. For the survivor to continue to see and feel himself still living in, and related to, the dead life of the other it is necessary for him to reconstruct his image of the other; but in doing this he must also rethink who he himself is, at least in so far as he relates himself to the dead person. This constitutes an essential part of the social-psychological processes of the living during the transition of death.

The cemetery provides the living with a sacred realm they have created by means of their social control of divine power, a function of sacred symbolism, in which they can deposit the impure and unclean corpse in a grave that belongs to it not so much as a corpse but as a sacred person, in a grave which also belongs to them, the living. The grave with its markings is a place where the living can symbolically maintain and express their intimate relations with the dead. There is a kinship of kind, too; today's dead are yesterday's living, and today's living are tomorrow's dead. Each is identified with the other's fate. No one escapes.

The grave is marked so that the living can approach it as something that belongs to a separate personality; it is not merely a symbol that refers generally and abstractly to all the dead. The cemetery is a symbolic meeting place for the dead and the living, for the realms of the sacred and profane, for the natural and for the supernatural. It is a social emblem, whole and entire, yet composed of many autonomous and separate individual symbols which give visible expression to our social relations to the supernatural and to the pure realm of the spirit. It is a meeting place which faces out to death and the sacred absolute and back to the secular realities of the finite and the living. In it the time of man and the time of God are united. It is a "final resting place" where the disturbed and bruised sentiments of the living members of the society mark the natural death and ultimate disposition of an individual organism and its detachment from the species, thus fixing a place in time where the living can relate themselves in human, understandable, emotional terms to the spiritualized personality now in the timeless realm of the supernatural other world. The members of the societies of the living and the dead meet here as "God's children" and are accordingly one people. The cemetery as a collective representation repeats and expresses the social structure of the living as a symbolic replica; a city of the dead, it is a symbolic replica of the living community. The spiritual part of the city of the Christian dead, often thought of as part of the City of God, is sometimes equated with the Invisible Body of Christ. For many Christians, each is an integral part of a greater mystery.

The social and status structures which organize the living community of Yankee City are vividly and impressively reflected and expressed in the outward forms and internal arrangements of the several cemeteries of the city. Just as cemeteries reflect in miniature the past life and historic eras through which the community has passed, so contemporary graveyards symbolically express the present social structure. This memorial of the living for the dead has been created in their own image.

During the field research we observed and described all the city's graveyards in Yankee City; several were studied intensively and systematically.[1] Their grounds and burial lots were plotted, an inventory was taken of the ownership of the various burial lots, and listings were made of the individuals and families buried in them. By interviews and through the collection of official cemetery documents, we were able to reconstruct their history and study the ongoing social processes. For obvious reasons all names of people, places, and particular cemeteries are fictional. To increase anonymity, the evidence from several of them has been combined into one composite statement.

The great importance of the elementary family organization as a fundamental and primary unit of our social structure is everywhere present in the collective representations of the cemetery. The configuration of the personalities in the family is reflected in the relative positions of burial of the various kin. The father is often in the center of the burial plot, but the mother occasionally occupies this position; father and mother sometimes hold an equal position in the center.

The use of stone borders to outline and define the separate character of the family plot emphasizes the basic unity and primary importance of the elementary family. Thus the live

1. I am very much indebted to Leo Srole and Buford Junker for their field studies of the several cemeteries. I am also in the debt of other members of the research staff for their observations.

facts of birth and procreation are reflected in their graveyard symbols. The conflict between the individual's family of orientation, into which he was born, and his family of procreation, which he has helped to create by marriage and producing children, are also clearly marked in the cemetery. By interview and by the disposition of the body, we were able to demonstrate that this competition between two families for its possession is clearly reflected in what happens in the graveyard. If the family of orientation is stronger, it is likely that there will be a large family plot with the father and mother occupying a more or less central position, with the male children and wives placed on each side of them and the grandchildren on the periphery. This is more often the pattern for upper-class position. If the family of procreation is stronger, or there is conflict between the families of birth and marriage, this family unit tends to break off by itself and the burial plot then may contain its male head, his wife, and their unmarried children. Although not confined to one class, this type of burial is most characteristic, as far as we could discover, of the middle classes, particularly those who have been upward mobile.

These two types of burial—the large, extended family and the small, limited one—represent the extreme differences in burial as they are related to the families of orientation and procreation. There are intermediate forms showing the variations that necessarily must occur in a society where there are differences among the several classes and there is opposition between the families of birth and marriage. When the family organization of extended kindred is as powerful as usual in the upper-upper class, it is likely that the family plots will record this class difference. When the lineage principle is powerful and the patronym is of real significance to a class, this too is likely to be reflected in the recognition of each in the arrangement of the dead and the inscriptions on the tombstones. Sometimes the lineage of the mother may be expressed by the inclusion of her maiden name on the stone. This may appear in any class, but it is more frequent with the upper class, where the patronym of the mother is of special significance to the social position of the family. As far as we could determine, it rarely appears in the inscriptions of the lower classes.

A Vacancy in Elm Highlands Cemetery

The symbolism of the graveyard, marking and expressing family conflict and solidarity, is well illustrated by the graves of the Worthington family. Jonathan Worthington, the son of an old Hill Street family, is no longer buried in the family burial ground, but in a small lot by himself on one of the low-rising knolls on the other side of the cemetery, a long distance from the family plot on the high hill where he was buried at the time of his death. His father had purchased the family lot when the children were young. Places were provided for his wife and all the children and their children's children. The family gravestone, a modest yet imposing shaft, was erected before Mr. Worthington's death. The graves of two of his children who had died when quite young were at one side of the plot, the small stones fittingly inscribed. Jonathan's older brother and his wife, the victims of an accident, were buried side by side within the family lot, near the father and the place that Mrs. Worthington would occupy beside him. She often said it was a source of satisfaction and comfort to her to know that some day she would be there beside her husband, with their children all around them. Once—but only once—she had said more literally, to the delight of the malicious and the vulgar, "I feel better when I realize my body will always be there beside my husband's." [2]

Jonathan had never been like the other sons. He disliked business and wanted to be a painter. Because of his delicate health as a youth his parents, after brief disapproval, had relented and allowed him to have his wish. After a period of study in Paris he had lived in New York. There he met and married a beautiful Polish girl who was earning her way through art school by modeling for artists. Although Theodora was American born, it had displeased his mother; she had hoped he would marry a daughter of one of the old families whom he had courted during prep school days.

2. The evidence comes from members of the immediate family. Before his death Jonathan had told us personally much about himself, his family, and the conflict between his wife and mother. Close friends of the family, as well as enemies, told the rest.

The fact that Theodora had lost her religious faith and no longer belonged or went to the Catholic Church was of some comfort to Johnnie's mother. When she agreed to Mrs. Worthington's suggestion that they have something more than a justice-of-the-peace wedding, and she and Johnnie were married again in an Episcopal church in New York, the event filled Mrs. Worthington with great hopes everything in time might work out all right.

When Johnnie and Theodora moved to Yankee City and refused to live with the mother in the old family house, but "took an old barn of a house" down on the river, remodeled it to provide studios for both, and lived a quiet life, refusing invitations to dinner and declining to be a part of the social world his family knew, Johnnie's mother's increasing hostility to his wife became a topic of gossip along Hill Street and among their friends on the "North Shore."

Only a few years later Johnnie's frailness turned into real illness demanding the attention of the family doctor. After a quiet visit from his mother the doctor urged them to give up their place on the river and move into the old Hill Street home where he could have better attention. To this he finally agreed. Here he and Theodora had a bedroom and sitting room in a small suite upstairs that could be separated from the rest of the house. The senior Mrs. Worthington, despite her anxiety about his illness, felt almost happy again because she had her son back under the family roof. She and Theodora were formally polite and, with a little effort, were able most of the time to avoid each other and to maintain a semblance of cordiality.

Johnnie and his wife had been at the old home only a few months when he became much worse. Suspecting that his health was poorer than anyone admitted, he finally persuaded the doctor to give him a frank report on his condition and was informed that he was likely to die within a short time. The mother and wife each had several tearful conversations with him, but neither was able to talk fully and frankly about what she felt or to speak of what might happen when he died.

One afternoon, shortly before his death, he asked to see his mother and wife together. When the two Mrs. Worthingtons had come in and the nurse had left, closing the door behind her, he said to them, "I want to say to both of you that you have been simply grand. I have been able to talk about everything to you. Some of it has been rough and tough for you to take. You both love me and I love you. My having to die now just when I think life is beginning to be something doesn't make sense to you or to me, but that's the way it is and that's the way it's going to be. But I suppose if I lived to be a hundred I would think I was too young to die right away. Anyway, we've been all over that one.

"There is something else that's bothering me. It seems a little silly for me, being the kind of man I am, to talk about it, but I've been thinking that I don't know for sure where I am going to be buried, and somehow I need to know where that's going to be."

The senior Mrs. Worthington moved her rocking chair back just a little and began rocking herself tentatively, as if she wanted to substitute movement for speech. She cleared her throat. Johnnie's wife looked down at her hands and then at him. Finally, she turned her face towards Mrs. Worthington. Mrs. Worthington spoke:

"Why, Johnnie, there has always been a place in the family plot for all of you children. Surely you know that." Johnnie looked at her anxiously and asked, "And that means that there will be a place for Theodora, too?" There was a brief pause before Mrs. Worthington said, "Yes, your father provided places for all the husbands and wives of our children."

When Jonathan died, Theodora was so overcome with emotion and uncertain of what was happening that many things perceived during the funeral and the burial did not have meaning to her until after several weeks had passed and she began to rearrange her experiences and think about them more rationally. During periods of weeping at the burial, she had noticed that Johnnie had been put in one corner of the burial ground and that his older brother was buried next to him. Later reflection made her realize that the traditional pattern of husband and wife being side by side was impossible unless the body of the brother was disinterred. In the springtime and after further thought about the matter, Theodora took some flowers down to Johnnie's grave. During this visit, after thinking about where the other members of the family would be buried, she realized that there seemed to be no place provided for her. She waited until an appropriate moment and faced Mrs. Worthington with the question as to what provision had been made for her own burial place.

Mrs. Worthington said she had not wanted to distress Johnnie at the time of his mortal illness, so had told him a "little white lie" about there being a place beside him for Theodora. No place was provided for her, because "no one would ever have believed Johnnie would ever marry." She informed Theodora that she would be very glad to make arrangements for a plot of ground as near to the family burial ground as possible. The conversation became more heated. Finally, when Theodora left Mrs. Worthington's room she rushed to her own, packed her bags, and made arrangements to have her personal effects moved to a hotel in Boston. Here, sitting in her room, she felt more lonely and isolated than since the early days of her adolescence, when she had realized that her outlook on life was different from that of other children her own age. She felt that she had lost not only the living Johnnie but the dead one and even the symbol referring to his burial. She finally decided to call a lawyer and discovered that she was within her rights to have her husband's body removed to another burial place.

Theodora purchased a small lot on the knoll far from the family burial ground and made the necessary arrangements at the cemetery for the disinterment. The lot had room for two graves; one is now occupied by Johnnie.

Johnnie died a number of years ago. Since that time Theodora has occupied herself once more with her profession and has been absorbed back into the art world. Here she has met men who have occasionally attracted her. At the present time it seems likely that she will marry a successful New York artist. She has told her friends that, although she still loves Johnnie, the new man interests her and life seems very lonely without a husband to share it with.

Meanwhile, there is a vacant place in the family lot of the Worthingtons which was once filled by Johnnie's casket, and there is also a vacant place in the new family lot which was to have been Theodora's when she died. The meaning of the separate burial places and the vacancy in each is not lost on those who know the Worthingtons. Just as family solidarity and the status of each member are usually marked by burial customs and their permanent symbols in the cemetery, so can deep conflict and hostility leave their own meaningful marks. Where the body of a man is placed when he dies tells much about his meaning as an individual, but it may tell even more about his social place and significance to those who survive him. The gossips of Yankee City do not use scientific terms to state what they think, but what they say expresses even more effectively what such terms should mean.

Collective Representations of the Sexes, the Several Ages, and the Institutions of Yankee City

Most institutions or associations leave their impress on the symbolism of Elm Highlands and the sign system of the cemetery. They are not merely imprints but meaningful sets of diverse symbols to which members of the various groups can repair at least once a year. The symbolic marks around which organized actions occur, and to which the mental attention of the members is given throughout the year, are placed there by the members themselves. The living mark the places of the dead with meaningful signs that refer to what the living want them to be, thus strengthening and freshening their memories about the dead past and maintaining it as a living reality in their thoughts and feeling. Such marks perform their share in maintaining the life of the social heritage.

The basic recognition of the superior and inferior statuses of males and females in our society is clearly reflected in the graveyard. The superordinate males are often given preference with larger and more prominent headstones, and their funerals give them greater ritual recognition. The eulogy, for example, when the corpse is a male, is likely to be more elaborate and the positive points in the life career of the person more fully developed. This is perhaps to be expected since the man of the family is more likely to have a recognizable public experience and record. But although the symbols of the graveyard—position, type of headstone, treatment at burial, etc.—formally give the adult male a superordinate recognition commensurate with his former status as head of the family and as father and breadwinner and the one whose patronym all members of the family carry, women are more fully recognized informally. The inscriptions on their tombstones are likely to be filled with deeper sentiments of attachment than those for males. The male inscriptions more often express the sense of respect and duty, whereas those for women speak of love and tender affection.

Age grading is clearly involved in the symbolism of all the graveyards. Those unfortunates who die as children have secondary places within the family plot. Their stones are small, commensurate with the "length" of their lives and the size of their small bodies. The inscriptions for subadult males as well as females are likely to be filled with expressions of love similar to those on the gravestones of females. The purity and innocence of the child are stressed, implying the young person's supposed freedom from the ultimate moral and supernatural responsibility for his acts.

The symbols of age in the graveyard unconsciously express the subordinate role of the child and subadult and the superordinate role of the adult; the social personality of young people and women is less developed and less important than the social personality of male adults. The overwhelming majority of the people of Yankee City would deny these statements, declaring that the souls of all are equal in the sight of God and in man's sight, too, when he faces God during the crisis of death. Yet our listing of the place and size of gravestones in the several cemeteries, as well as the evidence from the sentiments of the inscriptions, overwhelmingly indicates that the simple and subordinate social positions of females and children are clearly reflected in the mortuary symbolism.

The elaborate associational structure of Yankee City also becomes a symbolic part of the community of the dead and influences the cemetery as a collective representation. It does so in a variety of ways. Sometimes an association, such as the Masons, conducts the funeral. Symbolic plaques of a more or less permanent nature are placed on the graves of members. Yearly these plaques are refurbished—particularly for Memorial Day—to recognize the relation of the dead and living members of the organization. Emblems of such organizations as the American Legion, the Spanish War Veterans, the Women's Relief Corps, the Firemen's Association, Elks, Knights of Pythias, Moose, and many similar organizations are permanent parts of many graves. Many of these associations play a prominent role in the Memorial Day rites. Several associations have purchased burial plots where some of their members are buried; either because the member did not have sufficient funds or because his devotion to the organization was so strong that he wished to identify himself permanently with it. There are also associations which care for aged men and women of former good circumstances and superior class, which not only give them care while living but bury them in the association's burial plot.

The place of the church in the community is symbolized in the cemetery by a variety of usages. The church, the organization primarily responsible for maintaining and fostering the Christian religion, whose principal purpose is to help its members to achieve immortality through belief in the divinity of Jesus Christ, plays the most important institutional role in relating the city of the living to the city of the dead. The communicants of all the Protestant churches have common burial grounds. Catholics and Orthodox Jews usually have separate graveyards hallowed by their own rituals of consecration. The present inclusion of all Protestants in one cemetery provides a common sacred place where all sects can disregard their doctrinal differences. The funeral rites in which they participate without regard to their church affiliation also symbolically unite them. Moreover, the Christian afterworld to which such mortuary rites assign the souls of the departed is one place. For Protestants, the cemetery is increasingly a symbol which is helping to break down sectarian differences and unite them in one group. The sectarian holy ground once attached to each church now remains largely a memorial to a distant, respected past, though burials occasionally still take place in God's half-acre.

All the gravestones and most of the mortuary art of Christian cemeteries use Christian symbols, the principal ones being the Cross, the Lamb (either as Christ or as the Christian member of Christ's flock), and many other Christian representations found in most cemeteries. Some of the inscriptions on the stones clearly express the relation of the living to the dead and of the dead to the supernatural world. Among them are "Blessed are the dead which die in the Lord," "Sleep and take thy rest," "Asleep in Jesus," "More light, more love, more life

beyond." In other words, they emphasize the wish and the belief that the dead still live.

The several ethnic groups in Yankee City have left definite
marks on the cemeteries. There is, first, the dual cultural character of the several communities. Inscriptions often appear
both in English and in the ethnic language. There are wooden
crosses made in a form characteristic of the ethnic background
as well as headstones on the same grave. Sometimes there are
indications that the ethnic wooden cross has been removed and
replaced by an American headstone—clear evidence that the
new generation of American children of ethnic families are
exerting their influence on the family plot. Ritual objects having ethnic connotations are on some of the graves, often appearing rather incongruous to the eyes of native Americans. For
example, on one such grave there was an American flag beside
a small replica of a house within which could be seen wax
flowers and a candle. The whole of it was overhung with a
trestle. The more recent the ethnic group the greater the likelihood that such objects and ethnic variations will appear in the
mortuary art; the older the ethnic group the less difference is
likely to appear between its graves and those in the Yankee
part of the cemetery.

Perhaps one of the more significant symbolic variations is a
greater use of the American flag on all ethnic graves. Whereas
American tradition is likely to assign the use of the flag to the
graves of soldiers, recent ethnic groups often make no such
distinction. The flag seems to imply for many of them that the
deceased was a citizen, or the family believes he wanted to be.
Some ethnic associations are particularly active in making sure
that the American flag appears on the graves of their members.
There also seems to be some feeling that burials of members
"in American soil" gives the living a greater claim to being
American nationals. At some funerals it was stated that the
person had ceased to be only part American; his body was now
one with America itself. A few of the ethnic groups have separate sections set apart from the rest of the cemetery, which
are then redivided according to the family or extended family
groups. Some do not use formal arrangements but informally
place their dead near each other and in a separate part of the
cemetery.

Autonomy, Ambivalence, and Social Mobility

Perhaps one of the most interesting and significant activities found in the cemeteries of Yankee City is the removal of bodies from one part of the cemetery to another or their transfer from the cemetery where they were first buried to another. Such disinterments are not infrequent. They occur every year in most of the cemeteries. One caretaker informed us that he moved several bodies every year from his cemetery to Elm Highlands. When we examined the evidence to determine why these removals took place we learned that in some cases they were made because of changes in religious faith. Some occurred because the living members of the family had been socially mobile and had moved from the lower status the family occupied at the time of the person's death to a higher position. Motivated by embarrassment or strong love of parents and a wish to treat the dead as they might have done had opportunity offered earlier, the socially mobile living members of the family sometimes disinter their dead and place them in the "better" locations commensurate with their present social position. The values and beliefs which motivate such people and the reaction of some of the community to this behavior are perhaps best portrayed in the composite characterization I have called "These Bones Shall Rise Again" (the whole profile, here considerably shortened, is given in Volume I of this series).

Mr. Charles Watson (lower-middle class), the superintendent of the cemetery, squatted on his haunches while he supervised the pick-and-shovel activities of his two workmen. It was hot. He had removed his blue serge coat and laid it carefully over a gravestone. He loosened his tie and opened the collar of his white shirt. Dust rose from the dry earth. While Sam Jones (lower-lower class) broke the soil on one side of a burial plot, Tom Green (lower-lower class) shoveled the already loosened earth from the opposite side of the plot. The burial lot where these operations were proceeding was down on the flat ground in one corner of the cemetery. The headpieces were stone and rather small. Next to and just below this flat part of the cemetery was the area of wooden headpieces. Many had fallen and lay rotting on the ground. On the other side of the cemetery the stone headpieces were larger and increased in size until they reached the hill section, where there were some elaborate funeral urns. In this area a whole burial lot was often bordered with white marble.

The shoveler stopped his work and lit a cigarette.

"I can't understand that guy," he said. "Why the hell can't Phil Starr leave his old man and old lady rest in peace? Why, they been down in this here grave for thirty years, and now, by God, he's digging them up and running all over town with them. I say, once they're buried, let them stay buried. The dead ought to be left alone—they ought to rest in peace."

The pickman stopped and wiped his hands on his overalls.

"What makes me sore is it ain't because the old bastard had to get them out because of something else, like a new road being put through or city improvements, but he's doing it on purpose because he's got to be a big shot. Why, my own mother is buried right over there by that rosebush. It's good enough for her and there wasn't a better woman ever lived than she was."

The other picked up the conversation.

"Why, I remember the time before he made his dough in the Neway Shoe Factory when he didn't have a red cent. Why, that guy——"

"I think you men," said the superintendent, "aren't seeing this thing right. Mr. Starr is only showing his love for his father and mother. When they were alive he still had to make his money, and he couldn't do the things for them he would have liked. If he had had the money when they were alive, he told me, he would have moved them out of that little shack they had down there in the flats and up to his house on Hill Street. That's natural. Anyone who's worth his salt would want to do that for his pa and ma, especially when he's able to do it. But, you see, they died too soon.

"He told me just the other day he wanted to give them the best place to rest in that could be found in the cemeteries in this town. I tried to show him one of our better lots up on the hill but, 'No,' he said, 'only Elm Highlands will do.' He's putting them in a grave up there on the highest hill next to the Breckenridges and the Wentworths and all of those other old families. It's going to be his own lot. He's a-doing this for his pa and ma. Just what any decent American would do for his."

"Oh, yeah?" said the shoveler.

"That sounds okay," said the pickman, "but he ain't worried about this place not bein' good enough for his pa and ma. He's worried about it not bein' good enough for him. I bet that son and daughter of his don't like to come down here with him to decorate their grandpa's and grandma's grave."

"Sure," the shovelman continued. "It makes those kids remember that their old man is just one jump from the clam flats."

"I think you men are wrong," said Mr. Watson. "I sometimes see Mr. Starr at the Elks. He always stops and speaks. Last time he saw me he said, 'Charlie, how are you?' And I said, 'I'm fine.' 'How's your missus?' says he, and I said, 'She's okay, too.' "

The two workmen said nothing. They resumed their work. Mr. Watson went back to his small office. After he had gone, Jones spoke:

"Christ, Charlie'd kiss anybody's ass for a quarter."

They went on digging.

The efforts of Mr. Starr to assemble "all" of his family in a place favorably located to give effective expression to his recently acquired position in the class system of Yankee City portray some of the social and psychological conflicts in the family and status structures of Yankee City. The successful climb of a man from the low status of his birth to a superior position, which results in his family of procreation, including his wife and children, occupying a higher class level than that of his parents and the family of his birth, inevitably puts severe strain on the relations between the members of the two families. Customary usages of the parents and children and other members of the family no longer fit all situations that arise. The funeral and burial rites, as well as other rites of transition during periods of crisis and stress, when experienced by families involved in mobility, accentuate the strain sometimes to the point of open conflict. On such occasions some of the deepest and most irrational feelings that possess men dominate and harass their lives.

At a time of death, the ambivalent feelings of hostility and

love which ordinarily exist in all families between such kindred
as parents and their children, brothers and sisters, as well as the
parents- and children-in-law, are carefully and smoothly
handled by our conventions and the traditional symbolic behavior of the death rites. In many societies the ambivalent love
and hostility of the living for the dead are expressed and controlled by beliefs that the sacred soul of the departed is hostile
to the living. Consequently, the mourning ceremonies allow
both the grief of love and the aggression of hostility to be symbolically expressed. Among Australian aborigines and many
other peoples, the dead are believed to have two souls: a friendly
good one and an unfriendly bad one. The funeral and mourning rites express affection for, and carefully guide, the good
soul to the sacred totem well while frightening the evil one with
hostile threats away from the group.

The feeling in Yankee City is not that the soul is hostile to
the living; a sense of guilt felt by the living about some of their
hostility to the dead person is often expressed by regret as to
inadequate treatment of the person while he was alive. Whereas
the Australian aborigines use sacred symbols to control the
souls of the dead in order to eliminate them and be sure they
are transferred to a place safely away from the living, the people of Yankee City turn their graveyards into sacred realms of
love and respect, where only positive and affectionate sentiments are expressed for the deceased. [139a] The dead are
kept, as it were, intimately close to the love of the living. They
are carefully protected and the cemetery is a familiar part of
the town.

Often relatives appear at funerals, express their grief, and
confess their "unwarranted" enmity for the dead man whom,
while he was alive, they strongly disliked and avoided. Formal
and informal behavior during funerals sometimes results in old
feuds being settled and rebellious members reintegrated into
the family. This is accomplished by the hostility of the secular
living members of the family for the dead man being translated
into a feeling of guilt during the crisis and rites of death.
Meanwhile, the once ordinary living man, now dead, is transformed in their thoughts and feelings into a sacred person.
The ordinary living with their hostile thoughts feel inadequate

before the dead; external aggression is often turned inward on the (guilty) self.

Families which have not been disturbed by the social mobility of some of their members find the crisis and its transformations easier than those where mobility has existed. The man who has striven successfully to realize his ambitions to reach the top, and in effect, consciously or not, has rejected his parents, their values and way of life, is particularly vulnerable. When they die and guilt assails him he must have strong inner armament to protect his ego from yielding to the self-condemnation of his conscience. His moral self turns traitor and attacks what he is and what he has done to himself. Since much of his moral life lies deep within his unconscious and has its being there, surviving as such from the time of his childhood when he internalized many of the moral values and beliefs of his parents and made them part of himself, he is nakedly vulnerable and defenseless. What he has now become must be alien to what he once was. Despite the tough-minded internal controls he may have established, which permitted him to "leave home," in fact and emotionally he still feels the exaggerated guilt of a mobile man.

During life, while in competition for the success for which many Americans try, he may have defied his father and sometimes humiliated and shamed him; by his marriage to, and life with, a woman from a superior level he often made it heartbreakingly clear to his mother that for him she was inadequate. No matter how successfully they free themselves from maternal ties, few mobile men can guard themselves from the overwhelming sense of guilt which normal people feel in less violent form as the result of their ambivalent feelings for a loved person. The disinterment of the mother and father from their lowly graves and the removal of their bones to the mortuary splendor of "a burial on the hills of Elm Highlands" not only allows the guilty son to act out and sometimes free himself from his guilt, but also permits conspicuous display of his wealth before his less well-placed kindred, while placing his parents where they symbolically belong according to his present status needs.

Another painful factor operating during the crisis of death is accentuated in the feelings of the mobile man. Our society has always emphasized the values of individualism; the freedom and rights of an independent conscience and intellect are fundamental parts of our basic democratic dogmas. We train our children, particularly in the middle class, to be self-directed autonomous persons, yet deep within our moral and religious life there is strong condemnation of anyone who disobeys the traditional communal rules of the group. If a sense of sin is a result of the infractions of the sacred rules which are believed to unite man, society, and God, and such rules are believed to be formulated by, and an expression of, God, then the autonomous man during his early development must either internalize the social world about him in such a way that a personality is produced which is never at variance with God and society —an impossible task—or he must constantly face the pain of internal and external conflict. He will not find a place of harmony, for what he is as a moral and intellectual self and what he must be as a person withstanding the pressure exerted on him by the rules of his secular and sacred worlds cannot come to terms. The pain and guilt felt by the "sinful man" whose autonomy has directed him from the traditional moral rules are the inevitable results of the conflicting values our society has about him and his kind. We encourage autonomy and train the young for it, but we covertly and sometimes openly condemn those who make themselves into autonomous persons. The strong, successfully mobile man develops defenses against it, but his armor can never be quite sufficient to save him from a feeling of guilt "for doing and having done what he needed to do." When his parents or other loved ones die, he inevitably feels a deeper sense of egoistic guilt than the non-mobile person who has obeyed the rules, reduced his internal decision-making to a minimum, maximized his obedience to external social directions, and thereby fitted himself into the conventional places provided for his kind by the social traditions.

Transition Technicians—the Funeral and Other Rites of Transition and the Power and Prestige of the Professions

From the above considerations it is clear that the symbolic significance of the cemetery as a material artifact reflecting the community life of Yankee City and the private worlds of its members cannot be fully comprehended by an examination limited to the grave itself. The symbolic rites which relate the living to the dead are integral parts of the whole life situation.

The movement of a man through his lifetime, from a fixed placental placement within his mother's womb to his death and the ultimate fixed point of his tombstone and final containment in his grave as a dead organism, is punctuated by a number of critical moments of transition which all societies ritualize and publicly mark with suitable observances to impress the significance of the individual and the group on living members of the community. These are the important times of birth, puberty, marriage, and death. The usual progress of all such rites of transition, as Van Gennep has demonstrated, are characterized by three phases: separation, margin, and aggregation. The first period of separation consists of symbolic behavior signifying the detachment of the individual from an earlier fixed point in the social structure; during the intermediate period of margin the status of the individual is ambiguous—it is not fixed for him or his society—he moves in a world where he is no longer what he was nor has attained what he is to be; in the last phase, of aggregation, the passage is made complete. The individual is again in a fixed status and reintegrated into his society. He is in a new status—new for him, but a traditional one for the society, a status which the society defines as the end and goal of a particular transition rite. The society recognizes and consecrates the successful achievement of the passage of the individual. [54]

At the same time his change of status and the reordering of his relations with other members of the society are recognized and sanctioned. The transition phases of separation, margin, and aggregation always involve others who are in direct relation with the individual during this time. They, too, are in positions of uneasiness and confusion which are expressed in their feelings and actions. The different societies have developed traditional symbols which express the varying feelings of other members of the society, usually the family of the person concerned, and direct their actions to an attainment of the ultimate goal of each transition.

The informal and non-official behavior which is always a part of all transition rites is often a channel of expression for paradoxical emotions and sentiments which are not altogether inappropriate. The "tears of joy" at a wedding, symbolically a time of joy, may express feelings of loss, deprivation, and even hostility felt by members of the two families; the informal gatherings of friends and relatives after the funeral for bread and drink among peoples where wakes are not sanctioned, when laughter and tears are intermingled, often allow feelings to be expressed publicly and relations established which the official funeral has not permitted. In our society the unofficial behavior of fathers during the period of birth and confinement of the expectant mother, often a source of amusement and a target for the satirist, is an informal expression of the social sentiments formalized by the *couvade* in "primitive" societies. These sentiments of anxiety about themselves in the crisis are not provided for in our symbolic usage at the birth transition.

The symbols of our *rites de passage* of birth, death, and the others occurring between them always operate at four levels of behavior and consequently involve sentiments, emotions, and values which are of the deepest significance to the whole social system and powerfully affect the participating individuals. The levels of behavior are: species activity, technological and social action, and the action system which relates men to the supernatural.

Throughout the life span and in all rites, the social personality of the living—the product of the individual's interaction with other members of the society and the sum of the social positions he has occupied while living in the social structure—influences, and is influenced directly and indirectly by, the rest of the society. This means that the effects of the social personality of each individual are felt by other members of the group and retained as part of their memories. Consequently, when a member of a community dies, his social personality is not immediately extinguished. His physical lifetime is ended, but social existence continues. It exists so long as memory of it is felt by the living members of the group.

As Chart 7 indicates, death does not destroy the social personality, for in the memory of others it continues to exist, and only disappears when all trace of it is obliterated from the memory of the living and it no longer exerts any influence upon them. Thus the social personality starts in the sacred realm, passes through a secular existence, and returns to the sacred world of the dead. Birthdays and anniversaries of marriage are symbolic recognitions of the original events. They usually function within the realm of the family, contribute to its solidarity by allowing its members to reassert their own values and beliefs about themselves, and allow the social value of the person and

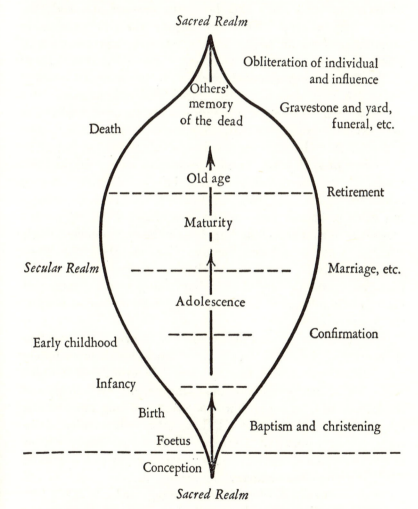

CHART 7. The Expansion and Contraction of the Social Personality (during the Passage of the Individual through Life)

the occasion to be reasserted in symbolic form by the group. The flowers given to a mother on her birthday or to a wife on a wedding anniversary, or placed on a parent's grave, revive and restate by yearly ritual the changing yet continuing meaning of an individual's life to him and his society.

Our complex western European society, during the long periods of its increasing differentiation, has developed a number of occupational statuses closely related to the several rites of passage which mark and define the passage of social time from birth to death. They are largely the older and more honored professions, which possess extraordinary positions of privilege, power, and prestige. Very early in the development of this culture they assumed functions in the rites and crises of transition that once were the duties and obligations of the families involved. Since the families of the changing individual are primarily concerned with his crises of change, it would be expected that their members might conduct the several rites. Although at such times family members are very active, professional men are called in to take charge: doctors, lawyers, ministers, priests, and, to a lesser extent, teachers assume leading roles in one or more of the several crises. They are the transition technicians standing by as the time conveyor belt transports and transforms those who compose its traffic. They manipulate the highly valued symbols and play their part in defining and establishing what is happening to the lifetime of each individual and what this means within the social time of the group.

The activities between death and burial are filled with tension, grief, and disorder in the social world which immediately surrounds the deceased. During mortal illnesses, fear mingled with hope in the thoughts of the dying person, his family, and the friends who surround him, has created strong anxiety and tension in the relations of all those intimately involved. For some, the sacrament of Extreme Unction provides a rite of transition which effectively separates and removes the soul of the living from the ordinary secular world, transports it, and places it in a position where it can be integrated into the spiritual world. Only a minority of Protestants now summon the spiritual aid of the minister to help them through the period of the death crisis. The feelings of fear and guilt which fill the emotions and thinking of family and friends often prevent them from calling in the minister, since his extraordinary visit might be interpreted as a sign that the techniques of science are no longer effective—that the minister as a representative of the sacred world is assuming the dominant place until then occupied by the doctor. His appearance could signify the certainty of approaching death.

There are significant differences between the relative status of priests and ministers in the community. The priest is of significance to the less as well as the extremely devout Catholics in all rites of transition. The fundamental human crises have been ritualized by the Catholic Church to the point where all the principal ones are raised to the ritual importance of sacraments. Five of the seven sacraments are directly related to times of crisis and transition in human life. The other two are also used in transition rites. Baptism for birth; confirmation for the child's passage from early immaturity to the beginnings of maturity—from the exclusive dominance of the family to a more responsible and larger participation in the society; the sacrament of marriage for sexual cohabitation and the passage of the individual from the family of his birth to his family of reproduction; and Extreme Unction for death: all are associated with transitions and life crises. For one devoted to a celibate existence, ordination is essentially a substitute for the marriage rite; it transforms the secular man of the world, living in the larger profane realm of the flesh, into a member of an adult spiritual order—a member of the sacred realm of the Church. Only the sacraments of the Eucharist and penance are not directly symbolic expressions of critical transition periods in which there is a marked change of the individual's status in the structure of the community.

The symbolic role and ecclesiastic authority of the priest in all these rituals are very great. The part he plays and the symbols he manipulates are of the very greatest supernatural significance, for they invest the transitional crises and the *rite de passage* occasioned by each of them with the absolute power of the Divine presence. Through the priest, the eternal Divine elements become part of, and are directly related to, a secular, mundane, transitory moment in one individual's life. The symbolic role and activity of the priest, backed by the authority of the Church and confirmed by the faith of the communicant, raise him to a position of highest professional rank.

The position of the priest in the Irish community as well as in the French Canadian group in Yankee City is very high. Since they belong to ethnic groups which rank below the old Americans and since their religion is considered inferior to that of the Protestants, they do not enjoy a status in the larger community commensurate with that held in the several Catholic communities of French Canada or southern Ireland.

Protestant ministers occupy a variable position in professional status and in class levels. They rank in social class from upper-lower to upper class, most of them being upper-middle. Despite the fact that the status of Protestantism is high (particularly certain indigenous forms of New England Protestantism) and the ministers largely of old American background and New England heritage, they cannot be sure of the secure place held by the priest within his own immediate community. Compared with priests, doctors, and lawyers, their position is weak. The reasons for this, although complex, are fairly clear. The role of the minister since the Reformation has been increasingly secularized. Many of the sacred symbols largely centered in *rites de passage* celebrating events of importance in the lives of the people have been destroyed, and those that remain are often weak and not of great importance. When the great system of sacred symbols was broken or destroyed by the forces that produced Protestantism and the absolute power largely removed from those which remained, much of the authority inherent to the cloth disappeared. God's vicars need his signs to make manifest what it is that they and he are. Words are important symbols, but the mysteries of the Word need other symbolic usages to manifest the full power of God.

Most of the symbols visible and perceptible to the senses have been removed by the hostility of Protestant reform. Vivid and sensuous ceremonies that capture the inner world of the individual, colorful images that elicit and contain the fantasies of his private life, have been abandoned and condemned. The Protestant minister, weakly armed with an anemic liturgical apparatus and devitalized spiritual imagery, has had his spiritual power reduced; the reinforcement of visual drama often needed to make his words significant to his congregation has been taken from him. He is often reduced to the use of verbal symbols, now impoverished by the debilitating effect of two centuries of science. Their potency with a Protestant audience, now highly secularized, is dependent not only on supernatural sanction but on their scientific and rational validity. He is in the awkward position of having to make sense with the symbols he uses, not only to the sacred but to the most secular part of the profane world. In the various times of transition the minister is often humiliated by having to compete with undertakers for the central role in burying the dead, with justices of the peace for the marriage rite, and with a varied assortment of speakers representing all parts of society at high school and college graduation exercises.

Although the liturgical life of the Protestant church has not disappeared but is still alive and in many ways vital, even in the Evangelical churches it does not possess the symbolic strength nor the validity of faith that it has among the Catholic faithful. Although verbal symbols are significant and necessary parts of any great liturgy, they are not by themselves as effective as those which depend on visual symbols as well as those appealing to the other senses.

For most Protestants, funeral orations and sermons by the minister are still believed necessary and important. An analysis of a number of them indicates that the primary function of the eulogy is to translate the profane person in the feelings of those who mourn from secular living into the sacred world of the dead and of Deity.

The funeral oration must reassure the living that immortality is a fact, that the personality of the dead has not ceased to exist, and that spiritual life has no ending, since death is only the transition from life in the present to eternal life in a spiritual world. The establishment of these spiritual truths in the minds and emotions of the audience prepares them for the next important step: the transformation of the total person, once a living combination of good and bad and of spiritual and profane elements, into a spiritual person who is a certain, or at least very likely, candidate for immortality. Thus his lifetime, bound by ideas of transition, is transposed into the eternal time of death. Essentially, from the point of view of what is being done to the dead person, the whole is an initiation rite and compares very closely with the initiation rites which many pass through in life.

Since at most funerals the whole group of mourners is composed of individuals who have considerable knowledge of the habits and activities of the deceased, each individual if questioned could often mention traits of the deceased which as evidence might cause an entirely just—not to say harsh— judge to refuse the candidate admittance to a happier life. The task of the minister is a delicate one. He must touch lightly on the earthly traits of the dead and then move gracefully over to his positive virtues and his spiritual qualities. Since he possesses an immortal soul given him by God, and since those most lacking in spiritual grace and moral competence are never categorically evil, these small and often insignificant positive traits of the personality are easily substituted in the words of a skillful speaker for the whole person, and the transfiguration takes place. The symbolic functions of the eulogy are to transform what are memories of the secular living into ideas of the sacred dead, and to re-form recollection of the personality sufficiently to make it possible for everyone to believe that entrance into heaven or any of its contemporary vague substitutes is not blocked or impossible.

The symbolic activities of the audience are minor but sufficient to allow them some participation, at least to the point of permitting them to affirm informally what the speaker asserts. The accompaniment of the casket in a funeral procession to the cemetery and the brief ceremonies there allow the living to demonstrate their love and respect to the end.

The doctor plays one of the more sympathetic roles of modern science. He is able to personify its optimism and insistence that all problems must be solved, for the public believes that science has its own miracles which can effectively pull back dying men from the edge of the grave. As long as the doctor continues to function as the central figure during a serious illness, everyone concerned can continue to believe that the sick person has his chance to live.

The role of the physician at the death of a patient who is a beloved member of a family is very complex and often difficult. Ordinarily he functions as a friend and an expertly trained professional who, with life and death in his hands, solves all problems and keeps human beings alive; but at death this role must be relinquished. His own conception of his role and his professional oath demand that under the most pessimistic circumstances, where death seems certain, he try to keep the patient alive and "hope for the best." His dominant position in the death crisis makes it difficult for him to shift openly from the role of the protector of life to one who prepares the family for approaching death by predicting its likelihood. Yet in many instances this is what he must somehow do. The tremendous pressure placed on him by those who transform their hope for the recovery of their loved ones into a firm belief that a hopelessly ill person will not die often makes it impossible to prepare the family for the imminence of dissolution. The doctor, to function in the combined role of scientist, friend, and citizen, must be a symbol of life rather than of death.

Despite the doctor's being the scientist and the "man in white" who brings new miracles to the sick to make them well and who, as the family physician, is friend and confessor, with intimate and privileged knowledge about family members and the relations among them, his role is not entirely positive. Although the formal symbols which surround him are positive and life-giving, the informal ones are negative. There is often a feeling af ambivalence, hostility, and distrust mixed with the faith, trust, pride, and genuine affection among members of a family for the profession. In Yankee City the grim jokes about the undertakers' being beneficiaries of the doctors' mistakes, the stories about various instruments being left in the body after the operation or excessive charges and pink pills and bottles of highly colored liquids being no more than chalk and colored water, as well as the sexual jokes about the doctor shifting from his professional, bedside manner to an all too human masculine one, all testify to this feeling of ambivalence about doctors.

The gossip about various doctors which appeared in our interviews again testified to themes of fear and hostility about them—tempered, it must be remembered, by willing submission to their "fatherly authority" and by genuine trust in their skill and love and respect for them as persons. The ambivalence towards doctors is usually divided symbolically into two types of concept, one being "my doctor" in whom I take pride and the other the "sawbones" who is suspected of varying infractions of the moral code, professional incompetence, and exclusive interest in his fees, as well as malpractice. Doctors in the intermediate position between these two types, when known by the informant, are likely to be well thought of or treated with indifference.

When a patient dies, a doctor must be sure that the family and other members of the community do not saddle him with responsibility for the death. In one sense, the physician is in a strong position because he is the professional expert who alone can make final judgment of the causes of the event. Professional ethics and mutual protection demand that his colleagues speak approvingly, keep quiet, or defend him, should gossip and rumor attack him. The surgeon, because of his central role in a dramatic situation, is particularly subject to threats of unpleasant criticism.

The doctor can announce the cause of death, sign the death certificate, and usually depend on the community and its officials to accept his pronouncement. But, given the various types of personality among those who grieve and feel guilty about their covert or open hostility to the deceased, the doctor must play his role carefully and well to make sure he will not be blamed and possibly have his reputation and career destroyed. His professional reputation must be reinforced by moral authority. Should there be doubts about his private moral life there may also arise questions as to his professional competence. Since doctors receive little or no training in problems of human relations, it is clear that each learns informally and by trial and error how to handle this difficult problem; sometimes by the quiet, sardonic advice of other doctors. Moreover, the society itself helps to protect the doctor, for, after all, its members believe—and must believe—that the profession is necessary to heal the sick and prevent death. Individual faith and trust are needed by all who use doctors to reduce their anxiety and conquer fear. It is not strange that most members of the community have a personal interest in protecting their faith in their own doctors by helping to protect the community's faith in the medical profession.

The doctor, particularly the surgeon, must take care of his own internal psychological problems. He must learn how to convince himself most of the time that he has done everything to save the patient or he may find it impossible to cope with the moral pressure of a succession of unpleasant outcomes. Self-confidence is often attained by allowing the role he plays for his patients to convince him that he is what they believe him to be. Since any doctor must always play a positive public role for his clients and act out beliefs and sentiments he may not feel, but which he knows are expected by his patients and their families, whose fear and anxiety demand constant reassurance from his deportment, he often learns to allow his experiences with his patients to convince him that he is what they think he is. His conception of himself in time largely corresponds with the role in which the public sees him. If he cannot achieve this he pays an intolerable and sometimes tragic price internally for his efforts to manage his own self-evaluations.

The authority and significance of a doctor for his patients and their families is clearly related to the class position of each. We made a careful statistical study of the clientele of each doctor in Yankee City. It demonstrated that patients, largely unconsciously, tended to select doctors who belonged to the class just above them. As such, the doctor was sufficiently superior to have superordinate value to the patient and yet near enough to allow the patient and his family to have confidence that he understood their needs. In Yankee City there were fifteen doctors; four were in the upper-upper, three in the lower-upper, and eight in the upper-middle class. The ethnic factor, while operating to some extent among the lower classes, did not seem to be of great importance in the middle and upper classes in their choice of doctors, whereas social class was of great importance.

The lawyer, the doctor's principal competitor for status, plays an important but usually not a central and crucial symbolic role in any of the important rites of passage. His symbolic activities at times of birth, marriage, and death are of secondary significance when compared to those of the doctor, but still his role is of great secular importance during these various crises.

Of crucial importance in understanding a lifetime from the point of birth to the point of death is the exact place where the professional role fits into the social system itself. Doctor and lawyer are usually private enterprisers. They relate themselves "voluntarily and freely" to their clients through such institutions as the hospital, their offices, and other business enterprises. In Yankee City they are independent and free, whereas minister, priest, and teacher are functionaries within organized hierarchies. The positions of the latter are dependent on the prestige and power of the structure to which they belong and to the status assigned to them within the structure's hierarchy. When the prestige of a church is very high and the minister is the powerful and active head of his organization, his position in the community is likely to be high, but when the sacred symbols of religion are not fully trusted or highly regarded, and when in addition the church itself ranks low in the community, his position must be correspondingly low. In Yankee City the Episcopalian and Unitarian churches ranked higher by a notch or two than did other Protestant churches. Although they had parishioners from all levels of the society, they were considered the upper-class churches, whereas the Presbyterians and Congregationalists were somewhat less highly ranked and Baptists and Methodists were well below. The social position of ministers generally corresponded to the prestige of the church. This is so partly because of the church's reputation and its social place within the community and partly because its members select their ministers and are likely to choose men who fit their own criteria for suitability.

The Undertaker

The role of the undertaker, as everyone knows, has developed very rapidly in the last few generations and is likely to continue to increase the social area it controls. Whereas it was once customary for the family with the help of friends to "lay out the dead" and prepare the corpse for burial as well as to "sit up" with it to show respect and indicate that duty, honor, and love were being bestowed upon the dead person's memory, the undertaker is now called immediately after death to take charge. At death the second phase of the general period of crisis begins; the first being the period of the last illness and the second the time between death and burial. The mortician has developed his place by satisfying a need for which those in distress were willing to pay. Basically he is a private enterpriser who will do the ritually unclean and physically distasteful work of disposing of the dead in a manner satisfying to the living, at a price which they can pay. He sells his goods and services for a profit. His salesmen, applying the sound logics of business enterprise, attempt to sell his goods—coffins and other mortuary paraphernalia—at the highest price possible, and he buys at a price low enough to maximize profit. As a business-man he advertises, enters into civic life, and engages in other activities businessmen use to increase business and compete successfully with their rivals. As an enterpriser he hires employees—drivers and other skilled workers—and by steadily increasing the size of his work force and the effectiveness of his sales organization, enlarges his business, profits, and importance in the community. [58]

As a skilled artisan he uses the expertness of the embalmer, thereby drawing upon some medical knowledge. He must also be proficient in the art of the beauty shop and the cosmetician to perform the last toilette of the corpse. This, of course, includes washing, powdering, painting, the use of paraffin, and other devices of the beauty shop. He must see to it that the corpse is properly clothed and that it conforms to the expectations of its audience, particularly the bereaved family. In this he functions to save responsible members of the family and their friends from performing the menial and unpleasant tasks necessary to prepare a body for burial. He does the physical work of taking the ritually unclean, usually diseased, corpse with its unpleasant appearance and transforming it from a lifeless object to the sculptured image of a living human being who is resting in sleep. The contemporary image of the corpse is that of a human being temporarily resting with his eyes closed, or perhaps someone who has but recently gone to sleep and will soon waken.

The corpse, although a dead human being, is supposed to "look well." Those who pass by in procession to look upon the deceased want a glorified, or at least peaceful, image of the live person they knew and loved. The undertaker closes the staring eyes, the gaping mouth, strengthens the sagging muscles, and with the aid of cosmetics and the help of soft silks and satins in the coffin's interior provides the central character of the tragic ritual with the proper appearance. Some of the favorite expressions of those who pass by "to pay their last tribute" are: "He looked very well—" "He looked just like he did when he was well—" or "You would think he was taking a nap or was resting his eyes for a minute." The people of Yankee City do not use formal death masks to look at what they want to see in death. But the skill of the undertaker provides an informal one which says that the dead who wear it look like life, that they are only asleep and will soon awaken. The art of the undertaker, despite its extreme secularity and its traffic with the impure things of this world, provides a symbolic product which fits very neatly into the needs of the symbolic life of Yankee City.

In performing these ritually unclean tasks the undertaker reduces the horror the living feel when in contact with the cold and "unnatural" remains of a loved person, particularly during the uncertain in-between stage of the funeral rites of passage, when anxieties are greatest. The undertaker helps to remove the pollution and corruption of death at less emotional cost to the living. In the language concerned with rites of transition, he allows the living to pass through the phases of separation and margin with less pain than if he were not present.

The staging and arrangements for the funeral ritual are largely in the undertaker's hands. He must place the coffin and arrange the flowers so that their dramatic effect is most easily brought out. He must be unobtrusively responsible for making certain that during the moments of intense emotion and sorrow no awkward situations arise. He must be sure that family, near kindred, and friends are properly placed in the audience, that pall-bearers are chosen who are symbolically correct and physically capable. He must be certain that all arrangements have been made with the proper officials at the cemetery and with the police escort for the funeral procession. Above all, he must be the competent stage manager and impresario who conducts the ritual of the tragic drama, beginning with the mortuary chapel, church, or home, that continues and coheres as a tragic procession across the crowded streets of the city to the open grave in the cemetery. In one sense he is the producer who fashions the whole enterprise so that other performers, including the minister, the eulogist, the organist, the vocalist, family, and mourners, can act becomingly and get the approval and praise for the funeral's success and receive the sensuous satisfaction that the funeral's symbolism evokes. At the same time all this must be performed in such a way that the uncontrolled grief and random behavior of the living when they face the dead will not destroy the form of the ritual.

Despite the fact that the undertaker performs a necessary, useful service and provides necessary goods for an inevitable event, that the skills and services he brings to bear are of a high order, and that he is usually well paid and very often successful as an entrepreneur, there is considerable evidence that neither he nor his customers are content with his present symbols and status within the occupational and social hierarchy of Yankee City. There is an increasing tendency on the part of the undertaker to borrow the ritual and sacred symbols of the minister and other professional men to provide an outward cover for what he is and does.

His place of business is not a factory or an office but a "chapel" or a "home." Its furniture and arrangement often suggest the altar and auditorium of a church. He frequently dresses in ritual clothes reserved for roles of extreme formality, high etiquette, and prestige. His advertisements, while cautious and careful not to use symbols indicating a particular sect (unless specialized for that purpose), tend to borrow from the language of religion. The brochures and other attendant literature used to advertise the functions of the enterprise skillfully draw on the traditional symbols of the church.

Although the social processes continue to turn the role of the undertaker from that of businessman into professional mortician, there is a considerable hostility to it. It cannot be forgotten that he handles the unclean aspects of death while the minister controls the clean and spiritual phases of it. The undertaker makes a business profit, whereas the minister is given a professional fee. The deep hostilities and fears men have for death, unless very carefully controlled and phrased, can turn the undertaker into a scapegoat, the ritual uncleanliness of his task being identified with his role and person. The thousands of undertaker jokes that appear on the radio and in other mass media as well as in informal gossip, which relate him to the more despised and feared features of death, are ample testimony to this fact. To hold this hostility in check it is necessary for him to surround his functions with sacred symbols and to profess a very high code of ethics. These uplifting efforts are often successfully attacked. For example, in Yankee City an undertaker was the principal sponsor of a non-denominational Easter service on one of the historic hills of the community. Although popular, the service met with considerable ambivalent "kidding" and comment about his skill in advertising his business and putting himself right with everyone so that he would get their trade. This despite the fact that he was known as a conscientious Christian. Undertakers have become the modern target of many of the same jokes as were once directed at grave-diggers.

Unless the place of the church and its supernatural symbols increases in importance, it seems likely that the professional role of the undertaker and his use of sacred symbols will continue to grow. His present prominence demands that his business enterprise receive the protection of professional ethics as well as the social form of sacred symbols. It is even possible that in the more remote future the church may incorporate the mortician into its system of functionaries or perhaps take over his functions as part of its own duties; in some sects the custom of referring members to an undertaker of the membership, presumably holding harmonious and trustworthy religious views, already approaches this. Death being at the very center of the sacred life of any society, the functionary who plays a prominent role in its rites is likely to become heavily ritualized and develop a sacred role.

The Life Span of a Cemetery and the Continuing Life of a Community

As long as the cemetery is being filled with a fresh stream of the recently dead it stays symbolically a live and vital emblem, telling the living of the meaning of life and death. But when the family, the kindred, and other members of the community gradually discontinue burying their loved ones there, the cemetery, in a manner of speaking, dies its own death as a meaningful symbol of life and death, for it ceases to exist as a living sacred emblem and, through time, becomes an historical monument. As a symbolic object it, too, is subject to the meaning of time. Its spirituality then resides in a different context, for it becomes an object of historical value in stable communities rather than a sacred collective representation effectively relating the dead to the living.

The active cemetery, funerals, and mourning symbols ritually look to the sacred life of the future while marking the secular end of the lifetime of the individual, while the "dead" cemeteries look backward to the life of the past. Their gravestones are not so much symbols of a man's death as the fact that he and the others once lived and constituted in their aggregate a way of life and a society. If a cemetery holds no future for *our own* deaths to mark our passage from the living to the dead—if we cannot project the life of our time into it—then its dead belong to the *life* of the past. The gravestones become artifacts that refer to the past; the cemetery becomes a symbol speaking of the people of the past to those of the present and stands for the regard of the present for its own past. But man's hope for immortality, his hope for the future, cannot be evoked by such historical symbols. They must be projected into cemeteries and into other symbols which represent man's beliefs and feelings about himself.

There are eleven cemeteries in Yankee City. Each has been filled with the city's dead for part or all of the period from the 1600's until the present. Only six were decorated on Memorial Day. The others were neither repaired nor decorated and were no longer being used as burial grounds. The graves were filled with the ancient dead. Their living descendants did not recognize them for a number of reasons: the family had moved west or gone elsewhere; the intermediate kindred connecting them with the living were buried in more recently established cemeteries, which did not extend to the earlier generations, but received the homage of the living; the dead had no living representatives, or the living representatives had no interest in, or knowledge of, their ancestors. The last two reasons are really one, for connections with the dead are always present but the knowledge or interest to trace these relations may not be.

Although these graveyards did not receive family recognition, it might be supposed that the associations would decorate them, but none did. Yet these same graveyards had been the objects of considerable attention and much ritual only a few months previous to the Memorial Day exercises we first studied. The answer to this paradox has already been suggested in the chapter on historical rituals, in the transforming symbolism of present and past. It is sufficient to say here that the very old graveyards lose their sacred character and become objects of historical significance and are accordingly recognized.

Two semi-active graveyards were in this process of change. They were the oldest cemeteries in use. Large areas were filled with undecorated graves which, except for Memorial Day, were not cared for by the cemetery authorities. They were becoming less sacred and most of the sections involved were not sufficiently "historical" to have fully acquired a new set of values. In a stable community such as Yankee City there is little chance that they face an ultimate loss of all value and that their land will be captured for business enterprise. Such seems to be the fate of many cemeteries in rapidly changing and growing communities where the social structure and population are unstable, this instability in the social system being reflected in the people's disregard of the cemetery as a collective representation to express either their sentiments for the dead or their feelings about the past. In an unstable community, where the changing social structure is reflected in disregard of the cemetery as a collective representation and it no longer has sacred value, the sentiments attached by social groupings such as the family and association disappear. The community loses its values for itself as a totality. Without traditions and a feeling for social continuity, the living lose their feelings for the social character of the graveyard.

When cemeteries no longer receive fresh burials which continue to tie the emotions of the living to the recently dead and thereby connect the living in a chain of generations to an early ancestry, the graveyards must lose their sacred quality and become objects of historical ritual. The lifetime of individuals and the living meanings of cemeteries are curiously interdependent, for both are dependent on an ascription of sacred meaning bestowed upon them by those who live. The symbols of death say what life is and those of life define what death must be. The meanings of man's fate are forever what he makes them.

PART IV

SACRED SYMBOL SYSTEMS

INTRODUCTION

The "myths," rituals, sacraments, creeds, and ceremonies of the several Christian churches of Yankee City, Protestant and Catholic, are here examined as collective representations and evocations of man's moral and organic (species) life. The traditional core of · Christian symbolism is explored. Particular attention is devoted to the symbolism of the Catholic and liturgical Protestant churches, and less to that of evangelical and Calvinistic Protestantism, still the principal and dominant faith of Yankee City. This is partly in order to present and interpret the basic symbols of Christian tradition as well as those of a powerful and populous faith; partly to help us with the difficult task of analyzing the diverse faiths of the many Protestant sects.

Although voluminous interviews were collected on the varieties of individual belief and practice, the evidence and analysis of beliefs and practice are limited to officially sanctioned documents and observed rituals performed in the several churches. Thus certain central tendencies are stressed and the problem of limited page space solved. Parenthetically it may be added that the materials on motion pictures, radio, books, etc., also had to be cut because of space requirements; see pp. 378–421 of Volume *1* of this series, *The Social Life of a Modern Community*, for the beginnings of this study. The analysis of sacred symbols presently given applies not only to Yankee City, where the data were collected, but generally to Christian belief and practice.

The several chapters interpret the structural significance of the Puritan revolt against the traditional sacred order. [141] They analyze the meanings of the sacred Mother, Father, and Son as well as dwelling upon the vital and crucial role of the

323

family in determining Christianity as a symbolic system. The holy sacrifice of the Dutiful Son and its significance to man's tragic condition and his hopes of overcoming it are examined. The meanings of time (see Part II) are restudied in the light of the meanings of the symbolic structure of the sacred year. Although these and all previous chapters have to do with theory, they tend to be limited to the immediate subjects under analysis; those in Part V deal entirely with theory and with its more general and abstract aspects.

The evidence for Part IV comes from interview and observation. All the clergy were interviewed many times, sermons were collected, congregations observed, and their members interviewed. Church histories (there were several good ones) and other religious documents were collected. In a society that does not have writing, such as that of the Australian aborigines, the field worker's ultimate authorities on religion are the old men of the tribe. They cite the ways and words of their ancestors to validate and sanction their own sacred beliefs and actions. In a literate community those who know and care have their own religious beliefs and practices which can be heard and observed, but citations for ultimate authority and the more profound truths, particularly for the clergy, are also in sacred and semi-sacred books and the written works of theologians and holy men. The several Catholic and Protestant versions of the Bible are of course the best examples, but the Roman Missal, the writings of authoritative Protestant and Catholic theologians, liturgical and other "guides" for the church seasons and Sunday sermons are important data for the field study of American religion. Evidence from all the above categories was collected and used in this analysis.

The term *myth* as used here refers to a verbal symbol system which is the outward expression of an inner system of sacred beliefs and values. Ordinarily in most cultures myths are related to rituals, the latter being symbolic practices which give overt expression to the feelings and beliefs contained in the myths. For the anthropologist the term *myth* applies to the sacred beliefs of all cultures, including our own. As used here, the word does not in any way imply that its meanings are true or false. At present such judgments are beyond the realm of science. I do believe that the social and psychological sciences have given insufficient attention to the problem of using the vast and overwhelmingly powerful beliefs and values of religion. There is need to bridge what I believe to be the unnecessary gap between them. Theologians have given much more thought to the meanings of science for religion than scientists have to the significance of religious values and beliefs for understanding man. I hope Part IV may make a modest beginning in this latter direction.

CHAPTER 10

THE PROTESTANT REVOLT AND

PROTESTANT SYMBOLISM

They Gathered at the River, Separately

On a spring day of 1635 they came down the river and landed. Pushing through the salt grass onto high ground they fashioned rude shelters for their families and then built a meetinghouse for God and their own collectivity. These Puritan founders of Yankee City were devout, hardheaded men. They knew what they wanted. Yet with all their reliance on common sense, logic, and their own ability to "figure things out" they, too, were driven by non-rational forces which surged through them and others like them in Europe and America—forces beyond their control or understanding. An autonomous conscience separated each of them from the English collectivity, and what a later prophet of their faith called self-reliance took them away from their homes across the Atlantic to an unknown wilderness. They were now "free" to order the unordered world around them in the image of themselves. This they proceeded to do. [102a]

Together and separately, in conflict and peace, these pious men founded a Protestant city and with other settlements established Protestant New England. [96] Here the values, sacred beliefs, and moral ideas of the Protestant revolt against the rule of established authority and the sacred symbols sanctioned by this authority grew and matured.

Contemporary Protestant churches of the community, some of them lineal heirs of the "first parish," others more recent and intrusive, reflect most of the diverse tendencies of American Protestantism. Despite the Reformation, some liturgical Protestant sects, such as the Episcopalian and Lutheran, cling tenaciously to the ritual style and much of the basic doctrine of the traditional church. Some have moved in diverse theological directions away from the ancient core; others have gone to the

limits of secularity, leaving little to distinguish them from
many secular organizations. Indeed, lodges and secret societies, such as the Yankee City Masons, are more religious in
doctrine and ritual than certain modern churches. However, the
churches to which we will give our present attention, including
the Congregational, Presbyterian, Baptist, Methodist, and at
times the Unitarian, all well established in Yankee City, possess
soundly founded theologies and public ceremonies, including
the Lord's Supper and baptism. The ritual usages of the
Unitarians in Yankee City largely depend on the minister and
the dominant parishioners. In some cases Communion is a
regular part of the service, expressive of the ancient doctrine
of the sacrifice held by those who participate; in others the
sermons are intellectual kin to the lectures of a modern psy-
chologist or social scientist.

Despite the great diversity in belief and ritual among Protestants, it is possible to ask and hopefully seek answers to
the following questions: What is the nature of Protestant
symbolism? How does it differ from Catholic signs and their
meanings? Why are many Protestant beliefs and practices different from, yet very similar to, those of the liturgical faiths? [1]

When the first new church was built and Yankee City
founded, the parishioners placed their own authorities within
the new house of God. They not only brought the absolute authority of the Holy Word with them but paid two pastors, a
junior as well as a senior, to help them interpret it. They controlled, and in turn were controlled by, their local clergy. From
the beginning the two ministers and their flock fought against
the "elders" in Boston who ruled the colony's Calvinistic
theocracy, refusing "obedience and subjection" to them as "the
duty of brethren."

Soon a few families moved several miles inland, still on land
granted to the original settlers. Their new settlement "demanded the right to establish a parish" and be independent.
A half-century of contention passed before they were allowed to
do so. Meanwhile, coastal trade and the building of small ships
developed a third settlement, which became Newtown or the
Port. It emerged as the urban center of Yankee City. In New-

1. It will be obvious to the reader that I am indebted to Weber, Tawney,
Lecky, Freud, Jung, Durkheim, and many others.

town "the seeds of a mercantile and shipbuilding aristocracy were beginning to sprout." They, too, demanded a separate parish. The first parish tried and failed to prevent it; not until 1722 was reluctant approval given for a separate church. [47*a*]

Thus, revolt against authority and the need for local and individual autonomy continued to stir those who had begun the struggle in England. [102*b*] Within them their internal conflict and the ethics of revolt were brought to America. From the very beginning the local settlements fought against central authority, established by those who once led the revolt which resulted in the founding of the colony. Yet, when confronted with the same separatistic spirit in their midst, the parishioners of the parent settlement of Yankee City fought tenaciously against the demands of offshoot settlements for freedom of worship and self-control.

From its beginning "the decaying and languishing state of religion was of deep concern" to the pious of Newtown. An association was formed "to redress in themselves and families any irregularities, and next to admonish their neighbors of the same." According to one of the accounts, to strengthen the state of religion in Yankee City the members of the association called on the young communicants of the church

. . . and endeavored to counsel and advise them to continue "in the sincere practice of those duties that are incumbent upon them by their public confession of Christ." A committee was appointed to "converse with ye wife of" one of the parishioners, "concerning the disturbances she gives him, when he is going to perform family prayers." One of the committees visited "ye taverns by ye water-side" and reminded the landlords of "ye order required to be kept in their houses" and ordered the constable to walk "ye streets after the evening exercise is over on the Lord's day, that the Sabbath may not be profaned."

A local church history reports that "the religious hysteria of the time was more violent in Yankee City" than elsewhere in that part of Massachusetts. The Rev. Caleb Cushing, lineal ancestor of a great family in Yankee City and the nation, commented at the time, "Many New Lights and new doctrines and corrupt errors threatened to overrun the country. Indeed, the many trances, visions, and dreams and wild extacies and enthusiastic freaks and phrensies, which have abounded in some places, have cast a great damp on the work and much cooled the fiery zealots, and we hope God will in mercy prevent the growth of those errors which seem to be creeping in space . . . and spare his people, and not give his heritage to reproach, Etc."

The great English evangelist, the Rev. George Whitefield, at about this time visited Yankee City. He was often obliged as the apostle of the "great awakening" to preach in barns because the conservative churches were closed to him. Because of his evangelism, sixty-odd families left the first and third parishes and, in what is locally called the Presbyterian Schism, founded the fourth church. In 1746 they built the Old South Church, one of the most beautiful structures in New England. (The bones of Whitefield lie in a vault beneath the pulpit.) A chronicler of the times, a member of the first church whose family remained loyal, calls Whitefield an "astonishing fanatic (who) in his sermon entitled 'The Seed of the Woman and the Seed of the Serpent' classed the people of (this) Parish with evil spirits, and is kind enough to inform us that a council of the Trinity was called to decide upon the creation of the lovely creature Eve. . . . He was accustomed to stigmatize (women) as weaker vessels, as the means whereby sin entered into the world . . ."

Still later divisions took place, and in the nineteenth century other churches including the Catholic and Greek Orthodox invaded this Puritan sanctuary.[2] The Irish and French Canadians each established a Roman Catholic church, the Jews a synagogue, and the Greeks an Orthodox church. Slightly under half the people of Yankee City are now Catholic, but the predominant spirit of the town is Protestant and the dominant people in the community are largely Protestant.

The principal Catholic church, although drawing from all class levels, is largely composed of members with ethnic backgrounds. By actual count it is low in membership from the two upper and two middle classes, but has a high proportion from the two lower levels. The three Congregational churches have a

2. See Warner and Lunt [139c], pp. 356–66, for a discussion of the churches of Yankee City.

significantly high membership from the lower and upper-middle classes. St. Paul's Episcopal church has a high proportion from the two upper levels and a low representation from the two lower levels. The Unitarian church also has a sparse membership from the two lower classes, but more than would be expected by chance from the lower-upper and upper-middle classes.

Oral Protestantism and Visual Catholicism

The church buildings located throughout Yankee City, consecrated and ritually set apart, contain the sacred places where those who believe come together to communicate with, and offer public respect to, their god. Extending high above the other buildings, the white spires of many of them gleam in the sun's rays against the dark borders of the river. The simple, unadorned lines and obvious utility of many of these meeting-houses give them an aloof, pure appearance—an aesthetic grace by which their builders strove to satisfy the spiritual needs of their congregations. All are beautiful, but some are architectural treasures, cherished and proudly cared for by the faithful. Within their walls the sacred world of the community lives and takes on collective form. The powerful Father, the gentle Son, and sometimes his lovely Mother are here to be found by those who seek.

Not far from Hill Street stands a sacred building that is different in architecture and beauty from the other churches in Yankee City. Its style is not traditional in New England; the congregation is comparatively new in Yankee City. Yet the massive church building gives an appearance of being older than the simple traditional New England churches. It is the principal Roman Catholic church of the city.

Entering it one sees a huge painting of Christ over the altar, a very physical Christ, nailed and bound to a heavy, almost threatening wooden cross. The human flesh of his face and body show the cruel marks of man's sadism. Crucified and dying, he dominates the whole shadowy interior of the building. Below and to one side of the altar is a smaller representation of the Christ, his body taken from the cross and cared for by his sorrowing Mother, the Virgin Mary. The building is named the Church of the Immaculate Conception. Thus even in name it is set apart from the others.

The Protestant pulpits are bare and largely free of decoration. Sometimes flowers grace them during services on Sunday. Despite the artistic excellence of the interiors of these churches, there is a bare quality about their walls. Their enclosed, precisely defined pews express a cool restraint and aloofness. In these consecrated edifices, Catholic and Protestant, separated from the profane world of secular life, men go to find and communicate with their god. Whom do they find there? What is the sacred world they enter? Who are the sacred beings they worship? And, for the social scientist, what is the meaning of what they do, think, and feel?

Let us enter this world with the reverence and respect it demands and is due. But let us examine it with detachment to make sure we give the facts of religious life the same scientific respect paid those from the other realms of man's collective life. Perhaps in so doing we will learn more fully why the symbolic world of the church holds truths which modern science must learn if it is to understand and help man to know himself.

The worship of the Catholic Church emphasizes visually connected symbols whose basic appeal is non-logical. The worshiper participates in the drama of man and his fate acted out before him while watching the symbolic actions of significant sacred characters. He hears the sacred words as part of this visual action system. The words themselves are important, but their communicative functions are tremendously strengthened by the context of visible symbols. The collective rite incorporates all the worshipers. For those who officiate at the daily Mass, the principal Catholic rite, all the senses of the body are directly involved. Vicariously, and sometimes directly, the worshipers also participate with all their bodily senses. They, too, see, taste, smell, feel, as well as hear, when they experience the sacred relation with God. They, too, vicariously and sometimes directly, and with the whole body, act out what is symbolically defined for them to think and feel. The *whole* human body, as well as all the senses, may be involved in public (group) worship with other members of the community and the species. Thus the act of communication with God by the communicant can be a total one; all of him can be involved.

Protestant worship has shifted the use of sensuous visible symbols to a minimum and oral-auditory ones to a maximum. For the clergy and the congregation the sermon, prayer, and hymn are the central parts of Protestant ritual. Muscular movements are minimized, the unobservable movements of the tongue being those principally used, reinforced by bodily gestures which tend to be signs equivalent to those of sign language. More often the gestures are those of the individual minister rather than prescribed and officially sanctioned symbols.

But the Protestant final symbol of authority is the *written* word. The oral word is reduced to written form. The marks of a written word are often symbolic substitutes for oral words which are symbolic substitutes for the sacred drama, itself a symbolic form. The activity of the eye and its field of vision are held to the limitations of the words on a page. Form, shape, color, texture, movement, rhythm, and all the varieties of visual imagery which stimulate the whole man are transformed into the arbitrary arrangement of a mechanical alphabet. Gratification from symbols expressive of immediate visual perception is greatly reduced. The sensuous, visible world around him has disappeared. The eye must first accept the emotional and mental discipline of written words. What words stand for may arouse deep emotions, but the principal intrinsic virtue of written alphabetical word-signs is that they in themselves have nothing to excite the emotions or the imagination. The written or orally communicated word may be a non-rational symbol, but it tends to stand for rational concepts more often than the dramatic, visible action symbols displayed to communicate to others.

Sermons, prayers, and hymns—as we said, the principal forms of Protestant public worship—are founded on the written word of the Bible. Each emphasizes oral, none visual, communication. In them the sensuous satisfactions of life are rigidly limited. To arouse the communicant's emotions these several ritual forms are dependent on the evocative qualities of words (and their meanings) and on the (animal) tone qualities of those who speak and the emotional significance given them by those who listen. The lyrics and music of the Protestant hymn provide the greatest opportunity for the evocation and expression of feeling. The non-rational feeling systems of the whole man can be involved by "a good rousing hymn." The sermon and prayers of some ministers may violently stir the passions of a congregation.

In the values of Protestantism, the reliance on "the word" is not only an expression of increased "rationality" but, more importantly, an exacting way of reducing the use of the several senses, for controlling the bodily needs and containing the appetites once satisfied directly or vicariously by dramatic symbols. When the visual signs are largely banished and the learned word substituted, the whole man—the man of the · species—is held in stricter control. When the rational mental life is emphasized, in some churches, the non-rational world of the species is largely eliminated.

Visual schemes of thought that are intuitive and come most frequently from within the organism,[3] often characteristic of the symbolic order of sacred rituals, are not easily reducible to referential language. In daily interaction they are used most often by children. They readily communicate feelings about bodily experiences with the inner and outer world with other beings like themselves, so that those who feelingly respond to these communications can fully understand and respond to their impact. But those who try to make referential sense out of such words usually fail to learn what the child means— children ‑understand children but adults supposedly better prepared for understanding, to whom the same communications may be sent, often fail.

The symbols of non-rational communication help to order the varieties of experience felt by organisms, and though such symbols may report on outer reality, their central task is to communicate the sensuous feelings of the whole body and the accumulated experiences of the species. They do not atomize the world into discrete units or reform and transpose it into the rigid, abstract mental structure of rational life. For example, the meaning of a man's love for his mother permeates all levels of his being. The sacred world and its symbols incorpo-

3. Piaget [110a], pp. 43–9.

rate all of man; they have to do with entireties. The mysteries of life, including man's love of God, always involve the entire meaning of man. These include man the animal, as well as the moral and spiritual being. Such symbols, including art and religion, express men's relations to each other and their place in the great physical world and the greater supernatural universe surrounding it. These mysteries do not and cannot yield to rational inquiry. They need, and respond to, non-rational understanding in which the whole man communicates and can be communicated to. The non-rational symbols which express these mysteries can be only partly understood by rational inquiry. The realities they express when translated into logical and scientific discourse lose much of their significance. The very process which attempts to make them logically meaningful may destroy what they really express. The expressive "language" of art and religion is most often successful in ordering these meanings into communicable forms.

 Protestant churches, particularly the "respectable" middle-class ones, are often perplexed by problems raised by their stern limitation of worship to oral rites and symbols. Some churches—the more emotional ones, such as the Holy Roller, the Shouting Baptists, and those of the Pentecostal faith—have evolved systems to provide for species expression. The congregation, led by their pastors, abandon rationality and the logical meanings of words, substituting violent gestures, bodily movement, and shouting, which permit the faithful to express what they feel and allow them to believe they have evoked the Holy Spirit. These "excesses" disturb the respectable and since, more often than not, such churches have a lower-class membership, they often arouse the scorn of middle-class Christians. It seems probable that the poverty of symbolic expression characteristic of the ordered worship of Protestant churches which minister to the lower classes makes it impossible for the cravings, longings, wishes, desires, and frustrations of the faithful to be expressed in sanctioned forms. The older symbols, characteristic of the traditional liturgies, which evoke and express the species and impulse life of man are lost to them. Some of the ecstatic emotional outbursts where the emotions of the whole congregation burst forth, where strange tongues are spoken and men and women writhe on the floor in

spiritual ecstasy, are most likely to be the compensatory substitutes of the less inhibited and more emotional lower classes
for the satisfactions they once felt in church rituals.

The solidly respectable upper-middle-class churches which
emphasize decorum and the use of the rational word sometimes
find that many of their own parishioners are little involved in
the sacred symbols used. Many fail to find the spiritual resources either in themselves or in the forms of worship to feel
confident that there is real communication with the sacred
world. The cold, alien rationality of science more easily invades
their sanctuaries. The seminaries, the ministers trained by
them, and the laity who feel their influence are often vulnerable
to the persuasive power of scientific materialism, for the mental
world of their sacred life is strongly founded on a faith in
rationality and logical communication. Such a condition often
disallows the grace to believe; it eliminates the sacred and
spiritual symbols from the mental life of many of those who
once believed.

The Symbols of Masculinity, Femininity, and Procreation in Protestantism

The Calvinists who founded New England and their descendants are regarded by most scholars as worshipers of a
masculine God; the Puritan faith usually is characterized as
"masculine." Lecky declared Puritanism to be "the most masculine form that Christianity has yet assumed." In his *History
of European Morals* he says that ". . . in the great religious
convulsions of the sixteenth century the feminine type followed Catholicism, while Protestantism inclined more to the
masculine type. Catholicism alone retained the Virgin worship,
which at once reflected and sustained the first." He added, "It
is the part of a woman to lean, it is the part of a man to
stand." [4]

During the Tercentenary celebration of Yankee City, as we
have seen, a sermon to commemorate the spiritual significance
of the event was preached by a leading Protestant clergyman.
Among his other remarks he declared, "The Christianity . . .
brought to Massachusetts . . . adapted its adherents for every

4. Lecky [78], p. 368.

kind of human endeavor that was adventure, self-reliant, rugged and idealistic . . . The masculinity, the strength and ruggedness in the Puritanism which formed us are the absolutely essential ingredients of any religion which is worth while . . . Puritanism brings people not to their knees but to their feet."

Although such statements about the masculinity of Puritanism are largely true, they fail to grasp the real significance of the Protestant revolt. Manifestly it did eliminate "worship" of the Virgin Mary. The Mother was removed from the temple and her many feasts and vigils destroyed. At the manifest level it is true that the male and his virtues were extolled and such values reified into the attributes of divinity. Yet these, important as they were, are dependent on, and expressions of, a more important revolt against existing values and their symbols.

The Protestant revolt against the reified symbols of the traditional social structure, particularly that part of the liturgy which expressed and bestowed moral approval on the species, greatly modified the ritual and belief system of Christianity about sexual life. It was not represented or freely expressed by Protestant sacred symbols. Liturgical life was reduced to a few crisis events believed to have occurred in the life of the male Christ. The longings, feelings, and deep physio-psychological attachments that had been a part of mediaeval and late Roman Christianity and the great religions that preceded them became suspect and were violently attacked and abolished. The moral revolt against female symbols of the species increased through time until the mother and the woman largely disappeared from worship and only the male Jesus and the other male figures of the Trinity remained.

The fundamental movement was against the great value placed on species life by the traditional church. The meaning of eternal life as it flows through the species and finds its most significant expressive act in human procreation was and is a mystery of the most sublime importance in the symbolic life of the traditional church. Females and males fulfilling their symbolic functions in procreative acts were necessary and central parts of the most sacred level of its belief system; not males or females as moral beings only, but males and females entire in all their procreative life-giving and life-fulfilling significance.

Although woman was banished from the Protestant pantheon, the revolt against her was not so much an attack on her for what she is in herself as a person but as the procreative partner and the one who symbolizes and arouses the erotic impulses of men. The revolt was not against her as the mother but as the central symbol of species life. The celibate priests can cry, "Hail Mary, full of grace, the Lord is with thee," and know at that solemn moment he is speaking of the procreation of God in a human female womb and that he is a male "other Christ" participating in a symbolic act expressive of the impregnation of a woman. But the Protestant minister, in status male and sexually active, cannot be so mentally free as to perform such a ritual lest his manifest sexuality affront the moral values of his congregation. To the priest, Mary with "the charm of virginity" *is* the queen of purity, "the eternal idea of true chivalry." To the Protestant minister, sexually free from the vows of the celibate, it is congruent that she be the remote and distant woman necessarily accepted, for she is recognized in the Holy Word.

The elaborate and growing cult of the Virgin, which will be discussed later, symbolically and non-logically expresses the central and focal point of species life: the procreative, fecund woman sexually conceiving, bearing, and caring for her child. Her sacred symbols reinforce species existence and make it manifest and meaningful in sacred form. More importantly, they greatly strengthen the masculine symbols of species existence. Her cult makes it easier for most men and women to "understand" and feel at the unconscious levels the significance of the Divine mysteries. Her presence as the Divine woman more fully involves men as males in the sacred world; the male aspects of God functioning as procreator and procreated are more clearly stated, thus providing a more unified emotional experience for the morally trained organism. The symbols of the whole family, male and female, father and mother, are represented and become channels of expressive significance for the worshipers.

With the female largely eliminated, there is less scope in Protestantism for male sexuality to express itself in religious symbols. The Lord God Jehovah is there and present but he tends to be a distant Father. The Holy Ghost has lost his significance as the symbolic spiritual being of masculine creativity. The Christ remains a male but an "asexual" one. These symbols of species life, focussed on the procreative function uniting males and females and maintaining the physical connection of the generations of men and women, have greatly weakened. For the very reason that Catholicism is strongly influenced by the female values and symbols, the male role is strengthened, not weakened, in the drama and myth of Christian life.

During the early periods of Christianity, following the Jewish theological system, women were not of positive importance at the sacred level. They were reduced to a subordinate sacred position. The spread of Christianity through the Mediterranean, where it felt the warm, sensuous influence of Grecian, Italian, and other cultures gradually increased the position of women until the role of the Virgin became of great importance and finally one of the central positions in the Christian pantheon. During the Middle Ages the secular ideals of chivalry and courtly love came to full flower in the aristocratic values and beliefs expressed by the symbol of the unattainable, perfect woman. More importantly, for our present purposes, it was then, too, that the long development of the sacred symbol of the Virgin, an ascetic and sensuous sacred ideal of womanhood, received great recognition by the faithful. While the secular troubadours were singing the knight's chivalrous and perpetual love of the unattainable woman, using symbols of erotic love, the clergy and the laity were offering prayers to the sacred woman whose cult as the Virgin and Queen of Heaven flowered in the rites of the Church.

Tristan's "love of love" dominated the passion of the knight for his unattainable lady. Sublimated desire, transformed to the highest secular level of moral purity, transfigured passion into images of moral perfection. Huizinga in *The Waning of the Middle Ages* says, "The knight and his lady, that is to say, the hero who serves for love, this is the primary and invariable motif from which erotic fantasy will always start. It is sensuality transformed into the craving for self-sacrifice, into the desire of the male to show his courage, to incur danger, to be strong, to suffer and to bleed before his lady-love. . . .

The man will not be content merely to suffer, he will want to save from danger, or from suffering, the object of his desire." [5]

Some writers believe the use of the symbol of the sacred woman was deliberately fostered by Church authorities; it seems more likely to have been an integral and "natural" expression of the non-logical, emotional needs of the Church and its celibate priesthood.

From the middle of the twelfth century onwards [says De Rougemont] there was a succession of attempts to promote a cult of the Virgin. It was sought to substitute "Our Lady" for the "Lady of Thoughts" of the heretics. At Lyons in 1140 the canons instituted a Feast of the Immaculate Conception of Our Lady. . . . It was all very well for Saint Bernard of Clairvaux to protest in a famous letter against "this new feast unknown to the custom of the Church, disapproved of by reason, and without sanction from tradition . . . a feast which introduces novelty—the sister of superstition and the daughter of fickleness"; and it was all very well for Saint Thomas, a century later, to declare in the clearest terms that "if Mary had been conceived without sin, she would not have required redemption by Jesus Christ"—the cult of the Virgin filled what the Church felt, in face of the danger threatening it, to be a vital necessity. [6]

The chivalrous courtly knight and the unattainable, perfect woman on whom his unfulfilled desire was expended, the celibate priest and the pure and undefiled Virgin in whom the clergy found a perfect symbol for its own chivalrous love, are the secular and sacred symbols and statues which express the moral ideals of Christians.

The secular structure of society has changed, the chivalrous way of life with its knights and ladies has long departed, aristocracy has lost its unchallenged noble position. But the great hierarchical structure of the Catholic Church has remained and its celibate clergy still venerate with combined filial and chivalrous feelings the sacred and unattainable symbol of the Virgin. She, lovely and beautiful, as the Queen of Heaven and the Mother whom no man has sexually possessed, is still the perfect symbol for the celibate expression of sub-

5. Huizinga [66], p. 67.
6. De Rougement [119], p. 111.

limation and unfulfilled desire perpetually unsatisfied. "Romantic love," Bertrand Russell declares, "as it appears in the Middle Ages, was not directed at first towards women with whom the lover could have either legitimate or illegitimate sexual relations; it was directed towards women of the highest respectability, who were separated from their romantic lovers by insuperable barriers of morality and convention." [120*b*]

The ideals of courtly love survive, transformed and weakened, in the arts and in the frustrated wishes of most contemporary women. The knight in the tournament competing in physical combat for the approval of his unattainable lady was gone long before Yankee City was founded, but he still survives there in the secular world of the motion picture, television, and other mass media. There in costume dramas he still appears, combining the thrills of love and death to satisfy the wishes of those who yearn for perfect love and the need of men to feel the vicarious pain of the sacrifice of self. Here the cowboy, too, on his great horse nobly rides forth to battle, to kill and be killed, to rescue pure womanhood from villainy. Honor and self-sacrifice dominate his thoughts and control his actions. The violence of the tournament is transformed into gun battles in the never-never land of the Old West, where the hero and his mounted horsemen, contemporary Tristans and Knights of the Round Table—still champions of purity and morality— fight and conquer the champions of evil and villainy. The Lone Ranger today, Sir Galahad yesterday; once Lancelot and Tristan, now Gary Cooper and Gregory Peck in "High Noon" and the "Gun Fighter."

The revolt against the sacred life of the traditional church and the non-logical, emotional order of the species has been carried beyond Protestantism to its ultimate extreme in the Marxian philosophy, now the state religion of several nations. The Marxian symbol system reduces all their sacred symbols to the dull logic of a technique and the discipline of a technology.

The symbols of the family and those of the species expressing themselves in the forms of sexual, filial, and parental relations were ruthlessly attacked in Marxian literature. [46] The ethics, morality, and doctrines of family life were subordinated to those of getting and sharing food. Those hostile critics who say Marxism reduces man to an animal or perhaps to the alimentary canal are wrong. In this materialistic doctrine emphasis is not on the nature of the animal but on the development of new technical *controls* over the environment through the social evolution of *new forms of technology*, thus changing the symbols and values of the group without counter-controls of the species and the society operating to control the technology. The technology in this new theology is primary and dominant. The ethics and basic social values of the group are officially reduced to the dependent position of being weak effects of this elemental First Cause: the Holy Ghost of Marxian mysticism.

The Freudian movement is in part a secular revolt against the extremes of "protestantism" as it is felt by modern men whether they be Jewish, Protestant, or Catholic. Although founded on the individual rather than on the group and the species, Freudian concepts lead modern men to recognize the worth of species life. Freudian thinking is still technological, perhaps necessarily in a scientific age. The rationale of the psychological interview reduces feeling to the mechanism of the libido and the feelings and affective life of the unconscious to the mechanical control of personality constructs. Personality becomes a "topological" mechanism; nevertheless, sexuality is recognized, accepted, approved, and allowed expression.

Some of the Protestant churches in Yankee City have staged a counter-revolt. There has been a resurgence of the sacred symbolic life. A liturgical renaissance has flowed through the worship of such diverse groups as the Episcopalians and Unitarians as well as Methodists, Congregationalists, Presbyterians, and Baptists. The *use* of non-verbal symbols to refer to the world beyond the symbols of reference—to the world made meaningful by the deep feelings men have as members of the species and as participants in the ordered daily events of their society—now seems to be increasing.

There are many indications that we have reached the limits of the Protestant revolt and that a counterrevolution supporting and using evocative symbols is developing. The present may be the extreme limit to which the technological symbols of Marxism and similar systems will take us. It may be the high-water mark of what was once called the Protestant revolt. No social system, no matter how great its needs for rational conduct, can carry a rationality founded on technological empiricism to the point where the needs and demands of the physical and social life of the species are no longer recognized and sanctioned in the symbols and values expressing the spiritual life of the group.

Mother's Day: the Return of the Woman and Her Family to the Protestant Pantheon

Perhaps one of the most significant changes in the contemporary Protestant church has been the recent introduction of several special family days into their sacred calendar—all of them coming out of the influence of the laity on the church. The church calendars in Yankee City now give an official place to the mother. There is an ófficial Family or Mother's Day on the second Sunday of May—coincidentally the month especially dedicated to the Virgin Mother in the traditional liturgical calendar. Mother's Day began as a secular holiday to allow sons and daughters to express their feelings for their mothers ceremonially. Its observance spread very rapidly throughout the United States. It became one of the most popular of all holidays. Ministers incorporated it into their Sunday services and preached sermons devoted to the mother. Many of these sermons express most of the sentiments and values evoked by the Mother of God in Catholic rituals. Some ministers interrelate the symbols of the human and divine mothers.

The Congregational liturgy suggested for Mother's Day and used in Yankee City includes a poem in free verse, "For All Mothers—A Litany" which not only comprehends "what is divine" in a mother's love and establishes the image of all women in the form of each man's mother, but also remembers the mother of Christ and views all women in her image.

MOTHER'S DAY

Scripture Reading: Ruth 1

For All Mothers—A Litany

From slowness of heart to comprehend what is divine in the
    depth and constancy of a mother's love,
        Good Lord, deliver us.

From the unreality of superficial sentiment, from commercial exploitation, and from all lip service to motherhood while we neglect the weightier matters of justice and mercy and love,
> *Good Lord, deliver us.*

By our remembrance of the mother of our Lord standing by the cross of her well-beloved Son,
> *Good Lord, deliver us.*

That it may please thee to open our ears that we may hear the Saviour's word from the cross, "Behold thy mother,"
> *We beseech thee to hear us, good Lord.*

That it may please thee to give us grace from this hour, with the swift obedience of beloved disciples, to take unto our own every woman widowed, bereft, hard-pressed in life,
> *We beseech thee to hear us, good Lord.*

That it may please thee to touch our hearts that we may behold our mother in every woman—

The Virgin Mary as the Mother of God with her own day and month assigned to her in the liturgical churches has been welcomed back, again the sorrowful mother who stands "by the cross of her well-beloved son." Indeed it would be strange and difficult to understand in a country with a secular cult rapidly becoming sacred if in time she were not recognized and her cult re-established. Furthermore, it seems probable that the original Mother may have some of the new values attached to her image in the rituals of the liturgical churches. Instances are at hand in some communities (not Yankee City) of statues of the Madonna being displayed by Evangelical churches on Mother's Day. Mother's Day is still a festival to celebrate the moral worth of the human mother, but now she is an idealized figure securely placed in the ordered worship of most Protestant churches and a significant part of liturgical revivals. It seems possible that this mother symbol may draw closer to, and again be identified with, the Virgin Mother of God. Whatever may happen to the symbol of the mother, the family through her inclusion is once more ceremonially honored in Protestant public worship.

Along with the recognition of the mother by a day set apart there has been a movement, although less popular, to give the father recognition. Some churches have instituted a children's day. Thus the whole family, mother, father and children, is being structured once more into the symbol system of Protestantism. A few years ago the Puritans in Yankee City did not so much as recognize Christmas or Easter; today their descendants are giving ritual recognition to collective symbols expressive of the whole family structure—the strongest being the mother's. Species life and the family structure are indeed reasserting themselves; in new images, the mother and her family have returned to an honored place in the Protestant ceremonial calendar.

Despite losing many of its functions in contemporary life, the family still organizes much of the emotional and species life of the individual. As such, it is a basic creator and referent for systems of common and uncommon evocative symbols whether they be sacred or secular. As world religious or political ideologies spread over the earth, becoming more universal and less tribal, they must increasingly depend for their evocative meanings and emotional validity on symbols which have universal sentiments back of them. The family is the only social institution which provides men of all cultures with such powerful and compelling experiences. It seems probable that as family life becomes more private and less public and increasingly the source of affection and emotional development of the individual, and as other institutions take over more of the practical functions of the family, its symbolism will increasingly dominate the sacred life of this and other groups.

The Protestant Revolt: Sex, Status, and Symbols of Power

Since the Protestant revolt at the moral and secular level was against authority, and since the authority system was masculine with descent of prestige, power, and position from father to son, it might be supposed that its attack would have been against the power and moral ascendancy of the father. Furthermore, since the movement was successful, it might be assumed that the status of the father would have been reduced and limited. It was not; the Puritan father, as well as his successors in New England, was an all-powerful tyrant. The pastor, the father of his flock, was also notoriously authori-

tarian and autocratic. The theocratic rule which dominated
the early years of Yankee City and long after informally
exercised powerful control demonstrates that the father and
male rulers cast in his image were very powerful men. Meanwhile they were reinforced and sanctioned by the authority of
the sacred male symbols; the virtual elimination of the cult
of the Virgin had left a father god all-important. Why was the
father not attacked? Why were male statuses, created in his
image, strengthened and given power by this "reform" movement? What was the moral part of the revolt against? [7]

It was not against male authority as such, but the *form* of
this authority; the target of the attack was the system of fixed
status for men. In feudal society the family functioned to fix
permanently the place of the individual. He was born to, and
stayed in, one closed position. The fluid Renaissance Protestant
and industrial societies, all terms for the several aspects of one
basic change, emphasized the movement of free individuals and
openness of status. The Puritans who came to Yankee City to
improve their *economic* and *religious* status also came to improve their *social* position. All were integral parts of a systematic change from an old to a new system. Birth into a family
of a given status no longer fixed the entire career of the individual or all of his activities within one status. He was freer
to do what he might to be the master of his fate. He could
move.

The woman's position remained largely fixed. She did not act
on her own but according to her family status. True, given the
new freedom of men to marry outside their status she, too,
could marry above or below her status. In American culture
women have always freely changed family status at marriage
but until recently, long after the tide of Protestant revolt had
reached its limits, they have been subordinate and under male
dominance in the family roles which fix their status in the
whole community. Masculine dominance limited a woman's
right to make individual decisions running contrary to the
rigidly defined roles of mother, wife, daughter, and sister. It
should be noted that, with one exception, each of these roles
in varying ways denies her sexuality. Daughter and sister are

7. My problem here is a structural & symbolic one. It is not my purpose to
examine the problem of corruption within the Church.

asexual and taboo. In daily life the moral attitudes toward the mother exclude sex; she, too, is taboo. Only the role of the wife is openly defined as sexual. Sexuality, impulse life, and the relaxed indulgence of the physical life of the organism were subordinated by Protestants to the harsher demands of daily tasks, sensuous pleasure to the virtues of work. Thus the emphasis on work as an end in itself, the disapproval of pleasure and idleness, the fear of impulsivity and joy in the senses and their condemnation as sins, are parts of a larger concern: the limitation and control of species life, denying it full expression at the moral and sacred levels.

In Yankee City, during the early years, there were additional reasons for the rigid control of women. Its social system was founded on the family; in fact, it was more fully dependent on the family to maintain order than was the older system. The loose social organization of Protestantism, largely free of the hierarchy of social, political, and church ranking, was more in need of the family to insure stability and security than the previous one where the controls of the larger systems of ranking unified and held people together. Each local society in early New England was greatly dependent on the autonomous family for order. The male's free movement, his increasing freedom to choose for himself, to move from role to role, from place to place, to change his functions and status, all helped to loosen this fluid system. Tightening the controls and limiting the position of women and the relations of men and women served as a counterforce, hence the rigid rules controlling a woman and her behavior in her several family roles, particularly her relations with men. The firm regulation of the status of the woman and the relations of men to it provided a foundation for the masculine moral and symbolic worlds. Free her and chaos might result; subordinate her and the fluid economic and social worlds largely inhabited by males could increasingly develop and absorb the physical and psychic energies of men. But within the family, usually the socially approved haven for the intimacies and indulgences of species life, the stern father rules his sons and daughters in relations of obligation and duty; the dominant husband and the submissive wife perform their procreative duties to be fruitful and multiply. We must remind ourselves that the difference between the culture of Calvin and the Latin culture of Catholic Rome are of degree only, for the latter, too, has its own asceticism. Yet, no matter how far the similarities of these two subcultures are credited, the great difference between them as to how they morally order and symbolically express the non-rational world of the species must be recognized as an important and significant characteristic.

We have spoken earlier of the ascetic rules controlling the celibate priest and his release in the sublime symbols of the Virgin Mother and her heavenly family. We need to examine such sexual controls in relation to the priest's place in the structure of the Church and his delegated authority to control sacred symbols of absolute power. We must then compare the status of the priest with that of the Protestant clergy to understand something more of the meanings of the Protestant symbol systems.

The status of the celibate clergy, a rigidly controlled sexual position, slowly developed in the Church structure as an expression and integral part of the ascetic, negative Christian ideals controlling the relations of the sacred and profane. The rules governing the position "married the clergy away" from their biological families into the body of the Church where the entire person is encompassed in one status. To understand the present condition of the clergy, a glance at the past is necessary. Originally celibacy, as most people know, was not required and the clergy married, yet throughout early Christianity there were strong feelings about the impurity of sex; [89] consequently the clergy, as the professionally purest of men, were felt to be most subject to ascetic ideals. As the structure of the Church grew more powerful, ascetic ideals forced celibacy on the entire clergy. At first celibacy "was an act of virtue," later it was "an act of duty," and by the fourth century marriage of the clergy was considered criminal. Yet "marriages" of the clergy continued to be openly celebrated. Lecky comments, "An Italian bishop of the tenth century epigrammatically described the morals of his time, when he declared, that if he were to enforce the canons against unchaste people administering ecclesiastical rites, no one would be left in the Church except the boys; and if he were to observe the canons against bastards, these also must be excluded. The evil acquired such magnitude that a great feudal clergy bequeathing the ecclesiastical benefices from father to son, appeared more than once likely to arise." [8] It was not until late in the Middle Ages that the power of the pope and the feelings of the faithful were sufficient to force celibacy on the clergy. Today this ecclesiastical status is now entirely extricated from the family system and community control.

The hierarchical organization of statuses to which the parish priest belongs, as a member of the lowest ecclesiastical rank, is a rigorously organized system of authority in which power supposedly resides at the top and flows from the absolute power of God himself. By virtue of ordination, spiritual power enters the status and person of the priest as part of the Church structure, lifting him above the laity who occupy no official position in the hierarchy. The symbolic tasks he performs, the symbols of his habiliments, and his way of life outwardly manifest the structural realities of the Catholic social system and the relations of the clergy and the laity.

The Catholic doctrine of infallibility by which the pope for certain purposes speaks as the voice of God and as an ultimate and final authority is part of the structure of spiritual absolutes making up the symbolic life of the Church. This infallibility of the pope and the doctrine of the "real presence" allow pope and priest within rigidly defined limits to talk with the spiritual authority of God himself. Symbolically each doctrine reinforces the others. Ultimate truth always and forever resides in the worldwide local use of the symbols of the Mass. In this ceremony the Church, the clergy, the hierarchy of local bishops, the pope, and countless congregations express their unity in a miraculous, magical symbol that makes them one.

The priest who performs the ceremony of the Mass does so through the absolute sacred power vested in him by his bishop and through the sacrament of ordination, the latter a principal rite of passage of the Catholic Church which sets the man who is a priest apart so that he is "another Christ." The apartness not only transforms him spiritually but socially and biologically. When he takes vows of celibacy to remove himself from the moral and biological claims of procreation, he acknowledges the authority and discipline of the sacred hierarchy of conse-

8. Lecky [78], p. 330.

crated officials which ultimately connects him in ritual union with the pope and through him with the absolute power of God. Historically, through some two thousand years and many generations of ordination, it is believed he is "one with Peter" and related to Christ himself.

When it is firmly believed by the faithful of Yankee City and elsewhere that the spiritual power of the symbols the priest controls are so great that he can bring God himself to the altar and incorporate him into the physical bodies of men, a number of consequences follow. The principal ones are that the priest himself, within the limits of his status in the hierarchy, exercises absolute spiritual power and authority; but the hierarchy, composed of ascending levels, each under the discipline of an immediately superior status, often removes decision-making from the local community of Yankee City and places it far from America in an alien culture. Through the priest the faithful are spiritually oriented to a local and a world society. The priest, as a being set apart, is removed from the immediate control of the family and community structure, this by training and by the symbolic separation. He is by personal training and the status he occupies in a better position than the minister to perform his difficult tasks. That he is a human being and sometimes fails must be recognized, yet more often he succeeds.

The Protestant clergy, on the other hand, are bound locally to the family life of the community. Through their wives and children their lives are inextricably interwoven with the biological and social cycles of procreation. Protestant clergy are locally controlled. Protestant hierarchies, if any, tend to be nationally rather than internationally centered. Power tends to be local. The congregation can "hire and fire" the clergy. The clergy are less set apart than priests. The symbols they manipulate have no absolute power *within* them; their sacerdotal authorities, if any, do not speak with symbols of intrinsic authority. Ministers must depend on their moral autonomy if they are to exercise control. The structure which weaves localities together being loose and often weak, a personally powerful local pastor, as the histories of the churches in Yankee City demonstrate, may become dominant and wield great power to the point of schism. But the sacred symbols he controls are intrinsically weak. God is not in them in the same way as he is believed to be in the Catholic Mass. The minister can never exercise the power the priest can express daily.

Because of the belief of the faithful in the power and influence of the symbols of the several sacraments, the Catholic hierarchy accumulates and controls great power. Because of man's dependence on its symbols, the church itself is a reservoir not only of great spiritual strength but of temporal power. Since most of the sacraments have to do with the spiritual sanction of human crises and their rites of transition, including birth, marriage, and death, or with maintaining graceful relations with sacred power, and since the sacraments controlled and performed by the clergy bring God himself into the immediate situation, the dependent and subordinate position of the vast mass of the laity is very great. This condition can exist only so long as the laity are faithful and believe. When faith goes, power departs, too. Because they refuse to recognize the power of faith and belief, the economic determinists and those who interpret power as only economically founded fail to understand many of the phenomena of contemporary and historical America and Europe. It might well be argued that it is the power of faith in an economic system which maintains it, or that the lack of a powerful faith in an economic system results in its abandonment. Obviously, not all change can be accounted for by this interpretation, nor is this intended. Yet scientific exploration and interpretation of the persistence or modification of many economic and social systems must also be founded on moral, spiritual, and symbolic, as well as economic, evidence.

Concomitant variation has continued from the time of the Reformation and the Protestant revolt; the sacred symbol system has shifted, the status order has changed from fixed to open, the technology from early hand to later machine; the division of labor from simple to complex; all concurrently, so that they are synchronized into a socio-technical-religious order in which the changing parts are moderately, if sometimes discordantly, congruent with each other. To say that one necessarily *caused* another is scientific nonsense. That technological shift and economic change *caused* the social and symbolic shifts or that a religious ethic shifted the economy, I believe, is false.

That radical changes in the technology will affect the social and symbolic orders obviously follows, for a moderate degree of congruence, equilibrium, and cohesion between them are necessary. However, that a new symbol system and powerful social order can change the technology of a culture has been demonstrated by no one better than by those who, following Marx, believe exactly the opposite: the Communists in Russia.

The Protestant reaction against the close attachment to the family of birth and social orientation and its fixed status in the group, combined with the feeling of repugnance for too open symbolic expression and satisfaction of the emotions, expelled the woman from the holy pantheon. The man who leaves his fixed status in fact or attitude is likely to be the man who emotionally "leaves" home. [61c] The deepest emotional, if not social and legal, tie to the family of birth is the mother. If the individual is to be freed from his family of birth and if fixity of status is to be reduced and freedom of movement increased, the intense attachment to the mother must be reduced. Her meaning to her children must be changed. They must be able to free themselves from her and get away. It is probable that the revolt against the closed and fixed position (of the men) of feudal society and the elimination of the Virgin from Protestant worship were both parts of the larger changes which resulted in a more flexible western European culture. All are integral parts of the shift in the treatment of the species in the moral and symbolic life of Yankee City.

CHAPTER 11

SACRED SEXUALITY—THE MOTHER,

THE FATHER, AND THE FAMILY

IN CHRISTIAN SYMBOLISM

The Family and Christian Symbolism

Although the sacred order must be rationally defended by rational men who are believers, its ultimate validity is forever founded on a non-rational base where men know what is true and real because they *feel* they know what is true. In those cultures which prize rationality, each religion must have its St. Thomas Aquinas, its Scotch theologians or their equivalents, who belatedly prune and domesticate the ancient beliefs and primitive practices of believing men to conform to the rational norms of civilized men. Thus rational men make what is essentially a non-rational matter "rationally" acceptable to them. They are often not so much apologists as translators, yet for St. Thomas, as for all believers, the central facts of his own beliefs were mystical and non-rational.

If religious symbols are collective representations, reflecting at the supernatural level the collective realities of the group, most of those present in the sacred world to which Christians ritually relate themselves are formed by, express, and reinforce the family structure. What the Church is, Protestant or Catholic—its own self-conception—the image in which its members conceive themselves, as well as the sacred way of life which orders their relations to the Church and to God—in short, the supernatural order of Christianity—is formed in, and nourished by, all or part of the family as a social and biological system. The Church, its rites, beliefs, and practices, would not exist if the family failed to survive. The Church, forever dependent on the family for its existence, expresses more concern about, and exercises greater moral influence on, the family than on any other human institution. The sanctions exercised against extramarital sexual life, the breaking of the marriage tie, birth control, and the deeper incest cravings are more than sacred interdicts of disapproved conduct; they are also expressions of the anxiety of the Church about its own sacred symbolic life. Should the present form of the family disappear, the Christian Church would necessarily undergo revolutionary changes. The hostility of contemporary revolutionary movements against both family and religion is not happenstance. [46] The values and beliefs of the two institutions energize and strengthen each other. Religion and family are at the center of the eternal, ongoing group life of man. They conserve and cherish the indwelling unity and human identity of a thousand generations and a multiplicity of institutions of the most diverse peoples. It will be one of the tasks of this chapter to show why this is true.

The concern of the Church with the control and regulation of sexuality and the family is not simply because its symbols reflect and reinforce the morality of the group. The mental life of the Church is also deeply dependent on the feelings and actions of the mated pair, of parents and children, of brothers and their sisters, both as models and factors in the processes of reification which transfigure the beliefs and values and feelings these persons have about themselves and their mundane life into the sacred symbols of Christian belief. The negative and positive beliefs and values surrounding the sexual act, with its pleasures and satisfactions, including the identification of such behavior with sin and the ambivalent acceptance of it under the marital control of the family, are expressed by and permeate some of the most important Christian symbols. Mary, the Mother and Virgin with no sexual experience; Joseph, her human husband, many believe without sexual contact with his wife; Jesus, their son, unmarried and with no sexual experience, the human offspring of a sacred impregnation in which there was no sin or male physical contact; all are, paradoxically, part of a family symbol system. A mother whose own conception is held by many to have been without the stain of original sin is part of this sacred system. Mortal man could not understand this immortal society or feel its significance were he not a mental and physical creature of his own family. The meaning of a mother who is a virgin may be difficult for rational men to comprehend, but it is easily felt and non-rationally understood by them as sons of mothers who are wives of all-too-human husbands. The struggle to control their animal emotions in a moral order is reflected in the symbolism of the Church and in its basic theology.

Christian doctrine recognizes many sacred as well as secular forms of the family. They are all interrelated and interdependent, moving from the physical through the social to the sacred levels. Even the mysteries of the abstract and abstruse Holy Trinity through its three Persons are involved in the family order and are felt by Catholics and others to be more clearly understood by the one human who had the closest family relations with the three, the Virgin Mary. "The ineffable mystery of the Holy Trinity," Cardinal Mindszenty declares, "was unlocked to her [the Virgin Mary] more than to all other human beings. The first tie binds her to God the Father whose eternal Son became her son. . . . The second heavenly tie binds her to the Son who is in truth her child. . . . The third heavenly tie binds her to the Holy Spirit, Whose espoused and pure bride she is. Hence, she was created as a most pure and untouched virgin." [1]

For Christians the most significant fact in the relation of the sacred and profane realms is the birth, life, and death of the Son. The Word is made flesh—a *spiritual* God is made *incarnate* in the symbolic form of his human birth as a son to a human family. His Father so loved all men that he gave his only begotten Son to them, that those among them who could believe would live forever. His only Son was born to a woman who was a virgin, who had been impregnated by him through the power of the Holy Spirit. The Son (in human form) lived, suffered, and died, slain by those he came to save from suffering and death, his spiritual kindred as potential sons of God, though far from kin in spiritual development. The depths of human depravity could not be more powerfully represented. Yet all men can be saved from death because by their evil actions and his spiritual ones Christ "redeemed" them and showed them the way to Heaven and eternal life.

The ultimate, most perfect conduct man can imagine—this in sharp contrast with his own depravity—is achieved when his brother-god, whom he has slain, rescues him from his own deg-

1. Mindszenty [97], p. 72.

radation and from the power of death. Furthermore, his gentle "older" brother intercedes with the stern father for him and by his atonement establishes a new order which for all time and for all men guarantees them the chance of redemption, salvation, and eternal life. It is significant that it is believed that man's greatest evil act, when he crucified his brother-god, was also the greatest act of God's goodness. Sacred evil and sacred good derive from the same horrible deed; the ultimates of human understanding are thus founded on family sentiments.

Distinctions are sometimes drawn by theologians between Christian concepts of love. The love they attribute to God often shows the unlimited love of a parent who can love his children unheedful of their deserts and yet remain "sovereign" with (parental) authority. The love of his children is "dependent" and filled with a "desire of good for the self." Dr. Anders Nygren, in his book *Agape and Eros, A Study of the Christian Idea of Love*," which distinguishes between love as Agape and love as Eros, declares that "Agape is God's way to man—Eros is man's way to God." [2] Agape does not recognize value but creates it. On the other hand, "Eros is determined by and dependent on the quality of its object—Eros recognizes value in its object and therefore loves it." The Loving God, like loving parents, can love and bestow value on wayward children.[3] [103]

For Christians, life is dually conceived, the sacred and profane realms are separate and distinct, their forces opposed and antithetical, yet one. Simply put, the more traditionally minded Christians believe that far *above* profane, mortal man is the sacred, immortal, supernatural world. Such lesser spiritual beings as the saints, the angels, and the souls of the born and unborn are members of this higher order of existence and subordinate to, and ruled by, the three great male personae of Christian Deity, the austere Father, the gentle Son, and their everpresent and always active Holy Spirit. They are the Three who are also the One. Beneath all of them in the ordinary secular realm of human beings, it is believed, the eternal struggle of good with evil for supremacy over flesh and matter is fought within the moral world of each man. In Yankee City and elsewhere in

2. Nygren [103], pp. 81, 87.
3. See *ibid.,* "The Content and Idea of Agape," pp. 75–81.

human society, it is a conflict that is never won, yet never lost.

Despite the hostility between the spirit and the profane flesh, the two are, and must be, in Christian thought mutually dependent and interrelated halves of a larger physical and cultural unity. Much of the meaning of the "flesh" in Christian belief has to do with the bodily actions and human emotions of males and females, the moral beliefs and values related to the two sexes and their acts and emotions, and the implications of sexuality for the spiritual order. We will first examine Christian thought about the relation of the church to the moral order of the family, and to the family as a species order consisting of the procreative pair and their offspring.

The faith of many of the Christian churches of Yankee City asserts, explicitly or implicitly, that men and women should be sanctioned by God "to enter the sexual domain." While some Protestants believe that marriage is no more than a civil and legal act, which a church wedding may celebrate, most hold with all Catholics either that God enters as the third party to the marriage rite or that the vows themselves are sanctioned by God through the rites of the church. The marriage rite may not be a sacrament, but for most Protestants it is a holy ceremony involving God. The rules of the moral order and the species life system are thus reinforced by supernatural sanctions.

Biological survival in such a system is thus made dependent on the approval of a father-son God, a single symbol combining the procreating and procreated life process and the actions of his human surrogates. In the past, and present, he and they have disapproved of a large variety of sexual unions because of the biological and spiritual nearness of the pair or for various social and spiritual disabilities.

For man to survive the two sexes must come together, copulate, produce, and protect their offspring. The social institutions which directly control this vital nexus of species life— the relation of the copulating pair and of this same procreative pair and their dependent offspring—control the source of human life. They give social form to, and are charged with, the vital energies which actuate human existence and dominate the basic forms of interaction in which human animals become human beings and emerge as moral, reasoning members of the social order. [16]

The customs and conventions of Yankee City, expressed in the formal and informal rules which regulate marriage, surround the "sexual domain" with a wall of negative values, symbols, and sanctions forbidding and interdicting every other form of sexual experience except those reached by the marriage gate and the domain into which it opens. The rules are often broken, yet their spirit is a powerful, coercive force in the life of everyone. Perhaps the most powerful repressive rule regulating sexual contact is the family incest taboo which forbids sexual relations between such kindred as mothers and sons, fathers and daughters, and brothers and sisters. The incest interdictions are the most important social inhibitions established on man's physical conduct, setting up immeasurably powerful broad controls over the sexual and procreative life of the species which greatly modify natural species organization and make harsh and rigid demands on the early learning experiences of each individual. [85b] The fact that many able scientists until Freud believed the feelings expressed by the incest taboo to be instinctive and not learned or socially derived indicates how quickly and effectively the human family system trains its young to obey automatically the taboos of incest. The sources of their power and efficacy lie far below human consciousness and contribute to the reduction of competition and open conflict within the family. They channel internal aggression into the larger society, thus protecting the social foundations of human moral existence. These feelings and attitudes, which are continuing, integral parts of the family structure, are necessarily given expression in the sacred symbols of the Christian faith.

Sexuality, Procreation, and Marriage in Christian Symbolism

The bond between the several secular and sacred forms of family life is clearly recognized in Catholic doctrine. We shall examine the beliefs to establish the symbolic form of the believed relations. The meaning and function of the social and biological family in Christian symbolism will become apparent. The biological family, hard, enduring, and central to all life, is the matrix from which the basic beliefs of Christianity emerge. On it are founded the eternal symbols of the truths of Christian faith.

Sexual intercourse, unsanctioned by marriage, according to church doctrine is of flesh and matter and as such (it is believed) evil and sinful, belonging to the realm of the profane. Wedlock, sanctioned by church and society, controls and disciplines man's species relations and places them within the moral *forms* of the social group. Here the basic moral order, sanctioned and in Christian faith instituted by God, justifies and sanctions the sexual act. The reciprocal exchange of rights and duties, obligations and privileges, between the husband and wife is initiated by the marriage rites through the mutual surrender of self, the sharing of each by the other, and the completion of each sex by the two becoming one in a marriage relation which controls the sexual act.

Marriage in Catholic thought—less so in Protestant—has three purposes: offspring, mutuality of the two persons, and the recognition of God. "The Church," says Von Hildebrand, "assigns three ends to marriage which St. Augustine sums up by the words *proles*, *fides*, and *sacramentum*." [4] The marriage act, sexual intercourse, is not only for the generation of children, but significant for man as a human being because it is the expression and fulfillment of wedded love and community life and therefore belongs to the moral order. It is also involved in the sacred because the utilitarian function of producing a new generation of men *in quantum animal* has been combined with the function of the sexual act as an expression of wedded love (*in quantum homo*) "because the two elements have been organically united by God." The bodily function of the marriage act, being for the generation of children, its continual focus is on the relation of the older and younger generations in the parent and child relation. For this purpose the copulating pair "in their mutual gift of self" submit to the moral control and social usages of human marriage. The family and the family systems are thereby integrated into and controlled by the moral order of the whole community. The species relations of the sexes too are ordered, disciplined, and confined to the

4. Von Hildebrand [62], p. 16. The quotations on the following three pages are from the same source, pp. 16–42.

rules and sanctions of the culture, and transformed and invested with the moral values of the society.

These Christian beliefs and values presuppose the possible emergence from the sexual act of new human beings, a new generation of men who will insure the persistence of the culture and the continuity of the group. The bodies of the infants resulting from sexual intercourse are the products of semen and ovum, but their souls are God's own creation. The sexual act is therefore a spiritual mystery in Catholic belief and among many Protestants because it means the mysterious creation of a body and a soul—"a body that receives its *form* from the soul and transforms it from mere matter into a human being . . . the parents procreate a human body destined for the most intimate union with an immortal soul and from which it actually receives its form." (*Anima forma corporis;* the soul is the form of the body.)

Some Protestants view the sex act as secular, subject only to moral control, unless conception takes place. Conception having occurred, the problem of the soul, and the new body and soul as God's child, is the same sacred problem for these believers as for other Christians. The more extreme rationalists among them reject its significance by taking a "scientific" explanation of personality (and the soul), but most face it or tacitly agree to it as a sacred event in which God is involved.

The second end of Christian marriage is mutual assistance, meaning that rights and privileges are mutually exchanged and duties and obligations reciprocally assumed by the procreative pair. This bond is founded on love, and wedded love is separated from other forms of physical love because the relation of the husband and wife lies within a moral order established, or recognized, by God. "The church sees in married love," declares Franz Walter in *The Body and Its Rights in Christianity* (quoted by Von Hildebrand), "the mutual attraction of the two sexes, implanted by the creator in human nature and the foundation and indispensable condition for the most intimate and indissoluble community of life between human beings of different sexes and as such it gives it her blessing."

Between the social bond and the bodily union there is "a profound organic unity" because sex is unique and central within the individuals involved in the act. "The sexual gift of one person to another signifies an incomparably close union with the other and a self surrender to him or her. . . . The sex union is a concrete expression of wedded love which intends the mutual gift of self."

Sex (it is believed) belongs to the innermost being of each person and is entirely private. When two individuals reveal themselves to each other in a sex relation they surrender their selves to each other and initiate each into the other's secret. From this moral fact the bonds of matrimony are created, and within them the human quality of sex is created. When the sexual act takes on human quality it takes on *form*, and "form is the soul and spiritual quality." This is the relation of sex to the soul and of flesh to the spirit and God; this is the essence of the sacrament, the third purpose of marriage and the Christian element.

It is also significant that an essential part of marriage for the church and the secular order is that sexual intercourse must take place, and semen must be deposited in the uterus. Thus signifying that marriage, in being a "will to unite" and a benevolent feeling for the beloved, is also for the purpose of generating children. A bride is not a wife and a bridegroom is not a husband until they have completed the sexual act.

The three levels of the sexual act—physical, moral, and symbolic, and the equation of each to the several levels of adaptation later described—are illustrated by Chart 8. The upward-

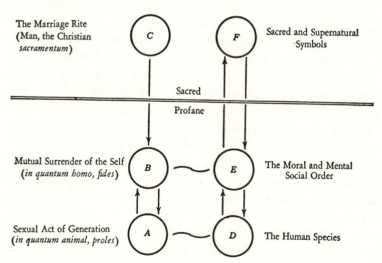

CHART 8. The Three Levels of the Sexual Act (according to Catholic Dogma and Its Scientific Equivalents)

pointing arrows indicate that the sexual act influences the bond of wedded love and the moral order; the downward-pointing ones show that the animal act is controlled and formed by the moral order. The downward-pointing arrow between circles *B* and *C* indicates that the "quality of wedded love" is under the control of "the pre-established harmony of Christian rites."

The interconnected circles on the right represent the several levels of human adaptation to which the different parts of the sexual life are equated. The horizontal double lines on the left separate the Christian from the moral and animal realms, and the ones on the right remove the sacred and supernatural symbols from those of the secular and profane world. Furthermore, the arrows connecting the circles *E* and *F* indicate that the sacred symbol system is directly under the influence of the moral order which helps control the secular life of the family.

The marriage ceremony which sanctions and consecrates the relations of the sexual pair and symbolically marks the relation's inception as one ritual act is not sufficient to maintain the relation's spiritual quality throughout its existence, for sexual activity within the marriage bed ranges from mere sensuality to behavior which transcends the flesh and approaches the spirituality of its divine model. Such variation ranges from the impure to the pure, from flesh and matter to the spiritual activity of a being capable of participating in the divine life. But the pure man or woman is not lacking in sexual desire. On the contrary, it is officially held that the man or woman who is insensible to sex is not favorable to purity. Men and women who do not feel sexual desire are merely weak sexually. Pure men and women control and transcend the demands of the flesh; they recognize the spiritual and human qualities of sexual desire and relate themselves to each other sexually as persons within the spiritual and benevolent bonds of marriage. The sensual man indulges his animal desires for themselves and experiences an animal pleasure in the use of another person. The weak man or woman lacks an essential element of purity: the will to unite. Impurity consists in the abuse of sex. It is both a desecration and a degradation, a desecration partly because it abuses the sanctity of one of God's children, and a degradation of the person who desecrates another. In such a relation the soul is made captive of the flesh, particularly in any unsanctioned union, and accordingly is lost to God. Under these conditions it is literally submerged in matter.

Although sex implicates the higher nature of man, it has within it intrinsic dangers which threaten man's spiritual existence. The orgasm, with its violence and fury, tends to overpower the spirit and swamp it, for, with the exception of death, the orgasm is the most profound physical expression of which man is capable.

The pure man understands that sex belongs in a special manner to God and that man can only make use of it as explicitly sanctioned by Him. In the rite of marriage, man is given "divine permission to lift the veil of the mystery," and he cannot directly abandon himself without restraint to the pleasures of sex. Throughout the sexual period of each marriage, in every marriage act, men and women must be forever aware that they are moral beings in wedded relations with another person. Such sexual relations are pure, removed from the control of the flesh, and formed on supernatural foundations. Their mutual concern about the welfare of the other, the knowledge that they participate in the mystery of the possible creation of a new human being, and the benevolent love of the husband and wife ennoble sex.[5]

The family of souls created by the rite of human marriage is believed to be founded on, and an expression of, the Mystical Body and, as it were, "a mystical body in miniature." For the Catholic Church "Christian marriage is a sign or symbol of the Mystical Body of Christ. In origin they both come from God, in structure, both are one and indissoluble . . ." "By marriage there is established in each family, as it were, a mystical body in miniature."[6] For St. Paul, marriage is not so much a fact in its own right as a symbol of the union of Christ with the Church.

> "Husbands, love your wives, as Christ also loved the Church and delivered himself up for her, that he might sanctify her, purifying her in the bath of water by means of the word, and that he might present her to himself a glorious Church, not having spot or wrinkle or any such thing, but holy and without blemish."[7]

5. *Ibid.*, pp. 97–105.
6. Ellard [45], p. 309.
7. Ephesians 5:25–28 [11e].

The Mystical Body, the Bride of Christ, some theologians declare, was formed at the time of the crucifixion "when She came forth from the wound made by the lance when he was crucified." Like the first woman, Eve, who was taken from the side of her husband, Adam, so the church came from the side of the New Adam, Christ.

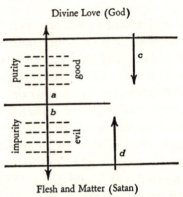

CHART 9. The Relation of Marriage to the Sacred and Profane

Let us recapitulate and analyze what has been said by use of a chart (see Chart 9). The moral world of man extends from the inferior realm of flesh and matter to the superior world of God and the supernatural. There are varying degrees of purity and impurity, of good and evil, in the sexual act, the increasing purity approaches the supernatural (arrows *a* and *b* pointing up and down). Divine love, the foundation of purity, extends into the moral world (arrow *c*) and can and should become part of man's wedded life, or man can degrade himself to such a degree of impurity that his moral world is submerged into flesh and matter (arrow *d*). Thus, we see that the moral life of man as a sexual creature is a constant struggle between the spirit and the flesh, the moral rules sanctioned by sacred belief and the pleasurable satisfaction of uncontrolled sexual appetite—in brief, between the forces of good and those of evil.

The family as a moral system is an arena where the forces of God and Satan meet in an endless struggle. Within their sexual relations men and women carry on a moral struggle to conquer impurity and transform themselves into pure beings who participate in divine love. A moral universe is made out of the treatment of the sex relation; it is dualistically conceived in terms of purity and impurity, the first being joined with the forces of good and ultimately with the Christian God, and the other with the powers of evil and, for some, with Satan. Sexual intercourse, the basic bond and creator of the links of species life, for the Christian occupies a central point of incalculable importance in the moral and spiritual life of man. Only in marriage, as *one* of the social relations which compose the family structure, is it permitted to take place. And the family of the wedded pair is firmly placed in the larger moral context of a family system of parents and children, and this larger family unity under the moral control of society and God.

We have presented the traditional Christian (particularly Catholic) ideology of the relations between the sexes and of human marriage and its place in the human family. There are several other forms of marriage which exist beyond the limits of ordinary life in the symbols of the supernatural world, and which are of crucial importance for understanding the sacred life of Christianity and the relation of the Christian to his God. The two principal officially recognized ones are the marriage of the soul, as bride, to Christ the sacred bridegroom; and the marriage of the Church (as bride) to Christ her sacred spouse. We shall see that these two symbolic forms are closely related to sacredly sanctioned human marriage and that these supernatural forms are not understandable without knowledge of, and experience with, human marriage and sexuality.

The Bride and Christ: Symbols of a Symbol

The soul of each man and woman in Church doctrine has a twofold, direct relation with Christ, as an autonomous soul and as an integral part of the mystical body of the Church. The souls belonging to human males and human females, being alike and feminine in form, are receptive to God, the giver, very much as women are open and receptive to men. The souls of men and women are therefore female, open and ready to contain the masculine creative sacred principle. "In the natural order woman represents, in contrast to man, the receptive principle," says Von Hildebrand, ". . . In relation to God, however, this characteristic of predominant receptivity is not confined to the female sex. Here, . . . where God and man meet, the man as an individual soul is as purely receptive as the woman. Here God [the male procreator] alone is the giver, the creative and fertilizing principle . . . And this is preeminently true in the supernatural order of the soul as the bride of Christ, the God-man." [8]

The soul, as a sacred Christian being intimately related to Christ, as we have said, is feminine. Its relation to Christ is further defined as that of the wife to her Divine husband or, more particularly, as the passionate young bride yearning for the love of her bridegroom. The singing of the love of the new bride for her husband and of the bridegroom for his beloved in the Song of Songs, once a poetic folk drama, is symbolic of the emotions that exist in supernatural marriage. Most Protestant and all Catholic Bibles as well as their sectarian interpreters identify the bride as the Church or the soul, and their bridegroom as Christ.

Just as the soul is feminine and in a nuptial relation with. Christ, so the Church is also feminine and also the bride of Christ. "Like the church herself, every member of Christ's mystical body is a bride of Jesus. Jesus is the bridegroom," Von Hildebrand declares, "of every soul which is a member of his mystical body," which means of every soul that has been baptized into the Church. However, the Church as the spouse of Christ is at the same time a virgin. An examination of this factual contradiction but symbolically congruent belief in which "virginity and wedlock are united with Christ" will lead still deeper into the meaning and significance of Christian symbols.

The female church is controlled by males, priests who are created in the masculine image, in effect the other Christs who are the husbands of the church as well as the heads of the family whose worshipers are its children. Finally, in the Catholic Church, the pope, the ultimate head of the hierarchy, is the "papa" for the entire church on earth. Meanwhile, the Church eternal in heaven is the spouse of the bridegroom, Christ, and their relationship is that of the bride and groom where her feelings for her husband are most effectively stated officially in the

8. Von Hildebrand [62], p. 124.

Song of Songs. On earth the Church contains, and is comforted by, the masculine Holy Ghost.

The relation of the Church to Christ as founded on human marriage and the husband-wife relation is clearly established by St. Paul:

> For the husband is the head of the wife as Christ is the head of the church, his body, and is himself its Savior. . . . Husbands, love your wives, as Christ loved the church and gave himself up for her . . . husbands should love their wives as their own bodies. He who loves his wife loves himself. For no man ever hates his own flesh, but nourishes and cherishes it, as Christ does the church, because we are members of his body. "For this reason a man shall leave his father and mother and be joined to his wife, and the two shall become one." This is a great mystery, and I take it to mean Christ and the church.[9]

We must now allow certain philosophers and doctors of the church to ask these profound questions: Why is the Church a virgin? And what does her virginal character signify? These Catholic writers declare that "the mysterious glory which invests mystical love and its perfection as the crown of human relationships has nowhere been depicted so vividly as in the Song of Songs." It will be remembered that in both Catholic and many Protestant Bibles, the bride calling passionately for her loved one is the Church and her bridegroom is Christ her Lord. (As everyone knows, there are several interpretations of the significance of the Song of Solomon. They vary from that of a romantic love song to a symbol of the relation of Christ and the soul, or Christ and the Church. The notations before each chapter in the King James Version, which for two hundred and fifty years influenced Christian thought, gave it the latter interpretation. More recent interpretations frequently do not. Catholic thought always emphasizes it. We will continue to examine the nuptial interpretation.)

The holy union of each soul with Christ is both a sister and a wedded relation. The Song of Solomon, the Canticle of Canticles, widely regarded as an authoritative and divinely inspired

9. Ephesians 5:23, 25, 28–33 [11c].

book, does provide a powerful foundation for the symbolic form and much of the emotional substance of the relation of the soul and Church as brides of Christ. Many other books of the Bible give evidence used by Catholics and often Protestants to substantiate this nuptial interpretation of the perfect relation between men and God. An introduction to the Song of Solomon in the family Bible of a Presbyterian home in Yankee City, for example, states an interpretation common to a number of Protestant churches. The notations at the beginning of each chapter of the book are similar to those found in the Bibles of many of the churches in Yankee City. The Song of Solomon, the introduction declares, is "a dialogue in which the speakers are Jesus Christ, the blessed bridegroom of souls; the church which is his body and bride . . . The scope of it is to represent Christ and his people's mutual esteem of, desire after, and delight in one another . . . the bride denotes either the church in general or a particular believer . . ." [11*b*]

In Chapter I in the Canticle of Canticles, according to the interpretative introductory notes of the King James Version, the "Church's love unto Christ" is passionately announced. [11*d*]

> Let him kiss me with the kisses of his mouth: for thy love is better than wine.
>
> Because of the savor of thy good ointments, thy name is as ointment poured forth, therefore do the virgins love thee.

"The mutual love of Christ and his Church," the cry of the loved and loving nuptial pair, is revealed in Chapter II:

> He brought me to the banqueting house, and his banner over me was love.
>
> His left hand is under my head and his right hand doth embrace me.

In this same chapter, "the profession of the Church, her faith and hope" about the bridegroom, is also stated:

> My beloved is mine, and I am his: he feedeth among the lilies.
>
> Until the day break, and the shadows flee away, turn, my beloved, and be thou like a roe or a young hart upon the mountains of Bether.

In Chapter IV, according to the interpretation, Christ "sheweth his love to her":

> Thou hast ravished my heart, my sister, my spouse, thou hast ravished my heart . . .
>
> How fair is thy love, my sister, my spouse! how much better is thy love than wine!
>
> A garden enclosed is my sister, my spouse; a spring shut up, a fountain sealed.

The Church is at once sister and bride to Christ in this seemingly contradictory role, a female symbol of the sister surrounded with moral rules and negative sanctions forbidding all sexual expression ["a garden enclosed"] and, on the other hand, the bride who like the hart longs to be united with her loved one. What can be the meaning of this sacred symbolic statement which seemingly contradicts some of the basic human values at the very foundations of human moral life? [10] To find our answer we must examine one other form of supernatural nuptial relations: the marriage of the consecrated virgin with Jesus Christ. Here we find this sacred theme and its values in their most extreme and detailed form and can examine them more easily. Moreover, since the sacred symbol of the consecrated virgin exists in substantial human form, the rules and regulations which order her life, the rituals which initiate her into the status, and those which continue to relate her to Christ are observable and recorded. It is therefore possible to obtain more explicit knowledge of the nature of this wedded relation of the sacred part of a human being to Christ and derive a better understanding of the meaning of the wedded relation of a brother and sister.

Marriage of the Consecrated Virgin

"Among the ritual blessings having to do with the official worship of God," says Michel in the *Liturgy of the Church*, "the consecration of the church and the consecration of the chosen spouse of Christ are most imposing." The marriage of the virgin to Christ is presided over by the bishop who is the "highest liturgical dignitary" of the Church. The ceremony

10. Ancient historical kinship factors having to do with the special use of sister also are involved.

occurs in the Mass, "so that the obligation of the virgin's soul may be immediately united with that of the spotless Lamb on the altar." [11]

The candidates, escorted by previously dedicated virgins, enter the church; a priest who is the assistant to the bishop sings, "Ye prudent virgins, prepare your lamps, behold the bridegroom approaches, go to meet him."

He presents the candidates to the bishop. The latter, as the representative of Christ, speaks to them: "God and our Savior Jesus Christ helping us, we choose these virgins, to present and consecrate them and to wed them to our Lord Jesus Christ, the Son of the highest God." The "brides" are then asked: "Do you will to be blessed and consecrated and betrothed to our Lord Jesus Christ the Son of the all highest God?"

They reply, "We will." In the ritual which follows each virgin is married to Christ "Come, my chosen one," the song of the bishop calls to them, "thy King longs for thee. Hear and see, incline thy ear."

"I am a handmaid of Christ," the virgins reply, "therefore am I vested in servile habit."

The bishop demands, "Will you persevere in the holy virginity that you have professed?"

"We will," they vow.

Each virgin is now a wedded spouse of Christ in eternal union with him. The perfect marriage on earth anticipates what will continue to be the perfect marriage after death in heaven.

Pure men and women in the marriage bed must control themselves and not yield to lust and abandon themselves to animal pleasures. Restraint and discipline are necessary if their wish to unite is to stay within the pre-established spiritual harmony and receive God's sanction. But no man or woman united sexually to another creature can ever completely escape from the lust of the senses and the vanities and snares of the world. Therefore, greater and further purification is necessary for any soul that yearns to achieve a more perfect state. Only ascetic practices can achieve this and allow such an individual to effect a perfect union with God. The vows of poverty, obedience, and chastity provide a way of life that by *self-denial* purify the individual. The symbolic fiesh is reduced and

11. Michel [94], pp. 258–63.

some of it "removed" and the realm of the spirit expanded, thereby creating a larger opening and symbolic womb in which Divine love can enter and be contained. The ritual life of asceticism lays the foundation for a closer relation with God, but "the motive is no longer purification but undividedness in the strictest sense . . . The *inner .emptiness,*—indispensable if we are to be filled with God—is complete inner freedom." Finally it is necessary for God to recognize the renunciation and make it acceptable to Him when "He and love for Him *fill the void* [italics mine] that has been left . . . He who invites the soul to the state of perfection will fill her with Himself if she obeys his invitation." Thus the marriage of the consecrated virgin, the bride of Christ, is spiritually recognized, emotionally experienced, and consummated.[12]

In this sacred marriage "there is delight and sacrifice for the beloved, and she leaves her worldly life just as the ordinary bride leaves her home to follow the man whom her love has chosen . . . Likewise, the soul that is inebriated with love of Jesus desires to forsake everything for his love, to stand before him naked, listen for his voice alone, draw his glance into her heart, and with loins girt and lamps burning await the bridegroom . . . The soul chooses suffering . . . that she may . . . celebrate with him the bridal of pain . . ."[13] This union is one of the highest and most spiritual of which human beings are capable. It is a living relation which completely surrounds and infuses the bodies of those involved in it so that such human beings are confined entirely within the limits of the sacred symbol, a sacred symbol of a sacred symbol, which in its turn is taken from moral man and his species life.

The marriage of the virgin to Christ reveals what the sacrament of marriage and the union of Christ and the Church signify. For the Church, the marriage sacrament in human marriage is an expression of the ecstatic nuptial union of the Church and her Lord. The marriage of the consecrated virgin indicates the emotional depth and moral form of this relationship in more explicable, concrete form. Furthermore, this sacred symbolic union states these facts in their most extreme form.

12. Von Hildebrand [62], pp. 158, 185–6. See also pp. 150–6 ("The Ascetic Significance of Virginity") and in general pp. 183–91.
13. *Ibid.,* pp. 177–8.

Such a person removes herself completely from the world, "dies to it," and devotes herself entirely to a life of consecrated purity within the loving arms of her Divine spouse. This human symbol of a symbol, set apart as the consecrated virgin, spouse of Christ, by her surrender to Christ as the symbol of the bride, emphasizes the extreme form of spiritual purity and expresses the emotional significance and the moral values of human marriage. The soul of the consecrated bride is wedded to Love Incarnate as a member of the Church, as a human soul, and as an entire person. She, made open and empty by ascetic practices and thus capable of containing more of incarnate love and closer union with God, can give and receive more of the love of the God-Man. Yet to most fully achieve this state of grace and earthly bliss she must be fully equipped with the sexual qualities of a human being. "The more fully a soul possesses the qualities of an earthly bride," says Von Hildebrand, "the better fitted is it to become a bride of Christ." [14]

Something of the emotional experience of the individual involved in such a mystical union is expressed by St. John of the Cross in a poem called "En Una Noche Oscura." The human lover's relations with the Divine Lover are deeply felt and explicitly stated.

> Once in the dark of night,
> My longings caught and raging in love's ray
> (O windfall of delight!)
> I slipped unseen away
> As all my hall in a deep slumber lay.
>
> . . . .
>
> There in the lucky dark,
> Leaving in secrecy, by none espied;
> Nothing for eyes to mark,
> No other torch, no guide
> But in my heart: that fire would not subside.
>
> . . . .
>
> O dark of night, my guide!
> O sweeter than anything sunrise can discover!
> O night, drawing side to side
> The loved and Lover,
> The loved one wholly ensouling in the Lover.

14. For this entire section see *ibid.*, pp. 258–63.

There in my festive breast
Walled for his pleasure-garden, his alone,
The Lover remained at rest
And I gave all I own,
Gave all, in air from the cedars softly blown.

. . . .

Quite out of self suspended—
My forehead on the Lover's own reclined.
And that way the world ended,
With all my cares untwined
Among the lilies falling and out of mind. [57]

The problem becomes still more paradoxical when we ask (at the sacred level) how it is possible to convert the forms of social life into sacred symbols which express the values and beliefs of human society when these symbols of purity place husband and wife in the incest images of brother and sister? Any attempt to use rationality or the logic of evidence and propositional order to explain this situation is certain to fail. Nor will justice be done to the meaning of these evocative and mythic symbols if we force them to submit to the rigid demands of logic and science. These mythic symbols are part of the *social logics* which may or may not be concerned about the requirements of evidence and rationality. They express real meanings and an inner constancy which communicate powerful and convincing truths to those who can accept and feel them. Their systems of mental life and moral order lie beyond the rational part of mental life and more often than not beyond the precepts and rules of official and formal morality. As religious collective representations they reflect and express, as Durkheim demonstrated, the moral and mental life of the group. Sometimes there is a mirrorlike reflection of its logic and even its most repressive morality, but more often than not such mental and moral symbols are part of the larger non-logical and non-moral context. Here there is something more than the social group ritually relating itself to the sacred representations of its own image; here life demands and gains full right to express what seems to be needed by men as members of this ongoing animal group we call the human species.

The several relations between the sacred symbolic life of Christians and the family structure are depicted in Chart 10.

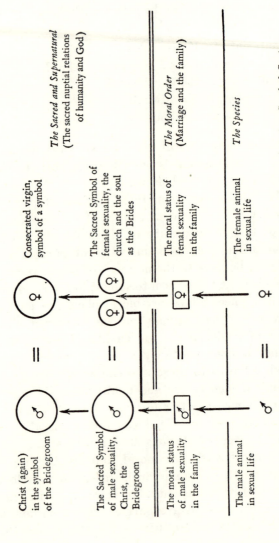

Christ (again)
in the symbol
of the Bridegroom

Consecrated virgin,
symbol of a symbol

The Sacred and Supernatural
(The sacred nuptial relations
of humanity and God)

The Sacred Symbol
of male sexuality,
Christ, the
Bridegroom

The Sacred Symbol of
female sexuality, the
church and the soul
as the Brides

The moral status
of male sexuality
in the family

The moral status of
femal sexuality
in the family

The Moral Order
(Marriage and the family)

The male animal
in sexual life

The female animal
in sexual life

The Species

CHART 10. Man's Sexual Life and Family Structure in the Christian Symbol System

374

This chart and the discussion which follows are founded on the more general one (Chart 8) and the theoretical foundations previously discussed which it represents. The upward-pointing arrows on the left connect the species level of the human male animal and his sexual life with the status of male sexuality in the moral order of the family and, higher still, with Christ and the symbol of the Bridegroom, the sacred and supernatural symbol of male sexuality in the moral order. The equal (marriage) signs show the male part of this basic dichotomy related to the female (this chart should also indicate that the male line of symbols, statuses, and creatures is, in Christian values, superordinate to the subordinate female line). It does indicate that the same relations exist among the female parts of species, moral, and sacred orders as on the male side. However, at the sacred symbolic levels in the female line several developments take place that are significant. The symbol of male sexuality, Christ the bridegroom, in the two circles at the top of the chart, remains the same in his marriages, but the female symbol changes: she is the bride, the individual consecrated virgin, a ritual symbol of the Church as the bride; she is the soul of a man or woman; and at the same time she is the Church in holy nuptial relations with her Lord. This symbol of a symbol in the "logic" of evocative, non-rational symbols provides, as it were, re-enforcement and symbolic validation of the vaguer and less easily felt and understood symbols of the Church as the mystical body and the soul.

The appearance of the two sacred symbols is an expression of the relation of the individual to the Church and the community and of the social principle underlying the relation of the secular and sacred Christian orders. The mystical body of the Church is composed of all the souls who have been initiated into it through the "rebirth" of baptism, which is also the "adoption" of Christians into the family of God. Christ is the Head of the mystical Body just as the husband is the head of the wife. "The husband," says St. Paul, "is the head of the wife, as Christ is Head of the Church." The mystery here is great. The husband is recognized as spiritually and morally superordinate to the wife at the moral level and, at the sacred, the symbol of the bride is subordinate to the superordinate male spouse, Christ. This sacred symbol dominates and controls the moral and animal worlds beneath it in the values of Christian thought.

The symbol, head, in this context has two important references, logically impossible, but metaphorically and evocatively sound and meaningful. The head of the family is the husband status, and it is the "physical" head, the directing and authoritative part of the mystical body. The congregation in its relations with Christ's vicar, the pastor of a church, is in a subordinate role to his leadership as is each of its members. The status of the pastor in Christian thought is male in relation to his flock. He is both father and husband; consciously he is always father; unconsciously and sometimes with difficulties resulting, husband to his congregation. At the altar and in the Mass as priest he at times represents, and is identified with, the female congregation—the mystical body—and partly plays a female role. As an individual soul he is always female. However, at other times he is identified with Christ and is one of the "other Christs" who compose the priesthood.

Thus the laity are female and the clergy are symbolically male; being so represented, they are made emotionally meaningful for all times, all places, and in all cultures. The significance of their male and female relations can be felt and understood everywhere. The Christ who enters the spiritual life of the community and separately enters into the private world of each of its members as the heavenly spouse can be felt and accepted by all. The human being's subordinate yet blissful relation with Him is easily acceptable, for the soul can live in everlasting bliss and intimacy with her heavenly spouse. In the contemplations of the living, the pure soul at death, when separated from society, will not be alone or subject to the anxieties and desperate fears of the person who has lost his group, for as the bride of Christ such a being has special and altogether intimate relations with God himself. Moreover, the soul is always a part of the female body of the Mother Church into which she is first taken by the initiation rites of baptism and, through the rituals which separate the newly dead from the living, finally joined at death.

The ritually male priest as another Christ is the leader and authoritative father to his children who, as members of his congregation, are brothers and sisters to each other and children of God in the Christian world family. The higher clergy, bishops, cardinals, and the pope, are all fathers, each with an increasingly numerous and more widely extended family, until the world society of the Christian collectivity is joined with the one father as the head of the mystical body of one human community. He is the father of all fathers.

The images of what men are as sacred entities shift from family status to family status, but all of them are in the form of a family member. These spiritual identities are logically and scientifically impossible, but there is complete mythic congruence because the "logic" is structural and non-rational. Their diverse forms in a congruent symbol system are based on man's feelings and beliefs derived from his experiences within the family structure; they are expressions of his emergence as a person within the family's all-powerful matrix. In the human family, as we all know, an individual can be and usually is at one and the same time a child to his or her father, a spouse to his or her husband, and a father or mother to his or her sons and daughters. In the family, males and females share an infinite number of common formative experiences which not only differentiate them morally as sexual beings, but often encourage them to be, and mold them into, one likeness where sexuality is not recognized—this because as children of the same parents they belong to the same family. As siblings they are equivalent, which means that from the point of view of the larger society they are very much alike in status and in person. In the values of the sacred symbol system, functioning in part to integrate and hold the collectivity together within its reified system, which expresses common values and beliefs, the common qualities of kinship are stressed and differences often disregarded. The superordination of males to females may be expressed in a symbolic world of this kind in the dominance of the sacred spouse over the sacred female or of brother over sister, or it may be that authority will be given the form of the father as image for the enforcement of moral rules in the lives of his children.

One other major factor in the formation of these sacred marriage symbols which relate persons within the family such as brothers and sisters in spiritual sexuality must now be examined. The evidence from the psychoanalytic study of personality in family life is most important. The Church for Christians is also the Mother Church, yet she is sister and virginal as well as spouse; but she is mother to her children, the individual members of the congregation, and spouse and sister to her husband, Christ. The testimony of psychoanalysis and other evidence demonstrates that the strong negative rules

which prohibit sexual relations between all family members
who are not husband and wife are not "instinctive" nor a mere
polite expression of man's "innate" goodness, but that these
moral injunctions constantly function to forbid and prevent
the powerful cravings of human beings to satisfy their species
longings within the family. The emotional attachment of sons
to their mother, daughters to their father, and brothers and
sisters to each other, can only be recognized at the respectable
level of precept and principle in socially acceptable sentiments.
But at the deeper levels, in fantasy and in dream life where
the evocative and emotional meanings are hidden from the
scrutiny of the moral order, the non-moral and non-logical
values of the species continue their existence and demand expression. The force of their existence can translate and transform the mental and moral system into fragments which are no
more than parts of the non-logical and non-moral orders. Wish,
desire, craving, emotionally remembered pain, and anxiety
dominate here. Within them the moral and mental orders can
be transfigured into symbols whose meanings on first inspection
appear to be logical and moral but whose real significance
belongs to the evocative world of species life.

The mythic, evocative symbols, related as they are to man's
hopes and fears, to his wishes and anxieties about the risk of
living and the certainties of death, to his desire for unfettered
gratification of his longings as well as for immediate satisfaction of all his species appetites, allow man, under the highest
and most revered auspices and sanctions, to express his species
life and, at the same time and with the same symbols as moral
representations, to project and act out his ordinary moral life
at this sacred mythic level.

Thus the strict moral rules governing sexual life and marriage and the incest rules rigidly forbidding the relations of
brothers and sisters at the mythic and sacred symbolic level
can be congruently connected and given full honor and respect; yet the incest cravings in perfect non-rational congruence can also be expressed and used to help re-enforce the
moral life of man. The whole man and the whole system of
species and moral life are projected and expressed in the symbols of the sacred level. Logical and moral contradiction do
not matter: the virgin is mother, incest is not incest, the in-
corporeal spirit implicates human flesh, yesterday is today, and

today is yesterday or tomorrow, the one is the many and the many are one: these are the reality of mythic life.

The meanings of these logical contradictions are of vital consequence in the mental economy of man's existence. The evocative symbols at the sacred and mythic levels "talk" to man about *all* of himself, about *all* of his being; they speak from the profound depths of his species life and only secondarily from the superficial level of logic and thought. In the mythic symbol the species life of man in society and the values and beliefs of society in man are transformed and transfigured. They are made one in the sacred symbols of Christian society. When the several levels of the communicant's symbolic life are merged and joined with the sacred symbols of Christian society, an inward unity is achieved. To the believer this unity is felt as an integration of his own organic and moral life, but in each individual it is also an expression of the species and moral life of the human collectivity.

Mary, the Virgin Mother, Symbol of the Perfect Woman

The sacred symbol of Mary, the mother of Christ, is a collective representation in Yankee City and our society expressing in ideal form the culture's opposing and antithetical beliefs and values about women. For those who are Christians and believe, it embodies basic, non-logical beliefs at two extremes of our values about women which state and define what women are and are not and what they should and should not be, to themselves, to men, and to God. The symbol carries within itself a series of implied negative and positive sanctions, a series of threats of punishment and promises of reward for approved or condemned sexual and moral conduct. It also expresses and gratifies the deep wishes found in each individual which are part of the species life of the human group. The threats and promises are addressed to men as well as women. To present, meaningfully and evocatively, the sexual and social definition of what a woman is and should be, not only is it necessary to define her to herself and all other women in extreme terms that are understandable, but it is also necessary to define her to the men who are in varying relation to the several basic statuses of women in this and other societies.

The figure of Mary, the Mother, is in many ways the most controversial one in the whole of Christian symbolism. The

Catholic Church officially venerates her and many of its communicants worship her. Most Protestant churches recognize her position as the human mother of Christ who at the Annunciation conceived Jesus and gave him birth on Christmas Day. Yet for most Protestants and Catholics the amount of attention and significance given the Virgin Mary, the mother of Christ, is a crucial test of what it means to be a Catholic or a Protestant. In considering the father-son relation at the symbolic level, it is not difficult to speak generally about Protestants and Catholics. The role of the Virgin Mary is different. As the mother of Christ she is accepted officially by most Protestant communicants. At Christmas she receives their recognition, but it is largely secular in character, for she has lost her high official position and her rites no longer fill most Protestant church calendars. Meanwhile in the Catholic Church not only has she continued significant, but her place has increased in importance. Her rites have developed and the Church, by new dogmas, has strengthened the sacred quality of her symbol and its position in the Catholic pantheon, her immaculate conception without the defilement of original sin and her assumption into Heaven without the necessity of "death" being the most recent. They are co-relative, since the two combined change her into a symbol like Christ's, for she is—conceptually speaking—without beginning (birth without the human consequences of original sin) and without end (deathless). Her symbol, too, resolves the contradictions of eternity and of changing time, of immortality and mortality. She now is nearer the "being" of her Son. Her conception by a human father holds her to an earthly role bound by the limits of space and held within the changes of time.

The symbol of Mary is that of a woman who feels all the emotions of a woman, who yearns for her spouse and suffers the humiliations of her son and the pain of his and her death. However, the Immaculate Conception removes the feelings of guilt and shame associated with sexuality from the symbol. The sin of sex being removed from her creation, Godhead in the act which created Christ does not touch an impure thing. Mary becomes a pure object. The Immaculate Conception transforms her in very much the same way as the ritual of the Mass transforms the chalice in which Christ is recreated and born again. Ritually speaking, the forces of impurity and the forces of the profane are pushed beyond the immediate generation to a previous one. They are effectively walled off from the realm of the pure by the ritual force of the belief in the Immaculate Conception.

Mary was born without sin, to be the perfect receptacle of the semen of God (his essence, as the Holy Ghost) and the woman who would carry the foetus of Jesus and give birth to a supernatural being, a member of the Trinity and a Son to his godly Father. This immaculate collective representation strengthens the forces of ritual purity and the supernatural. God is further removed from the impure and the natural and ritually safeguarded from uncleanliness and pollution. The Annunciation purified the sexual act that produced a Son of God and removed male, but not female, sexuality from it.

When the mystery of the Immaculate Conception took place in the sexual act of Mary's father and mother, no male God intervened and implanted his impregnating energies within Anne. Her spouse was allowed to be the father of his child, but the ritually unclean forces present in the predetermined succession of sexually connected generations as conceived by Judaism and Christianity and founded symbolically on the prototypical Eve and Adam, were removed by the intervention of Divine forces. The Holy Ghost did not enter her womb as he did Mary; rather the effects of the pollution were removed from the procreative act.

The great strength of such ritual symbols of pollution and purification is that they mobilize the feelings and values and beliefs we possess about sexuality, sexual intercourse, and the institution of marriage and family life, and relate them to the hopes and fears we possess about our present condition and future prospects. The feelings of guilt and moral inadequacy of everyone are transfigured and reformed into the pure symbols related to Divine sources. Thus each feels cleansed and reassured, his anxieties are reduced, and his hope for ultimate satisfactions and future reward maximized. He is saved today, and by the happy consequences of the efficacy of the sacred symbols' guaranteed victory over his greatest fear: death and obliteration of the self.

The difficulties of bridging the great impossible divide of

the sacred and the profane are accomplished, yet the communicant retains the strength of the feelings that flow unretarded from species behavior and, at the same time, gains life-filling vigor from the increased hope of immortality through the intervention of the all-powerful forces of the Divine and the supernatural.

In the earlier pagan religions of the Mediterranean Osiris' mother, Isis, was also his much-beloved wife. This same incestuous relation exists in many of the great religions, where members of the immediate sacred family who under secular circumstances would observe the rules of incest are conceived as perfect sexual mates. Christianity modified this. Although Christ is the Son of Mary and God, he is not conceived as the *spouse* of Mary. The idea of Christ being a second person in the Trinity and the Son of God the Father, whose Holy Spirit impregnated Mary, divides the Godhead into three separate roles and thus saves Christianity from worshiping what is in effect an incestuous god. But God is not the Son in sexual relations with the Mother nor is he the Father in direct intimate relations with Mary, the Mother. But it is his other spiritual self, the Holy Ghost, the symbol of his procreative strength and his intermediary with man, who becomes her sexual partner and is the male responsible for Christ's sacred conception.

Despite this Divine division, there is a very close parallel between the conception of the Virgin Mary as Christ's *mother* and the Church as the *bride* of Christ. Many of the same passages in the Bible, used to refer to both, indicate this incestuous conflict. "Christ is called the bridegroom of the Church," Mindszenty declares in his book, *The Face of the Heavenly Mother*, "That is why she is our mother. Her heart beats with the Holy Spirit. She conceives us in her womb. Joyfully, she brings us with our brothers forth to a new life. We are children of a sublime mother. New born in baptism, we may take the path to a new life." [15]

The Virgin Mother, for those who are conventional Christians and particularly for those who are Catholic, is a symbol of the ultimate and unattainable, yet always approachable, woman. As the Virgin she is the figure of sexual purity, taboo, highly desirable but as the Mother symbol always beyond any

15. Mindszenty [97], p. 131.

thought of sexual contact; yet at the very center of the incest feelings and beliefs, she is a woman who is necessarily—if not sexually, then procreatively—experienced.

Two ineffable beauties [Mindszenty declares] are united in Mary: the charm of virginity and the dignity of motherhood. Mary is, therefore, the crown of nature, the wondrous flower of the new heavenly order. The charm of virginity does not disappear, the bright untouched snow of the distant virginal mountains does not melt away, but she becomes a mother. God is born into the world, the virgin proceeds in her blessedness—no man has intervened. She becomes a mother and remains a garden enclosed. She brings a child into the world not through desire of the flesh, but through obedience of the soul. . . . She stands alone in unspeakable dignity. Lovely virginity and sublime maternal fertility! [16]

Mary represents the two highest moral virtues that women can possess, symbolizing the basic contradictions implicit in the evaluations and symbols that we have of womankind in this culture. For men and youths, she is the queen of purity, the eternal idea of true chivalry. For if she is profanely touched, for those who are unwittingly involved there is a deep sense of guilt; better said, there is greater guilt for those who feel guilt in their basic emotions toward members of their family. The holy mother, for her earthbound sons, is perfect. She conceives and bears a child without sexual experience with her sexual mate. Her husband is not the feared sexual rival of her sons.

"Wholly of God," says Mindszenty, "is the fulfillment of this blessed wonder: mother and virgin at once. And virgin before, during, and after child-bearing! Virgin in body, virgin in soul, virgin for all time. . . . According to Hippolytus of Rome: 'The Pure One, in a pure manner, opened the womb of the virgin.' After her maternity, she remained untouched in soul and body, as though she had never been a mother." [17]

Mary also is always the yielding, soft, loving person. She forever acknowledges and accepts this superior masculine spirituality and power. She yields unresistantly to the male God.

Although as the Queen of Heaven, the spouse of god, and

16. *Ibid.,* pp. 32–3.
17. *Ibid.,* p. 34.

the mother of Christ she receives the veneration of those who love and believe in her, she does not receive the worship given the Son who was also flesh. Perhaps it is not without significance that he was male flesh.

As the good woman, Mary is obedient and yielding to masculine superiority, as the wife of Joseph, as the spouse of God, as the mother of the Divine Son, and as the dependent and bereaved mother of the dead Jesus, while under the sponsorship of John the Beloved. But as the sorrowful mother standing before the cross, suffering the final and ultimate pain as she watches her own son suffer and die to pay for man's sins, she becomes the ultimate appealing figure of the mother of all men. As her sons they can express their own love and the guilt they feel in the presence of all mothers who unreservedly give them their love.[18]

> Stood the Mother, stood
> though sighing,
> Tearful, 'neath the cross,
> where dying
> Hung her only Son and Lord.

The virgin mother is provided with a husband, Joseph, who is her protector and moral representative in the larger world; God, the Father, acting through his agent, the Holy Spirit, impregnates her. The question arises as to what is involved symbolically that made it necessary for the male head of the family to be divided into two persons: Joseph and God. The immediate explanation that comes to mind is important but insufficient. Joseph, the human being, primarily in the role of the husband, and God in the role of the father and procreater— the one person being split into two—conveniently express this division in their persons. But why is this division necessary? It is not because God was too sacred and spiritual to be permitted symbolic human form, for Christ was one with him in the Christian Trinity and became human and suffered the degradation that all humans fear and never understand. It must be added that powerful gods of other religions have assumed human procreative roles and maintained their sacred authority. It could be said that the required symbol of the

18. *The Roman Missal*, pp. 847–9.

father is likely to be more reserved, withdrawn from his children and felt to be further removed from human approach and, consequently, less capable of assuming a human symbolic form. There can be little doubt that these values about the father do operate and keep him from too close contact with fearful and always distrustful man, but other societies have possessed family systems where the father was feared, yet they have worshiped father gods who were human procreators.

The principal factor is what might be called symbolic congruence. If sacred symbols express the idealized beliefs and practices of the social structure and are saturated with the idealized feelings and values human beings have for the statuses and relations which compose the various parts of the structure, then it would be expected that the several parts of the sacred belief system would eliminate conflict between the parts and harmonize them or provide satisfying explanations. Thus conflict at the human organizational level is less likely to be part of the ideal organization expressed in the sacred symbols.

For Joseph to be a human husband and a procreative god would make him far too substantial. His human sexuality would arouse the very conflicts which, intrinsically a part of the values and feelings of the human family, are most difficult to face and cause the greatest pain. To these ends, the present symbolic arrangement accomplishes several vital effects. It eliminates the husband, Joseph, as a father and sexual being and thereby removes the feelings of distress about the sex relation of the mother and father. It reduces the feared figure of the human father to a very secondary place. It increases the ease of accepting the mother of Christ as a virgin whose immaculate conception makes her the perfect expression of a moral purity which flees from the distress of the human sexual act. It elevates the role of the father as an authoritative figure to a spiritual place where, although greatly feared, he can be fully accepted.

This arrangement of Divine and human persons creates two highly approachable intermediaries, Jesus and Mary, who are far more able and much better situated to gain spiritual favors from a father who is always difficult to approach and who by his very nature arouses the very fears and anxieties that need to be assuaged. His very remoteness now contributes to his closeness. For the mother and her earthly son can intercede with this distant figure who no longer need to be the threat to man's basic sense of self-reproach. The structure of emotions within family life, particularly those which forbid and enjoin sexual expression, are thus idealized and the conflicts present in the ordinary world are by this symbolic phrasing eliminated in the sacred world.

The roles of the pure virgin and the saintly mother, combined in the figure of one woman, create a symbol of ideal simplicity to arouse and evoke the deep oedipus love of all males, particularly the love of those men who in fact retain their unloosened attachment for their mothers. The love for their own mothers is contained and bound by the worship of virginity. No other woman threatens the tranquility of this original love. The symbol of the virgin is strengthened and maintained by the deep attachment to the mother. It is quite possible that her worship by such men may release them from the guilt and terrors of the too deep attachment and the pain of a love of the mother that will not permit them a wholly satisfying attachment to someone else.

The Freudian conception of oedipus pain and the complex emotions underlying it being essentially psychological and *individually* oriented, loses sight of, and does not completely comprehend, their destructive power for those in the *group* in which such an individual operates. There can be no doubt that psychoanalysts have understood the grief and sorrow of those immediately attached to such a person, particularly the wife and children; but if it is a tragedy for Oedipus to suffer incest longings it is also a tragedy for Jocasta, his mother and wife, and for Laius, his slain father, and for Thebes, his community. All must suffer, since they are part of the society where such incompletely socialized men can never make satisfactory adjustments to those who are capable of living normal lives. It is possible that one of the principal functions of the sacred symbols of femininity is to help sublimate many of these asocial and antisocial longings and fears and drain them into areas that are approved and not dangerous.

It is probable that many in the celibate priesthood may feel a particular attachment to this wholly satisfactory sacred feminine symbol. They are officially urged to venerate her as first among the saints, second only to the Divine persons of the Trinity. "No created being can attain to so intimate a union with God as she. The saints live in the order of grace, but Mary shines in the order of the incarnation of Jesus." They are men capable of the same emotions as other males but under the strict ascetic discipline of celibacy. Yet scandal now rarely touches any member of the clergy. The love of the human mother can continue unmodified, and much of it without transformation can be passed over to the love of the Divine mother. Cardinal Mindszenty declares, "To the priest, a human being consigned to loneliness, the Lord gave Mary as mother when he gave her to His beloved disciple: 'Behold thy Mother!' The priest finds that warmth every heart needs in Mary. The priest, therefore, is obliged to love her with all the strength of an affectionate heart." [19] It will be recalled that it is officially stated that the perfectly pure man is not one without sex drive but he who learned how to control it and rise above it. The same statements, of course, hold for the attachment to the symbol of the female Church and, as we saw earlier, for some mystics in their relation with Christ.

The virgin part of the symbol of Mary reduces and largely eliminates the hostility to her. As such, she is not in the ambivalent position of human mothers. She is without immediate or original sin. She is innocent of sexual desire and accordingly the perfect mother of the perfect child. She is soft, warm, loving, merciful, and affectionate. She is the self-sacrificing, yielding mother who needs the love of her children. God, the father, fortunately remote, is harsh, unyielding, inhuman, largely without pity, the moral judge who punishes without mercy according to the harsh laws of a masculine universe. Their son, although masculine, is born in the image of his mother, yet he is also like his father. Christian doctrine has recognized him in both roles. As the gentle Lamb of God, he is the soft, innocent one who inherits the personality of his mother. As the fearful judge who will condemn the wicked to eternal torment, mentioned in the Gospels and the liturgies, who will preside on the Judgment Day at his second coming, he is created in the stern and fearful likeness of his father. Since he

19. Mindszenty [97], p. 76.

is both, different ages and different peoples have emphasized one side or the other of his personality. It is now fashionable to think of him only as the loving God, compassionate, and the source of loving kindness in human behavior.

God, the strong father, strikes terror in the hearts of men. Should they disobey his stern commands, he may condemn them to everlasting torment or personal obliteration. The mother continually appeals to the merciful side of her son, asking him to persuade his father to act in behalf of her weak human children who, as members of our species, forever misbehave morally and forever are sorry for their misdeeds. She can do this because, during the nine months she carried her Divine son in her womb—from the time of her impregnation by God at the Annunciation until his birth on Christmas Day—the blood and life forces of her human body nourished him, and her breasts comforted him and the milk drawn from her body fed him and became part of the infant—the same Jesus who, himself, grown into the mature male Christ, sought to save and redeem sinful man.

The harsh, not to say cruel and vengeful, qualities of the father image are transformed into the gentle, loving, peaceful son of the woman. The fighting, aggressive, male Jehovah becomes the gentle peaceful male Christ, capable of loving men as well as women, not in an erotic way but within the limits and bounds of the moral rules of a brother. In Christ as the brother, men and women are protected from sexual anxiety and fear because they share common incest bonds with him. He obeys the moral rules as they themselves hope they will act in any situation.

CHAPTER 12

THE SYMBOLIC STRUCTURE

OF THE SACRED YEAR

The Problem: Time Symbols and the Sacred Year

Since in the rational and non-rational thought of Yankee City notions of time are basic and penetrate all mental life, and since faith in Christian symbols, founded on the family and the species, permeates most of the collectivity, it would seem that an inquiry into the possible interrelations of the two systems of signs and the worlds of meaning they represent should give us increased understanding and possibly be rewarding, too, with a view of some part of the master plan which holds the several systems of belief and value within one mental universe. The worship of the Christian Trinity brings forth the deepest and most persistent primitive emotions of the animal world of the species and relates them to those from the moral and spiritual orders which are the highest and most recent achievements of man's collective life. The notions of social time, largely founded on the cultural adaptations that men make to each other, and the constructs of objective time, [56] products mostly of technological adjustments to the outside world and the universe, are united in Christian symbolism, [21] as in all systems of religious thought. The youngest school child in Yankee City knows that "Christmas comes but once a year" and that Easter Sunday is different from all other Sundays of the year. [7] Still others in many of the present Protestant congregations of the city know about and are fostering the "liturgical revival" and the institution of sacred seasons and holy days and an ordered public worship in their churches. Meanwhile, the Catholic Church continues to maintain the yearly liturgical cycle of seasons, with Advent leading to Christmas, Lent to Easter, and the other holy seasons with their own days of significance. In them the symbols of time and those of the Christian supernatural join and are one, and in so doing become something more than what they are separately. [94]

To examine this problem, direct our inquiry, and determine our theory and choice of method and relevant evidence, we will begin by asking a series of questions: How are the several notions and symbols of time related to the Christian symbolic structure and the non-logical mental world it expresses? What is the scientific and social significance of this relationship? Given these answers, what can we learn that will provide explanations about the mental life of the society? The several answers will be derived from, and refer to, several levels of thought and behavior. To begin our inquiry we must briefly review the relevant facts about the signs, seasons, feasts, and fasts and their relations to each other in the sacred calendar. The visible sacred calendar, a sign system which refers to the Christian signs of public worship, will be a major part of our evidence. The variations among the evangelical, non-liturgical and liturgical churches, including Episcopalians and Catholics, will be considered and the variations and uniformities noted. [40, 128]

We will ask about the meanings of these signs as representations of the rhythms of collective life and how their meanings are related to those of social and objective chronological time. Since the holy days and sacred seasons advance not as cold arithmetical numbers, as they appear on a secular calendar, but in dramatic rhythms of emotional intensity and modes of emotions, we must learn what the emotional rhythms are and inquire about the significance of the recurrent periods of affective intensity and relaxation, even perhaps apathy. What are the periods of sacred joy, sorrow, love, and other human emotions? And what are the meanings of their rhythmic evocations to the functioning of the collectivity?

We will begin by examining the present state of yearly public worship in the several church calendars of Yankee City. The evidence runs from the great liturgical structure of Catholicism, which has held firmly to the holy days and seasons of the past and has added to and strengthened them, through the liturgical Protestant churches such as the Episcopalian, with its prayer book and outward signs of sacred worship, to local and national variations of the evangelical churches and the Unitarians. Furthermore, these differences and similarities cover a history from the time when the Congregationalists and others in Puritan times destroyed all liturgical worship to the present and what we are here calling the Protestant Counter Reformation and liturgical revival in Yankee City and America.

Stafford in his *Christian Symbols in the Evangelical Churches*, discussing the "restriction of the forms and symbols" of Christian tradition, says,

The various Catholic, Episcopal and Lutheran churches are professedly liturgical and make extensive use of the traditional forms and symbolism inherited from the early Christian Church, or developed in the period of magnificent flowering of medieval religious art which preceded the Reformation. During the early stages of the Calvinistic Reformation, much of this heritage was thrown into the discard by wrathful reformers, who wrought havoc on priceless treasures of religious art in Scotland, England and other parts of Europe. Of three hundred sixty Celtic crosses, said to exist in Scotland prior to the Reformation, only two exist today. John Calvin permitted gratification of the ear through poetry and music, but denied gratification of the eye. Genesis 1:31 was overlooked. In attempting to uproot "superstitious" and "idolatrous" usages, the Calvinists committed many destructive excesses and, for the sake of stark contrast to Roman Catholic custom, kept their churches almost completely bare of everything that might appeal to the imagination and the esthetic sense of the worshipers. Every candid student of history will admit that they had much provocation. Nevertheless, it now appears that the catharsis was too severe.

The present liturgical renaissance, after a passage of time, he says,

. . . has brought the inevitable backward swing of the pendulum from the extreme Calvinistic position regarding forms and symbols, and today we find a considerable number of Presbyterian, Congregationalist, Baptist and Methodist churches introducing enriched forms of worship, altars, crosses, candles, vestments and other ecclesiastical equipment that would have been darkly frowned upon, even as late as the beginning of this century. Apparently a concomitant of all this is a deepening of reverence for the sanctuary as such. . . .[1]

The liturgical renaissance in the evangelical churches such as the Congregational and others in Yankee City, once the icon-breakers of Puritan times, makes it less easy to draw sharp distinctions among churches about the use of the liturgy in public worship. The present *Guide for Members of Congregational and Christian Churches,* used in Yankee City and cited to our research to describe what Congregationalists do, declares, "The observation of the Christian Year goes back to the very earliest days of the Church . . . when the Christian religion became established . . . the celebration of memorial days significant to the Christian religion grew in importance . . . Within a few hundred years the Christians had developed the observance of two great seasons—Lent, the period preceding Easter, and Advent, the period preceding Christmas." The Puritan Reformers, in their efforts to free themselves from the control of tradition "retained only the Bible, some of the hymns, and the observance of Sunday. . . . They rejected," the *Guide* continues, "the beautiful and symbolic ideas which have helped to make the older churches places for reverent worship . . . In New England this attitude went to the extreme of preventing by law the observance of Christmas."

The Protestant liturgical revival has reached the point where the Congregational *Guide* in Yankee City provides a full calendar for the Christian year with a liturgy of over sixty pages presented for the sacred season (see Chart 11). "The Congregational and other non-liturgical bodies," it declares, "have been making a study of the values in historical Christian culture . . . Christian symbolism is [now] being used, the cross appears in many churches. The revival of interest in the observance of the great days of the Christian year is of special significance to the worship program of the Church."

Despite the surge of new interest and liturgical manifestations in the "non-liturgical" churches and the present elaboration of full liturgical seasons, including many of the great

1. Stafford [128], pp. 21–2, 24.

Catholic [a]	Episcopal [b]	Congregational [c]	Presbyterian [d]	Methodist [e]
Advent	Advent	Advent Season	Advent Season of Expectancy	Advent Season of Expectancy
Christmastide	Christmastide	Christmastide	Christmastide Season of the Nativity	Christmastide Season of the Nativity
Time after Epiphany Septuagesima Remote Preparation	Time after Epiphany	[Sundays] After Epiphany Three Sundays next before Lent	Epiphany, Season of the Evangel	Epiphany, Season of the Evangel
Lent .... (Holy Week)	Lent (Holy Week)	Lent (Holy Week)	Lent Season of Renewal	Lent, Season of Penitence and Renewal
Paschal Time Eastertide	Paschal Time Time after Easter	The Sundays from Easter Day to Whitsunday	Eastertide Season of Resurrection	Eastertide Season of Resurrection
Time after Pentecost	Time after Pentecost	Whitsuntide the week following Whitsunday	Whitsuntide Season of Holy Spirit, Expansion of Church	Whitsuntide Season of Expansion of Church
		The second half of the Christian Year from Trinity Sunday to the Advent Season	Kingdomtide Season of the Kingdom of God on Earth	Kingdomtide Season of the Kingdom of God on Earth

a. Dom F. Cabrol, O.S.B., "The Liturgical Year and Prayer of the Time," *The Roman Missal,* in Latin and English (P. J. Kenedy and Sons, 1922), pp. xiv–xxi. Rt. Rev. Fernand Cabrol, O.S.B., *The Year's Liturgy* (New York, Benziger Brothers, 1938).

b. Calendar for 1952, *The Living Church Annual,* Yearbook of the Episcopal Church, 1951 (New York and Chicago, Morehouse-Gorham Co.). *The Book of Common Prayer* (New York, Oxford Univ. Press).

c. Calendar, the Congregational *Guide* (Pilgrim Press, 1952).

d. Calendar of the Christian Year, 1952–53, *Presbyterian Plan Book.*

e. "A Calendar and Lectionary for the Christian Year," *The Book of Worship* (The Methodist Publishing House, 1945), pp. 209–12.

CHART 11. The Seasons of the Sacred Year

festivals (the Annunciation of the Virgin Mary on March 25th, for example), the evangelical churches have yet to develop the elaborate rituals and accompanying myths with detailed biblical and traditional references that are common in the Catholic and liturgical Protestant churches. The forces of rationalism and revolt are still strong. However, this new Counter Reformation in the Protestant Church, emphasizing the visible signs of sacred thought to communicate the non-rational mysteries of the spiritual world more effectively than words, continues to gain strength.

The Protestants, once fearful of the distortions and "earthly impurities" believed to come from the generations of churchly men and women who, in the thousand-odd years after the "books" of the Bible were written, added their own signs to the liturgy, are now filling the old liturgical seasons with their own feast days and their liturgies with words and sentiments and interpretations of sacred life now considered appropriate for a given season. Meanwhile they are reincorporating the older liturgical symbols and seasons into their calendars (see the earlier discussion of Mother's Day). These include days of significance to the Church and those taken from the larger collectivity's holidays. For example, in the Christian year of the Congregationalists are "Race Relations Sunday" to be celebrated on the Sunday nearest February 12, Lincoln's Birthday; Independence Day, "the Sunday next before July 4th"; Labor Sunday, Thanksgiving Sunday, as well as Forefathers' Day "in honor and memory of the Pilgrim Fathers." Reformation Sunday is placed on or near October 26th by the Presbyterians.

The testimony of some of the local ministers brings out the Protestant situation in Yankee City and provides evidence about the liturgical movement and the surviving sense of local independence and concern about visible sacred signs. "There is a strong liturgical revival in the Protestant churches here in Yankee City. We wish to bring in more beauty," the minister of the largest Congregational Church said (1952). "There is a general feeling that it is a good thing to bring the old symbols back into the church. For the last ten years we have been following the Congregational Calendar [see Chart 11]. Both we and the First Church follow it entirely. If you get the church calendar it will tell you exactly what we do. We also place more emphasis on the ordinances. The two [he used the word sacraments later] we observe are Baptism and Communion. Marriage can either be an ordinance or a sacrament according to the decisions of the minister."

The minister of the liturgical Episcopal Church (1952) said with considerable satisfaction that "all the churches in Yankee City are beginning to reinterest themselves in the liturgy. A number of the liturgical seasons are being recognized again, particularly Advent and Lent, by such churches as the Congregational. The Episcopal Church here has always followed the seasonal cycles of the prayer book and observed all of the ordinances and sacraments that the Episcopal Church has always observed."

The Presbyterian minister stated that "we follow local judgments about what will be done and not done to celebrate the seasons. Although we don't place much emphasis ourselves on the liturgical seasons, I myself follow the *Presbyterian Plan Book* (see Chart 11) of the General Assembly of the Presbyterian Church. We pay attention to such days as Christmas, Easter, Thanksgiving, and sometimes Pentecost [Whitsuntide]."

It was clear from the general tone of the interview that he took pride in the local independence and freedom from what he thought might be domination from outside sources. However, it was also apparent that he used the information sent out by the central authorities to guide his selection of topics appropriate for the several seasons of the liturgical year.

Catholic authorities testify that the liturgical year "is one united whole"; the most cursory examination shows that it traces "the different phases of Our Lord's life from Advent to Pentecost," and thereafter the development of the Church and its relation to the Holy Ghost.

The several seasons usually recognized in the various churches are: Advent, Christmastide, Time after Epiphany, Septuagesima (Period of Early Preparation), Lent, Eastertide, and Time after Pentecost or Whitsuntide (see Chart 11 for each church). The several periods (the Catholic Missal says) "are regulated by the three chief feasts of the year, Christmas, Easter, and Pentecost"; the first appearing on a fixed date, December 25; the second, a movable one, on the first Sunday after the first full moon of the vernal equinox;

and the last appearing fifty days after Easter, also a movable feast, dependent on Easter. Advent, with four Sundays, is a period of three to four weeks from Advent Sunday to Christmas Eve. The length of Christmastide is dependent on the time of Septuagesima Sunday, which may fall on any day from January 16 to February 22. It includes all Sundays after Christmas "to the number of six." [2] (See Chart 12.)

The extent of Septuagesima is only three weeks; "the duration of the season is invariable," but its beginning is dependent on the position of Easter. Lent is always a period of forty days, extending from Easter Sunday (March 22 to April 25) back to Ash Wednesday (see Chart 12). Eastertide extends forward from Easter Sunday for fifty days to the Feast of Pentecost or Whitsunday. At present it is the practice in some

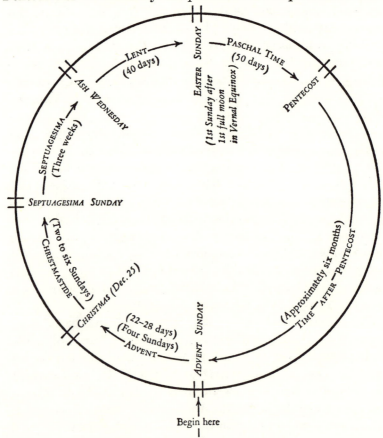

CHART 12. The Sacred Cycle of Time

2. *The Roman Missal* [117], pp. xiv–xx.

churches to extend it "to the Saturday before Trinity Sunday." Time after Pentecost, the longest liturgical period—approximately six months—varies in length depending on the date of Advent Sunday and the end of Paschal Time (certain churches divide it into two seasons). This season, of secondary importance, expands or contracts according to the demands of the more important ones directly related to the great feast days celebrating the two crises in the life of Christ: his birth and death.

Starting with Advent, it is immediately evident that the liturgy follows very closely a series of irreversible events directly related to the life cycle of Jesus. Beginning with the preparation for his birth and continuing thereafter with his childhood, his presentation in the Temple, later fasting and similar events, and ending with the last few weeks of his life, the liturgical drama exactly parallels the biblical accounts. The last periods portray his passion, crucifixion, the events of his resurrection, his ascension into Heaven, and finally, at Pentecost, the descent of the Holy Spirit from Heaven to the apostles and the birth of the Christian Church. This whole period, from the beginning of Advent to Pentecost, can be viewed as one sacred cycle. The feast days and other liturgical events after Pentecost are not chronologically arranged. They may or may not follow an objective time order.

As symbols the central and minor characters of the Christian calendar are infused with the ultimate values and beliefs of the moral order and the emotional needs of the species. Each year they act out a story which narrates and expresses in material form the symbolic significance of man's existence and the meanings of the social and natural world which invade and surround his species. The human attribution of meaning to them is not merely individual projection but the group using common symbols which it has produced. In them the psychic needs of men are fulfilled.

The sacred characters and their actions, the Father, the Son, the Holy Ghost, and the Mother of the Son, being signs of man's long experience as a social species—a species whose physical acts are never free of social and spiritual infusions, whose spiritual life is filled with his physical and species nature—are collective expressions which are multi-determined. To take a parallel from another culture, the meanings of Bapa

Indi, the great python god of Australia, is at once a deity, a snake, the weather, one of the seasons, the male half of the age-status structure, several clans, as well as one of the moral and spiritual forces of the whole society. [139a] Jesus Christ, the Son of God and the second Person in the Trinity, is not only a male with a human body born of a woman, the friend and leader of man, but the abstract Word and the summation of modern man's spirituality and supernatural beliefs. The Holy Spirit, the Ghost of God, the least corporeal of the three Persons of the Trinity, is a moral being who is the Comforter, Paraclete, and Christ's substitute in man's present life; yet even so he is infused with physiological and species significance, for in his most important act he is the symbolic energy and spiritual power which impregnated the Virgin. The differences, great as they are, between the Holy Ghost and Christ, the God-Man, as well as between God, the Father, are of degree, not of kind. All three Persons of the Trinity, in the liturgy in varying degrees refer to and evoke feelings and beliefs which express all levels of man's existence.

The efforts of the logicians and some theologians to explain God's significance in a set of propositions are as futile as they would be dangerous should they be effective. The yearly story of the life of Christ expresses and evokes some of the deepest and most significant emotions men feel about themselves and the world in which they live. The great drama necessarily releases them from quandaries and dilemmas for which rational and moral values have no answers. Social and technical sources, in the ultimate sense, have no adequate solutions for man's will to live and his need to die. Furthermore, since the world of man is fundamentally a species world, to be significant the basic symbols which organize his private world must be images whose meanings remain close to the meanings of his individual membership in the species life of his group. This statement becomes dramatically true at crucial moments such as birth, marriage, and death, when the behavior of the species interconnects, or fails to interconnect, him and other (separate) individuals as ongoing beings in the flow of species behavior. At these moments there is the greatest concern, anxiety, and fear among those involved. The symbols of the death rituals, for example, express the sorrow and guilt of those who have lost someone they love and the anxiety of the survivors for their own anticipated death, as well as the disquiet and disorder felt by those involved. Rationally, morals and technical knowledge should suffice, but the brutal ultimate facts of death, felt and experienced at the animal level of species life, can be expressed only by the physical and oral acts of sacred ritual. A dead Christ brutally slain and his human body nailed to a cross, in fact once and in liturgical observance beyond count, can tell all that must be said; the identification of his passion and men's pain at their deaths allows each human animal to feel and know what it means to die. But since individual transience, in Christian drama, is merged in the myth of the collective Christ with the eternal myth of the eternal species, the pain of death is assuaged by the healing assurances of this symbolic transformation.

The liturgical calendar as a comprehensive system of signs relates the several non-rational time orders to each other and to the rational chronology of objective, solar time (see Chart 12). The sacred calendar is a sign system ordering certain events of the sacred myth into the form of a cycle beginning and ending at the same place. The sacred signs are meaningful directives to order the public worship of the collectivity. The sacred symbols, given linear time dimensions "bent" to the form of a circle, as Chart 12 depicts, are transformed into the *space* of a circle which is non-rationally given a beginning and an end. The beginning and end occur at the same liturgical point. The liturgical year covers the same length of time as the secular; like the secular year it, too, has its seasons; but whereas the natural year has four seasons, in fact or by ascription more or less equal in length, that correspond with the course of the sun and the changes in external nature *felt* and conceived to be of significance to man's adjustment, the seasons of the sacred calendar are more numerous, vary greatly in length, may or may not have close correspondence with the solar cycle, and are variable according to the usages of church denomination. All of them, however, have to do with the life crises of Christ.

The sacred calendar as a yearly structure of sacred symbolic events is represented in the circular representation of Chart 12. In it objective time with its beginning and ending, with duration in a linear series of unending days, is transformed into a sacred circle where duration is contained and forced to repeat itself in the preestablished eternal forms of sacred time. At the bottom, with Advent Sunday, the liturgical calendar starts and ends. The breaks in the outer circle (||) indicate the principal holy days when the seasons are said to start and end. The arrows running clockwise show the course of the seasons and their approximate periods of time. Some of the principal holidays of some of the churches are marked on the outer circle.

The liturgical year transforms the feelings of the species as well as technological and social time, conceptually and emotionally, into the powerful symbols of the life span of a godman. Social and technological time is thereby securely bound to, and confined within, the significant emotional crises of human individual experience. The cold, desireless technological time of recurring nights and days, of equinoxes and solstices, extending from infinitesimal divisions of a second through a mathematical order into eternal duration, yields to the fantasies and wishes, the hopes and fears, that are intrinsic parts of the crises of birth, life, and death. The rhythms of our social order, expressed in the social calendar's weeks and months and other secular conceptions, are transformed into symbolic birthdays, deaths, and other important days of Christ and those who surrounded him. Thus social time is transfigured and "raised" to the sacred level through the individual time of incarnate God; accordingly it has become emotionally meaningful to everyone who believes, since everyone from his own experiences with his own life crises can project his private and public values and beliefs onto the action of this sacred drama. What is projected is not the idiosyncratic differences of individuals and the social world that they and others have experienced during their lives in the group, but the life cycle of Christ, God become human, who was born, lived, suffered, and died as a man, symbol of all men, although individually conceived, symbolically structured into a sequence of individual events that mirror the essentials of the life of the collectivity.

The sacred seasons, directly related to the symbolic structure of Christianity, and through it to the human social system and the species order, consequently evoke and express the nonrational meanings of life through its sacred symbols by the rational arrangement of objective time. Spiritually stated, the liturgy is said (by Pius Parsch, Augustinian canon) to have "a twofold function: to lead men to a worship of God pleasing to Him, and to conduct His grace to men."

For those who believe, the dull, discordant realities of ordinary existence are transfigured by the symbolic power of the liturgy. For them the fearful, separate beginnings and endings of human life are lifted from dark obscurity into circular, timeless tranquility. At this sacred level the brutal facts of secular mortality lose their harsh significance. They merge with and lose their meanings in the peace and quiet of the sacred symbols of immortality. The sequence of past events and their projection into the changing future disappear within the liturgical stillness of an eternal present. The self-contained sacred conceptual system expressed in the outward forms of the liturgy symbolically transforms yesterday and tomorrow into an eternal today. The recurring yearly feasts and festivals, forever in a self-contained, circular continuity without beginning and without end, express and refer to the eternal quality of the group and the human species. The liturgical circle of holy days and holidays celebrating the human life span and godly existence of Jesus Christ allows those who believe to escape some of the pain of life and their feeling of doom within this symbolic sanctuary. Here each mortal's fate is transformed by identification with the immortal fate of his God. Through the symbols of the liturgy one can say, borrowing from the theater, that "death takes a holiday," not for a brief interlude but forever and in all ways.

The system of sacred belief and ritual is not only an organized expression of the social and species life of the human individual and his group, but one of the effective controls exercised on the animal life of man. By use of it the ongoing species, with its interconnected members, maintains and controls part of the life of the group. The several types of ritual usage directly or indirectly constrain and control the physiological processes of the separate human organisms and the outward actions which interrelate them in time and space as members of the species. The biological crises, including those of birth, maturation, procreation, and death, and the feelings of the individual about them, the sensations of hunger, thirst, sex, and the satisfactions felt in eating, drinking, and copulation, as well as the feelings of cold and heat and other emotional reactions to the natural environment, in the liturgy are given recognition. The ritual usages employed are the several *rites de passage*, those of fasting and feasting, commensalism, and other forms of ritual eating, sexual prohibition, license, and the ritual usages of sexual contact.

The Sacred and Secular Rites of Passage—Reified Signs of Age and Ritual Status

Since the whole liturgy is a drama, or several connected dramas, it can be examined by a methodology similar to that used for historical dramas. As research materials the two are quite similar, the several elements being: (1) the principal sacred characters, Christ, the other personages of the Trinity, the Mother, and the human and divine, positive and negative, characters; (2) their actions and the involvements of the hero, those of his birth, life, and death; (3) the actions as plot (story line) in his, and our, tragedy and triumph; (4) the several scenes—for example, Bethlehem and Calvary; and (5) the emotional involvements, identifications, and evocations officially assigned to the audience and to the actors who present the drama. For the liturgical and some of the evangelical churches there are a series of directions for moral conduct and the control of physical activities. To learn something more of the significance of this little understood and vastly unappreciated mode of human understanding, the emphasis in the discussion will be upon deriving a clearer delineation of the non-rational clusters of sacred meanings.

The feast days of Jesus are the marks of his own rites of passage, conforming in broad outline to Van Gennep's classical conception of what they are in all societies. [54] They include birth, naming, circumcision, the miraculous events that mark his maturity, the Crucifixion, Resurrection, Ascension—and, in his other Persons, his conception at the Annunciation and the coming of the Holy Spirit at Pentecost. In Catholic myth the rites of passage of the Virgin, beginning with her immaculate conception and her nativity, through the birth of her son until her death and assumption into heaven, paralled those of her Son. They provide a spiritual age structure for women similar to the one of Jesus for men. The worship given to God by the faithful is paralleled by the veneration (hyperdulia), not to say worship, given the Mother. Through the two in Catholic worship, and the one in Protestant, the (felt) meanings of species events that flow through the family structure and their crucial moments are significantly marked and made symbolically meaningful. The sacred ceremonies of baptism, confirmation, marriage, and the death rituals symbolize the significance of these events in the life of the devout.

The sacred symbols of the family—the Father, the Son, the spiritual semen, and the Mother—exist outside the dimensions of time. They have their being in *eternal simultaneity*. As such they symbolically express the ever-present finality of the family system. As such their meanings are circular in conformance with being parts of a larger unity. It is only when the events in the life of one of them (Christ) are viewed in sequence, or when the sacred family is related to the reckonings of human collective time, that the linear time of past, present, and future enters. It seems likely that the logical and very abstract concept of simultaneity, a comparatively recent acquisition of logical thought, is little more than what was once only felt by the individual as the oneness of the sensations coming from his separate bodily parts and—collectively—as the primitive non-rational sense of those elsewhere existing now as do those who are (spatially) present. Passing events change all this, and for the individual age becomes the dominant mental organization of experience.

The several sacraments and ordinances, various in number according to denomination, reorganize the sacred symbols of the family into a linear order of the changing events of individual age and rechannel the notions and feelings they express about the life cycle for those who believe and are involved with them. [83] The unchanging yearly cycle of spiritual eternity is given human meaning by the projection of the significance of the meanings of the individual life span and human rites of passage onto those of Christ as a symbol of the general collectivity. The family structures, those of birth and orientation and of procreation, are represented in new symbolic forms. The factual events which establish parent-child relations are first transformed into the symbols of individual time and a linear time extension. Thereafter the symbols of the human life cycle are reified into those of the Christ cycle and as such they meaningfully interpenetrate. In Christian thought, as we stated earlier, the family and its extended kinship structures, along with the Church, stand for the total collectivity. The age crises of the individual, made sacredly significant in the several sacraments, and the Christ symbols of the collectivity as an age aggregate blend and merge in the liturgy.

The symbolic events in the life of the Virgin, for example, carrying the unborn child in her womb for nine months from March 25 to December 25—in the liturgy from the Annunciation to Christmas—her accouchement and period of recovery from the birth of Jesus, her flight with him into Egypt, all accent the age and species relations of Jesus and his mother. In one period he is physically connected with her, his human life dependent on her human life, a foetal member of the species and a participant in the ongoing, continuing behavior which commits him to the physical and social generations of men. The given facts of his foetal life and his mother's life during that time correspond with the natural age order of the species and of all men and their mothers. As a sacred drama, it is a series of interconnected acts involving human beings and their gods, the natural and the supernatural. The center of the whole drama is in the transitional rites of the family and the life cycle of each human being.

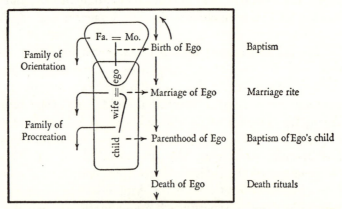

CHART 13. The Symbolic Recognition of the Flow of Species and Moral Events in an Age Status System

The flow of species events and the related structural changes in the family's moral order and their liturgical recognition are depicted by Chart 13. It shows how the changing feelings and sensations of the growing individual and the moral and symbolic structures are ordered in an age-time arrangement. On the left the interlocking families are translated into a time order, running from the generation of ego's parents, through his birth, marriage, and the birth of the new generation. Immediately to the right are the critical events, species and moral, and to the extreme right the symbolic age rites that mark the passage of individual time. Out of this intimate and, for those involved, easily comprehended system, a symbolic structure, world-wide in its distribution and existing ages before Christianity, takes form and attains non-rational validity. Species events miraculously defined, but humanly felt as portrayed in the collective symbols that comprise the life of Christ—birth at Christmas and Easter, death in the events of Good Friday and Holy Saturday—give human meanings in the collective worship of the liturgy.

The symbol system of the liturgy, responding to the significant cultural and species meanings of human facts, marks the objects and relations among them with ritual expressions, the sacred meanings of which are mysteries. At the points where the age and family facts of the ordinary world of natural reality are connected with the truths of religion, the church and religious tradition erect a symbolic marker pointing to the critical changes of age and interpreting their meanings with supernatural meanings. The liturgy provides an interrelated system of age symbols which refer to the facts and provide their supernatural meanings. When the logic of reason can apply, it is used freely; when it fails to correspond with the order of natural facts and provide a "reasonable" and "believable" relation between the sacred and natural orders, sacred symbolism is employed and the supernatural becomes the cause (the "pre-established" form) which explains the natural. Those who can avail themselves of faith readily move from the starting point and progress from ascertained fact to symbolic reified truth.

Chart 14, of the emotional rhythms of the sacred season, depicts the rise and fall of intensity of feeling as it is officially defined by the liturgy and by the human and family nature of the events symbolized; the symbolic seasons (moving from left to right) are listed and numbered. The degree of emotional intensity is shown by the height or depth of the seasonal curve. Below the list of liturgical seasons are the principal sacred characters and crucial actions occurring during the great divi-

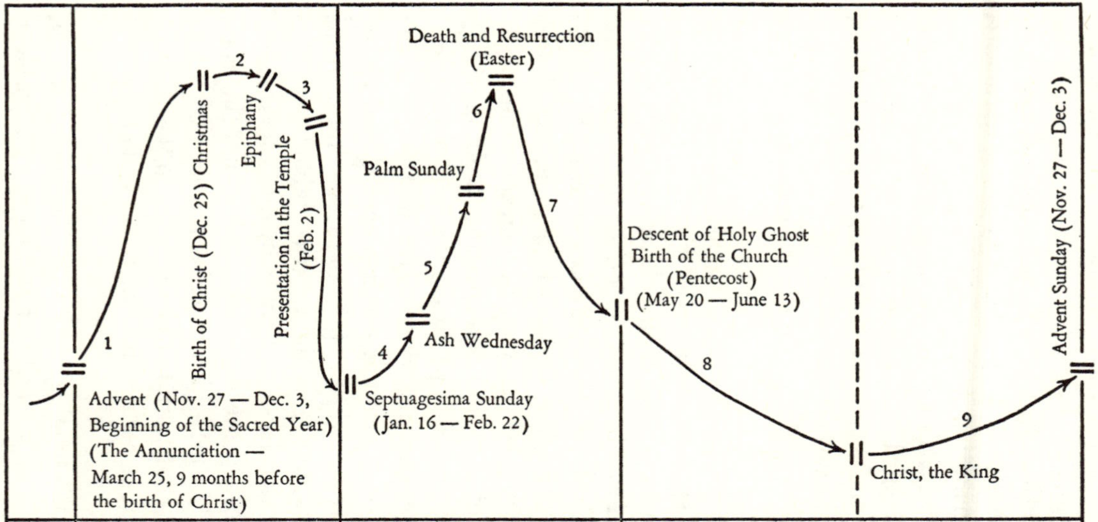

The table below (rotated with the chart) reads:

	Advent (Nov. 27 — Dec. 3, Beginning of the Sacred Year) (The Annunciation — March 25, 9 months before the birth of Christ)	Septuagesima Sunday (Jan. 16 — Feb. 22)	8. Birth of Christian Church, 8–9. Time after Pentecost.	9. Kingdom of God on Earth.
Seasons	1. Advent, 2. Christmastide, 3. Time after Epiphany.	4. Septuagesima, 5. Lent, 6. Holy Week, 7. Eastertide (Paschal Time).		
Characters and their actions	God the Father, Holy Ghost and Christ and Mary (and Joseph). Impregnation of Mary, birth and baptism of Jesus.	Christ, the Apostles, the Passion, Lord's Supper, Crucifixion, Resurrection, Ascension.	The Holy Ghost, the Apostles (Peter and Paul and John). Forming of the Church and conversion of Gentiles.	St. Paul and the Apostles. Expansion of the Church.

Labels within the chart:

Advent Sunday (Nov. 27 — Dec. 3)

Christ, the King

Descent of Holy Ghost Birth of the Church (Pentecost) (May 20 — June 13)

Death and Resurrection (Easter)

Palm Sunday

Ash Wednesday

Presentation in the Temple (Feb. 2)

Epiphany

Birth of Christ (Dec. 25) Christmas

CHART 14. The Emotional Rhythms of the Sacred Seasons

406

sions of the year. It will be noted that the principal holy days and the occasion for their celebration are given.

In general the emotions rise from Advent to Christmas and the birth of Christ and fall slightly thereafter; the curve for the Period of Remote Preparation (Septuagesima) that leads up to Ash Wednesday rises rapidly and reaches its highest peak at the death and resurrection of Christ at Easter, then lessens towards Pentecost and falls into the period of least interest, Time After Pentecost.

Dom Cabrol, one of the great authorities on the Sacred Year, in his commentary on Holy Week makes abundantly clear the emotional rhythm and the liturgy's increasing intensity from the Period of Remote Preparation to Easter. He says, "We might compare the time from Septuagesima to Palm Sunday to a long road, which has brought us by a gradual but continuous ascent to the summit whereon we now stand. The three Sundays before Lent and the five which follow them are all really a preparation for Holy Week." [3]

The significance of the family structure, and the species and non-logical significances given to the Easter period, most clearly marked in the rites of Holy Saturday are secondarily accented on "Low Sunday" after Easter and the rebirth of Christ. Remembering that the symbols of this period were of direct significance to the initiates who were to be baptized in the womb of the font, previously impregnated by the Holy Spirit (see next section), we see the joyous theme of the celebration following Lent expressed and interpreted by the joyful melody of that Sunday's Gregorian setting. "The newly baptized," Cabrol says, "are as new born infants, who already instinctively long for the natural milk, a symbol of the first element of the Christian doctrine."

Paschal Time following Easter is a time of joy. It is the Holy Fifty Days, "a long continuous feast," once so in fact, now only by sign and emotion. This period is believed to be the oldest of the liturgical seasons. On Ascension Day, fixed by the Gospel text as forty days after Easter, Christ ascends into Heaven. The Catholic Mass for the day makes its symbolic function clear: "Christ Our Lord, after His resurrection, appeared to all His assembled disciples, and, while they gazed at

3. Cabrol [21], p. 164.

Him, ascended to heaven, in order to make us participants in His divinity . . . it is on this most holy day that Our Lord, the Only Son of the Father, placed the substance of our fragile nature, united to His own, at the right hand of the glory of God the Father." The scriptural reference in the Congregational *Guide*, "The Ascension" (Mark 16), also provides the biblical significance of the day.

Whitsunday, fifty days after Easter, a date exactly set by scripture, "celebrates the Day of Pentecost, the gathering of the first church, when the disciples were met in the upper room in Jerusalem, and Jesus' spirit was manifested to them, making them realize again that he lived. This sending of the Spirit," continues the Congregational *Guide*, "marked for the disciples the great new day of Jesus' continuing leadership of men."

"With the Feast of Pentecost," Cabrol explains, "the Holy Ghost has taken possession of the Church." [4] The ritual is the same as for Holy Saturday on the night before Easter.

During Time after Pentecost the Catholic liturgy uses once more St. Paul's Epistle to the Ephesians on the Nuptial Mass which relates the belief about the feminine nature of the Church with the masculinity of Christ in wedded union with the love of human males and females in marriage.

Michel, in speaking of the liturgy of the Trinity, presents the non-logical cluster of meanings and their theological significance. "It is he [Holy Ghost] who is sent down to complete the fullness of Christ's mission, sent down by both the Father and the Son after the Son's return to the Father." He quotes Dom Grea to interrelate the scriptural metaphors about the relation of the Third Person to Christ as the Head of the feminine body of the Church: "The Holy Spirit could not be absent, and in the mystery of the Church united to her Head, he is given to the Church; he lives in the Church, breathes and speaks in her. And his presence in her is a mysterious necessity of the hierarchy, founded on the eternal necessities of the divine life and of the society that is in God. And as he unites the Son to the Father, so he unites the Church to her Head . . ." [5]

The Holy Ghost has an important role in several acts of the drama, particularly at the time of the Annunciation in the impregnation of Mary, where he represents God and, for this

4. In general see *ibid.*, pp. 197–204.
5. Michel [94], p. 36.

particular event, symbolically is sacred semen, and at Pentecost when he returns as one of the persons of the Trinity to the Church and once again, in effect, plays a similar symbolic role. This time, as with Mary at the Annunciation, he enters the Church and fills her with his spiritual power. The primary role of the Holy Ghost is essentially that of being a substitute for the other two major figures of the Trinity. In the Trinity, the unity and diversity of men in society are represented, the three separate autonomous personae made one in the collective image expressing the unity of the group—the Father, the Son, and their connecting principle, the Holy Ghost, separate yet one, the collectivity made in the image of the family. He provides an abstract and formless spiritual image for the more material forms of the other two when the presence of either in the sacred acts involved might be awkward or embarrassing to the sentiments of Christians. A too close and realistic representation of the impregnation of Mary by God at the Annunciation would be embarrassing and difficult for the faithful to accept. The appearance of the Holy Ghost on earth after Christ's departure makes it possible thereafter for the resurrected Christ to be felt as an ever-present reality, permitting the faithful to reduce their sense of loss and deprivation by his disappearance to the sacred world. The return of the Holy Spirit at Pentecost and his entrance into the female body of the new church and into the spiritual life of each Christian as the Holy Spirit provide an intimate, enduring relation of the sacred with the ordinary world of men.

Whereas the Roman rite repeats the coital symbolism of the early initiation of the Catechumens as new Christians at the celebration of Whitsunday (see next section), the Presbyterians list Whitsuntide as the "Season of the Holy Spirit and the Birth and Expansion of the Christian Church," thereby clearly recognizing not only the biblical account of the "fiery tongues" of the Holy Spirit descending into the assemblage of the Apostles but the *birth* of the Church from this mythical union. In keeping with this masculine-feminine symbolism they also place the Annunciation and the impregnation of the Virgin Mary by the Holy Spirit, which resulted in the birth of the other holy symbol, Christ, on March 25th, nine months before his birthday.

The liturgical drama acts out the Christian myth as it is told in the Bible; it is also clear that what it expresses are the deeper emotions of the species, particularly those of the family and the age-grade system.

Holy Coitus and Sacred Procreation

The present Catholic rite and many Protestant rites of baptism, originally sanctioned by Christ himself and by the appearance of the Holy Spirit when he was baptized by John the Baptist, are greatly dependent on the early Christian rites of initiation used for *adult* pagans who went through a long period of training to be crowned and completed by the Easter rites of rebirth. During the rites of the catechumens on Holy Saturday night the initiates died with Christ and rose with him from the dead. The Catholic liturgy for Easter preserves and makes symbolically explicit what the shortened and more oblique Protestant and Catholic baptismal rites express in condensed form.

The principal ceremonies of the night before Easter are the blessing of the new fire, the rites of the paschal candle, the reading of the twelve prophecies, and the blessing of the baptismal font.[6] All of these overt rituals and oral rites, some of them with an extreme degree of literalness, symbolize (among other things) the power and significance of man's sexual life as a member of his species. Let us examine and analyze the symbols of this most important ceremony.

The candle, a principal emblem in these Holy Saturday rites, with its light and fire is officially a "symbol of Christ," to "enlighten the minds of the faithful" where "grace enkindles their hearts." When at this very solemn moment of bleakness and stark darkness which symbolize death and the end of things, when all lights are out in the church, fire is struck from a flint, the priest blesses the new fire (as the symbol of beginning and renewal) and appeals to God for his aid as "the author of all light." Then the triple candle is lighted and blessed and the deacon sings, "Light of Christ." Once more every year a new world begins, an old one ends, and new life triumphs over the deaths of all men.

"The darkness of sin" is overcome by the light and spiritual

6. See *The Roman Missal* [117], "Holy Saturday," pp. 399–446.

splendor of Christ. The feared symbol of death and feelings of ritual pollution and darkness are defeated by the triumph of light, symbol of life and spiritual purity. This is the symbolic "night which broke the chains of death," and man, with Christ, "ascended, conqueror, from hell." It is "the time and hour when Christ rose again from hell and man and the world were sanctified." "It is the time when Jesus Christ," says the Roman Missal, "paid for us to his eternal Father the debt of Adam and by his sacred blood cancelled the guilt contributed by original sin. The sanctification of this night blots out crimes, washes away sins, restores innocence to sinners and joy to the sorrowful. It banishes enmities and produces concord . . ." [7] After the reading of the twelve prophecies of the Old Testament, including those having to do with ritual pollution when the sin and wickedness of the earth are washed away by the flood and the earth purified, and the destruction of the evil Egyptians by the waters of the Red Sea, the priest begins the solemn rite of the blessing of the font. Water, sanctified and transformed into a sacred symbol, washes away pollution and cleanses the sinful earth.

Some of the more significant passages from this aesthetically beautiful and symbolically significant rite of purification need further analysis. (The material used is taken from the Roman Missal.) In the rite, after the twelfth prophecy, Psalm 41 is quoted. "As the hart panteth after the fountains of water so my soul panteth after thee, O God. My soul has thirsteth for the living God." In the collect it is implored, "Almighty and eternal God, look mercifully on the devotion of the people desiring a New Birth who, like the hart panteth after the fountains of thy waters; so mercifully grant that the thirst of their faith made so by the sacrament of baptism sanctify their souls and bodies through our Lord." In the same collect, the priest invokes, "Almighty and eternal God, be present at these mysteries, be present at these sacraments of thy great goodness and send forth the spirit of *adoption* to regenerate the *new* people whom the font of baptism brings forth . . ." [8]

The priest continues saying, "O God whose spirit moved

---

7. *Ibid.,* pp. 399–406.

8. *Ibid.,* pp. 434–5. See the Missal for passages cited from the continuing ceremony.

over the waters of the beginning of the world that even the
waters might receive the virtues of satisfaction." He also says,
"God, by water, washed away the crimes of the guilty world
and of the deluge which gave the figure of regeneration."

The symbolic "fountains of water" which refresh the soul,
the primal waters over which the Spirit of God moved at the
beginning of the world, and the purifying water of the deluge
which regenerated sinful man, are all symbolically invoked and
with God related to the waters of the font of adoption where
the "new people" are to be brought forth and "adopted" into
God's spiritual family. The holy font is being formed into the
image of the other spiritual water symbols and prepared to
become the efficient symbol for the rebirth of the initiates. The
female symbol, water, is being acted on by the male representative of a male god.

The priest divides the water in the font into the form of a
cross and refers to God "who by a secret mixture of his divine
fruit may render this water *fruitful* for the regeneration of
man to the end that those who have been sanctified in the immaculate womb of this divine font, being born again a new creature,
may come forth a heavenly offspring, and that all that are
distinguished either by sex and body or by age and time may
be brought forth to the same *infancy* by Grace, their spiritual
Mother."

The officiant then touches the water with his hand. He says,
"May this holy and innocent creature be freed from all of the
assaults of the enemy" and "purified . . . by the operation of
the Holy Ghost, the Grace of a perfection purification." The
priest then makes the sign of the cross three times over the
font. He says, "Therefore, I bless thee, O creature of water by
the living ·God—by the Holy God—by the God who in the beginning separated thee by his word from the dry land, whose
spirit moved over thee."

During this ritual the water in the font and the font itself
take on a spiritually female significance, the priest being the
male representative of the male God. Meanwhile, the transformation of the water continues. The priest declares, "I bless
thee also by our Lord, Jesus Christ, his only Son who in Canaan
of Galilee changed thee into wine by a wonderful miracle of his
power—walked on thee dry foot—was baptized *in* thee by John

in the Jordan—and made thee flow out of his side—and commanded his disciples to baptize and to be baptized." The priest adds that the water's "natural virtues of cleansing the body are also effectual for the purifying of the self."

At this point the water and the font have not only become spiritually transfigured into feminine sacred symbols but have also been transformed into effective ritual instruments for the purifying of the soul when it is reborn and becomes Christian. For the first time the priest sinks the paschal candle in the water. While so doing he sings, "May the virtue of the Holy Ghost descend into all of the water of this font and make the whole substance of this water fruitful and capable of regenerating." The waters of the Jordan into which the Holy Spirit descended when Christ was baptized are likened to a symbolic womb, the water made fruitful and the font capable of regenerating sinners.

When the priest divides the water, he declares, "May he (i.e., the Holy Ghost) fertilize this water prepared for the regeneration of man by the secretive mixture of his light that by a holy conception a heavenly offspring may come forth from the spotless womb of the divine font as a new creature and may all who differ in sex or age be *begotten* by parent grace into one and the same infancy."

The sexual act is thus dramatized. The paschal candle inserted in the font overtly states it. The oral rite invoking the intervention of the Holy Ghost cries for a holy conception "in the spotless womb of the divine font." The rite of baptism is formed in, and validated by, the equated female symbols of the Annunciation and the waters of the River Jordan.

The priest withdraws the paschal candle from the water. He intones, "Here may the stains of all sins be washed away. Here may human nature created to thy image and reformed to the honor of its altar be cleansed from all the filth of the Old Man; that all who receive this sacrament of regeneration be born again *new* children of true innocence."

The people are sprinkled and the priest pours oil of the catechumens in the water in the form of a cross. He says, "May this font be sanctified and made fruitful by the oil of salvation, for such as are regenerated therein unto life everlasting." He pours chrism (consecrated oil and spices) into the font. "May this infusion of the chrism of our Lord, Jesus Christ, on the Holy Ghost, the Comforter, be made in the name of the Trinity." The officiant then mixes oil and water and baptizes the candidates in the usual manner.

The candle as· the symbol of the holy male God, Christ, is inserted in the fruitful waters of the "immaculate womb." The pure wax symbol of Christ (a product of the social labor of a community of bees), the spiritually potent chrism, and oil are dropped into the waters, and the spiritual womb of the ritual is thus made fruitful and capable of regenerating all men who come from it. They enter it sinful adults and come out innocent infants. But, symbolically, they do not come out of it for, by intent and ideally, they remain forever in the secure containment of the Mother's spiritual body. It need not be said that this rite and the beliefs which it expresses are a non-logical analogue of the Christian belief in the spiritual conception of Christ, the New Adam. Mary, the immaculately conceived, is impregnated by the Holy Spirit, the third person of the One God, and at this time she hears the words, "Hail Mary, full of Grace, the Lord is with thee. Blessed art thou among women and blessed is the fruit of thy womb [the Lord Jesus]."

The candidates, spiritual progeny of the baptismal symbolic sexual act, are "babes crying for the milk of salvation." The rite of baptism, an initiation of rebirth, is a symbolic statement of the marriage act, the resulting conception, and the birth of a new generation. More abstractly, it symbolizes the species relations necessary for biological continuity and the persistence of the social group. This rite dramatically acts out the spiritual union of Christ, the Bridegroom of the Church, with his holy spouse, and the spiritual birth and regeneration of the candidates. At baptism, Christ and the Church procreate a new Christian, recognize and mark this new creature as a member of their eternal family by "christening" him. The newborn in name, substance, and form, is in the likeness of the Father.

To go back to the ritual: meanwhile, the time being Holy Saturday, Christ lies dead in his tomb waiting for his return to life. The neophytes, too, are spiritually dead awaiting a rebirth to eternal life. On Easter morning they with Christ will come to life from death. The immaculate womb of the font of baptism "receives" the body which has "died unto sin," the initiate being immersed by the waters of salvation. The grave also receives the corruption of the body that has died and is to be reborn and, for many believers, restored as the same organism and the same person on Judgment Day. Thus birth and death are joined in the one transition rite. Moreover, both are related to the conjugal connection of Christ, the risen God, and the Church, his spouse.

Michel, in *The Liturgy of the Church*, makes this vividly clear: "The mystical union of the Church with Christ in his risen splendor puts her in a transport of joy that continues to vibrate through the liturgy of the whole Eastertide till the very consecration of this union on Pentecost Sunday. The newly baptized, who for this week will wear the white garment of their new bliss, rejoice at their rising with Christ to the new glory." [9]

There are several symbolic consequences of the symbolic transfiguration of death into birth. The open tomb of Christ and each human earthen grave out of which resurrected and reborn individuals come forth are implicitly feminine. The Christian symbols thus parallel, and are identified with, the idea of the earth as female and fruitful. In the rites of dedication for one of the principal cemeteries of Yankee City, which transformed secular ground into sacred soil, it was said to be the Mother and the grave, like Christ's tomb. The dead body like the sinful initiate polluted by the experiences in the world, following Christ's prototypical experience, and by use of the final rites and sacraments, would arise once more, born again from the womb of the earth. Symbolically death is but the beginning; it is the "conception" which becomes the final birth into the heavenly family of God.

The Non-logical Structure of Time—the Collective Product of Species Experience

Within the exact time-forms of the calendar, Yankee City's social and individual life rhythms ebb and flow, expand and contract; new experiences or old ones repeat themselves as the community's activities endlessly pour through its numbered days, its cycles of weeks, months, and years. Looking at the

9. Michel [94], pp. 138-9.

symbols of the calendar, Yankee City faces signs of reality; eternity flows through their ordered confines and finite existence is fixed and made meaningful. Their words and numbers are the visible signs of a system of concepts and values, a moral and mental order of social control, which organizes and gives meaning to much of the life of Yankee City and contemporary society. Its meanings reach beyond reason and the precise logical order of reference, stretch through the intangible, uneasy guesses of science and theology, and finally touch the edges of an unformed meaningless void which is nothingness. "Science is inevitably tied to dealing with time, but is ultimately driven to aesthetic or imaginative rather than logical grounds for selecting the way to formulate time relationships." [68]

Without the calendar, the contemporary life of Yankee City as it is now lived would be impossible; with it, the events of today and yesterday are invested with form and significance. People's fears for tomorrow become more bearable, their hopes and wishes for the future more believable, because their emotions about what might happen are subjected to the control and meaning of the calendar's precise and invariable sequence of well-known and securely connected words and numbers.

Objective time is forced on each individual by his culture, but its meanings are never given more than the right to remain in the vestibule of each man's inner life. Objective time must recognize and adjust to the non-rational levels of personality and of the collective mentality—to the time of the self and to subjective, social time. Within each of us, far below what are said to be the "realities" of logic and culture, lies that "obscure inaccessible part of our personality" which Freud called the id, where "there is nothing corresponding to the idea of time, no recognition of the passage of time and . . . no alteration of mental processes by the passage of time." [10]

The calendar (and the clock) divides duration into a manageable series of interconnected representative compartments and thereby transforms its vague meaningless expanse into a time that men can conceive and understand. "A calendar," says Durkheim, "expresses the rhythm of the collective activities, while at the same time its function is to assure their regularity. . . . Try to represent what the notion of time would be," he

10. Freud [51a], pp. 103–4.

exclaims, "without the processes by which we divide it, measure it or express it with objective signs, a time which is not a succession of years, months, weeks, days and hours!" "Time," he says further on, "is an abstract and impersonal frame which surrounds, not only our individual existence, but that of all humanity. It is like an endless chart, where all duration is spread out before the mind." [11] Time thus conceived is a yearly cycle which tidily begins, contains, and completes a unit of duration. Each yearly cycle is related at its two ends with connecting ones that form a chain conceived to extend in a line from the present back into the past and on into the future. Often a festival marks the point where one link ends and a new one begins, thus ritualizing the separation of past from future time.

The conception of the earth's yearly movement around the sun, used by Western man (as well as others) to give precise form and human significance to the bleak, unyielding, and unmeaningful extension of duration, provides fixed points that give accurate, safe places on which to put marks saying that a bit of meaningless duration ends and another begins. The marks of the repetitive movements give Yankee City and Western man a feeling of security, of being on familiar ground where they know, feel, and can be sure about what is likely to happen. Enclosed within this system, collective memories of yesterday become a reliable and dependable map for knowing what will happen tomorrow, thus reducing anxiety about the future's uncertainties. If the facts of reality are obdurate and will not yield to technical efforts for the fulfillment of all man's wishes, then they must be dealt with in some other manner to allow him to survive as a species and permit normal affective and physical feelings to express themselves. If man cannot control his fate, mold harsh reality to fit his creature wishes, and destroy the validities which feed his fears, he can do the next best thing by fitting the outer realities to the strict rational, conventional symbolic forms which he himself provides and controls. Many can go further and subject the rationalities of objective time to the evocative claims of the sacred year.

The non-rational ritual year, systematically related to the mathematically rational, objective time of the solar and lunar

11. Durkheim [42a], pp. 9, 10.

years, incorporates all levels of man's experience and mental life into a symbolic unity. As a sign system conforming outwardly to a time cycle founded on the movement of the earth and the planetary system, it gives "visible form" to what is believed to be reality. It embodies all forms of man's ordering of time and relates them to all levels of his mental life. Sacred time relates in one system the rational and verifiable references of objective time—of calendar, clock, and construct—to the feelings, moods, and significances of the emotional and non-rational orderings of social time and those of the species level. By reification it reconstitutes them and translates them into a divine and sacred order. The symbols of Christ's life become syncretistically interrelated with the physical changes of the earth, with the universe and the species, and with the non-rational world of the collectivity. The facts of species life, the earth, and the universe are transfigured into *signs* of meaningful sacred significance. Their meanings refer to the supernatural; it assimilates their multiple meanings into clusters whose cores have commonalities. The commonalities are modes of feeling, of pleasure and joy, of pain and sorrow, or of love and hate, security and anxiety, good and evil. The cores of significance and their feeling systems spread out to the several worlds of reality: the non-rational world of men and the rational one of referential objects.

Liturgical time is but another expression of the sense of time in men. In our culture, as we said earlier, are present the objective references that can be validated. These are to physical, social, and self phenomena. The non-rational expressive and evocative signs and meanings of time also have their physical, social, and self objects of reference. There is time felt and reacted to at the species level which is syncretistically related to the objects of the physical, social, and self environments. The species level, being limited by the nature of the species itself, determines what can be experienced, what can or cannot be accepted. Responses to cold and heat, to the opposite sex, to what is food, what is light and darkness, to hunger and thirst, are so determined, and their rhythms lend themselves to notions of time and thus contribute to their non-rational ordering in the self and in the mental products of collective life.

The nature of these non-rational clusters in the sign system of the liturgy needs to be further analyzed and broken down into objective and rational terms. But in doing so we must constantly keep in mind that, for purposes of translating them into the foreign universe of rational thought, the meaningful life and truth of such mental systems is being damaged. The system of non-rational thought holds man's entire universe together in a valid whole, where the species can live a full life and the rational worlds of both constructs and objects can be made useful in the sacred system of thought. For those who can believe and practice its beliefs and rituals, the liturgical year helps admirably to perform this function. We will begin our analysis of the several components by first examining authoritative statements issued by theologians.

There is a rhythmic ebb and flow running through the liturgical year as through all else in the world [Michel declares in *The Liturgy of the Church.*] The universe of the heavens has its changing cycles and periods; the solar system gives us our four seasons and the earth gives us the regular recurrence of night and day, the rhythms of which are copied by the various forms of life here on earth. In life itself there have been the vast cycles of species coming into existence in geological time and again disappearing; the stages of youth, maturity, old age in the individual; the seasonal changes in many forms of life; the daily periods of wakefulness and sleep . . .[12]

The figure of Christ is identified with the sun. "The liturgical year," says Cabrol, "is the revolution of the year around Christ." Dom Michel makes the myth's objective reference even more clear.

In nature the most resplendent, most beautiful object is light, and for us it is the natural light of the sun, which is also the source of the power of growth in life. Hence in the liturgy the sun is the symbol of Christ and of his light-giving mission, just as darkness represents the powers of evil and of sin. Christ appeared on earth as man in the midst of the darkness of night, both literally and figuratively, and around him as around the sun revolves the true life.

12. Michel [94], pp. 75-6.

On Holy Saturday the triple candle, lighted from the newly blessed fire, is saluted as the "Light of Christ." [17]

Colors related to light and darkness and to the solar year and change of night and day have their own sacred significance. White, the color of unrefracted light, "is the symbol of God, the father of Light, and of Christ, the Light of the World." White accordingly is the sign of purity, angels, virgins, and joy, and is used at the nuptial Mass. Black is the color of mourning and is used on Good Friday and in services for the dead.

Finally the end of the solar year arrives, the time of harvest and the death of seasonal life, entering the liturgy at the end of Time after Pentecost. Says Michel,

The Ember days of the September harvest time occur after the seventeenth Sunday [after Pentecost]. While the spring Ember days had to do with asking God's blessing for an abundant harvest, the September days are those of the gathering of the fruits, and they point to the final consummation of things. The harvest in time directs the Christian mind to the eternal one . . . It is within these last Sundays that the feasts of All Saints and All Souls occur, which are distinctly feasts of the next life . . . [and of death].[13]

In joyous anticipation of the birth of Christ, Advent, the opening season of the Christian year, once again starts the new cycle: death and its sad reveries are now forgotten. Since Christ's actual birth date is not known, any day might have been chosen. [45] The feast seems to have originated in Alexandria. January 6 was first chosen, but by the third century December 25 was being celebrated. [31] The latter date was connected with the popular festival of sun worship. By imperial order, the return of the sun after the passing of the winter solstice was the occasion for a great pagan feast. Christmas took its place. [7, 140]

It is necessary perhaps only to mention *The Golden Bough* of Sir James Frazer to bring the numerous pantheons of nature and vegetative gods to mind and see our problem in its larger historical and comparative setting. In his chapter on "The Myth of Adonis," Frazer summarily states that

13. *Ibid.,* pp. 77–8.

under the names of Osiris, Tammaz, Adonis, and Attis, the peoples of Egypt and Western Asia represented the yearly decay and revival of life, especially of vegetable life, which they personified as a god who annually died and rose again from the dead. In name and detail the rites varied from place to place: in substance they were the same. The supposed death and resurrection of this oriental deity, a god of many names but of essentially one nature, is now to be examined . . . In the religious literature of Babylonia Tammuz appears as the youthful spouse or lover of the Ishtar, the great mother goddess, the embodiment of the reproductive energies of nature . . .[14]

The several statements of the theologians about the sacred time of the liturgy interweave solar and objective time with those of the vegetative seasons, day and night with winter and summer. Heat and light alternate with cold and darkness, and these are given connotations of good and evil. Growth and development in nature and man alternate with decay, sterility, and death; and all of them with Christ, "the Light of the World" and Savior whose life and death atoned for man's sins and purchased Paradise for all men.

These syncretisms—which include all man's experiences as a species with all his non-logical relations and interpretation—can only be expressed by visual representations supplemented by textual descriptions and explanations. Two charts will display them. Chart 15 shows the clusters of species experience which have accumulated through time and taken on symbolic significance. The cluster of primitive, not to say species, feelings and notions at dawn, noon, sunset, and midnight are partly noted. They are notions, feelings, and sensations that the simplest societies experience and are possible in the communities of most primates. The syncretistic clusters, partially differentiated or not at all, are the beginnings of light, of brightness, at times of heat, the rise of the sun, the beginnings of day, and the end of darkness. In species-centric thought and feeling they involve the beginning of body and social activity, more effective use of the senses, particularly seeing things and seeing what it is one does as an active being. There is increased social participation and with it greater maximation of the self in the

14. Frazer [50], p. 325.

physical and social world about one. The group increases the amount and kind of its interaction; there is greater inter-stimulation and exchange of collective symbols. The quiet privacy of sleep yields to public life.

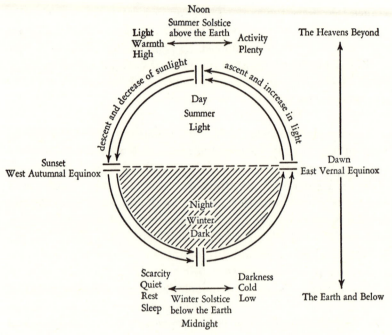

CHART 15. The Synchronized Meanings of the Sun Cycles

The sun moves and rises to its height at noon. The primitive undifferentiated feelings and notions of increased heat and brightness, of the apex and end of the rise of the sun, cluster together deep within the animal and non-logical life of the group and the individual. Non-logically it is the felt moment when things are least private and secret and most public.

The sun moves downward to sunset, leaves the world and is gone. In non-logical thought there cluster the notions: end of day, of light, the waning period and the beginnings of dark-ness, possibly loss of heat, usually individual withdrawal from public activity to purely private and family life. It is the begin-ning of the reduction of the full use of the senses and public use of symbols.

Midnight and night—generally when light is gone with the

sun and there is the greatest darkness, conditions are most private and least public and, during sleep, there is least use of the senses and intellect. The symbolism used then is private, unconscious, and non-rational. There is regression to more infantile stages when words are not used; the images are dramatic, mythic, not propositional and rational. In general there is a lack of form, of order and clear definition of things.

The notions of the yearly cycle (Chart 15) can begin with the vernal equinox when night and day, darkness and light, shadow and sunlight are equal. The sun is beginning to be nearer and more evident and the dark nights are shorter and less cold. Spring is starting and winter ending. There is the promise and expectation of more pleasant bodily sensations (and less of the unpleasant)—of warmer and more pleasant days. Seeds are to be planted, vines and trees bud and bloom, and new creatures are born. There is more food, the promise of abundance, and a reduction of the fear of scarcity—in general, an increased sense of individual and collective hopefulness and well-being. At the middle of summer (summer solstice) the sun is warmest, the days are long, growth is abundant, the plants and animals are ready to be food for man. At the autumn equinox the sun descends and leaves, it is colder, vegetation stops growing, crops are gathered, and plants wither and die. At the winter solstice, the sun is at its remotest angle, the days short, the nights long, and the weather cold. Annual vegetation is gone and men are less free and active. The feelings and notions of the yearly and daily cycle interpenetrate each other and form syncretistic clusters of meaning. These symbols accordingly are multidetermined. Space, time, feeling, sensation cluster tightly together. In the meanings the species gives to each there is something of all the others.

In Chart 16 the headings to the vertical columns list these external and internal influences felt by the species, perceived and evaluated by men, and syncretistically projected into the symbols and activities of the social world and on the self. Along the left side the horizontal columns are listed. They include the cycles of day and night, the seasons, light and heat, plant rhythms, annual life cycles, and that of the human species. A horizontal reading of day and night, for example, shows dawn, noon, sunset, and midnight. Of the human life cycle: concep-

	The Beginning	Transition	Transition	The End
Day and Night	Dawn Morning ↓	→Noon Middle of the Day	Sunset Evening	Midnight (→ to *dawn*) Night
Seasons	Vernal Equinox Spring	Summer Solstice Summertime	Autumn Equinox Fall: after summer and before winter	Winter Solstice Winter ∟→ to Spring
Light and Heat	Beginning of increase in light and heat and solar vitality	Maximum of light and heat and solar vitality	Lessening of light, heat, and vitality	Least amount or no light, least amount of heat and natural vitality ∟→ to return of light, etc.
Plant Species	First vernal signs of activities, early growth	Fruition, ripening of fruit and grain, full growth of plants	Changes in leaves, plants, drying of grasses. Beginning of decay	Decay and death, quiescence, disappearance of vernal life ∟→ to the beginning
Technology	Planting and sowing, animal breeding	Protection and care, cultivation, etc.	Harvest, slaughter	Harvest of plants Slaughter of animals for food
Life Cycle Animal Activities	Mating, animal herding and birth of the young	Full maturity, strength and power, greatest sexual and productive power	Decrease of power and lessening of sexuality	Old age, senility, and death
Life Cycle Species	Marriage, sex intercourse, birth, infancy and early growth, conception, children in the family of orientation	Growth to full man- and womanhood Height of sexual and productive power Parents in family of procreation	Decreasing strength and energies, lessening of sexual and productive power Grandparent generation	Old age, senility, and death Cemetery

CHART 16. Transitions and Syncretisms: the Species, the Seasons, and Solar Time

(Some of the influences on the species from the external environment as perceived and *felt* by man, evaluated and transformed and projected, along with influences of his social and biological world, back onto the external environment.)

tion, sexual intercourse, birth, infancy, and marriage, followed by later periods ending with old age, senility, death, and burial.

A glance down the left column shows dawn, spring, solar vitality, early growth of plants, the mating of animals, and the birth of the young equated with human copulation, conception, and infancy; and on the right, winter, night, low solar energy, the decay and death of plants, harvesting, and slaughter of animals, the old age and death of other species equated with senility and death for man. [140]

None of these equations is as exact as denoted here, but the clusters of meaning syncretistically expressed in the non-rational thought and symbolic expressions of men are vital and driving parts of the collective life and man's sense of what he is. These are the inchoate notions, the emotions felt, and the sensations which significantly motivate men and, by use of non-rational symbols such as those of the sacred year, find ordered expression.

The Church writers on the liturgy, with different objectives and interpretations in mind, clearly recognize these modes of thought. Professors and doctors of the Catholic Church through the two millenia have ordered and rationalized them. Thus Ellard says,

. . . man has his complex corporeal structure so closely linked to his spiritual powers, that when he thinks, his imagination, his bodily emotions, and his nervous system, all to some extent come into play. The more intense his mental operations, the more necessary also it becomes for him to give corporeal expression to them in some way . . . man does not hesitate to employ any word or tone, any gesture or posture, fire or water, light or darkness, oil or incense, or any object about him as an aid in expressing his religious sentiment . . . The symbolism of the liturgy is fundamentally natural . . . being the expression of the relation of the Author to nature itself.[15]

15. Ellard [45], pp. 60-1.

CHAPTER 13

SACRIFICE, SUICIDE, AND TRAGEDY

The Sacrificed God of Catholics and Protestants

For all Christians, Christ's death on the cross and his resurrection from the tomb after the brutal slaying are the climax and the wondrous denouement of the sacred drama of the gospel. [45] The public drama of the liturgies of Easter and Holy week, the Mass, and the Lord's Supper are some of the present ritual expressions of the dreadful ending of his life on earth and of each Christian's involvement in the horrible deed. They tell, too, of the triumphal return of Christ to his spiritual home and of man's assurance of life after death.

In such rituals as the Mass (since the bread and wine are not symbols but Christ Incarnated) it is believed that each time the sacrifice is re-enacted the God-Man is brought back to life on the altar and slain again. Thus he is made to suffer the cruelty and pain of man's depravity not once but daily throughout human history. Why was one time not sufficient? More broadly, for both Protestants and Catholics, why commemorate this dreadful horror? And, one must ask, theoretically, what is present in the feelings of men as they are expressed in Christian belief which demands that this gentle God continue to be the ritual victim of their sadistic brutality? Why is it socially and psychologically necessary now for men to re-enact this bloody and horrible event of two thousand years ago, when an innocent man was captured, humiliated, nailed to a cross, and killed because his human contemporaries collectively hated him?

Why do contemporary men, and the most devout, feel the need of continually remembering and re-enacting the great tragedy that their God was made to suffer when he was here on earth? Part of the answer, of course, is that he arose triumphant out of his suffering and thus, it is believed, reassured men that they could have eternal life. However important this reassurance is, at best it can be no more than one important part of the larger explanation. We must now further hypothecate that those of the faithful who are emotionally satisfied by this terror-filled drama—who unconsciously as well as consciously identify with the suffering God—not only receive vicarious satisfaction from his tragedy but, because they also unconsciously identify with the killers, can express their deep hatred of, and their desire to kill, their brothers and other members of the Christian and human collectivities. Moreover, their hatred is directed against themselves and what they are as moral beings.

We can also hypothecate that, by self-righteously loving their God and killing him, they can hate others and themselves and, through ritual usage, identify first with the hated human figures and later with the loved and valued God to forgive themselves for their hatreds and efficaciously release their feelings of guilt and self-condemnation. Such rituals as the Mass, later analysis will indicate, symbolically accomplish this transformation. The symbols of the myth of the Father and his Son supply the signs, buried deeply in the moral and species life of man, which evoke the human feelings that, when properly manipulated, accomplish this task. As long as this transformation can be done vicariously and unconsciously as a sacred act, the beneficial effects of such a mystical relation of God and man are incalculable, perhaps even beyond present human understanding, for to know what is meant is far beyond what we know now about the nature of life and about love and hatred.

The love of God for man and the effective form that it takes are expressed in such scripture as "God so loved the world that He gave His only begotten son that whosoever might believe would have eternal life." But there is a less recognized and unsanctioned set of feelings aroused, antithetical to the first, which are expressed in the sacrificial rites of the Church. In the drama man is put in the position of killing his God, his ritual older brother, and offering this slain kinsman to their father. The God, slain on his own altar by his human brothers, the human sons of Christ's own father, is offered to, and accepted with approval by, God himself. The whole of humanity's relation to Christ and all of its hopes and fears and all of its aspirations for itself are focused and contained in this relation of the adopted human brothers who, as members of the Christian family, are with Christ the sons of God. God not only accepts his Son as the slain Lamb but in varying rituals in the several churches becomes a member of the banquet table where all present dine upon the blood and flesh of the slain Son. The human members, refreshed, strengthened, and purified by this divine eating, receive grace and, by the efficacy of these most sacred rituals, are freed from a sense of guilt and the bonds of sin. How can this be so? How is it possible that such sacred beliefs and practices do free men from their feelings of guilt and do make them "whole again?" If this belief were newly invented and freshly presented to men and not sanctioned by sacred tradition and the churches, it is probable that contemporary men would draw back from it in horror and disgust. One must ask, What is this "myth's" deep appeal? Why should such beliefs become the very center of worship and the ultimate symbol of Christian belief? Why through it and its rituals do men feel cleansed and at one with themselves and with the members of their group?

In brief, what is the *meaning* of the myth and the several rituals of the Crucifixion and others having to do with Christ's death? How do they *function* in the beliefs and values of the collectivity and of each individual? Why are the beliefs and rituals efficacious? In sum, what is their validity in the non-rational mental life of the society?

To begin our analysis, we will briefly examine some of the variations of belief about the rituals of Christ's death and resurrection. When the wine and bread of our Lord by the ritual action of transubstantiation become the Blood and Body, they have their own particular significance to Catholics and some Episcopalians. As the sacrament of the Lord's Supper for many Evangelicals they "convey the Gospel in dramatic form" and "portray forgiveness and life which Christ imparts in response to personal faith. The sermon is in the Supper. In accepting the Sacrament we remember His death. It brings to mind the redemptive death of Christ; it is an expression of Communion with God, as we have access to the Father through Jesus Christ, the one mediator between God and man; it is an expression of fellowship among the disciples of Christ, emphasizing their oneness in Him. In the word 'Eucharist' we express gratitude to God for redemption and dedicate our lives [to

Him] and lastly 'The Sacrament brings assurance to us of the ultimate completion of our redemption when the Christ comes again.' "

For the authority of the Holy Word such passages as 1 Peter 2:24 are often quoted: "Who his own self bore our sins in his own body on the tree that we, being dead to sins, should live unto righteousness; . . ." Even better known are those from John 6:54–57:

> He that eateth my flesh and drinketh my blood hath everlasting life, and I will raise him up on the last day.
>
> For my flesh is food indeed, and my blood is drink indeed.
>
> He that eateth my flesh and drinketh my blood abideth in me, and I in him.

Whatever may be the variation among Protestants about the meaning and ceremonial form of the sacraments, most churches of Protestant faith officially recognize only two—the Lord's Supper and baptism. Their retention by Protestants during the Reformation and after Puritan destruction of liturgical signs demonstrates their deep significance to all Christians. We have previously examined some of the meanings of baptism as they are expressed in the yearly liturgy on Holy Saturday before Easter Sunday. Here we will analyze those of the Lord's Supper and the Mass. Although different in form and symbolic intent, the sacrament of the Last Supper and the Mass are symbolically related to two significant forms of human experience, the sharing of food at a common meal of intimates and the fear and fact of human death. The symbol system of Calvary and that of the last meal of Jesus with his disciples in the upper room are treated as separate and yet as one in Christian ritual. The "meat and drink" of the Last Supper, the bread and wine, become one with the live Christ who died and lived again.

To further our understanding of the myth of the voluntary sacrifice of the Son to his own Father, and the Father's acceptance of the voluntary death through which all humankind were "redeemed" and given the gift of immortality, we must analyze the symbolic communication involved in the rituals of sacrifice.

What supernatural meanings do the signs of sacrifice convey in the symbolic dialogue between God and man? What functions do they perform? (Those who are theoretically inclined might read Chapters 14, 15, and 16 on symbolic theory before proceeding.)

The Mass—an Analysis of the Constituent Parts of an Act of Ritual Meaning

To arrive at a better understanding of the meaning and functions of the myths and rituals of the Lord's Supper and the Mass we shall first ask ourselves, What are the assumptions and methods followed in the act of ritual communication? How are the various elements in the communication—the signs, the communicators, and the objects—evoked and referred to and related to each other? How do its signs function? Why is the rite efficacious as a system of communication?

To accomplish our ends we shall analyze the whole interaction of the basic parts of the Mass and, by use of the methods described in Chapter 14, compare the component parts of the ritual with the ordinary forms of sign usage and acts of meaning.

As all Catholics and many others know, the Mass is divided into two basic parts, the opening half, or Mass of the Catechumens (the initiates of an earlier period who were not yet baptized), and the Mass of the Faithful (those who had been previously baptized). [45] Each is redivided into two parts. In the first part of the Mass of the Catechumens, the faithful (through the priest) give prayers to God and in the second part he, in return, gives instructions to them. The present ritual maintains the symbols of the ancient rite of initiation of adults into the mysteries of Christianity.

The first half of the Mass of the Faithful is the offertory of gifts and consecration to God. The latter part, Communion, is "the true enactment of the liturgical mystery of Christ's sacrifice." In the second part the "sacrifice-banquet" is God's return gift. (In official belief this rite is made effective by "our intimate union with Christ who is both God and man.") Formerly and prototypically, "the people went up to the altar of Christ, they placed themselves in their gifts on the very altar of the sacrifice as living oblations to God, and in the consecration they were most truly merged in the very passion and death of Christ, sharing fully in the redemptive action of Christ made really present in the liturgical mystery."

Thus there is a gift exchange, an exchange of signs and meanings in the two Masses; the reception by God of the gifts from men obligates each by the "intimate nature" of man's and God's relation to the Divine victim to exchange gifts. [88] Thus Michel writes,

The Mass is an interchange of gifts; we give to God and God gives to us. This double motive is the basis of the entire Mass-structure. It determines the division into two parts of both the Mass of the Catechumens and the Mass of the Faithful. In the Mass of the Catechumens we first give to God, in the prayer-part, and then God gives to us, in the instruction-part. Likewise in the Mass of the Faithful, the sacrifice-oblation is our gift to God, while the sacrifice-banquet is God's gift to us. In both cases the interchange is effected through our intimate union with Christ who is both God and man, according to the ever-recurring phrase: *per Christum Dominum nostrum:* through Christ our Lord.[1]

The obligations of the gift and gift exchange in the two parts of the Mass are illustrated in Chart 17. This symbolic interaction is the fundamental mold in which the ritual signs of the Mass are given meaning and efficacy for those who believe as well as for scientific analysis as we see in the Missal.

The priest offers the bread with the prayer: "Accept, O holy Father, almighty and eternal God, this host for the all-holy sacrifice, which I, thy unworthy servant, offer unto thee, my living and true God, to atone for my numberless sins of sinfulness and neglect; on behalf of all here present, and likewise for all faithful Christians, living and dead, that it may profit me and them, as a means of salvation unto life everlasting, Amen."

The exchange takes place at the altar which stands for God the Father, and for the cross of Calvary. It is here in the holy of holies that the consecration can and usually does occur. In brief, here while the Mass proceeds: (1) the signs of the bread and wine become Christ himself, (2) the priest becomes (a)

1. Michel [94], pp. 162-3.

Christ, the victim offered, and (b) the Christ who offers himself as the Son to his Father, and (3), through the efficacy of the rites and the original perfect act of love by the Son for his Father and for mankind, the audience of the faithful become one with the priest and with the Son, the entirety in the symbol of the Son being accepted by the Father. Lastly, in the sacrifice banquet the return gifts of immortality and fellowship with God are given by God to man. "In the sacrifice-banquet we receive back from God the gift we gave to him in the sacrifice-oblation but in the meantime it has been consecrated into the living Christ. Our acceptance of it is in the form of the Bread of Life. We thus assimilate ourselves most intimately with God, by uniting ourselves with the sacrificial victim." [2]

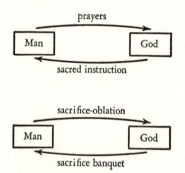

CHART 17. The Obligations of Sacred Gift Exchange
1. Sacred Sign Exchange in the Mass of the Catechumens
2. Sacred Sign Exchange in the Mass of the Faithful

The ceremony, although concentrated on the literal death and rebirth of God, "is also a celebration of Christ's entire life work—" including the mysteries of the human conception of Jesus, the virgin birth, his suffering, crucifixion, and resurrection and ascension. The audience vicariously lives through it all and is initiated into God's family; a collectivity of kindred made one in the holy birth and death partakes of the banquet at the family table.

Not only are the priest and the immediate *individuals* in the audience involved in this symbolic transformation, but the entire collectivity as a corporate body is assimilated into the signs of the bread and wine which as Christ are slain and offered to God. St. Augustine in *The City of God* states the official inter-

2. Ellard [45], p. 160. See also chart in *The Roman Missal* [117], p. xxv.

pretation: "The whole ransomed city, that is, *the Church and the communion of saints, forms the universal sacrifice* offered to God by the High Priest, who in His passion gave up His life that we might become the Body of so great a Head . . . This is the Christian's Sacrifice: we being many are one Body with Christ, as the Church in the Sacrament of the Altar, so well known to the faithful, wherein is shown that in that oblation *the Church is offered* [italics mine]." [3]

The bread, product of the many broken grains of wheat, and the wine from the bruised countless grapes, symbolize the unity of all in the signs of the Body and Blood of Christ. St. Augustine in an Easter sermon uses these symbols to express the supernatural significance of these earthly unities and to evoke the feelings of spiritual unity in the faithful.

When you were enrolled as catechumens [says the saint], you were stored in the Christian granaries. Later, when you handed in your names as candidates for Baptism, you began to be ground by the millstones of fasting and exorcisms [in the Lenten exercises of the catechumenate]. Then ye came to the font, and were moistened and made one paste; and then the fire of the Holy Spirit coming upon you [in Confirmation], ye were baked and became the Lord's Bread. See what you have received. See how this unity has been brought about, and be of one accord, cherishing one another, holding to one faith, one hope, one love . . . Thus, too, the wine was once in many grapes, but now is one . . . Ye now dine at the Lord's Table, and ye there share in His Cup. We are there with you; *together* we eat, *together* we drink, for we live *together* [italics mine].[4]

The symbolic gift exchange of sacred signs between man and God, depicted in Chart 17, is not just an exchange of signs which refer to separate objects, as it is at the secular level of communication. In the language of symbolic analysis, the signs (bread and wine) become the object (Christ), and the communicators (priest and congregation), through the efficacy of the changing signs, also become the object (Christ), and all are received and accepted by the other communicator (God, the first person of the Trinity; the Son being the second is one

3. Quoted in Ellard [45], pp. 124–5.
4. *Ibid.*, p. 199.

with Him). The sacred symbolic action can also be subject to the analysis of the theoretical chapters (see Chapters 14, 15, and 16).

To summarize, the supernatural communication involves two actions and results: (1) The signs and those who use them become one with the object and are so received by the (symbolic) receiver, God. (2) Their meanings, signs, and communications *transport* and *lift* them from the natural and profane level to the superior supernatural where they possess qualities in kind of the Trinity and Divinity.

When a man is "in Christ," forthwith He and Christ are vitally united, and Christ offers Himself and His Christian in Himself, and the man offers Christ and himself in vital unity, and God, looking upon Mass, sees both His Son and those who are "in one" with Him. Hence you cannot but perceive the incredible cogency of Mass. It is a gift that God cannot resist: the priest, and the layman too, since there is solidarity between them, have omnipotence in their hands. Mass is an act—not a prayer recited, not a ceremony contemplated, but the supreme act of history unequaled in the world.[5]

These products of supernatural communication, sign into object, communicator into communicated, and all into the One, are a supernatural aspect of the technical facts of communication. They are portrayed below in Chart 18. It will be noticed that everything engaged in the visible human process of communication moves from beneath the broken line and the realm of the profane and is transported, through the sacred efficacy of the ritual, to the supernatural realm, these including priest, communicants, and the signs of bread and wine. This is accomplished by "magically" identifying sign with object (arrow *a* in the present chart) and sender (priest) and human congregation with the transformed signs (see arrows *b* and *c*). Broken lines *d*, *e*, and *f* indicate the ritual identifications made possible: the congregation with the priest and both with Christ in direct relation with God the Father. In the rituals of "consubstantiation" (Luther) and the symbols of the Lord's Supper representing the history of Christ's life and death and

5. Martindale [87], p. 115.

man's redemption and immortality, the object does not become the sign, nor the sign the object. In the theology of consubstantiation, however, Christ, the object, moves through the actions of the sign's manipulation and is present, never becoming one in the substance with the bread and wine.

By the acts of meaning in the sacred dialogue of the Mass, the words and gestures are not only verbal signs but actions whose effects in the meanings of God who receives them *cause* change to occur in man's state. Ritual pollution is removed from sinful man and, in a state of grace and in the symbol of Christ, man moves from the natural to the supernatural, from mortality "up to" immortality. The purification is accomplished in the images of the slaying of a son as the Lamb of God and the communal eating of him by the family of God.

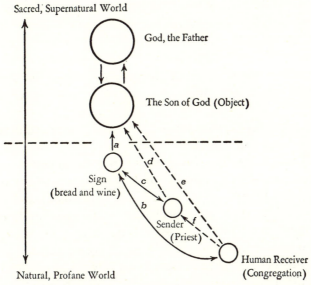

CHART 18. Sign, Object, and Sender Become One with the Receiver

Wherein lies the great validity of these symbolic themes? To repeat a question asked earlier in this chapter, What in us, expressed in Christian belief, demands that the God-man be the victim of attack? Why must men reenact these horrible details of a man being nailed to the cross? And, adding disgust to horror, eat the innocent victim?

The Father and His Son

Let us first repeat what is traditional knowledge; the rite of sacrifice is a very old and widely spread ceremony inherited in part by the Christians from the Jewish rite of the Passover. [67 b] This said, we can ask why the meal and the slain victim are now used as the central myths which provide the non-rational mental forms in which the collectivity has contained their meanings of the rite's significance and its public display of signs. The writings of Frazer, Durkheim, [42a] Hubert and Mauss, Freud, Robertson Smith, and others have been drawn upon to help us progress to the interpretations offered here. We will begin with Smith.

In his classic *Lectures on the Religion of the Semites* W. R. Smith establishes two types of sacrificial rituals. "Sacrifices slain to provide a religious feast, and vegetable oblations presented at the altar, make up the sum of ordinary religious practices of the older Hebrews." "The animal victim was presented at the altar . . . but the greater part of the flesh was returned to the worshiper, to be eaten by him under special rules."

"Everywhere," he continues, ". . . a sacrifice ordinarily involves a feast and a feast cannot be provided without a sacrifice." [6] Smith develops his analysis by his commensal interpretation that "those who eat and drink together are by this very act tied to one another by a band of friendship and mutual obligation." The sacrificial meal in which the community of men share their victim with the host, their God, is a "solemn expression of the fact that all who share are brethren . . . and the duties of brotherhood are implicitly acknowledged . . . By admitting man to his table the God admits him to his friendship . . . The very act of eating and drinking together was a symbol and a confirmation of fellowship and mutual social obligations." The circle of those obligated was "the circle of kinship" where . . . "the whole kin is answerable for the life of each of its members." Finally, the ritual action of the ceremony purged those who participated of their sins, bringing them into actual union with their god. According to Smith's

6. Smith [127], Lecture VI, p. 239.

account, when the small *kin* group grew into *national* aggregates there was greater need for reconciliation with God. Mystic religions then developed and man fled from divine hostility "by incorporating himself in a new religious community." [7] In such religions man atones for his sins through a holy victim, pure and sacrosanct; the ceremony commemorates a divine tragedy for which, like that of Tammuz or Adonis there was annual mourning.

These early rituals of atonement contributed their share to the myths and images of Christianity. Despite their historic significance, Smith's emphasis on the obligations of the kinship community is of most use to us. The divine father and his mystic family, in heaven and on earth, recognize mutual obligations and give mutual aid and brotherly care and affection to each other. The efficacy is in the signs of a shared meal where each incorporates the food of a holy victim into himself and thereby is so constituted that part of him is also incorporated into the others whose entirety make up the spiritual group of kindred. The symbol of the family meal that becomes a sacred ritual image and a sign of mutual aid and the obligation of God and his human kinsmen to each other is part of a basic myth all built on the family structure and the sharing of food at the family meal. The emotional efficacy of such symbols for understanding the meaning of the ritual relations to God and the feelings attached are clear. Their non-rational validity in the feelings of men is also satisfied by this analysis. But what isn't clear is how at the deep non-rational level of human mentality these images of kinship relations and the horrible killing of the holy victim are interrelated in such a way that they satisfy the celebrants and contribute to the felt validity that such rituals evoke in the minds of the faithful. We will first examine this problem by returning to the whole question of the sacred family, this time examining the relations of the father god and his son and that other principal father-son image connected with the supernatural: Adam, first son of God and father of all living.

The father-son relation with its many complexities and contradictions, with all the importance and the depth of its significance for society, is at the core of Christian life. It per-

7. *Ibid.,* Lecture X, p. 359.

vades all faiths, its mysteries involve some of the most important rational problems that beset metaphysicians and scientists, yet it successfully deals with the practical problems that constantly face men. "I believe in God the Father Almighty," the faithful repeat, "Maker of Heaven and earth; and in Jesus Christ His only Son our Lord who was conceived by the Holy Ghost, [and] born of the Virgin Mary, suffered under Pontius Pilate, was crucified, dead and buried . . ."

In Christ as the human Son of God, the hopes, fears, and dilemmas of creation and all existence are resolved in Christian thought. Through him the Eternal One becomes Father to that which is opposite to eternity, the human Son, who as a *person* of God in another image, is transformed into ephemeral man to live, die, and become a part of changing time and finite space. The unlimited and abiding Eternal is meaningfully articulated to, and expressed by, its opposite where there are a human here-and-now and beginnings and endings. Mortality and immortality are no longer antithetical and opposite, but one, yet still opposite and different.

These profound logical contradictions of existence are easily solved by the Eternal One becoming the Father to his other person, the Son, through the action of the third, the Holy Spirit, in the womb of the human mother, the Virgin Mother. Problems founded on rationality which are thus insoluble and their terms contradictory, when translated into the non-rational symbols of the family circle of relations, can be and are easily resolved. The great mysteries of life, often no more than contradictions based on external logic, which frustrate and frighten men, when translated into non-rational terms (social logics) are easily understood and accepted, for now they are founded on the known experiences of family life. Under these conditions, logical contradiction and the rules of rationality lose control and men's convictions are allowed to rest on empirical evidence and use the deep feelings which attach to beliefs founded on the persons of the family. Such symbols place human faith in a human family mold that is "feelingly" understandable to all human beings.

The Father and the Son are then meaningful and symbolically acceptable to men in all their most peculiar yet profound manifestations. A loving father who sends his son out in the world to be horribly crucified and a son who goes out from the father into a sadistic world and offers himself to be slain to return *obediently* to his father, although monstrous at the secular level, are easily accepted by the faithful at the sacred level. The moral, animal, and sacred orders are fused, and each within this undivided whole has another and fuller meaning. The loves and hatreds of men, the problems of discipline and authority, of social order and individual autonomy, the dependence of men on society and of sons on their fathers and families find expression in this magnificent drama of the Father and his Son. The earthly son's need to be with his father yet escape him and the right of access and help from him are portrayed. The oneness of the two in the family "blood" and in shared experience and *their unity and oneness in the spiritual semen of the Holy Ghost* are fully stated, yet their difference is made clear. The dependence of the Son on his Father, his need for his help, his freedom from the Father to make his own choices, even to being tempted by the Father's greatest enemy, are all acted out in the sacred drama of the Father and Son. Yet the discipline and authority of the Father are supported; the Son, after paying a terrible price, returns willingly to his Father. Thus God, "who so loved the world that he gave his only begotten Son that whosoever might believe would have eternal life," once more repossesses his Son. With him, when he takes him back, he accepts rebellious mankind. In the Son who loves perfectly, a hostile mankind, hating its fathers and its brothers, can momentarily find peace and a belief that transcends much of its daily experience and rises above the deeply buried hostilities of those who love.

Adam, as the first son of God and father of all human sons, in sacred symbolism is the image that expresses what man is that Christ is not. Whether he is believed to be true in the literal or metaphorical sense, the son and father symbols express some of the deeper meanings in the cluster which surround the human father. Adam is not only father to all mankind and husband to Eve, but he is the first son of God just as Christ was his only "begotten Son." Through Adam's husbandly relations with his wife, Eve, original sin, the curse of mankind, was

passed on to all succeeding generations of his children; thus
a father-god's curse on (his and) Adam's children becomes
part of man's eternal inheritance.

Adam, the son, autonomous and free and by free will capable
of knowing and choosing between good and evil, chose Eve
and evil and thereby rejected the father. It was then that he
was banished and cut off from his father. Christ, the other son,
refused to reject his father and, when tempted, resisted the
tempter, returning to sadistic mankind to suffer and be slain
that he might save his cruel human "brothers" and return to
his father. The hostility of a father to his son and of the son
to him is movingly portrayed by the image of Adam; but he,
too, is a son lost in a world his father made, yet which he, the
son, feels responsible for. He is the guilty man who lost perfection for himself and for his children because (he feels) his
father cannot forgive him. When he clung more closely to his
wife (and by implication to their own family) than to the
paternal family of his father, he thus chose earthly evil as
against heavenly good. But, in fact, Adam is also the father
who in the attitudes of his "sons" is blamed for the pollution of
all his progeny because of his relations with his wife, their
mother. When he is forced out of the Garden of Eden he is
thrust out of the household of God. He is the unforgiven son
with a father with whom man has not made peace. Adam, the
father, although blamed "by all mankind" for their human ills
and their destinies, is more important as the rejected son who
loses his first birthright and is cut off from the father. In him
the faithful can punish themselves and express opposition to all
fathers.

This image of Adam may be seen as a perfect fantasy of
what a spiritually rejected man should be, and wishes to be—
the model of thwarted physical, moral, and spiritual perfection. Adam before his defeat was the perfect man; in the
present interpretation he represents for those who believe a
projected dream of human perfection. In the beginning he
was ritually clean, not in need of prayers, sacrifice, or any
Christian rites which now symbolically relate men to God, the
present inadequate substitutes for the wholly satisfying direct
face-to-face relations believed once to have existed between
Adam and God. When he ate the fruit, Adam—symbol of man's

innocent self—became ritually unclean and therefore out of relation with the sacred world and his God. The pollution of all mankind and the inception of original sin occurred when Adam, by an oral and alimentary act, swallowed sacred, ritually forbidden fruit. Adam, the human father of all, becoming ritually unclean, pollutes all men generated from him. When Adam, image of all men, fell, man (the referent) fell too. Thus man's vision of his pure self is symbolically always accompanied by guilt and the moral accusation that he is inadequate because he cannot live up to his ideal of moral and spiritual perfection. For those who believe in these symbols, the biological generations listed in the Sacred Book, supposedly tracing their beginnings from Adam, validate their feelings about mystical contagion and transmission of spiritual pollution. "After Adam's fall, Adam's progeny is like a race of wingless birds still destined only for God's spiritual sky yet only able to crawl along the earth."

Sacrifice, Suicide, and Tragedy

The Christ symbol, "the New Adam," is the image of man's· moral self and the moral life of the collectivity stated in the form of family life and expressing much of it. In him men can give perfect moral love to their fathers and, through their kinship to him and the father, as brother to all others. Hostilities are suppressed. The images of the rebellious Adam and his attractive wife (mother of all men) functioning to express human faults and to evoke the deeper and forbidden fantasies of the non-rational levels are pushed aside and in the drama superseded. Each man and the entire collectivity are "saved" from themselves and their sense of guilt. The sons kill themselves and in the image of Christ as a "perfect act of love" voluntarily and vicariously offer themselves to their father. In this perfect act there can be no hatred. In him fathers and sons are one and brothers are united in heavenly grace.

Even as in the first Adam [Michel declares], the entire human race was virtually *persona ingrata et maledicta* (displeasing and accursed) before God, so in the second Adam, Christ, all mankind becomes virtually before God a *persona grata et bene-*

dicta (acceptable and blessed of God). Christ, replete with sancti-
fying grace and with charity not merely as an individual but
rather as head of the Church, as universal man in whom the entire
race is as it were condensed, achieved an act of perfect love of his
Father. As a result of this act he is ever the man universal in
whom all mankind is concentrated, the object of the infinite pleasure of his Father.[8]

The "family" meal provides a perfect set of images for
the evocation of the deep feelings involved. Food and drink as
facts are in the very center of man's feeling. [34] In the family
meal and sharing with brothers, sisters, and parents the food
assumes moral significance. Around it the meanings of family
life can be expressed and the moral authority of society made
significant. Here, too, the deep positive feelings of love that
men feel for each other can be expressed and those emotions
belonging to the deeper levels of the species which Kropotkin
categorically dealt with as "Mutual Aid" can be symbolized. [75]

And by them and with them their opposite, hostility and
hatred, can also flow and be purged in the symbols of the
brutalities of the killing on the cross. The elder brother is
killed and offered to a father, who, they implicitly believe, is
sufficiently in the fantasied image of their own families to
approve and demand such sadistic collective actions. The myth
of the Mass and the Crucifixion purges men of the pollution
of their own self and collective disapproval. Their guilty selves
can be free from the distress of each life and from the collective accumulation of generations. The competitive hostilities of organized life can be submerged or transformed into
the spiritual identification with the sacrificed son. Purgation of
hatred and guilt in his slaying and the assumption of grace at
the "banquet table" of kindred—perfect sons before a benign
father—are symbolized in the giving and the taking of the two
parts of the Mass of the Faithful. This is the dialogue, the
exchange of signs between God and man. The sacred image of
the family provides its powerful symbols to arouse the totality
of men's feelings and mobilize them for moral action.

Durkheim's conception of the altruistic form of suicide often

8. Michel [94], pp. 40-2.

found in the actions of human beings, [42*b*] Kropotkin's theory of mutual aid among the members of different species, including men, [75] and Freud's theory of totemism, [51*e*] help us to understand the positive factors contributing to the efficacy of the sacrifice and its emotional validity among those who believe. The altruist may give up his life for the good of the moral life of the collectivity or for the maintenance of a moral principle. Many species, including the other primates, "sacrifice" their own egoistic satisfaction to help or benefit others in the group. All is not competition and individual struggle for existence. This form of "love," a feeling for the good and benefit of others, in its extreme form is expressed by the sacred concept of Agape. Nygren declares: "Agape is spontaneous and unmotivated . . . a free gift" that is "indifferent to value" in evil or good men. It "freely spends itself." [9]

Complete unselfish love is the epitome of self-sacrifice and mutual aid carried to the point where the self may be destroyed for the collective moral order. In the Mass each son dies for the father, and in so doing subordinates self to the authority of the moral order. Since the rites surrounding the sacrifice are partly death rituals expressing the wish for immortality and the fear of death and the destruction of the self, they also allow men, by anticipating their own deaths and by voluntarily and vicariously living through His sufferings and death, to train themselves and thus prepare for death. This long preparation for death in the constant re-enactment of Christ's death helps to release their anxieties and control their panic. The myth of human triumph over the human tragedy of death, in the gift of the entire self to God through the image of the sacrificed Christ, allows each voluntarily to sacrifice himself and in so doing save himself.

When viewed as a drama, the Christian myth's basic theme is seen to be the fearful struggle between life and death for each man's destiny, and its climax: the ultimate triumph of life. The life of a Divine being—his birth, suffering, death, and resurrection—provides the plot. The efficacy of the sacred play lies in the dominant identification of the audience with the sacred hero and secondary identification with his adversaries. Just as the human members of an audience identify with the

9. Nygren [103], pp. 75–6.

human hero who triumphs, so the worshiper and the audience of Christ also triumph over death.

But this sacred drama represents the collective history of ten thousand years of authoritative fathers and submissive and rebellious sons and a multitude of cults and cultures. Its symbols contain the non-rational meanings of the species and collective life of men in societies. The truths it contains, the significant non-rational beliefs, feelings, and actions it expresses and evokes, cover the entirety of what man is and wishes to be. This kind of understanding is beyond the simple logic of rational men; too often, in this scientific age, men, proud of their disciplined intellects and rational inheritance, have dismissed it as unworthy equipment for those who seek to know the nature of reality.

The rational pursuit of knowledge of course must continue; its value is self-evident. Ways must be devised, however, by which men can enter the non-rational domain of human understanding and there find the secrets and strengths of individual and collective life. Through the ages our species has lived in the harsh realities of the world and collectively accumulated a store of understanding on which it successfully operates. This is a product of its organic evolution, its non-rational world of meaning and the thin crust of rationality. All of this knowledge is part of men's adaptation as a highly successful animal species. For the last few centuries we have partly succeeded in developing a scientific understanding of ourselves and the world around us. For further aid we need to turn to our non-rational collective and individual mentalities, for the tools of rationality are not enough. With equal ingenuity and skill, we must learn how to develop those deeper understandings of human beings. Perhaps when we do so we shall achieve even more spectacular results in our understanding of this subliminal world of belief and feeling than we have gained from rationality and logic. Myth and non-rational belief may need their own rules of inquiry. In them we may make new discoveries about the older meanings of man and develop new and better ways of solving his problems and determining his fate.

PART V

THEORY AND METHOD FOR THE
STUDY OF SYMBOLIC LIFE

INTRODUCTION

The mental life of Americans and human beings generally is examined in abstract terms. Symbols and symbol systems are treated theoretically as objects of study and as the most important form of collective behavior. Although the author follows in the path of Durkheim and Radcliffe-Brown, emphasizing the influence of the moral order on the creation and maintenance of symbol systems, the influence of the human species as an (organic) animal organization is also stressed. It is contended that only in this way can much of our adaptive mental behavior which is not mainly logical or rational be comprehended and properly evaluated and accounted for. It is also contended that efforts, such as Freud's, to found an organic theory of symbolic behavior which is confined to the individual unit distort the true significance of man's non-logical life; and that only when such theories and their research are reconstituted to include organisms in *collective interaction* as the basic unit of study can they contribute their full power to a science of symbols. Religion when viewed in these terms is not an "illusion," as Freud contended, but a reality of far greater significance than our present scientific competence allows us to understand.

CHAPTER 14

SYMBOLS AND THEIR SYSTEMS:

THEORY AND METHOD

Theories about the Nature of Symbols

In the foregoing chapters we have searched for the meanings and functions of symbols and their larger systems in the mental life of Yankee City and, given the ancient and pervasive nature of the systems studied, of the United States. We have confined our attention in most cases to the more traditional symbols of our sacred and secular life. Until now all our interpretations have been in terms of particular systems: Christian belief and practice and the family structure, the symbols of time and the calendar, the rhythms of collective life, the symbols of political strife and those of social class and ethnic membership.

The three chapters which follow present the results of using, modifying, and recasting the several existing bodies of theory about symbols through the necessity of making sense out of evidence collected. They attempt to state a general theory and method which re-form the several theoretical positions into one integrated theory about the nature of symbols, their signs, their meanings, and the varieties of logical and non-logical thought in the collective mental life.

In his now classical essay on symbolism, Edward Sapir declares that the term refers to such complex systems of reference as "speech, writing, and mathematical notations." Psychologists also apply it to any "emotionally charged pattern of behavior which has the function of unconscious fulfillment." Consequently it seems useful, Sapir says, "to distinguish two main types of symbolism. [The varieties of] referential symbolism . . . are agreed upon . . . economical devices for purposes of reference" and a "second type . . . equally economical . . . may be termed condensation symbolism, for it is a highly condensed form of substitutive behavior . . . allowing for the ready release of emotional tension in conscious or unconscious form." He observes that in ordinary life both types are "generally blended" and that "all culture is in fact heavily charged with symbolism, as is all personal behavior." [122*b*]

The semanticians such as Ogden and Richards [104] and Korzybski, [74*b*] and logicians such as Frye and Levi, [53] although with different purposes in mind, make a similar distinction, saying that "evocative symbols" are likely to "reinstate" the emotions involved in the original situation when the symbols were first encountered and learned, rather than the situation itself, whereas referential symbols are more likely to bring back the characteristics of the original situation or generalizations about it. Here their theory not only parallels Sapir's and others like him, but their implied learning theory partly interrelates with that of the Yale school headed by Dollard and Miller. [41]

Freud in his *Interpretation of Dreams* says that "a symbol comes under the heading of the indirect representations"; dreams being symbol systems which "give a disguised representation to their latent thoughts," their meanings must be found in the conscious and unconscious mental life. His symbolic formulation is essentially a theory of personality. In the mental world of the unconscious, bordering on the emotional and organic realm of the id, the categories of logic, time, space, and number do not exist. Meaning is a residue of emotion organized by the experiences of the organism. Here outer reality, human or not, is formed into a symbolic composition which expresses the wishes and anxieties, the aggression and submission, and the ambivalences of love and hostility.[1]

The French school of sociology led by Durkheim, [42*a*] social psychologists such as Jean Piaget, [111*a*] and social anthropologists such as Radcliffe-Brown, [114*b*] Malinowski, [85*a*] Mauss, [88] and Kluckhohn, [72*a*] on the Continent, in England, and the United States respectively, have also contributed importantly to symbolic theory with the notion of the collective symbol or representation. The latter, as all of us know, is a social symbol created by the collective actions of the group, which represents certain realities of group life. The categories of logical understanding, said Durkheim, are religious in origin. "Religious representations are collective rep-

1. Freud [51*c*], pp. 339–53, 368–97.

resentations which express collective realities; the rites are a manner of acting which take rise in the midst of assembled groups . . ." For example, in the case of the notion of time "it is not my time that is arranged; it is time in general"—the latter a matter of "objective signs" created by the mental actions of the collectivity; the former—"my time"—more often a matter of sensations and impressions. It is only when the individual through experience has learned the time of the group that he knows what time it is.[2]

The theories of George Mead are both social and psychological. The sign only becomes meaningful to the individual when "by taking the role which is common to all, he finds himself speaking to himself and others with the authority of the group . . . The significant symbol is then the gesture, the sign, the word which is addressed to the self when it is addressed to another individual." And obversely when it is spoken to the self meaningfully it is in a form in which it can be addressed to others. The "significant symbol" in the individual is a product of public experience and an achievement of socialization. [90b]

The theories of Freud, Mead, Durkheim, and the others will be considerably modified; not so much because they are not adequate or useful but because they are, and their idea systems need to be correlated as necessary parts in understanding the nature of the mental life of the collectivity.

Objects and Signs—the Marks of Meaning

As has been said elsewhere, although signs constitute the observable evidence, the search for the nature of symbolic life should start with the component of meaning, for meaning is the central fact of human life. [104] This precious product of man's long collective experience as an animal and social being is always active—and only alive—in the ever-present here and now, in the actions of each man and each society. The ordered accumulation of meaningful responses which all individuals learn to make as they give attention to themselves, to others around them, and to their natural environments persists through the changing generations; yet all systems of meaning are forever being transformed in the immediate activities of

2. Durkheim [42a], p. 10.

the present as they move into the future. [90a] The attribution of common agreed-upon meanings, of giving and receiving signs, is a necessary part of all social action. [90b] "Knowing" what men and the world are is adaptive and crucial for the survival of a society and for each individual in it. [90c] When the members of a society assign meanings to themselves, things, and their own actions they are acting together even though no overt activity may be displayed. Society, so conceived, is a system of meaningful acts commonly shared. Meaning can only be understood as a vital and necessary human activity. Like Heraclitus' river of time, meaning in a society is forever the same yet forever different. To enlarge his metaphor, the "water" in the context of that river is not the same as the "water" in the quiet borders of a natural pool or in the saving grace of the baptismal font. Paradoxically, although protean and changing in time and context, most meanings hold constant and unchanging. The meanings of the "water" of salvation, of Heraclitus' river, and of Old Man River, as well as the water pouring into the morning bath or spreading across parched acres from an irrigation canal, are all different, yet they have a common core of significance.

Signs mark the meanings of things. Men exchange these signs within and among themselves. They can be publicly offered and received only so long as the members of a society continue to agree among themselves about what it is they signify. The symbol systems of a society such as Yankee City define and limit the world of men. They represent the thinking and feeling which correspond to the limits of man's knowledge. The symbols of a people set up limits to the extension of their knowledge about themselves and about the world of nature outside themselves. The so-called reality which the individual learns is provided by the symbols of the culture he learns in various situation contexts. [95]

The central task of the analyst of symbols and their systems is to understand what their meanings are and learn how they operate in the lives of individuals and societies. He must learn their common and diverse meanings and relate them to the actions of men. To relate them to the life of men he must know what they mean to those who use them and find out what they do and signify within the contexts of group life. Strictly speaking, signs are symbols when they are being used, for only then do they have meaning. Since they are used by social animals, their study must never be divorced from the internal and external activities of these human animals who are social beings.

Meaning is culture-bound and species-bound. The contexts of the society and the species where particular signs are used must always be considered. Meaningful existence within the organic species and a cultural tradition is controlled and determined by each of these closed systems. The adaptations of each to the rest of nature are necessary and have most important influences, but the experiences felt, the effects achieved, and the meanings of the world outside man and his culture are always mediated and transformed by the limitations and needs of the human organism and its cultural context. Direct experience with nature is necessary and unavoidable, but the meaning of the experience, and what lies beyond those who experience "reality" outside man, is always transformed into what is significant to the animal and social life of the group. A changing American culture spreading its expanding technology across and into the natural world of things constantly increases its store of meanings for natural reality; yet the experiences felt, recorded, and known are transmitted through the changing, yet traditional, cores of meaning of that culture and bound within the organic limitations of the species. Scientists should not forget that myth and "scientific reality" alike attribute meaning to human life or nature only as man experiences each within the confines of his own species.

The humans involved in any society, Yankee City included, are integral parts of the life of the human species and the onward life-flow of interconnected species events. [3] As such, by their very nature they must and do live within the limitations imposed by the social structure upon their species. The outward acts and gestures which relate physically separate individuals are a combination of species acts, which join the individuals and thus maintain the continuation and biological survival of the group. These outward acts are accompanied by inner feelings and emotions, expressed and interpreted by the individual partly as a separate being and partly through the exchange of gestures which interrelate him with other mem-. bers of the species group. Such acts (or their sequences) as copulation, pregnancy, birth, caring for the young, foraging, eating, digesting, and defecating, accompanied by their feelings, are some of the more obvious elements of species behavior. The changes of behavior among individuals during maturation, senility, sickness, and death are also species events which, in varying degree, influence and are part of the life of the species. They are all necessary for the survival of the group and the production and maintenance of new individuals. They must and do occur whether the species possesses a culture or not. Man, the other primates, and the higher animals in varying ways share species characteristics as parts of the condition for their existence. Cultures, no matter how variant and bizarre, can, by extending or contracting the potentialities of these several components, do no more than modify this central species core of man's life.

As a result of suppressing and reducing certain aspects and accenting and increasing others, or variously combining the parts, extraordinary variations among societies do occur. In a cultural sense the simple hunting and gathering peoples who use stone tools and worship their totemic gods differ enormously from America with its industrial, scientific, and multidimensional controls over its natural environment, its complex social alignments, and the individual worship of a "monotheistic" deity. Detailed inspection of the two types of culture increases one's realization of their vast differences, yet a community of hunting and gathering Australian totemites and the industrial and scientific community of America are more alike than different. The culture of each can be no more than the symbolic expression, moral control, and technological instrumentation which modify the species behavior of each group. The rational and non-rational life of the group and the individuals who compose it are the product of accumulated experience. The felt and known meanings which compose its entirety are necessary parts of the action system of each group and the entire species.

Each society possesses its special system of meanings. Despite the fact that each individual has his own world of meaning, much of it private to a point below consciousness, symbolic meanings could not exist in him or in others were not he and they members of a society. Each society has its own things

—marks, colors, forms, actions, and movements—which can be seen and identified, to which agreed-upon conscious and unconscious meanings have been attached and maintained through time. Each culture has its own sounds, noises, and silences which arouse the attention of its members and have agreed-upon significance. [122*a*] There are complex systems of sending and receiving sounds and silence, which also are the complex oral and auditory muscular disciplines we call language. Other human senses have their "marks" of meaning: "good" and "bad" smells or friendly handshakes and primitive face-slappings are olfactory or tactile signs of agreed-upon connotation.

Such "marks," whether noises, acts, absence of action, smells, or anything else perceived by the several senses in the manner described, are signs of meaning, which in turn depend on how they are interpreted and used. For their users, to make their own meanings known to others, are dependent on these marks of meaning. [27]

Signs and their meanings, combined, we call symbols. The meaning conveyed by a sign may or may not be that of some other object or an idea. It may do no more than express the feelings of those who exchange it. [24*b*] Whether it expresses feeling or refers to some objective thing, we call a combination of sign and meaning a symbol, thus distinguishing the principal component parts of a symbol while recognizing their unitary character.

Objects in nature when not being interpreted, it should go without saying, are without meaning; they signify nothing; it is only when they are interpreted that they have meaning and become signs. All signs by definition are dependent for their existence on a community of interpreters implicating them— both signs and interpreters—in a system of meanings shared by those involved. The meaning of a sign, however separately perceived, always involves and implies the meanings of other signs. The meaning of one sign can be understood only when related to the meanings of other signs; a sign is always a part of one or more sign systems.

The interpretation of an object may be limited to only the agreed-upon "facts" about what it is as it confronts those who interpret it. [22] Its meaning in this case is no more than what it is; it does not connote anything other than itself. When an object is known merely for what it is, its characteristics are treated by those who know it (its interpreters) as a sign or a system of meaningful signs in itself. Its assigned meanings, which limit it to being only what it is, are unavoidably dependent on the larger system of meanings possessed and shared by the members of the community. The object may be discrete and separate from others, but its meanings are necessarily integral parts of the larger network of meanings maintained by each group.

When it is not being interpreted, a dead lamb lying alone on a hillside is without meaning. The members of a community of human interpreters, or one of them using the meanings of his culture, may view it as no more than a dead lamb. Its meaning is no more than what this object is. Those who identify it as such, do so by meanings which separate it from the rest of the world around them, classifying and placing it within the total accumulated meaningful experiences of the group. They identify it with a set of agreed-upon characteristics. These become the outward signs which—combined—stand for the general meaning they attribute to it. They know what it is because they know what these traits mean. They *believe* they know what a dead lamb is because they accept the agreed-upon, customary meanings of signs which tell them that the object lying on a hillside is a dead lamb.

The community (of interpreters) not only agree upon the separate signs which they translate into the meaning "dead lamb," but also—usually without conscious effort—to a set of limiting stipulations which indicate the content of interpretation. The degree of agreement and of conformity in a group about the meaning of an object may or may not vary greatly according to the signs used and the contexts of interpretation. Usually the immediate action situation in which the interpreters of the moment are operating is decisive in determining the sign content and the amount of agreement.

The meaning of a sign may be something more than, or entirely different from, its object; sometimes it is both to those who interpret it. When an object stands to its interpreters for something beyond itself, and is not limited to what it is inherently, its usefulness to its interpreters lies precisely in the fact that it is not what it is, and—acting cooperatively—they can use it to mean something else. A community's stock of signs, as we observed in the historical chapters, circulates back and forth, within and throughout its social system, being forever refreshed, changed, and strengthened. Old symbols are transformed into new symbols or cease to be, and new ones become old as those who send and receive meaning by this means repeat their attributions and deepen the connotation. Meaning is created out of, and is a product of, man's experiences; without the mutual exchange of attributed meanings he and his world would perish. Yet this exchange, on which his existence largely depends, itself rests upon signs which can be individually and collectively used. Once it is "agreed" that an object is filled with meaning it can carry its load and have it received by all those whose learning has bound them to the "agreement."

The typographical marks—the English letters—which compose the *words* "dead lamb" refer to something beyond what the marks are. The agreed-upon, conventional meanings among our community of interpreters allow these several marks (letters of the alphabet) to be sent and received within a context which decrees that they may be in themselves almost meaningless, while that to which they point is significant. This is possible because they are in use by a community where there is agreement among the members as to how these signs shall be used.

There is also agreement on how they fit into a larger system of interdependent meanings and actions. The same dead lamb lying alone upon the hillside may have meanings beyond those limited to the object confronting the eyes of the interpreter. It may be the symbol of the slain Lamb, the Son of God, once and forever sacrificed on the cross as an acknowledgment of man's guilt, an expiation, and an offering of repentence: a sign of the meaning of man, his God, and their mutual relations in a Christian community. The sacred meaning of the dead lamb is partly dependent upon the meanings directly attributed to the object itself, partly upon the cluster of meanings related to it—among them the significance of death for all living things, including the death which waits for all those who give meaning to the sign. Its meanings may include feelings of guilt and many other similar emotions having to do with good and evil.

The process by which a natural object becomes a mundane

sign, and the latter in turn becomes and remains a supernatural one, are discussed elsewhere. What is important here is that the immediate signs identifying what the dead lamb should mean to those who interpret it· at different times and places must depend in part on the larger sign and meaning context in which it is placed. Whether it is to be interpreted in a system of natural signs or refer to something more than itself—even man's hope of victory over death through the events of Calvary —rests upon the contextual conventions.

Since everything we think we know is a sign of meaning, to make the term "sign" useful it is necessary to limit the meaning of this all-inclusive word. We can start by saying that all meaningful things may be divided into signs and objects. Objects mean what it is believed that they are. Signs stand for, or express, something which is not present in the sign itself. Objects "contain" all the meaning attributed by their interpreters; none goes "elsewhere." They are what they are and mean only what they are. Signs do not mean what they are in themselves; none of the meaning attributed to them is contained in them but is assigned elsewhere. The meaning of the word (sign) "cat" is not on the printed page or in the voice but attributed elsewhere. The live cat confronting us as an object on the hearth can mean what it is.

Signs and objects diverge from the two extreme types just indicated; for purposes of symbolic analysis at least two varieties of each may be usefully distinguished, composing four types of things to which meaning is attributed—in other words, four types of attribution of meaning. Type I, or Pure Sign Meaning, stands for and expresses something which it is not. In Intermediate Sign Meaning (Type II), most of the meaning is directed beyond the sign; it stands for and expresses something which it is not, but in addition part of its meaning refers to, or expresses, itself.

The meaning of Intermediate Object, Type III, in the range of attributed meaning is an object where most of the meaning attributed to the object remains there, but dependent meanings cluster about it which are not limited to it. The object is what it is, yet it also has secondary meanings reaching beyond it. Type IV, or Pure Object Meaning, is what it is and means only what it is. The range of the four types of attribution of meaning is represented on Chart 19.

Theories about the nature of symbolic behavior start with the outward signs and move their discussion on to inward meaning. While this is understandable, since signs can be perceived and the present has inherited this disposition to so treat the

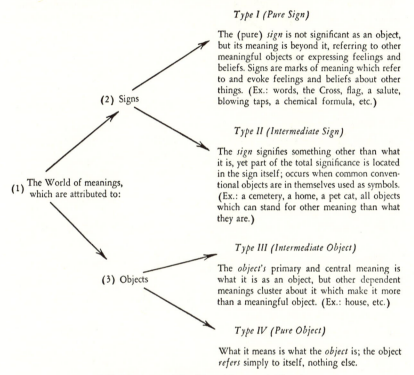

Type I (Pure Sign)

The (pure) *sign* is not significant as an object, but its meaning is beyond it, referring to other meaningful objects or expressing feelings and beliefs. Signs are marks of meaning which refer to and evoke feelings and beliefs about other things. (Ex.: words, the Cross, flag, a salute, blowing taps, a chemical formula, etc.)

(2) Signs

Type II (Intermediate Sign)

The *sign* signifies something other than what it is, yet part of the total significance is located in the sign itself; occurs when common conventional objects are in themselves used as symbols. (Ex.: a cemetery, a home, a pet cat, all objects which can stand for other meaning than what they are.)

(1) The World of meanings, which are attributed to:

Type III (Intermediate Object)

The *object's* primary and central meaning is what it is as an object, but other dependent meanings cluster about it which make it more than a meaningful object. (Ex.: house, etc.)

(3) Objects

Type IV (Pure Object)

What it means is what the *object* is; the object *refers* simply to itself, nothing else.

CHART 19. The Four Types of Meaning

problem from past treatments such as the word being followed by its meanings in the dictionary, this procedure has usually led to erroneous results and awkward and unreliable methodologies. Here we have emphasized meaning as primary and signs and objects as secondary. Chart 19, The Four Types of Meaning, represents the active attribution of meaning through signs and objects. On the left at (1) this world of meanings which are attributed to Signs (2) and to Objects (3) is connected by arrows which lead on to the range of meanings from Pure Sign to Pure Object.

For a devout Christian, two crossed sticks may be the cross referring to Christ and his sacrifice and not two crossed sticks (Type I). The *words*, "my dog," refer to, but are not, the animal itself (Type I). The chemical formula, H_2O, refers to water but is not the water (Type I).

A physical house and garden may be meaningful as my family home. In this sense its primary significance is more than the physical plant or dwelling; its meaning has to do with a set of beliefs, values, and feelings that far outweigh the value of the physical object, yet a residual part of the home (when so used by the interpreter) is the meaning of the house as an object (Type II).

Perhaps a particular house may be under inspection by a potential buyer. The principal meaning to this interpreter may be that it is a house, but in the total immediate impression there may be other dependent meanings of "attractiveness," "well kept," "superior neighborhood," etc. When the major and dominant impression of the house as a meaningful object is that it is a physical object of a particular kind and the other meanings are dependent and quite secondary, it falls into Type III of meaningful objects.

When a chemist views a chemical element in a laboratory the object's meaning to him can be what it is (IV). To some interpreters it might mean more, but to the chemist working in an experiment it may mean what it is as an object and nothing more. For most interpreters such exact application of meaning is difficult, if not impossible. Probably special training, and perhaps a particular kind of personality, are necessary.

Each of the two types of meaningful object and sign may have other signs added by the interpreter, so that a sign of a sign may refer to the objects classifiable under the four types. For example, a word may refer to other words, and they to the object. At one second, to the individual interpreting it, a given thing is an object only; at the next, a sign—or, as a sign, it can shift and become an object. The attributed meanings of the dead lamb on the hillside in a brief moment can shift back and forth through all four types from one extreme to the other. The interpreter within the realm of his culture is seemingly free to determine what it means. Yet closer inspection of what he is doing when he attributes meaning to a sign or object demonstrates that his choice is usually most limited, and—given the necessary evidence—largely predictable. The individual variations, the extent of his freedom of choice, the cultural and species domination of his attribution of meaning are all considerations that must be included in any methodology for the study of meaning and symbol systems.

The semantic rule that the word is not the object is true; but not always, for sometimes the word (sign) can become the object, as its meaning shifts and the marks themselves become meaningful. The separate alphabetical marks, *D, O,* and *G* can be objects of intelligent scrutiny by the linguist, but the meaning of a word for a household pet—"dog"—is not attributed to them.

Most behavior, to those who engage in it during their daily lives, or at night when they sleep, belongs to sign situations of the first three meaningful types. The meanings of pure signs which refer to strictly delineated objects—and, of course, pure objects—often belong to the professional disciplines, particularly to the scientist and the logician. Night and day dreams are likely to use signs of Type II. The meanings of words and signs in ordinary daily intercourse move back and forth among all four types.

CHAPTER 15

SIGNS, SYMBOLS, AND

MENTAL ACTION

The Anatomy of Acts of Meaning

All meaningful things which are not "objects" are symbols. All signs and their meanings which conceptually or expressively refer to something beyond the sign itself are symbols. Symbols are substitutes for all *known* real and imaginary actions, things, and the relations among them. They stand for and express feelings and beliefs about men and what they do, about the world and what happens in it. What they stand for may or may not exist. What they stand for may or may not be true, for what they express may be no more than a feeling, an illusion, a myth, or a vague sensation falsely interpreted. On the other hand, that for which they stand may be as real and objectively verifiable as the Rock of Gibraltar.

The essential components of a symbol are the sign and its meaning, the former usually being the outward perceptible form which is culturally identifiable and recognizable, the latter being the interpretation of the sign, by a person or persons, usually composed of concepts of what is being interpreted combined with the positive or negative values and feelings which "cluster about" the interpretation. [104] The sign's meaning may refer to other objects, or express and evoke feelings. The values and feelings may relate to the inner world of the person or be projected outward on the social and natural worlds beyond. Feelings and values, when expressed in the sign behavior of the individual, always connect with his past and present experiences. Since his experiences are organized into his person, and most such experiences are socially expressed, the ideas, values, and feelings attributed to a sign and discharged upon it inevitably indicate meanings whose entirety is privately defined in a public universe.

The other components of the act of attributing meaning to

a sign are the *objects,* real or imaginary, material or not, concerning which the sign has significance for those who interpret it; *the levels of awareness,* conscious or not conscious, [72b] including varying degrees between the two extremes; the *kinds* and *intensity of feeling* and the *contexts* of situation in which the symbols are being, and have been, used. [51c] These several components are given full treatment in this and the following sections.

Each of these components has a ramified and connected environment of its own: signs with signs, objects with objects, feelings with feelings, and contexts within ever-widening clusters of context, etc. Man in his species totality, as social and animal being, is the ultimate total environment of a symbol.

For some purposes, to complete the problem of understanding a sign it is only necessary for the analyst to recognize the culturally attributed meanings. But to fully grasp what is involved in the act of attributing meaning, the relations of all the parts to each other must be known and understood. This is particularly necessary for studying symbolic behavior in the community, where—fortunately for science—it is not easy to

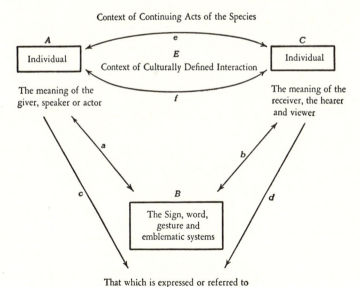

CHART 20. The Attribution of Meaning

maintain the usual fiction that one can find the significance of a symbol by studying an individual in isolation.

For the purposes of clarity and brevity in explaining what symbols are and how they function, at first we shall confine the hypothetical community and social situation to only two people who are communicating by sending and receiving signs. To keep all the parts and their complex relations in mind we will use Chart 20 as a model. It shows how symbolic interaction takes place between individuals *A* and *C*. When individual *A* talks to *C* or *C* to *A*, the chart indicates that the action is reciprocal and the exchange of signs mutual. The arrow pointing down from *A* to the rectangle labeled *B* shows that he acts by attributing (spoken) meaning to a word, gesture, or other sign. Individual *C* interprets the sign sent by attributing meaning to it (hearing and understanding). Line *b* pointing to the "meaning" of the hearer or viewer indicates this fact. Lines *c* and *d* pointing down to *D*, the thing referred to, indicate that the meaning of the speaker of the word or the gesture of the actor has been successfully sent and received by the listener or an audience because the object referred to is the same for each.

Line *a* not only points to the sign *B*, indicating that he uses it as actor and speaker, but also points back to *A*, indicating that he interprets the meaning to himself as he communicates to *C*. Line *b* is also double-arrowed, indicating that he acts outwardly to attribute meaning to the sign and inwardly relates it to himself. For communication the sign must be public and available to both.

For purposes of graphic simplicity, *E* has been made to represent several parts of the symbolic process. The double-headed arrows *e* and *f* on the chart are labeled "the context of the continuing acts of the species" and "the context of culturally defined (sign) interaction." As such, they represent the ongoing eternal flow of species events interrelated with the culture in which meaning is attributed and in which sign *B* and all other signs are interpreted. *E* also stands for the immediate action context where the exchange of meaning and sign interpretation occurs. If the object *D* were part of the immediate action context, it might have been placed within the context of *E*. To be precise, the sign *B*, too, might be represented as part of *E*.

The social act of attributing meaning consists in the *public* giving and receiving of signs. When the act is private, as in internal conversation or dreaming, there is individual interpretation in which signs are presented and interpreted. Such private and individual sign interpretation is largely dependent on the previous use of the sign in public exchange. The individual, although he may treat it in a private manner, learns what the sign is from public sources. A sign is publicly maintained only because by forthputting and reception it is exchanged. For purposes of further exposition we will continue to limit the whole web of society's relations to that between two individuals and allow them and their relation to represent the totality. The "anatomy" of an act of meaning is depicted below (p. 466), beginning with the context between individuals *A* and *C*. The several movements of the act of meaning in their symbolic interchange of meaning are numbered (1–5) beginning with *A*'s sign offering (1), through to their reception by *C*. Dyadic Interaction shows the internal and external reception and sending of meanings.

A major part of human interaction, including the biological and social levels, consists of symbolic interchange, the giving and receiving of symbols. The attribution of meaning to things transforms what they immediately are into signs capable, or potentially capable, of exchange in a social context. The attribution of meaning in social interaction consists of the presentation of the sign, the bestowal of meaning to it by the giver (sender), and the meaningful reception and incorporation of it by the receiver into his own sign context. The acts of receiving and sending a sign between two or more people involve internal and external behavior in each organism. Each individual influences the other and himself in the exchange. Meaning is inwardly bestowed on the sign by the sender; thus modification takes place within himself as he presents the sign to the other, who may or may not receive it. He may fail to perceive or recognize it. If he does recognize it an action takes place in which the sign is made over to him and incorporated by him into his own system of meaning. The reception of the sign by him re-influences the original giver. The outer behavior of the sender and the receiver may constitute the sign itself, the object to which meaning is attributed, the immediate context surrounding the sign involved in the interaction, or it may be both sign and context. Sign exchange, involving as it does attribution of meaning by two or more people, is circular; in fact it consists of several interdependent circles of meaning and be-

Dyadic Interaction: A Social Act in a Relation between A and C:

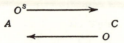

(s = sign)

1. A makes some oral sounds (the external, objective thing—internally there is neuro-muscular behavior):

$$A \ O^s \longrightarrow$$

2. A hears his own sounds, to them he attributes meanings: To him they are, for example, a word signifying *dog*. The word has meaning to him in saying, hearing, and as a total act of his own speech. The sounds are transformed by him into something more than they were when they were sent:

$$A \longleftarrow {}^sO$$

3. C also hears the sound (he is stimulated auditorially—internally there is neuro-muscular behavior):

$$O^s \longrightarrow C$$

4. He receives and incorporates the sounds by attributing meaning to the sound-objects. (He transforms the oral act of A into the meaning of the word *dog*.) The allotment of meaning is a modification of his behavior:

$$O^s \longrightarrow C$$

5. The modification of C's behavior (he receives or fails to receive the sign, the oral noises of A are meaningfully transformed or not) sends back meaningful signs to A:

$$A \longleftarrow O^s$$

6. The chart below shows the total process of the attribution of meaning to signs in social interaction. (1 to 5 refer back to the several parts of the process.) They constitute symbolic interaction within a social context:

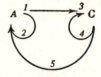

If individual A did not speak but thought *dog*, there would only be the neuro-muscular behavior and private, internal communication of A to A. The attribution of meaning might be to no object present in the environment or any other environment, or it might refer directly to an object or objects.

If individual C were not present the oral act of individual A would constitute an unheard soliloquy (1 and 2).

havior. Let us examine the several parts and then see how each is related to the total process.

The attribution of meaning to an object by an individual depends on previous experience of the individual with the object itself or with signs of the object. If it is with signs of the object ordinarily he will learn from others and be trained by them to bestow their meaning to the sign and thus to the object. If it is directly with the object the meanings of others will be reinforced or modified by his own experiences and by the meanings of the signs they use for it. The basic core of meaning for most signs and objects is acquired in infancy, childhood, and adolescence. However, the meanings of signs and objects shift throughout the individual's and the society's existence. The meaning of the Cross in the years 33 and 1954 A.D. is different and its meaning to a child being confirmed something other than to a dying man.

The situation so far depicted illustrates *successful* exchange of signs. It implies that there is no important difference in the meanings of the speaker and the listener. But the listener (audience) and the speaker or actor may have quite different meaning and fail to communicate. If this is true, lines *a* and *b* will not interrelate *A* and *C*. The double arrow for each will still express the outward attribution of meaning to sign *B* and the inward interpretation of it (Chart 20). The object (word or gesture) used as a *sign* would be the same as a perceptible object, but it would be no longer the *same* meaningful sign to both. Furthermore, the lines *c* and *d* would no longer point to *one* object, *D*, but to at least two quite different things for the two people.

Many other variations of this kind are possible. Let us mention but a few: The actor in a play, radio, or television show (or a priest standing before his congregation) sends words to a large audience. The individuals in the audience may have quite different meanings for the symbols sent, some agreeing with the actor and the director and some not. Moreover, the dramatist who provided the script may have other meanings in mind for his characters and their actions and the play's denouement. Quite possibly the actor may use secondary meanings of the symbols provided rather than those considered primary by the author. The play, as they say, can be interpreted or slanted. Or there may be varied objects and meanings attributed to the sign given, yet a common core of meanings may relate the variety. This is very often true, since most people who grow up in a culture have experiences which furnish them with a common core of understanding on which they have developed variations.

Other possibilities in the symbolic situation and the relation of meaning to sign need to be mentioned here. The communication between *A* and *C* may be indirect rather than direct. The painting on the wall of a public library may be "sent" by an anonymous worker under the direction of a long-dead donor and be viewed by a passing stranger. The painter, too, may be unknown—a member of a different culture; yet indirect, and possibly non-intentional, communication and sign-exchange have occurred. And it is also *delayed* sign-exchange. Those who learn to read the hieroglyphics carved on a stone by members of a dead culture are involved in this kind of sign-exchange. Such signs, like all things in time, can move only one way. To represent this, the lines and arrows on the chart need to be changed.

Then, too, the sign used may be contained within the reveries or "internal conversation" of one individual. It is hidden from all others. Individual *A* on the chart stays in context *E;* object *D* may be present and referred to by sign *B;* but *B* is not available to *C*, or *B* may be public and available to both, while each privately attributes his own meaning to it.

The sign *B* may be the "manifest content" of a dream known to no one but the dreamer. [51c] It expresses emotions which relate to the unconscious and "unknown" world of meanings inaccessible to the dreamer's conscious levels of meaning. The meaning attributed to the dream-sign and its context of situation are different when the sign is used in public exchange. However, even when publicly used at the conscious level, its unconscious meanings and contexts are related to it. The negative and positive feelings and values attributed to it are always an accumulated amalgam of individual experience and cultural definition. During sleep the society's present control over the use of the sign is greatly reduced, but the society's past influences are integral parts of the meaning and contexts of all dreams. During sleep the impulse life of the species with its wishes and attendant hopes and fears has greater opportunity to express itself by the use of symbols ordinarily not available for such purposes. But the dream world of a community is no less a social reality than the rational and non-rational one of daily life. Sleep merely reduces the arena of meaning.

For analytical purposes we have divided signs into two perceptible varieties: the public, conventionally defined forms existing in sensory reality and the hidden sign, internally but not externally recognized by an individual—manifest to the one who experiences it, but until made explicit by him not available to anyone else. [72b] Other intermediate varieties, sometimes necessary for analytical purposes, are those with less explicit public form, which are more vaguely and loosely defined by convention. Examples of the first major sign-type include oral and written words, available to everyone in the culture; through previous learning experiences with them everyone has learned how to interpret them in social interaction. The elements of a liturgy or religious service, such as those of Communion, are visible, perceptible, and available to a group of worshipers. Examples of the hidden type include such sign phenomena as the manifest content of a dream just discussed, the visual and other signs of daydreams, reveries, fantasies, the phantoms of supernatural experience, the manifestations of a vision. The use of words in internal conversation during contemplation, without visible and perceptible signs being present, are also hidden signs. But in all these examples of the second type these non-material, non-perceptible forms are treated by the user as if they had a visible or auditory or other sensible form. Indeed, the meaning attributed to the sign—the manifest content of a dream, for example—projects it into a form that assumes an imagined explicit existence for it. Ordinarily in such experiences the meanings of the signs attached to objects in a dream or reverie do exist in some form of reality.

Thoughts and feelings about a non-visible sign in a society can be given objective form in visible symbols. The culturally (or naturally) formed design on a ritual object such as a cross or animal totem can beome the conventional projection of an inner state of feeling and belief. Once such a relationship is established, the design and its object can become the means of invoking and evoking and recreating the feeling and belief in those in whom the meaningful relationship has been previously established, for men need signs as outward forms to organize, and give a sense of reality to, the fleeting feelings and beliefs that crowd through their mental life. Concrete signs, being subject to the immediate and continuing scrutiny of their interpreters' senses, belong to the world of sensible "reality." They are objects as well as signs. The conscious "recognition" of an "objective" reality beyond the "subjective" self—a basic categorical dichotomy of this culture— where the meaning of what is being interpreted is felt to *come into* the interpreter from *outside* him—dangerously disguises the other fundamental fact that the person, as a product of his culture and an item of his species, attributes their meaning to them. There is an investment of the self *into* the sign. The self, expressing the innate impulse needs of the organism as experienced in the culture, has modified them and made them subject to its constrictions and expansions. The sign-object's concrete perceptible reality increases man's belief in the immaterial images and thereby reduces anxiety and increases his sense of security.

Signs vary in clearness of definition, fixity, and strength and durability of structural form, from those of extreme rigidity, firmness, and lasting quality to those whose structure is so intangible and lacking in definition, in unity as well as continuity, that they seem almost beyond the limits of observation and scientific inquiry. Yet the latter shadow-like patterns, momentarily present in the rushing flow of the human mind or in the passing emotions of a crowd, are real, significant, and fundamental parts of human symbolism. The images of a fleeting daydream, the vague reverie, or the confused remnants of last night's dream are as real symbolically—as accurate as indicators of meaning and as significant as conveyors of feeling and belief—as the symbolic gadget with its interchangeable and refillable containers we call the calendar.

The intensity of negative and positive affect discharged on a sign varies within different individuals, social contexts, and levels of awareness. Various techniques, including interviewing, projective techniques, and attitude scales may be used to measure the degree of intensity.

When meanings are attributed to signs in the context of the inner world of the individual, the whole symbolic activity is private and hidden. When they are invested in signs within the context of the outer world in which the individual exists, the "whole" is public. Such meanings may disregard time, space, and the logical categories because they are non-logical and depend on social logics for their significance. This means that their structure and ultimate validity rest on an order provided by the social and species systems. Discussions about the Church and Christ, the Bridegroom, use symbols and a social logic based on the family structure and the species life it organizes. Their assumptions and conclusions are human understandings founded on experience derived from these contexts.

Meanings may also disregard time and space categories by logical methods, when what is attributed is significant precisely because it is "known" to be out of time and space. The eternal nature of God, the believed-to-be timeless and spaceless nature of beauty and truth, and the "Existence" of certain philosophers are outside the meanings of time and space.

Let us examine some of the kinds of meaningful acts the analyst must take into account when he studies the attribution of meaning to signs in action contexts. The *direction* of the meaning may be inward. The context in which the word "mother" may be interpreted has to do with thoughts about his own mother; feelings of pain, grief, and guilt may suffuse them. Or the direction may be outward. The sign "mother" may be interpreted in a public context and refer to "the mother of F.D.R."

If the meaning has a *locus* in space and time several analytical types may be usefully employed. Our culture divides time into the past, present, and future; it divides space into the immediate here and localities of ever-increasing distance. In everyday life the two are combined into meanings such as the here and now and somewhere else at some other time.

Meanings may be non-logically attributed to signs and employed in contexts where time and space are disregarded and inner and outer directions fused. [52b] Many reveries, dream-signs, and religious symbols are of this character. [69a] Attention may be applied to signs within contexts which are outside the interpreter which attribute "here and now" to what is meant. The words, gestures, and other signs being used stand for some or all of the immediate action context. The gentleman bows and kisses the hand of a lady in a drawing room at a formal reception. The manager dressed in white shirt, tie, and business suit gives orders to a worker garbed in greasy coveralls. Biggy Muldoon in Yankee City socks the mayor in the jaw in His Honor's office at the City Hall. The kiss, the bow, the order, the sock on the jaw are signs whose meanings are to be found in the "here and now" of an immediate context. Their larger significance is located in other times and places.

Signs may stand for, and operate in, contexts where the locality is immediate but the time is past. The old friend who appears after twenty years in the same drawing room, kisses the lady's hand, and bows as he once did arouses emotions and memories of the romantic moments of a distant past. The presence of the signs in an immediate action context may cause meanings to be assigned which have to do with anticipated future events. Their interpreter may apply meanings to them in terms of fears, hopes, and expectancies of what may occur here but after now. They stand for what is to be but is not yet. The husband standing by, watching the wife respond to the bow and kiss, may imagine future consequences while the signs for the two involved evoke past memories.

Signs may stand for (refer to or express) some other time and place context far away and long ago or nearby and recent. The mature man finds a letter written in another language, dated many years before, signed by his mother's name. He reads it and cries. The action context is here and now, but the meanings are evocations of a time and place far away and long ago. The action observed is now and here, but the attributed meaning places the sign in a very different context.

The difference between the present example of a different time and place and the salutation to the lady by the gentleman with meanings of present locality but past time is one of degree. If the sign suffused the man and the woman with emotion so that they were both unaware of present time and place and only aware of another place in the past, then it would be similar to the situation of the letter. But the significance of the first sign-event is that the past is brought to bear on a present in the same immediate context, while the letter "carries" the meaning of the reader to other times and other places. The analyst observes what takes place. The solitary man reads a letter and cries. The signs and its immediate action contexts are significant as such, but the interpretative act has evoked a distant past that is far away. On the other hand, the interpreted sign may evoke anticipations which attribute meanings to somewhere else, tomorrow. The jealousy of the husband may be so deeply aroused and his fantasies so intense as he watches the sign exchange of response to the kiss and bow that for the future he will imagine his wife being unfaithful to him.

All or several of the types of context mentioned (others are possible) may be combined, and were so in the report on the symbols of Yankee City in an observed set of activities. The meanings attributed can be directed inwardly and outwardly, to the here and now or elsewhere and some other time with split-second rapidity, as we all know. Each of the outward situations listed may be inwardly duplicated by the inactive individual while indulging in reveries, internal conversations, or some other form of private mental activity. Furthermore, the "here and now" meanings are in fact never completely separated from memories of things past or anticipations of what is to come. Nor can the meanings of signs about the future or those of the past —except for analytical purposes—be freed from the meanings of the present. Signs of the past are always implicated in contemporary meanings. The hieroglyphs telling of an ancient Egyptian dynast are forever subject to the limits and power of the meanings of today. Signs of the future cannot reach much beyond the present and past meanings on which they are founded.

The forms and functions of attribution must be determined. Are the meanings rational or non-rational (see Chapter 16 "The Structure of Non-logical Thought")? Do they have real or imaginary objects of reference or are they expressive, evoking only feelings? For our purposes three types of meaning will be distinguished. The first includes referential and scientific concepts, the logic of propositions and rational discourse, where the meanings are stipulated and their relations precisely fixed; they convey information and are verifiable. At the other extreme are the evocative, expressive, and affective meanings, the non-rational meanings whose validity does not depend on empirical proof, but on feeling or perhaps on ways of knowing and understanding beyond ordinary experience. Between these two extremes is the type which in varying degree combines the two in the ordinary world of practical life. Most meanings attached to most signs and objects in the ordinary practical world of daily life are of this type. [104]

Whenever several symbols of the same or different kinds, with the same or different functions, are coordinated into a recognizable unity they constitute a symbol system. The many ancient and recently invented symbol systems our society possesses, although recognizably unitary, clearly interpenetrate each other. In a symbol system such as an Easter ritual, literary and art systems are integral parts of the ceremony. Gesture, word, song, and emblematic systems intermingle with a prescribed choreography. Each of these separate symbol-assemblages may be integral parts of several other systems, yet be functioning parts of, let us say, an Easter service. The identification of such systems depends partly upon who is recognizing them, the circumstances under which they are being used, and the purposes of the observer. Some of the conventionally and more generally recognized systems are the various forms of art and popular culture: drama, radio, television, the comics, news stories, novels; play and games, ceremony, dogma, creed, sacred and secular ideologies, etiquette; as well as vague and more implicit forms such as reveries, daydreams, and dreams during sleep.

Symbol systems function in part to organize individual and group memories of the immediate and distant past and their expectancies of the future, and by so doing strengthen and unify the persistent life of each. Those symbols which evoke memories of past events for the individual or the group are greatly contracted and condensed, often modified beyond the power of the individual or group to recognize what their full references are. Such condensed systems arouse the emotions of individuals and the sentiments of the group; the emotions and sentiments aroused range from overwhelming intensity to slight feelings with only minimal significance to those who have them. They may range from the indifference of an onlooker passing a highway sign in a swiftly moving car to the devoted involvement of the initiate holding the Communion cup.

Generally speaking, living symbols which direct the attention of the individual or group to the past and relate him to it tend to be non-rational and evocative rather than rational and referential. Often for the individual they express memories of past events which are deeply buried in the transpositions of "condensation." [51c] This statement, properly modified, also seems true for the society. The symbols used to arouse memories of Armistice Day and Memorial Day, for example, carry a charge directly connected with the emotions of World Wars I and II and the Civil War, but convey only a blurred, condensed notion of what those events were felt to be by those who directly experienced them. In being related to the whole body of past experience which makes up the life of the group at the time, to be continually modified by the new experience of the group and individuals who compose it, much of a symbol's original meaning—both evocative and referential—while transmitted by the older generation into the minds, thoughts, feelings, and expectancies of the younger, is condensed and transformed. The social relations involved in this transmission, including those of parents and children, sex and age groupings, the economic and political orders, and the society generally, each with its own needs, values, and previously acquired symbols, refashion and sometimes transfigure the words, signs, and meanings of original events in the symbols used for them, which come to have a new significance, functioning to produce new and different effects in the individual and the society.

Symbols which evoke *sentiments* proper for contemporary ritual recognition of the memories of an occasion often have little to do with recreating the beliefs and ideas involved in the actual event. They become condensed versions of much that we have felt and thought about ourselves and the experiences we have in living together. But the *effect* of what has been forgotten remains a powerful part of the collective life of the group.

Such basic groupings as the family order transform and store traditional meanings as part of the physical conditioning of the organisms which are members of the interactive group. The conscious and "unconscious" symbols we retain are present expressions of past experiences, related and adapted to the ongoing life of the species, the society, and each individual.

At the time it is taken, a family photograph of a young mother and father and their several small children may be a representation of what they are in so far as a camera can represent them as human, physical, and social objects. But to the children grown old, with the parents long since dead, the picture may be no longer a representation but a memento, now acting as a fetish does in ritual life to arouse conscious and unconscious feelings and beliefs they have about themselves and their family. To *their* own children, it may evoke at most only feelings of family solidarity and pride. The once representational and referential "individuals" in the photograph may to their great grandchildren become symbolic figures which arouse, portray, and focus the new generation's values, feelings, and beliefs about themselves in the manner of the inward, non-visible images of a dream. They portray a reality of feeling and social value for what the person viewing the photograph in himself is, rather than what the individuals once were to whom the picture refers.

These statements are *not* meant to imply that there is a *racial* unconscious. They do indicate that part of the non-rational symbolic life of the "far away and long ago" world of past generations—forever refreshed in the same kind of mold from which it came—continues and lives in the present.

Every interpretative act is but one momentary event in an infinite series. The flow of evocative meanings of hate, fear, pity, and love, of confident hope and anxious dread and all the other meanings of men is forever being transformed in the present minds of those who interpret; yet, being the ongoing symbolic activity of the human species, it remains fundamentally the same. Tomorrow's meanings are prepared by those of today; those of the present are firmly founded on the meanings of yesterday. The meaning of an interpretative act must always be sought in the present, as the past is momentarily caught, rushing into a previously structured future.

The Meaning of Signs in Immediate Contexts of Action

Each sign to which meaning is attributed by those who interpret it must be seen by the research analyst not only in an immediate action context but in the larger community where the action takes place. The context consists of actors, actions, objects, and signs in relations of mutual influence. In the circus poster incident on Hill Street, some of the actors involved were: Biggy, the authorities, the Hill Street men and women, and the passing public. The actions consisted of Biggy's placing the posters on the Hill Street house, the response made by those who approved or disapproved, and the counter-responses of all concerned in the conflict. The principal signs and objects, such as house and poster, have been mentioned. The larger context was Yankee City and those people beyond its borders who, because of the influence of mass media, became involved.

At the beginning of the action on Hill Street the objects had meanings which referred largely to themselves, but they were transformed by what happened and operated as symbols to evoke responses beyond their meaning as objects. The house became a sign whose meaning referred to something else in the mental processes of the interpreter. For many it stood as a symbol of the aristocracy, of stability and security; for others, as a sign evoking resentment of the upper class and its "snobbery." What the house stood for as a sign was not just what it was as an object. The whole action context of factual events was transformed into systems of signs which evoked meanings for the larger public—expressing feeling and values about a world of ideas far beyond the empirical significance of the incidents or objects themselves. The whole context became a symbol system functioning to evoke and express emotions, much as a scene in a drama does for its audience. In the symbols of the mass media, the action context changed from an object situation (Pure and Intermediate Objects) into a symbol system (Pure and Intermediate Signs).

Thus in each action context there are several kinds of meaning. The observer must take account of them all. The actors in each context have meaning for each other in the action system. Meanings are ascribed by each actor to himself and to his own actions, to the other actors and their actions, and to the non-human objects and their treatment and relation to the rest of the context. What takes place in the context will have conventional significance conforming to the traditional core meaning of the society about which almost everyone would agree. Less universal meanings consciously held by members of subcultures and segments of the society are also present.

Finally, the scientific observer, by use of his theory and method and techniques of analysis, through interpretation of each of these meanings derives still other meanings for them when he transfers the evidential meanings of individuals and those of the society and its subcultures into his scientific conceptual context. During the several phases of this transformation of the observed meaning, he may develop several kinds of meaning. For example when, for purposes of analysis, he relates the several meanings attributed to the house by those in the Hill Street conflict, and connects them with the conventional core and subcultural meanings, he may find that the generalities present in the variety of meanings give him a different notion of the meaning of a house for people of this culture.

The observer inevitably has his own *personal* system of meanings about the context and—being a scientific observer—also possesses a set of concepts and scientific operations he can use to make scientific sense out of what he observes. The personal meanings may or may not help his scientific endeavors, yet may sometimes be better than the Procrustean bed of an inadequate science.

The person who reads a book, sees a play, hears a radio program, or views a television show is also in an immediate action context; the author of the book or play, the "sender" of the radio or television show, may not be present, but the signs he has created and sent are active—in varying ways and differing circumstances they are received and their meanings interpreted. The reception of the signs is only delayed. The meaning ascribed to such a sign by the receiver may be very different from that of the sender or very much the same, just as the meaning of persons in face-to-face interaction within a context may or may not coincide. More often than not, because all who send and receive the "same" signs are members of the same culture, there is a core of common meaning present.

The basic problem of interpreting signs and their meanings does not change in situations where members of contemporary society exchange "mass" symbols. The observer can be satisfied, for certain purposes, with the reactions of the reader to the words of a book or a radio program. He can make scientific meaning out of a comparison of the meanings of a particular type of audience studied with the common meanings of the culture for the same words, gestures and pictures. For example, he can compare the meanings attributed by lower-middle and upper-class levels, to determine similarities and differences and their significance. If the problem is differently posed, he may want to interview the author, director, and actors to learn what they believe they transmitted, and examine the program itself as well as the responses of the audience to discover as far as possible the significance of the various meanings involved or to determine the nature of communication as a human process.

The meaning ascribed by each participant to the action elements of the context is derived by treating the several elements and the total context—consciously or unconsciously—as objects and signs which he interprets. [152] They have significance for him, just as a highway sign has, in its cruder, more concrete form. The meanings will be feelings, beliefs, and values about himself, the other actors, his and their actions with each other, and the other "objects" in the context. The meaning he assigns may be privately understood or given public expression. It may be conventional and part of the generally agreed-upon cultural meanings of the sign, or may vary individually from such norms. The meanings he holds may be at several levels of awareness: they may be consciously known or unconsciously significant to him. Generally, and perhaps always, they are both. The response to the several signs may have a minimal or maximal amount of emotion in them. The emotional intensity may or may not be overtly expressed, and may be only unconsciously felt.

The meaning he derives from each sign may be that each is no more than an "object" in its own right, or it may be significant to him as referring to something that is not the object itself. In either case the object before him at the moment is something he interprets and which has meaning for him. Both forms of meaning should be learned by the observer, since each is significant evidence for his scientific understanding of the action context.

Each action context is part of the larger action system whose totality makes up the community. Every actor in the context is part of, and comes from, the larger action system. These systems of action can be, and have been here, analyzed in terms of moral, symbolic, and technical systems. For our purposes their entirety will be referred to as the social system of the community. Each of the several actors occupies one or more general and specific statuses within the social system. Some or all of these statuses are significant in determining what the signs mean to him within the context. Some or all of them may be directly involved in the immediate action context. Biggy Muldoon the son of Mary Muldoon, Muldoon the property owner, Muldoon the candidate for mayor, and the man of a social class from the wrong side of the tracks are some of the statuses directly involved in the Hill Street conflict. So are the members of families and households on Hill Street, the property owners in the region, the people belonging to the "better classes," as well as the several local and state political authorities.

Beyond these are the people of Yankee City as a whole, using rules, values, and symbols which influenced, and were influenced by, the context and which were also directly related to each of the actors in their participation in the larger life of the community. For an actor or participant, the meaning of each sign in a context will involve the present and past influence of this larger environment on him, the other actors, and the objects involved, as well as the meaning he ascribes to all of it for the whole community and the pressure he feels from its members.

If the observer can determine the meaning ascribed by each actor to what takes place in the action context, he of course knows what he is investigating. The observed overt behavior is the sign system of the actors and a part of the systems of meaning they ascribe to what they are, what they do, and the effects contributed to the action context. They, and the context itself, have become signs for the observer, whose own carefully developed meanings are also part of his evidence. Certain researches could be complete at this point. The problem for us is, what do they signify beyond the meanings ascribed by the participants in this context.

Each science has its own universe of sign and meaning, and each interprets its relevant data accordingly. The political scientist and the economist derive their own sets of meaning from Biggy Muldoon and his world. Our efforts, while finding a knowledge of these approaches necessary, follow a different path.

Once the objects, signs, and meanings of the immediate context are interrelated, it is then necessary to connect this system of signs and meaning to other action contexts. This can be done by relating the symbols of the context to those used in other symbolic contexts, by examining the same symbols in different social contexts and determining their meaning in different contexts, and finding the meaning of different symbols in this same context. The meaning of the context can then be studied as one of several which form a larger cluster of contexts and their meanings; this last procedure to be followed by a comparison with the known meanings our society conventionally ascribes to the symbols being studied.

Ideally, to interpret what took place in Yankee City in terms of context, we needed to know: (1) where the action context fitted into the social system of the town and American culture generally; (2) where the actors fit into its family, political, economic, class, and larger social life; ideally but rarely practical, (3) the social history of the city as it is related to the action context being studied; and (4) the social and psychological development of each participant. Fortunately in Yankee City, because of previous work, we had evidence on the first three and some of the material necessary for the fourth. [155]

We were interested in all symbolic contexts, but most particularly wanted to determine the functions and effect of various action contexts in the social system of the community and their effect on symbolic behavior. We also wanted to learn more about the several complex sign and meaning systems which form parts of various symbol systems. Although language is the most basic of all our symbols, we did not study it as a system, but of course it was an element in all the symbolic situations examined.

Types of Action Context

The action situations in which symbols operate are distinguishable by the *type* of context in which they occur. The immediate social context, where the symbolic event occurs, may be in a family, clique, theater, or situation when the individual is alone. Three broad contextual types, the technical, moral, and supernatural, should be distinguished. The many contexts which comprise the technical type in our society always function to adjust men to the external world by use of tools, instruments, machines, and skilled behavior to manipulate them for a utilitarian purpose. They are simply what the observer sees. They form an interconnected action system. Lying back of them is an organized knowledge, largely rational, consisting of signs and meanings related to the skills and tools.

The moral type of context—often non-rational—functions to adjust men to each other; consisting of norms of right and wrong, it re-orders, defines, and controls species interaction among the individual organisms who compose the group.

The supernatural context, always non-rational, relates men to God and to sacred things. It consists of sacred belief, ritual, and an organized group which is believed to relate men to the sacred world.

The technical contexts are empirical, pragmatic, and more dependent on testing than the moral and supernatural ones. [148] They are forever being modified to fit the hard realities of the outer world. Symbol systems fitting such contexts need to be largely denotative and referential. They must refer largely to actions and things and their operational relations to produce the necessary effects for man's survival.

In our society the symbol systems of science, with their emphasis on proof; on systematic, planned testing of the symbols by relevant, observable evidence; on planned prediction; on generalization based on the characteristics of objects and their relations, and continual inquiry into the real relations of words, things, and events—these are the best examples of symbols belonging to non-moral, non-mythic, technical contexts. [120a]

There is, of course, an interdependent relation between our developing and expanding scientific symbol systems and our expanding and developing technology. Consequently, there is a connection between the increase of detached, empirical, and logical thinking about the world around us, and what we are in relation to it. Despite the great importance of this expansion, we must not overlook the large amount of non-logical, effective thinking and feeling which is still attached to our technical contexts. The mere mention of food, clothing, and shelter—all items in our technical system—indicates how strong emotions remain closely related to the rational aspects of our technical systems. [149]

The moral type of context which organizes the relations of the members of the species into ruled behavior governing man's existence is characterized by obligations, duties, rights, privileges, and attendant values and sanctions. Our moral order is highly complex, consisting of a great variety of identifiable social contexts. To deal with it adequately, one must consider whether the context has certain kinds of statuses and roles, what relations exist between them, and what kind of family, political or economic groups, and formal or informal organizations are parts of the context of situation.

Since the relations involved are those which organize intraspecies behavior, the deep affective, non-rational needs and demands of species life are exceedingly powerful and important. The symbol systems related to these contexts express and evoke basic human emotions which are part of the onward flow of species life. Even so, the realities of the natural environment are felt there and need to be satisfied. The technical parts of the economic life of man are closely interrelated with such phenomena of social life as the sharing and use of goods and services. In this and other contexts, the opposition of rational and non-rational concepts and values is expressed in symbols combining both sets of values.

In our complex society, with its extreme division of labor, development of methods for ordering the relations of people to facilitate collaboration around common problems are more necessary than in the simple societies. The signs and concepts of time, space, number, class, quantity, velocity, as well as logical method itself, need to be increasingly used to help keep order and effectively interrelate this diverse, heterogeneous social world. The symbols operating in this complex social context range from the highly rational to those which are almost purely non-rational; from the detached and reflective words and symbols of the philosopher to the non-logical symbols of affection used by lovers or by parents with their children. [149]

The supernatural, or "sacred," type of context is composed of interrelated sacred beliefs and rites and their attendant values. Sacred beliefs are verbal and thought symbol systems; as such they may be called myths. A myth, narrowly defined, is a system of sacred belief. It is composed of verbal signs. The signs are interconnected and for those who interpret them they refer to and express meaningful things. To those for whom the signs refer to real experience, they express their feelings and beliefs about the sacred and help relate these believers to the sacred world. Rituals are symbol systems composed of interdependent words, actions, and emblems which under appropriate rules relate men to their gods and the sacred world beyond the natural. According to Durkheim,

Religious phenomena are naturally arranged in two fundamental categories: beliefs and rites. The first are states of opinion, and consist in representations; the second are determined modes of action. Between these two classes of facts there is all the difference which separates thought from action . . . [The] division of the world into two domains, the one containing all that is sacred, the other all that is profane, is the distinctive trait of religious thought; the beliefs, myths, dogmas, and legends are either representations or systems of representations which express the nature of sacred things, the virtues and powers which are attributed to them or their relations with each other and with profane things.[1]

The wishes and hopes, the fears and anxieties about life and death, the strong physical demands which constantly drive the members of the human species, all the feelings of ill- and well-being determined by the events and social values of the varying social contexts, are symbolized and expressed by sacred symbol systems. The social and species life of man, given form and symbolic substance, are each projected into this sacred, reified level. Here the symbol becomes the imagined "real" object, and the object is what man fears he is and will be, as well as what he hopes he is and may be. Modified by the moral and technical forces of the social group, the species gives expression to all its fears and longings in the reified mythic symbols of the supernatural.

Sacred symbols are largely non-logical, evocative, and expressive. They speak of feelings and mythic beliefs, not neces-

1. Durkheim [42a], pp. 36–7.

sarily true or false, which lie deeply imbedded in the ongoing emotional life of the species. The words and concepts of a religion may be logically organized and systematically arranged according to the tenets of some of the greatest of the logicians, yet all such sacred systems are ultimately based on the non-logical feelings of man. Ultimately, proof and validity are not to be found in any kind of empirical testing, for the ultimate meaning of such mythic symbols lies beyond ordinary experience.

Attempts to prove or disprove mythic beliefs as true or false by the methods of empiricism are foolish and unjustified. The truth of such symbol systems has nothing to do with the thinking and methods of empirical verification. Their truths are to be found in the larger experience of man and his species. To be valid they do not need the support, or criticism, of rational thought. Mythic symbols and their truth or falsity are not dependent, nor can they be, on the methods of science. They represent a different order of reality. They tell of older and more fundamental facts of man's poor existence. Science is not equipped to test the truth of their meanings. The basic "truths" our species has learned and transmitted through living millions of years on earth, expressed in an infinite variety of sacred signs and reified symbols, belong to an order of reality beyond the concepts and methods of contemporary science. Science can only know them in its own terms and imperfectly translate them into a symbol system often contrary to their nature. But for the scientist their natural meanings can be discovered only in what they represent, what they evoke, and how they function in the social and species life of man. Sacred collective representations are symbol systems which for the members of the group express and refer to their collective life. They reflect and evoke what people feel and think themselves to be in times of social action. They symbolize what the values and beliefs of the group are. The group being a social and species system, such collective representations symbolize for men what they feel and think about themselves as animals and persons.

The three types of context and their significance as adaptive orders in which symbolic systems operate are best understood by use of a visual representation. Chart 21 shows the various contexts and their interrelations and indicates some of their significance.

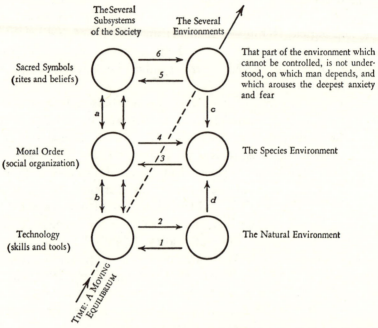

CHART 21. The Human Environments and the Adaptive Cultural Contexts in Which Symbols Are Used

The three adaptive subsystems—the technology, moral organization, and the rituals and beliefs of the sacred order—are represented by the circles in the left-hand column. The first two environments (see the circles on the right) are that part of the natural environment which, for purposes of survival, is satisfactorily controlled by the skills and tools of the technology and the species, including its innate capacities, limitations, and the animal group life regulated by the rules, values, and sanctions of the moral organization. The third environment—imaginary or not—consists of the threatening, fearful, uncontrolled and rationally unknowable world of nature and man which lies beyond the power of the technical and moral orders, where death and disaster are forever present—these being assigned by men to the ritual control of religion and its sacred symbols.

The double-headed arrows connecting the circles in the left-hand column, *a* and *b*, indicate that the several subsystems are in relations of mutual influence and make up one unified system. At the right, the single-headed arrows pointing toward the central circle indicate the influence of the other two environments on the species and show how their influence is felt in the adaptive system.

The two arrows which show the relations and influences between each type of adaptation and its environment need to be carefully noted, for they provide the foundations for understanding the symbolic forms and meanings of this and other societies. The empirical and pragmatic knowledge governing the skilled manipulation of tools which transform the natural environment and increase man's control of it also broadens and strengthens the rational foundations of man's mental life. The increasing accumulation of knowledge from experience with the rest of nature not only broadens his understanding of the real world about him but leads to propositions about what nature is and what man is in his relations to it. This is all part of the process by which the ego subsystem is founded and structured into the personality of each individual.

Horizontal arrow 1 shows the influences of the natural environment in man's technical system; arrow 2, the control of nature by the technology. At the next level arrow 3 shows that the biological relations and their feelings and gestures among the members of the species influence the moral order, although held in check and partly controlled by the learned precepts and the rules and sanctions expressed in the usages of the social order, which gives cultural *form* to all biological relations (arrow 4).

The symbols of the moral order—which convey the group's meanings for the rules governing human conduct and express their beliefs and values about right and wrong, good and bad, and what is to be rewarded or punished—are integral parts of the basic moral relation of the culture with the organized animal life of the species.

The moral order, by its direct involvement with the interaction of members of the species, helps to channel the feelings of individuals in species interaction into meaningful and cohesive relations—thereby permitting the powerful life energies of the species to be culturally expressed. In this matrix the growing individual learns the rules and experiences the negative and positive social sanctions of criticism, physical punishment, and bodily rewards for acting or failing to act according to the precepts of the moral order. The moral order aids the technological in helping the individual to learn, use, and invent symbols which refer to and express outer reality. The environmental forces of animal life are felt by the moral order, and the knowledge of the technology presses heavily upon it and forces it to adjust itself to the natural environment. Social control of the species and the natural environment must be constantly synchronized, the consequence being a constant adjustment between them.

Changes in the skills of the technology, in man's moral relations, or in his sacred symbols influence all other parts of the sacred system. It is not until attention is turned to the sacred symbol system that the purest form of symbol system is found, combining species and social symbols. This system of supernatural adjustment reduces and helps to control the anxieties and fears felt by the species because of insecurity in the natural and moral environments. Man's inability to control parts of the environment on which he depends for his individual and group survival is the source of his deepest anxiety and accordingly a prepotent influence on sacred rituals and beliefs. It need only be mentioned that his anxieties come from his experience with the real threats of his natural environment and the equally real ones of his species existence, as well as from the fearful fantasies of his moral and social life.

The supernatural level combines and re-expresses the values and beliefs of the moral and technical orders; here they are charged and powerfully motivated by the animal life of the species. Here the wishes, hopes, fears, and pent-up longings of species life, combined and molded by the conventions of the mental, moral, and technical orders, hold sway. Here the deeply buried fantasies, the covert symbolic life of man, driving for a mastery over nature and his species which the social system does not provide, and a well-being which man rarely experiences in fact and can only find for the most part in imagination—here these hidden elements find not only expression but confident encouragement. Here man's wishes to conquer death—to provide food, shelter, and creature comforts in abundance—can be completely satisfied. Here the haunting fear and growing anxieties about his health, moral worth, and personal persistence can be assuaged. The oral and action rites publicly and privately performed by his group fill him with confident hope that their supercontrol over the supernatural environment makes possible. His faith in these reified symbols expresses the "eternal" and infinite power of species and cultural life as they are felt within himself as part of his existence in the group.

These considerations place Durkheim's collective representations in a somewhat different setting. So viewed, the sacred world is not just a reified symbolic expression of the realities of the society, but is also an expression of the ongoing group life of the human animal. Men can fully realize all they are as members of a species and a society at the supernatural level. Here they can love and hate themselves as gods and be loved and hated by the deities they have created.

The faith of the group in supernatural symbols, the sense of "integration," of "oneness," and the sacrifice of self for the survival of these sacred symbols now become meaningful. Whenever an individual can identify sacred symbols in which he believes with the integrated socio-species symbols of his ordinary life he can have enough faith to believe in their supernatural efficacy and power. The source of their power is in and beyond him; these symbols unquestionably express for him a feeling of belonging to a vital eternal world which is all-powerful and—although beyond human understanding—knowable and true because of what he feels the symbols have "within them" and express for him.

The knowledge of science is necessarily limited and incomplete. Part of the great authority we presently grant it is given because it, too, reduces anxiety and maximizes our sense of control over nature. Until now, when the symbols and skills of science have marched into a new area of man's adjustment, the sacred symbols of religion have retreated. The rapid advance of science and the confused retreat of religion in recent history have given to some the impression that science will ultimately conquer the whole world of religious life. This may be a false impression. Science, a recent superstructure built on the solid foundations of empirical knowledge supplied by earlier technologies—a product of realism—cannot be directly related to, and fused with, the evocative symbols of species life. The two systems can only be bound indirectly and mediated through the moral structure of the society in each individual. For example: the science of psychoanalysis cannot be a total way of life, although some of its adherents attempt to use it as such. At best it can only heal an injury to the human psyche resulting from the dislocation of species life from the moral and technical life of the group. The individual who has lost his faith can no longer express his hopes and fears, his sense of belonging and togetherness and thereby his feeling of "wholeness," for the sacred symbols which combine the emotional world of the species and the moral world of the society are the only ones now available that can function in this manner.

Those who have faith may be on more solid ground in their understanding of reality than those who cannot find a way to believe. What they *feel* in their thinking may refer to a larger reality—mystical and supernatural or not—which speaks of truths beyond the present power of scientific thought. That this may be so should do no more than make the scientist truly humble and deeply respectful of other kinds of knowing; it should in no way influence him to abandon or reduce his efforts to know and understand.

Only passing attention has been paid here to the meanings of non-logical, evocative symbols and the systems of mental life in which they exist. We have briefly defined what was meant for our purposes by species behavior and the "ongoing flow of species events." Since both phases are important for our analysis, and the two are interdependent, we shall devote the next chapter to their significance for the proper development of theory in the study of mental life and symbolic behavior.

CHAPTER 16

THE STRUCTURE OF

NON-RATIONAL THOUGHT

The Significance of the Species Group for Understanding Non-rational Symbols

Human beings cannot be understood when studied as separate units for, although separate in space, each is a dependent and interconnected part of the species. In their physical entirety they compose a biological ongoing system of interaction at the subcultural level. The actions of all individuals, from the time of conception, are dependent, integral parts of the continuing actions of the species. During their lives they closely interact with other human animals within the limited framework of species life. The observable actions and cries of the bodies involved in the interplay of species life are only the manifest parts of the whole action system, the rest taking place as it were subcutaneously in the internal physiological processes of the bodies involved. [3]

The infinitesimal, momentary, individual speck in the infinite species expresses and reflects what the nature of his species permits him to do and learn to do. The private world of each individual is largely the product of the efforts of our society's moral order to control and constrain the non-moral and non-symbolic continuity of species behavior and to channel some of these somatic energies into technological, moral, and supernatural contexts. [59]

Since men are cultural animals, the influence of species behavior and its contexts on symbolic life can be studied only by analytical and indirect methods which conceptually separate the species way of life from culture. Since symbol systems by their very nature are social, they can be understood only as integral parts of the larger social systems which they express, interpret, record, refer to, and help to maintain for members of the group. But symbol systems must also be recognized as belonging to the varying kinds of species action groups which are given affective expression by the several forms of symbol system.

The principal species action groups are the family of procreation, the sexual pair, the parents and offspring; the food-gathering and using groups; and the physically and sexually mature and immature. [100] Since man is physically most like certain other primates which do not possess symbols of language or culture—for example, the chimpanzee—the contexts of species behavior which infra-human primates exhibit are useful indicators of what man's species groupings may be. [33] Many studies of groups of monkeys and apes demonstrate that they possess and "recognize" in their behavior the simple family group consisting of such relations as the procreative pair, parents and offspring, the relations of siblings, and the external relations of this kind of group to other members of the band and other subgroups within the larger one. [156] In addition, other groupings can be recognized in primate behavior, including sex and age groupings as well as feeding and defense groups. [154a]

The social groups discernible in the behavior of members of such simple and loosely organized human territorial cultures as the Andamanese, Paviotso, Negrito, and many other primitive tribes approximate the simple biological grouping of the other species of the primate order. [64] Our own society, despite its great complexity, has a common core of basic groupings which seems to correspond with those mentioned for the simple and primate societies. Certainly our system of social interaction is still strongly founded on the elementary families of orientation and procreation and the closely interrelated age and sex divisions. For the purposes of our present analysis, no more evidence of species contexts is needed than those just mentioned. [41]

Each individual of the infra-human primates (and presumably man) by nature grows into, and learns by experience to be, an ordered and functioning member of an orderly persistent group. [73] The non-symbolic, non-moral ordered life is maintained through time. [13] The animal energies of each species are expressed and discharged in an animal organization. There is very little that is amorphous or a "cauldron" of seething emotions about the life of an ape. His sexual life is ordered, his child-rearing conforms to a developmental pattern, and his feeding and eating conform to the status usages of his animal group. The uncontrolled violence hypothecated for the uncontrolled id when free of the constraint of the cultural ego and super ego is not observable. The adaptations in behavior necessary for animal interaction for survival have been made. It seems probable that man during his transition from a non-cultural to a cultural and symbolic animal brought these adaptations with him and that they continue important and crucial factors in the social and biological life of man. The resulting order reduces individual variability, decreases immediate satisfactions of unfulfilled desire, and restrains the immediate satisfaction of pleasurable "wishes."

It is reasonable to assume that our species, since it is closely similar to many other primates, possesses a core of non-verbal and non-symbolic meanings and gestures closely related to our animal nature, which express many of the needs and demands, the fears, satisfactions, and deprivations, the frustrations and gratifications found in these other primate species. [95] It seems equally reasonable to infer that our cultural symbols and the non-verbal animal symbols are integrally interrelated and that some of the former are more fully suffused with the meaning of our animal signs and meanings than others. The meanings derived from our experiences with what a mother is, for example, must be in large part a product of the early animal behavior with her in which her gestures, sounds, and action systems became cues interpreted and responded to at the non-verbal level. The taboos, restraints, and limitations which later became a part of her meaning and the meaning of "mother" as a sign are part of the moral order of our culture. [109]

If the cries and actions of the animal group directly express the meanings of the species and these become integral parts of the accumulation of such symbol systems as language and moral rules governing the relations of the sexes, of parents and children, and of the dominant and the dominated, it must be supposed that much of the meaning of some of the more basic parts of man's symbolic life must be sought beyond the signs and meanings of the conventions of culture. It must be looked for within the signs and meanings of species behavior and within the physical world of the human animals who embody its biological composition.

Furthermore, the non-logical expressive symbols which make up most of our symbols used in daily action—particularly those of religion—will be valid for those who use them, not because they can be proved to be true or false or logically congruent, but because they make emotional sense and are emotionally valid for those who *feel* them.

Moreover, if this is true, rational and scientific truth can be no more than one form of "knowing" reality and—this being assumed—reality as now defined can be no more than one form of what is real. The non-symbolic species behavior is the result of millions of years of accumulated adaptation. [51e] What the species inherits biologically and each individual member learns socially at the non-symbolic level, and is felt and experienced by the individual organism and by the organized responses of the group—being outside the realm of reason and its logical and scientific operations—contains orders of significance and truth far removed from even the suppositions of rational thought. The accumulated, condensed experience transferred and integrated into the species and its behavior and felt intensely by its members, individually and collectively, has meanings and validities and forms of truth for men beyond the capacity of rational thought to conceive and to order into sense-making symbols. Man's sense of what he is cannot ever depend solely on rational thought; too much is left out of what we know.

Non-rational Symbols: Their Development and Function in Species and Social Life

The meanings of non-rational and rational symbols, conscious as well as unconscious, emerge in the internal world of the individual during his development. They become part of his self and his relationship with those around him, being fitted inwardly into the structure of the personality and outwardly into his relations with his species, his society, and the physical world. [95]

For the natural environment, the signs and contexts reflect previous and past learning situations of what is present beyond the organism. "Outward" experiences with the natural world are somewhat different from those within the world of the species. Outwardly there are no immediately shared contexts of direct experience. The gestures of others, and one's own, do not here become intermeshed and blended in common, simultaneous interpretations which in themselves re-influence the situation and become part of the stimuli helping to redefine it. The inanimate world can be experienced as something to adjust to purely on the technological level—as something to manipulate and handle or not handle. Of course, members of a society can and do "share" these relations with the outside world, but here the relations can be direct, denotative, and in terms of what the object is and what I do and do not do with it. This may be done through the tools and the skills of the technology. The inanimate environment may also be defined indirectly by the symbols of the social order and conceived of as something alive, either like other non-human living things or in the image of human beings, living beings which are not human, or beings which possess human attributes. Or the biological world may be divided into those who share some but not all of man's social nature. Usually such conceptions of other species are redefined and re-expressed at the supernatural level.

In the species environment the individual's experiences take place with other members of the species; interaction among them is primary; the only reality is the peculiar nature of the species itself. Each individual is directly involved in the learned and learning contexts of the others. Each member of the species is implicated, as George Mead indicated, in the other's meaning by being involved in his own. What is learned by each is how to act towards the other, and in so doing how to act towards himself when acting in relation to the other. The species cues and acts are interchanged in a continuing series of adjustments interpreted and organized by the participants. The action is composed of continuing, adapting acts of each as integral parts of the continuing acts of the other. [152] The learned context of each includes much of the learned contexts of the other.

For men, therefore, the sign situation for one is similar to, and part of, the sign situation of the other. The significant cries and other significant gestures which refer to what is going on inside and outside both organisms can later refer to what has taken place and express and evoke for each what was felt at the time. When similar cries and actions are heard or seen and become symbols and symbolic gestures whose meanings are found in previous contexts of social and species interaction, each individual will have shared in a core of similar yet different meanings. The accumulation of such shared meanings among all members of a society, past and present, constitutes its living heritage. The continuing investment of these mutual meanings in objects, signs, and their relations transforms the world and men into a significant whole.

From the very beginning of each individual's life, what he feels, sees, hears, smells, expresses, and does, and his intensity of feeling are directly related to what other humans experience and do in the situations in which he finds himself.

The mother's initial meaning, for example, is not only the taste of warm, satisfying milk, the hard feel and tactual pressure of the nipple on the soft lips, the soft feel of a breast against the baby's face and fingers, the filling belly, and the satisfaction and support of her arms and lap, and the sound of her voice. She is also the soft voice saying something to herself. She is (to herself and others) the woman who holds the child in her lap and bares her breast to feed her child as a nutritive and loving gesture to a being sexually constituted but one with whom overt sexual experience is forever taboo. The reciprocal sounds and gestures and other overt acts compose the socio-species interaction of the mother and the child. Each has shared meanings and the significant actions, gestures, and sounds of the other. Each internalizes part of the other in the context of a common experience. The two share a species relation defined in the social context of a family. Although the relations and experiences are different with others in and out of the family, the infant learns from them by a similar process.

The child learns what the mother (and others in his immediate environment) is as an object to feel and know. The mother learns what her child is to feel and know, while at the same time the woman who is mother learns what she is as a mother, and more generally what a mother is while the child is experiencing her as a mother, in the same context of experience and defined social situation. The interdependent actions implicate the other in this mutually defined context of social and species experience. The shared experiences of each internalize part of the other in each. [16]

When these basic and continuing experiences take place within a previously defined cultural context—in which a mother, father, or sibling [80a] is defined as someone who, according to the rules and feelings and beliefs, is a person who must do this and not do that, and where a child must learn to to do this and not that—symbolic usages are internalized into the behavior of the child and the mother. [37] The meaning of child becomes son or daughter to a mother and father, with a specific name to designate this person with whom they share certain experiences, responsibilities, rights, and privileges. For example, the actions of the mother in which the child's behavior is implicated are learned in time, and implicitly and explicitly the meaning of mother for him becomes one with whom he has shared certain kinds of experiences, felt certain obligations, certain privileges, and whom he has recognized with a set of symbols. The symbol for mother must forever reflect the mutual experiences of the two with each other, experiences which are different, yet the same, but always experiences molded in a context of "permanent" meaning socially defined. [95] Through the family the vast, infinitely powerful, and largely unknown, forces of species life flow into the moral forms of the society and human personality. [150]

When a baby makes a sound or a gesture it expresses one or more emotional states. These sounds, as Malinowski pointed out, are signs which have meaning to adults—to people who have learned the culture. The emotion of the child has to do with his situation as it is related to the internal workings of his organism, his outer environment, or a combination of the internal and outer environments. Sound behavior which expresses emotion breaks up into units of sound. The actions of the child in time also break up into parts which are significant gestures. As this differentiation proceeds in time, the growing individual is acting by sound as well as by muscular, overt behavior. Sound-making and certain gestures get sign-attention from adults and cause action to take place in the immediate interpersonal environment. Most of this behavior occurs in the family context. Adults, particularly family figures, give aid and comfort to the needs of the child. Gradually sound-making and action gestures are roughly adapted as signs to the surrounding adults and to the emotional and mental states of the child. These adaptations have pragmatic validity, since they work to relieve the child's tensions and irritations. Thus an anatomically helpless infant is socially adapted and becomes a more effective part of the action system of the species and the social group. The child acts through the parents and instigates acts through them by sound and other appeals which later become verbal and symbolic. From the time the child uses words, they not only express feelings but are a form of action. [85c]

A biological arrangement of sound-making and overt acts permits words and gestures to produce the effect that they mean. Words, as one form of sign, are active forces and instruments to relate the individual to social and species life. Words and symbols relate the child to the realities of life, not just because the child has learned to use them but because social tradition has given them common meanings as ways of interacting and as objects which refer to the rest of the world around them. Such symbols when used with the child not only attract but also repel. They act as controls over the interpersonal relations of an individual, and they give others control over him.

While the growing individual learns the various systems of symbols, he does this for the most part unconsciously—which is to say, he is not aware of what he is doing and rarely separates feeling from concept. The child uses the name of the object to express an emotional bond. The expressive jargon for a toy does not depend so much on its properties as on the feelings the child has because of his experiences with it. The meaning of a thing and its signs are the total set of experiences a child has had in using them. Such meaning is part of the meaning that other people attribute to the symbol and the object for which it stands. It is probable that in most cases the meaning of an object or symbol for each person will be similar to its meaning for most other persons who live and have been trained in similar contexts.

Although conscious symbols vary greatly in meaning among the members of the community who interpret them, they do have a common core of agreed upon and customary meaning. Even though the unconscious ones are always important parts of each individual's social interaction, and usually possess significance which is generally felt and implicitly understood, they rarely become explicitly meaningful. [24b] There may be a little conscious agreement about their ideational meanings in the community, but the degree of emotional agreement among those who respond to their stimulus is high, despite the fact that they may be unaware of the significance of their responses. The testimony from the psychoanalytical couch as to the meanings of various dreams shows strong resemblances among the meanings attributed to various kinds of private symbols and the unconscious responses elicited by them. The typology of implicit meanings found in the unconscious symbols produced in the responses to the various projective tests, including the TAT, the Rorschach, and similar tests, clearly shows that there is a whole submerged world of general implicit meanings where collective agreements are not referential so much as emotional and evocative. The processes of socialization have reduced them to a submerged life fitted below rationality, embedded in the feelings related to species behavior. The increasing demands of the technology in our society have decreased the social area where such evocative and expressive symbols can be explicitly used. Consequently, they live a hidden life in the demi-world of human thought and can only be understood by translation into rational thought by a scientific interpreter.

The testimony of research in the mental and moral life of children demonstrates a pattern of non-logical thinking and behavior. Piaget's research led him to the conclusion that the child was *egocentric* in his thinking and that the logical thinking of the society only appeared after the child was socialized. The egocentric thinking and moral behavior of the child, he said, must be stripped of what he called *personal schemas* of analogy and supplemented by the thinking of the group. The "motivated" individual thinking must give way to the "arbitrary," obligatory, abstract thought of the society. The problem he poses is one of the *individual* child becoming socialized and a thinking member of the group. [111a]

A re-examination of his concept of egocentrism leads to a reformulation of the problem. The egocentrism of the child, according to Piaget, occurs when he does not distinguish himself from the world around him. He interacts as an organism with other organisms about him without distinguishing *himself* from the *others*. He treats cultural things and organizes them "syncretistically" into his own affective way of life.

And what is this way of life? The infant and young child act largely according to the action systems of the species. They interact in the group more as members of a species than as self-directed socialized beings. The action system of the biological family still operates as a powerful influence on what the child thinks and does. The insistent needs and wants, pleasures and pains, of the body related to other bodies dominate the feeling system of the child. The meanings of things are organized in the pattern of the feelings of species action systems, always under the continued and increasing influence of the cultural system.

The social symbols are present and used, but they are used according to the feeling order of the organism behaving within species action systems. Their significance and ordering are largely determined by the species context and only secondarily by social contexts. They are not irrational but non-logical. Their validity lies not in testing but in feeling and conviction.

Freud's and others' evidence about the nature of dream symbols and the mental life of much of the unconscious, where logic and rationality do not organize the mental life, adds further demonstration of the relation of non-logical order and species life. The mental world of the child—a feeling system which in early life dominates each person—continues to exist in the life of the adult individual and the group. The feeling system operating in the interaction of human animals as part of the action system of the species lies below the reality system of the ego and the society. Although Freud conceptualized mental life in individual terms, he treated it within the context of the family. The family is a biological and species system for the child, but for the mature it is dominated by the moral order and incest taboos of the society. Freud's "id," touching and being charged with energies from the organism, the source of our strongest feelings, indicates how the non-logical feeling system operates as part of the social life of man. [51b]

Such symbols as dreams, reveries, hallucinations, many of the ordinary symbols of everyday life, those of many of the arts, and supernatural symbols such as myths—Durkheim notwithstanding—can be understood only when referred to the context of species relations and events. They are never free from cultural influence, for the symbols have a cultural *form*, but the feelings they express are largely those of the ongoing species life.

There are at least two classes of unconscious symbols: those which operate covertly in the inner world of everyone, evoking emotionally charged similar meanings among sizeable proportions of the population of the community; and a second class, still unconscious, or largely so, which functions quite differently in the life of some individuals and the society. The latter type, instead of being powerful forces integrating the society and relating the individual in a deep, meaningful way to those around him, separate the individual from his fellows, distort prevailing relations, and create problems wherever they exist. These private symbols and the irrational emotional meanings they attach to the flow of private and public events are usually born in experiences which tear painful lesions in the inner world of the persons who have them. Although they are evocative and charged with the powerful energies of species life, belong to the type of expressive covert symbols first referred to, and emerge from the same milieu where the species life and the moral order merge and normally interpenetrate each other, they prevent the individual and others around him from discharging their emotions as "adjusted" animals. They force their emotionally powerful but distorted interpretation on what takes place, so that the maimed individual cannot adapt easily to the present or the future. They are irrational and usually result in non-adaptive behavior, whereas the non-rational type supports, strengthens, and provides the foundation of our social life. [139b]

The deep, unconscious, latent meanings connected with manifest signs during sleeping and waking must be considered as more than the unique and hidden symbols of an individual.

They, too, are part of the total action context in which other individuals are involved as animals and persons. Their full meaning can only be learned after similar knowledge about conscious and unconscious signs from *all* individuals in an action context are interrelated as integral parts of the meaningful whole. Their full meaning can only be found by studying the rest of the system of unconscious understandings out of which the individual ones have been taken, and in which they were learned and have been maintained.

Much of the collective life of man is carried on by an exchange of signs part of whose meaning is unconscious, and whose function allows the animal life of man to be expressed. The expression may be entirely hidden, or it may find a vehicle in collective signs, whose conscious conventional meanings are so related to unconscious meanings that they are accessible for their expression. Psychoanalytical techniques allow us to learn how to study them as part of the action system of a society. Research must learn how to relate them to the conscious collective signs of the community as a system and—at the other extreme of the mental life of man—to the sociological behavior of the ongoing species. The findings of Freud and other depth psychologists must be reconceptualized. The deep, unconscious id of each individual must be conceptualized, not so much as a component of individual mental life, but as an integral and significant part of the action life of the species—as a segment of our mental life, much of whose meaning must be sought within the context of the action groups. What are called the ego and super ego are not only individual phenomena but integral parts of the society; of the moral and sacred relations of group life. The interconnections among the three should be viewed in the total context of the life of the species as it exists in the groups which compose the observable eventful life of men.

The underlying themes of non-logical symbol systems, to be learned by research through an examination of the special parts, are basic arrangements of dominant meanings expressed in varying designs at the sign level. The motifs (themes and their designs) are patterned in traditional or newly invented forms. The proportionate amount of thought or emotion involved in the construction of an art product, liturgy, or whatever the symbol system may be, varies greatly. The form may be professionally sophisticated or naive and simple. [19] The response of the interpreter also may be simple and folk-like or highly sophisticated. There is no necessary relation of similarity between the forms of response and the degree of artistic professionalism. The simple folk-like creation of an early blues song or cowboy ballad may receive a sophisticated or folk-like response, depending on the interpreter and on the context in which he is acting when the response takes place. Part of the satisfaction in slumming, by both white and Negro sophisticates, in a "hangout" where popular jazz is played is not only to feel superior but to give the direct, immediate, naive response that the unsophisticated give, and "do it like gone guys" among others who can only respond in the naive, direct way.

All popular arts are capable of being translated into the rhetoric of the sophisticate. The oral action rites of the emotional religions of the crowd in time may develop a style expressing greater use of thought and professional competence. When this change occurs in a religion it usually means that the leader, and later the congregation, has moved up in class position, that the concepts of God expressed by the leader and felt by the congregation have changed and acquired a new set of meanings; as a consequence, many lower-class members, to receive the symbols they need, must once again go to another church.

When "rhetoric" is said to be present in a symbol system, professionals have usually entered either as creators who give thought to the evocative signs and their relations and to their meanings, or as critics of folk and other unsophisticated products, attributing a rhetoric which may or may not be present in the way they assert. [20b] Essentially such a process usually indicates that the art forms of the masses are being translated into "fine" arts acceptable to the superior classes, to those aspiring to such levels, and to a few of lower station who have learned to appreciate them. [20a]

The popular arts that satisfy and engage the attention of the masses are the rallying points where the people arrive at the common points of meaning and feel again the deep memories of past experience. Here diverse adults can find, re-live, and re-feel the central areas of what they themselves are and the emotional core of their culture. The fine arts allow many in the superior classes generally, and a selected few among ordinary men, to withdraw from the meanings of the common world to an aloof and protected one where they enjoy what they experience and at the same time are rewarded by a feeling of exclusiveness and superiority.

The creators of all types of symbol systems in effect first define the meanings of the meaningful forms they have produced. The interpreters in the audience in varying degrees accept or reject these meanings. The signs, objects, and their environments to which the "producers" refer may or may not be the same as those assigned by their interpreters. Ordinarily the audience and producer, in the immediate context of interpretation, are not identical (in dreams they may be). The problem of how much the meanings of the product for its creator and those who interpret it coincide is a special one and need not presently concern us. What we must consider are: (1) the meanings signs have for an audience as judged by an analysis of their conventional meanings and the relations of signs, meanings, and audience to each other as part of a whole symbolic assemblage; and (2) the meanings the signs have for the varying kinds of individuals composing the audience. Consequently, to adequately cover and collect evidence, the skills and instruments of the field investigator must include those from the social and psychological disciplines.

Non-rational symbols are basic parts of the animal organization of man. They express and evoke the feelings and sensuous observations of animals in an interactive group. The signs and gestures used are not private but part of the basic sociality of man. They relate to his deepest emotions. Within them flow the vital energies and emotional significance of species behavior. When individuals grow up these symbols are not "stripped" of their egocentric meanings, but undergo modification and become part of the symbolic equipment of mature men and women, remaining deep within their mental and moral selves. Such symbols are not unadaptive because they are non-rational; on the contrary, these evocative symbols, directly related to the species organization of man, allow this part of man's essential nature to be expressed and justified without the restrictions of cultural and moral life interfering. With their aid, man remains a *full* participant in the life of his species. Without their help he encounters painful difficulties. A logical mind is not a good one to reinforce the pleasures of sexual communication. It will not increase and maximize the exchange of sign and gesture which enhances the physical and moral worth of the sexual act to the participant pair. The language of love is non-rational; its symbols are evocative. They arouse and evoke some of the deepest and most profoundly significant feelings and "understandings" of what man is to himself and others, but they do not need the denotative symbols of logical speech.

These symbols are part of, and refer to, the species organization of man, culturally reformed but still lived and expressed in the social organization and in the person. The constant pressure of the natural environment, beginning long before man was a symbol-using animal and up to this moment, modifies his full expression of his species urges. Obviously, as an animal acting in direct relation with other animals, he does not directly attend to any reality beyond that of his species.

The way of life identified as egocentric does exist as a phase of individual development, and it continues to exist and is an important and vital part of all human existence. But it is not so much egocentric as species-centric; it serves as a vital part of species interaction. Species-centric symbols in human beings are largely family ones. They find their freest and easiest expression in the arts and religion. Here, sometimes hidden but often in very transparent disguises, they are available for the full charge of animal emotions released from the moral restrictions and logical controls of secular life. Men can murder their brother gods—the father can be accused of knowingly permitting this, incest can be indulged in, and the father can become the son and the son the father, each with one woman as mother and wife.

The suppressed species life partly excluded from expression in the moral life of the community takes refuge in the sacred symbols of religion and art. Unfettered by the conventions and inhibitions of social and cultural isolation, the family unites the understandings of men—sometimes thousands of years apart—by creating persons who share a common core of human experience. Great literature, great drama, many of the other arts and much of religion rely on the shared meanings of family life to permit communication and understanding across the barriers of cultural diversity and long passage of time. When men of the age of steel and atomic fission see *Oedipus Rex* they easily respond to its beauty and to the thoughts and feelings of a dramatist who lived many years before Christ's birth.

What makes it possible to arouse their sympathy, their fear, and pity, and gives human meaning to Oedipus, the man "who-walked-in-pain," is the shared experiences and feelings that all men, ancient Greek and those of Yankee City, must have by virtue of living in families. All people, however primitive or civilized, deep within them hold these fears in common. Each of us can walk in pain with Oedipus, since we share common feelings and a common conscience with him. Through this human symbol, born out of myth and fashioned by the literary arts, we are allowed to express that which we cannot say. Oedipus' fate of marrying his mother, killing his father, and the awful tragedy he experienced as a moral being when he learned what he had done arouse the deepest emotions in men of every culture. Everyone can understand and share in the tragedy of such a man:

> His staff groping before him, he shall crawl
> O'er unknown earth, and voices around him call:
> "Behold the brother-father of his own
> Children, the seed, the sower and the sown,
> Shame to his mother's blood, and to his sire
> Son, murderer, incest-worker."

The meanings of the moral and sacred orders in all cultures more often than not lie deeply bound beneath rational existence in the solid core of species life. It is no accident that most religious beliefs are fundamentally based on the simple realities and on the relations of family deities. These figures, coming out of the unity of the family, express, as no other human symbols can, the desire of all men to be one, yet separate, for as the sons of God in His family they can all be, or could be, brothers. The most diverse peoples can understand and feel the ambivalent meanings of hate and love, conflict and cooperation, for they are all basically molded in the moral and species structure of family life.

ACKNOWLEDGMENTS

The acknowledgments and dedications published in the four preceding volumes hold for the present one. It is hoped that the reader will relate them to the present recognitions of indebtedness. Throughout this and the other volumes, footnotes to the several chapters have given inadequate credit to the young men and women, most of them then undergraduates at Harvard and Radcliffe, now prominent in many activities of American life, whose field work as part of the research team contributed so much to the success of the Yankee City research. Most of the work was done without pay, for the intellectual excitement of learning something about how to study American life. Through the years my love and respect for them, present from the beginning, have not only continued but grown and strengthened.

To these names must now be added those of the late John Shea of Yankee City and Mario Wagner of São Paulo, Brazil.

I am indebted to Professor John Thomas, S.J., of Washington University in St. Louis, and Professor James Luther Adams of the Harvard Theological School for their criticisms of the manuscript, particularly for their comments on the chapters on sacred symbolism. I must acknowledge the advice and excellent critical comments given me by Professor Clyde Kluckhohn of Harvard University; Professor Charles Warriner of the University of Kansas; Professors Allison Davis, Robert Havighurst, David Riesman, Edward Shils, and Richard Wohl, of the University of Chicago; and John Marquand, of Newburyport and the United States. Each has generously given the manuscript careful attention and helped with valuable advice.

For what John Dollard has contributed to the whole "Yankee

City Series" I must say here what I have said previously: To John Dollard of the Institute of Human Relations of Yale University we owe a very special debt of gratitude for his recognition of the significance of the scientific problems we attacked and for his help in the solution of many of them. The searching questions he asked us and the generous acclaim he gave our research have been deep sources of scientific and spiritual strength to all of us.

I also wish to thank Alice Chandler, Mildred Warner, Roberta Yerkes, and Annabel Learned for their critical advice and editorial skill in preparing the manuscript for publication.

Above all I wish to express appreciation for my colleagues and myself to the citizens of Yankee City who generously gave their knowledge of the community and maintained a cooperative interest in our work. To protect the anonymity of these people and their community, no one actual individual or family in Yankee City has been depicted in any of the volumes; rather, several individuals, several organizations, and many incidents have been compressed into one fictive individual, organization, or event. The justification for these changes lies in an attempt to protect those studied and to tell their stories economically. I have not hesitated to exclude all material which might identify specific persons in the community; and I have included generalized material wherever necessary to prevent recognition. In all cases where changes were introduced in the reworking of field notes I first satisfied myself that they did not destroy the essential social reality of the points of the original interview. Only then were such materials included in the text.

Some of the material on associations and Memorial Day has been published earlier. All of it was first written for this volume.

The sixth proposed volume of the "Yankee City Series," the data book, will not be published, since it is felt that sufficient evidence has been published in the first five.

I wish to express my indebtedness to the authors and publishers for their permission to use the quotations from their publications.

REFERENCES

1. ADAMS, HENRY. *History of the United States of America.* New York, Charles Scribner's Sons, 1921.
2a. ADAMS, JAMES T. *Provincial Society 1690–1763.* New York, Macmillan, 1927.
2b. ———— "The Historical Background," *New England's Prospects,* ed. J. K. Wright. (American Geographical Society Special Publication, Vol. *16.*) (1933), 1–13.
2c. ———— *The Founding of New England.* Boston, Little Brown, 1930.
3. ALLEE, WARDER C. *The Social Life of Animals.* New York, W. W. Norton, 1938.
4. ARISTOTLE. *Aristoteles,* ed. and trans. S. H. Butcher. London, Macmillan, 1911.
5a. ARNOLD, THURMAN W. *The Symbols of Government.* New Haven, Yale University Press, 1935.
5b. ———— *The Folklore of Capitalism.* New Haven, Yale University Press, 1937.
6. BALKEN, EVA R. "Thematic Apperception," *Journal of Psychology, 20* (October 1945), 189–97.
7. BARNETT, JAMES H. "Christmas in American Culture," *Psychiatry, 9,* No. 1, (February 1946), 51–65.
8. BEARD, CHARLES A. and MARY R. *The Rise of American Civilization.* New York, Macmillan, 1949.
9a. BERELSON, BERNARD R., and LAZARSFELD, PAUL T. *The Analysis of Communication Content.* (Mimeographed.) University of Chicago, 1948. Deposited in the University of Chicago Library.
9b. ———— and JANOWITZ, MORRIS, eds. *Reader in Public Opinion and Communication.* Glencoe, Ill., Free Press, 1953.
10a. BERGSON, HENRI L. *Time and Free Will. An Essay on the Immediate Data of Consciousness,* trans. R. L. Pogson. New York, Macmillan, 1913.
10b. ———— *Creative Evolution,* trans. Arthur Mitchell. New York, Macmillan, Modern Library, 1944.
11. Bible, editions of
11a. American Revised Version, New York, Thomas Nelson & Sons, 1901.

11b. Brown's Self-interpreting Family Bible, Edinburgh, Daniel Chadwick, 1778.

11c. Revised Standard Version, New York, Thomas Nelson & Sons, 1952.

11d. Riverside Parallel Bible, Boston, Houghton Mifflin and Company, 1885.

11e. Westminster Version of the Sacred Scriptures, London, Longmans, Green and Company, 1913–

12. BIRKHOFF, GEORGE D. *Aesthetic Measure.* Cambridge, Harvard University Press, 1933.

13. BLUMER, HERBERT. "Social Attitudes and Nonsymbolic Interaction," *Journal of Educational Sociology, 9* (May 1936), 515–23.

14. *Book of Common Prayer.* With the additions and deviations proposed in 1928. New York, Oxford University Press, 1951.

15. *Book of Common Worship,* rev. of Hugh Thomson Kerr and Others. Philadelphia, Presbyterian Board of Christian Education, 1946.

16. BOSSARD, JAMES H. S. *Parent and Child. Studies in Family Behavior.* Philadelphia, University of Pennsylvania Press, 1953.

17. BRIFFAULT, ROBERT. "Festivals," *Encyclopaedia of the Social Sciences, 6,* 198–201. New York, Macmillan, 1930–34.

18. BRYSON, LYMAN and Others, eds. *Symbols and Society.* (Fourteenth Symposium of the Conference on Science, Philosophy, and Religion.) New York, Harper, 1955.

19. BURCHARD, JOHN ELY. *Symbolism in Architecture.* Cambridge, Mass., Department of Humanities, Massachusetts Institute of Technology, 1956.

20a. BURKE, KENNETH. *Philosophy of Literary Form. Studies in Symbolic Action.* Baton Rouge, La., Louisiana State University Press, 1941.

20b. ——— *A Rhetoric of Motives.* New York, Prentice-Hall Inc., 1950.

21. CABROL, FERNAND, O.S.B. *The Year's Liturgy. The Sundays, Feriae and Feasts of the Liturgical Year.* Vol. *1* of 2 vols.: *The Seasons.* New York, Benziger Brothers, 1938.

22. CARNAP, RUDOLF. *Introduction to Semantics.* ("Studies in Semantics," *1.*) Cambridge, Harvard University Press, 1942.

23. CARPENTER, C. R. *A Field Study of the Behavior and Social Relations of Howling Monkeys.* (Comparative Psychology Monographs, *10,* No. 2) Baltimore, Williams and Wilkie, 1934, pp. 1–168.

24a. CASSIRER, ERNST. *An Essay on Man. An Introduction to a Philosophy of Human Culture.* New Haven, Yale University Press, 1944.

24b. ——— *Language and Myth,* trans. Susanne Langer. New York, Harper, 1946.

25. *The Catholic Encyclopedia,* ed. Edward A. Pace and Others. 16 vols. New York, Gilmary Society, 1936–

26. *Catholic Pocket Dictionary and Cyclopedia,* compiled by James J. McGovern. Chicago, Extension Press, 1906.

27. CHASE, STUART. *The Tyranny of Words.* New York, Harcourt Brace, 1938.

28. CIRLOT, FELIX L. *The Early Eucharist.* London, Society for the Promoting of Christian Knowledge, 1939.

29. CLARK, ELMER T. *The Small Sects in America.* Nashville, Tenn., Cokesbury Press, 1937.

30. CLARK, VICTOR S. *History of Manufactures in the United States.* New York, McGraw-Hill, 1929.

31. COUNT, EARL W. *4000 Years of Christmas.* New York, Henry Schuman, 1948.

32. CRAVEN, AVERY, and JOHNSON, WALTER. *The United States, Experiment in Democracy.* Boston, Ginn, 1947.

33. CRAWFORD, MEREDITH P. "Dominance and Social Behavior, for Chimpanzees, in a Non-competitive Situation," *Journal of Comparative Psychology, 33* (April 1942), 267–77.

34. CRAWLEY, ALFRED ERNEST. *The Mystic Rose. A Study of Primitive Marriage and of Primitive Thought in Its Bearing on Marriage,* ed. Theodore Bestermann. New York, Boni and Liveright, 1927.

35. CUNLIFFE, MARCUS. *The Literature of the United States.* London, Penguin Books, 1954.

36. CURTI, MERLE E. *The Growth of American Thought.* New York, Harper, 1943.

37. DAVIS, ALLISON, and DOLLARD, JOHN. *Children of Bondage.* Washington, D.C., American Council on Education, 1940.

38. DAVIS, ALLISON and ROBERT J. HAVIGHURST. "The Measurement of Mental Systems," *Scientific Monthly, 66* (April 1948), 301–16.

39. *Dictionary of American Biography,* ed. Allen Johnson. (Auspices of the American Council of Learned Societies.) New York, Charles Scribner's Sons, 1928–44.

40. DOBSON, JAMES O. *Worship.* New York, Macmillan, 1941. 1941.

41. DOLLARD, JOHN, and MILLER, NEAL E. *Personality and Psychotherapy. An Analysis in Terms of Learning, Thinking, and Culture.* New York, McGraw-Hill, 1950.

42a. DURKHEIM, ÉMILE. *The Elementary Forms of the Religious Life,* trans. J. W. Swain. New York, Macmillan, 1915.

42b. ——— *Suicide,* trans. John Spaulding and George Simpson. Glencoe, Ill., Free Press, 1951.

43. DWIGHT, TIMOTHY. *Travels in New-England and New-York,* Vol. *1* of 4 vols., New Haven, T. Dwight, 1821.

44. ELKIN, FREDERICK. *A Study of the Relationship between Popular*

Hero Types and Social Class. Ph.D. Dissertation, University of Chicago, 1951. Deposited in the University of Chicago Library.

45. ELLARD, GERALD. *Christian Life and Worship.* New York, Bruce Publishing Co., 1933.

46. ENGELS, FRIEDRICH. *The Origin of the Family, Private Property, and the State,* trans. Ernest Untermann. Chicago, H. Kerr, 1902.

47a. FARIS, ELLSWORTH. "The Sect and the Sectarian," *American Journal of Sociology, 60* (May 1955 supplement), 75–89.

47b. —— "Some Phases of Religion that Are Susceptible of Sociological Study," *American Journal of Sociology, 60* (May 1955 supplement), 90.

48. FAULKNER, HAROLD U. *American Economic History.* New York, Harper, 1931.

49. FRANK, LAWRENCE K. *Projective Methods.* Springfield, Ill., Charles C. Thomas, 1948.

50. FRAZER, SIR JAMES GEORGE. *The Golden Bough. A Study in Magic and Religion* (abridged ed.). New York, Macmillan, 1927.

51a. FREUD, SIGMUND. *New Introductory Lectures on Psycho-analysis.* trans. W. J. H. Sprott. New York, W. W. Norton, 1933.

51b. —— *The Basic Writings of Sigmund Freud.* trans. and ed. A. A. Brill. New York, Random House, Modern Library, 1938.

51c. *The Interpretation of Dreams,* pp. 181–552.

51d. *Three Contributions to the Theory of Sex,* pp. 553–632.

51e. *Totem and Taboo,* pp. 807–930.

52a. FROMM, ERICH. *Escape from Freedom.* New York, Farrar & Rinehart, 1941.

52b. —— *The Forgotten Language.* New York, Rinehart, 1951.

53. FRYE, ALBERT M., and LEVI, ALBERT W. *Rational Belief. An Introduction to Logic.* New York, Harcourt, Brace, 1941.

54. GENNEP, ARNOLD VAN. *Les Rites de passage.* Paris, Émile Nourry, 1909

55. *A Guide for the Christian Year (1951–60).* New York, Commission on Evangelism and Devotional Life, 1950.

56. GUNN, JOHN ALEXANDER. *The Problem of Time.* London, Allen & Unwin, 1929.

57. JOHN OF THE CROSS, ST. "En Una Noche Oscura," trans. John Frederick Nims. *Commonweal, 55,* No. 16 (January 25, 1952), 404.

58. HABENSTEIN, ROBERT W. "The American Funeral Director. A Study in the Sociology of Work." Unpublished Ph.D. dissertation, University of Chicago, 1954.

59. HAVIGHURST, ROBERT J., TABA, HILDA, and Others. *Adolescent Character and Personality.* New York, John Wiley, 1949.

60. HAYAKAWA, S. I. *Language in Action.* New York, Harcourt, Brace, 1941.

61*a.* HENRY, WILLIAM E. "Art and Cultural Symbolism. A Psychological Study of Greeting Cards," *Journal of Aesthetics and Art Criticism, 6* (September 1947), 36–44.

61*b.* ———— *The Thematic Apperception Technique in the Study of Culture-Personality Relations.* (Genetic Psychology Monographs, Vol. *35.*) Provincetown, Mass., Journal Press, 1947.

61*c.* ———— "The Business Executive. Psychodynamics of a Social Role," *American Journal of Sociology, 54* (January 1949), 286–91.

62. HILDEBRAND, DIETRICH VON. *In Defence of Purity.* New York, Sheed & Ward, 1935.

63. Hodges, George. *The Episcopal Church, Its Faith and Order,* rev. of James A. Muller to accord with the new prayer book. New York, Macmillan, 1932.

64. HOMANS, GEORGE C. *The Human Group.* New York, Harcourt, Brace, 1950.

65. HUGHES, HELEN M. *News and the Human Interest Story.* Chicago, The University of Chicago Press, 1940.

66. HUIZINGA, JOHAN. *The Waning of the Middle Ages. A Study of the Forms of Life, Thought and Art in France and the Netherlands in the XIV and XV Centuries.* New York, Longmans, Green, 1948.

67*a.* JAMES, EDWIN O. *Christian Myth and Ritual.* London, John Murray, 1933.

67*b.* ———— *Origins of Sacrifice. A Study in Comparative Religion.* London, John Murray, 1933.

68. JOHNSON, MARTIN. "The Meanings of Time and Space in Philosophies of Science," *American Scientist, 39* (July 1951), 412–21.

69*a.* JUNG, CARL G. *Psychology of the Unconscious. A Study of the Transformations and Symbolisms of the Libido,* trans. Beatrice M. Hinkle. New York, Dodd, Mead, 1916.

69*b.* ———— *Psychology and Religion.* New Haven, Yale University Press, 1938.

70. KEATING, JOHN F. *The Agape and the Eucharist in the Early Church; Studies in the History of the Christian Love-Feasts.* London, Methuen, 1901.

71*a.* KLAPP, ORRIN E. "The Creation of Popular Heroes," *American Journal of Sociology, 54* (September 1948), 135–41.

71*b.* ———— "The Hero as a Social Type." Unpublished Ph.D. Dissertation, University of Chicago, 1948.

71*c.* ———— "Hero Worship in America," *American Sociological Review, 14* (February 1949), 53–62.

71*d.* ———— "American Villain-Types," *American Sociological Review, 21* (June 1956), 337–40.

72a. KLUCKHOHN, CLYDE. "Myths and Rituals," *Harvard Theological Review, 35* (January 1942), 45–79.

72b. —— and MOWRER, O. H. "Culture and Personality," *American Anthropologist, 46* (January 1944), 1–29.

72c. —— and KLUCKHOHN, FLORENCE R. "American Culture. Generalized Orientation and Class Patterns," *Conflicts of Power in Modern Culture,* eds. Lyman Bryson and Others (Conference on Science, Philosophy and Religion in Their Relation to the Democratic Way of Life, 7th Symposium, 1946.) New York, Harper, 1947, pp. 106–28.

72d. —— and Murray, Henry A., eds. *Personality in Nature, Society and Culture.* New York, Alfred A. Knopf, 1948.

73. KÖHLER, WOLFGANG. *The Mentality of Apes,* trans. Ella Winter. New York, Harcourt, Brace, 1926.

74a. KORZYBSKI, ALFRED. *Manhood of Humanity. The Science and Art of Human Engineering.* New York, E. P. Dutton, 1921.

74b. —— *Science and Sanity. An Introduction to Non-Aristotelian Systems and General Semantics.* New York, International Non-Aristotelian Publishing Co., 1941.

75. KROPOTKIN, PETR A. *Mutual Aid. A Factor in Evolution.* New York, Penguin Books, 1939.

76a. LASSWELL, HAROLD D. "Propaganda," *Encyclopaedia of the Social Sciences, 12,* New York, Macmillan, 521–7.

76b. —— and Others. *Language of Politics. Studies in Quantitative Semantics.* New York, G. W. Stewart, 1949.

76c. —— and Others. *The Compartive Study of Elites.* Stanford, Calif., Stanford University Press, 1952.

77. LAZARSFELD, PAUL F., and STANTON, FRANK N., eds. *Communications Research, 1948–49.* New York, Harper, 1949.

78. LECKY, WILLIAM E. *History of European Morals, from Augustus to Charlemagne.* New York, D. Appleton, 1879.

79. LEE, ALFRED M. *The Daily Newspaper in America. The Evolution of a Social Instrument.* New York, Macmillan, 1937.

80a. LEVY, DAVID M. "Hostility Patterns in Sibling Rivalry Experiments," *American Journal of Orthopsychiatry, 6* (April 1936), 183–257.

80b. —— "Sibling Rivalry Studies in Children of Primitive Groups," *American Journal of Orthopsychiatry, 9* (January 1939), 205–15.

81. LÉVY-BRUHL, LUCIEN. *Primitive Mentality,* trans. Lilian A. Clare. New York, Macmillan, 1923.

82. LIPPMANN, WALTER. *Public Opinion.* New York, Macmillan, 1922.

83. MacCULLOCH, J. A., and Others, "Sacraments," *Encyclopaedia of Religion and Ethics, 10* (1919), ed. James Hastings. New York, Charles Scribner's Sons, 897–915.

84. McMASTER, JOHN BACH. *A History of the People of the United*

States, from the Revolution to the Civil War. 8 vols. New York, Appleton-Century, 1883–1913.

85*a*. MALINOWSKI, BRONISLAW. "Magic, Science and Religion," *Science, Religion and Reality,* ed. J. Needham. New York, Macmillan, 1925, pp. 19–84.

85*b*. —— *The Sexual Life of Savages in Northwestern Melanesia. An Ethnographic Account of Courtship, Marriage and Family Life among the Natives of the Trobriand Islands and British New Guinea.* New York, Liveright Publishing Corp., 1929.

85*c*. —— "The Problem of Meaning in Primitive Languages," *The Meaning of Meaning,* C. K. Ogden and I. A. Richards, New York, Harcourt Brace, 1936, pp. 296–336.

85*d*. —— "Culture," *Encyclopedia of the Social Sciences, 4,* New York, Macmillan Co., 621–45.

86. MANNHEIM, KARL. *Ideology and Utopia. An Introduction to the Sociology of Knowledge,* trans. Louis Wirth and Edward Shils. New York, Harcourt, Brace, 1936.

87. MARTINDALE, CYRIL CHARLES. *The Faith of the Roman Church.* New York, Sheed & Ward, 1951.

88. MAUSS, MARCEL. *The Gift. Forms and Functions of Exchange in Archaic Societies,* trans. Ian Cunnison. London, Cohen & West, 1954.

89. MAY, GEOFFREY. *Social Control of Sex Expression.* New York, William Morrow, 1931.

90*a*. MEAD, GEORGE H. "Social Consciousness and the Consciousness of Meaning," *Psychological Bulletin, 7* (1910), 397–405.

90*b*. —— "A Behavioristic Account of the Significant Symbol," *Journal of Philosophy, 19* (1922), 157–63.

90*c*. —— *Mind, Self, and Society, from the Standpoint of a Social Behaviorist.* Chicago, University of Chicago Press, 1934.

91. MEAD, MARGARET. *Sex and Temperament in Three Primitive Societies.* New York, William Morrow, 1935.

92. MECKLIN, JOHN M. "The Passing of the Saint," *American Journal of Sociology, 60* (May 1955 supplement), 34–53.

93. MERTON, ROBERT K. and KENDALL, PATRICIA L. "The Focused Interview," *American Journal of Sociology, 51* (1946), 541–57.

94. MICHEL, DOM VIRGIL. *The Liturgy of the Church.* New York, Macmillan, 1937.

95. MILLER, NEAL E., and DOLLARD, JOHN. *Social Learning and Imitation.* New Haven, Yale University Press, 1941.

96. MILLER, PERRY G. E. *The New England Mind. The Seventeenth Century.* New York, Macmillan, 1939.

97. MINDSZENTY, CARDINAL JOZSEF. *The Face of the Heavenly Mother.* New York, Philosophical Library, 1951.

98. MORISON, SAMUEL ELIOT. *The Maritime History of Massachusetts, 1783–1860.* Boston, Houghton Mifflin, 1924.

99. Morris, Charles W. *Signs, Language, and Behavior*. New York, Prentice-Hall, 1946.

100. Murdock, George P. *Social Structure*. New York, Macmillan, 1949.

101. Murray, Henry A. *Thematic Apperception Test Manual*. Cambridge, Harvard University Press, 1943.

102a. Niebuhr, H. Richard. *The Social Sources of Denominationalism*. New York, Henry Holt, 1929.

102b. ———— "Sects," *Encyclopedia of the Social Sciences, 13*, New York, Macmillan, 624–30.

103. Nygren, Anders T. S. *Agape and Eros. A Study of the Christian Idea of Love*. London, Society for Promoting Christian Knowledge, 1953.

104. Ogden, Charles K., and Richards, I. A. *The Meaning of Meaning*. New York, Harcourt, Brace, 1936.

105. Pareto, Vilfredo. *The Mind and Society*, trans. Andrew Bongiorno and Arthur Livingston. New York, Harcourt, Brace, 1935.

106. Park, Robert E. "The Natural History of the Newspaper," *American Journal of Sociology, 29* (1923), 273–89.

107. Parkman, Frances. *The Oregon Trail*. New York, Farrar & Rinehart, 1931.

108. Parrington, Vernon L. *Main Currents in American Thought*. New York, Harcourt Brace, 1927.

109. Pavlov, Ivan Petrovich. *Conditioned Reflexes*, trans. and ed. G. V. Anrep. London, Oxford University Press, 1927.

110. Paxson, Frederic L. *History of the American Frontier, 1763–1893*. Boston, Houghton Mifflin, 1924.

111a. Piaget, Jean, and others. *The Language and Thought of the Child*, trans. Marjorie Gabain. New York, Harcourt, Brace, 1926.

111b. ———— *Judgment and Reasoning in the Child*, trans. Marjorie Gabain. New York, Harcourt, Brace, 1928.

111c. ———— *The Child's Conception of the World*, trans. Joan and Andrew Tomlinson. New York, Harcourt, Brace, 1929.

111d. ———— *The Moral Judgment of the Child*, trans. Marjorie Gabain. New York, Harcourt, Brace, 1932.

112. Piddington, Ralph. *The Psychology of Laughter. A Study in Social Adaptation*. London, Figurehead Press, 1933.

113. *Presbyterian Plan Book*. New York, Department of Stewardship and Promotion of the General Council of the Presbyterian Church in the U.S.A., 1952–53.

114a. Radcliffe-Brown, Alfred R. "The Sociological Theory of Totemism," *Proceedings, Fourth Pacific Science Congress, 3* (1929), 295–309.

114b. ———— *Religion and Society*. London, Royal Anthropological Institute of Great Britain and Ireland, 1945.

114c. —— *The Andaman Islanders.* Glencoe, Ill., Free Press, 1948.

114d. —— *Structure and Function in Primitive Society.* London, Cohen and West, 1952.

115. RAGLAN, FITZROY R. S. *The Hero. A Study in Tradition, Myth and Drama.* London, C. A. Watts, 1949.

116. RIESMAN, DAVID, and Others. *The Lonely Crowd.* New Haven, Yale University Press, 1950.

117. *The Roman Missal,* ed. Fernand Cabrol, O.S.B. New York, P. J. Kenedy and Sons, 1949.

118. Rosten, Leo, ed. *Guide to the Religions of America.* New York, Simon & Schuster, 1955.

119. ROUGEMONT, DENIS DE. *Love in the Western World,* trans. Montgomery Belgion. Revised and augmented edition. New York, Pantheon Books, 1956.

120a. RUSSELL, BERTRAND. *Mysticism and Logic and Other Essays.* New York, Longmans, Green, 1918.

120b. —— *Marriage and Morals.* Liveright Publishing Corp., 1929.

121. SANDBURG, CARL. *Abraham Lincoln. The Prairie Years and the War Years.* New York, Harcourt, Brace, 1954.

122a. SAPIR, EDWARD. *Language. An Introduction to the Study of Speech.* New York, Harcourt, Brace, 1921.

122b. —— "Symbolism," *Encyclopedia of the Social Sciences, 14.* New York, Macmillan. 492–95.

123a. SCHLESINGER, ARTHUR M. *The Colonial Merchants and the American Revolution 1763–76.* New York, Columbia University Press, 1918.

123b. —— *New Viewpoints in American History.* New York, Macmillan, 1922.

124a. SIMMEL, GEORG. "The Sociology of Secrecy and Secret Societies," *American Journal of Sociology, 11* (January 1906), 441–98.

124b. —— "A Contribution to the Sociology of Religion," *American Journal of Sociology, 60* (May 1955 supplement), 1–18.

125. SMALL, ALBION W. "The Church and Class Conflicts," *American Journal of Sociology, 60* (May 1955 supplement), 54–74.

126. SMITH, JUSTIN H. *The War with Mexico.* New York, Macmillan, 1919.

127. SMITH, WILLIAM ROBERTSON. *Lectures on the Religion of the Semites.* New York, D. Appleton, 1889.

128. STAFFORD, THOMAS A. *Christian Symbolism in the Evangelical Churches.* Nashville, Tenn., Abingdon-Cokesbury, 1942.

129. SULLIVAN, HARRY STACK. "The Importance of a Study of Symbols in Psychiatry," *Psyche, 25* (1926), 81–93.

130. SUMNER, WILLIAM G. "Religion and the Mores," *American Journal of Sociology, 60* (May 1955 supplement), 19–33.

131. TAWNEY, RICHARD H. *The Acquisitive Society.* New York, Harcourt, Brace, 1946.

132. TOCQUEVILLE, ALEXIS DE. *Democracy in America.* New York, Alfred A. Knopf, 1945.

133. TILLICH, PAUL "The Religious Symbol," *Journal of Liberal Religion, 2,* 13–33.

134. TINKELPAUGH, OTTO L. "Social Behavior of Animals," *Comparative Psychology,* ed. F. A. Moss. New York, Prentice-Hall, 1942.

135. TURNER, FREDERICK JACKSON. *The Frontier in American History.* New York, Henry Holt, 1921.

136. VAN DOREN, CARL C. *Benjamin Franklin.* New York, Viking Press, 1938.

137. VEBLEN, THORSTEIN. *The Theory of the Leisure Class.* New York, Vanguard Press, 1928.

138. WACH, JOACHIM. *Sociology of Religion.* Chicago, University of Chicago Press, 1944.

139a. WARNER, W. LLOYD. *A Black Civilization. A Social Study of an Australian Tribe.* New York, Harper, 1937.

139b. ———— "The Society, the Individual, and His Mental Disorders," *American Journal of Psychiatry, 94* (1938), 275–84.

139c. ———— and LUNT, PAUL S. *The Social Life of a Modern Community.* ("Yankee City Series," Vol. *1.*) New Haven, Yale University Press, 1941.

139d. ———— and SROLE, LEO. *The Social System of American Ethnic Groups.* ("Yankee City Series," Vol. *3.*) New Haven, Yale University Press, 1945.

139e. ———— and LOW, J. O. *The Social System of the Modern Factory.* ("Yankee City Series," Vol. *4.*) New Haven, Yale University Press, 1947.

139f. ———— and HENRY, WILLIAM E. *The Radio Daytime Serial. A Symbolic Analysis.* (Genetic Psychology Monographs, *37.*) Provincetown, Mass., Journal Press, 1948.

139g. ————, MEEKER, MARCHIA, and EELLS, KENNETH. *Social Class in America. A Manual of Procedure for the Measurement of Social Status.* Chicago, Science Research Associates, 1949.

140. WATTS, ALAN W. *Easter, Its Story and Meaning.* New York, Henry Schuman, 1950.

141. WEBER, MAX. *The Protestant Ethic and the Spirit of Capitalism,* trans. Talcott Parsons. New York, Charles Scribner's Sons, 1948.

142. WEBSTER, HUTTON. "Holidays," *Encyclopedia of the Social Sciences, 7,* New York, Macmillan, 412–15.

143. WECKLER, JOSEPH E. JR. "Ritual Status in Polynesia." Unpublished Ph.D. dissertation, University of Chicago, 1940.

144. WECTER, DIXON. *The Hero in America. A Chronicle of Hero-Worship.* New York, Charles Scribner's Sons, 1941.

145. WEDGEWOOD, CAMILLA H. "The Nature and Functions of Secret Societies," *Oceania, 1* (1930), 129–45.

146. WEEDEN, WILLIAM B. *Economic and Social History of New England, 1620–1789.* Boston, Houghton Mifflin, 1890.

147. WELLER, FORREST L. *The Changing Religious Sect. A Study of Social Types.* Unpublished Ph.D. dissertation, University of Chicago, 1945.

148. WHITE, LESLIE A. "The Symbol. The Origin and Basis of Human Behavior," *Philosophy of Science,* 7 (1940), 451–63.

149. WHITEHEAD, ALFRED NORTH. *Symbolism, Its Meaning and Effect.* New York, Macmillan, 1927.

150. WHITING, JOHN W. M. *Becoming a Kwoma. Teaching and Learning in a New Guinea Tribe.* New Haven, Yale University Press, 1941.

151a. WHORF, BENJAMIN L. "Time, Space and Language," *Culture in Crisis. A Study of the Hopi Indians,* ed. Laura Thompson. New York, Harper, 1950, pp. 152–72.

151b. ——— *Language, Thought and Realty.* Cambridge, Mass., Technology Press, Massachusetts Institute of Technology, 1956.

152. WOLFF, CHARLOTTE. *The Psychology of Gesture,* trans. Anne Tennant. London, Methuen, 1945.

153. WRIGHT, JOHN K. "Regions and Landscapes of New England," *New England's Prospect 1933.* (American Geographical Society Special Publication, No. 16.) pp. 14–49.

154a. YERKES, ROBERT M., and NISSEN, H. W. "Pre-Linguistic Sign Behavior in Chimpanzees," *Science, 89* (June 1939), 585–87.

154b. ——— "Social Behavior of Chimpanzees. Dominance between Mates in Relation to Sexual Status," *Journal of Comparative Psychology, 30* (August 1940), 147–86.

155. YOUNG, PAULINE V. *Scientific Social Surveys and Research.* New York, Prentice-Hall, 1949.

156. ZUCKERMAN, SOLLY. *The Social Life of Monkeys and Apes.* New York, Harcourt, Brace, 1932.

INDEX

Action system, social, 454
Adam, 411, 437, 439-41
Adams, John, 176, 178, 183
Adams, John Quincy, 118, 132, 177-8, 180, 182-4, 186, 188
Advent, 389, 394-6, 397, 399, 406, 407, 420
Age grading, and symbolism, 294
Altar, 126, 261, 331, 376, 413, 430, 433; and Lamb, God-Man, 279, 370, 426-7; and Lincoln's sacrifice, 192, 265, 272-3
American Legion, 252-4, 266-7; Auxiliary, 267
American Revolution, 108, 132, 139, 141-3, 146, 154, 164, 168, 175, 186, 190, 192, 198
Ancestors, 107, 112, 113, 121, 124, 125, 128, 147, 161, 163, 164, 174, 176, 190, 197, 212, 218, 223
Anglican Church, 174-5. See Protestant
Annunciation, 381, 388, 393, 402, 404, 408-9, 413
Armistice (Veterans') Day, 248; in evocative symbols, 475
Arnold, Benedict, 86-7, 119, 165, 196, 198, 200-3
Art, as symbol system, 4-5
Ascension Day, 407
Ash Wednesday, 396, 407
Associations, 229; activities, 235-44; activities by sex, 243-4; activities by social class, 244-7; in cemeteries, 282, 294-5; in Memorial Day ceremonies, 248, 254, 258, 261; as segmentary groups, 231, 234; in Tercentenary, 123, 157, 197; in war, 275-7

Baptism, 284, 307, 328, 375, 382, 394, 403, 407, 410-14, 429
Baptismal font, 284, 407, 410-14
Baptist Church, 261, 314, 328. See Protestant
Bartlet, William, 141, 185-6
Bass, Bishop Edward, 174-6, 183-4
Beard, Charles, 127
Bible, 215, 262, 382, 394, 410; as autonomous word, 219; in visual communication, 333; as word of first settlers, 213, 218. See Song of Songs

Birth, 111, 229, 284, 398, 401, 402, 405, 414, 415, 425, 432. See Rite de passage
Blood: sacred, 411; in sacrifice, 254, 275
Boas, Franz, 241
"Boston Massacre," 164
Boy Scouts, 254, 259, 263, 267
Bradford, William, 173
Bride of Christ, 366, 368, 371, 376; as the Mystical Body, 364, 375

Cabrol, Dom Fernand, 407-8, 419
Calendar, sacred, 343, 390, 394, 397, 399, 415-16
Candle: on ethnic graves, 296; as "Light of Christ," 420; in Paschal rite, 410, 413-14, 420; as symbol of male God, 414
Catholic Church: architecture, 331-2; "idolatry," 165; in Memorial Day, 268, 279; in Tercentenary, 107, 123, 132, 176-7, 199. See Priest
Catholic Order of Foresters, 266
Catholics, 127; in associations, 277; by class and ethnic background, 83-4, 123, 330
Cemetery, 31, 32, 229, 249, 250, 258, 260, 264-9 passim, 279-86 passim, 415; death of, 318-19, 320; and family, 287-8, 297-9; as garden and city of the dead, 31, 282-3, 287. See Graveyard
Charter, Massachusetts Bay, 108, 132, 210, 213, 215, 217-19, 223
Chase, Aquilla, 156
Chekhov, Anton, 50
Cheverus, Bishop, 176, 198, 205
Chivalry, 339, 340, 341
Christ, 87, 119, 126, 172, 200, 201, 258, 283, 331, 337, 354, 363, 369, 370, 376, 380, 385, 388, 396, 397, 399, 400 ff., 404, 407, 408, 410-15 passim, 419, 421, 426, 431, 433, 440, 441, 443, 444; as asexual male, 339; as God-Man, 273, 398, 426, 435; as Lamb, 295, 370, 387, 428, 435; as Lord, 256, 372, 457; as new Adam, 364, 441; as Sacred Bridegroom, 365-8, 375, 414, 471
Christian, 126, 200, 203, 237, 272; con-